I0121071

A Unified Approach to Measuring Poverty and Inequality

OTHER TITLES IN THE ADePT SERIES

ADePT

Health Equity and Financial Protection: Streamlined Analysis with ADePT Software (2011) by Adam Wagstaff, Marcel Bilger, Zurab Sajaia, and Michael Lokshin

Assessing Sector Performance and Inequality in Education: Streamlined Analysis with ADePT Software (2011) by Emilio Porta, Gustavo Arcia, Kevin Macdonald, Sergiy Radyakin, and Michael Lokshin

ADePT User Guide (forthcoming) by Michael Lokshin, Zurab Sajaia, and Sergiy Radyakin

For more information about Streamlined Analysis with ADePT software and publications, visit www.worldbank.org/adept.

STREAMLINED ANALYSIS WITH ADePT SOFTWARE

A Unified Approach to Measuring Poverty and Inequality

Theory and Practice

James Foster
Suman Seth
Michael Lokshin
Zurab Sajaia

THE WORLD BANK
Washington, D.C.

© 2013 International Bank for Reconstruction and Development / The World Bank
1818 H Street NW
Washington, DC 20433
Telephone: 202-473-1000
Internet: www.worldbank.org

Some rights reserved

1 2 3 4 16 15 14 13

This work is a product of the staff of The World Bank with external contributions. Note that The World Bank does not necessarily own each component of the content included in the work. The World Bank therefore does not warrant that the use of the content contained in the work will not infringe on the rights of third parties. The risk of claims resulting from such infringement rests solely with you.

The findings, interpretations, and conclusions expressed in this work do not necessarily reflect the views of The World Bank, its Board of Executive Directors, or the governments they represent. The World Bank does not guarantee the accuracy of the data included in this work. The boundaries, colors, denominations, and other information shown on any map in this work do not imply any judgment on the part of The World Bank concerning the legal status of any territory or the endorsement or acceptance of such boundaries.

Nothing herein shall constitute or be considered to be a limitation upon or waiver of the privileges and immunities of The World Bank, all of which are specifically reserved.

Rights and Permissions

This work is available under the Creative Commons Attribution 3.0 Unported license (CC BY 3.0) http://creativecommons.org/licenses/by/3.0. Under the Creative Commons Attribution license, you are free to copy, distribute, transmit, and adapt this work, including for commercial purposes, under the following conditions:

Attribution—Please cite the work as follows: Foster, James, Suman Seth, Michael Lokshin, and Zurab Sajaia. 2013. *A Unified Approach to Measuring Poverty and Inequality: Theory and Practice*. Washington, DC: World Bank. doi: 10.1596/978-0-8213-8461-9 License: Creative Commons Attribution CC BY 3.0

Translations—If you create a translation of this work, please add the following disclaimer along with the attribution: *This translation was not created by The World Bank and should not be considered an official World Bank translation. The World Bank shall not be liable for any content or error in this translation.*

All queries on rights and licenses should be addressed to the Office of the Publisher, The World Bank, 1818 H Street NW, Washington, DC 20433, USA; fax: 202-522-2625; e-mail: pubrights@worldbank.org.

ISBN (paper): 978-0-8213-8461-9
ISBN (electronic): 978-0-8213-9864-7
DOI: 10.1596/978-0-8213-8461-9

Cover photo: Scott Wallace/World Bank (girl and child)
Background image: iStockphoto.com/Olga Altunina
Cover design: Kim Vilov

Library of Congress Cataloging-in-Publication Data
Foster, James E. (James Eric), 1955–
Measuring poverty and inequality : theory and practice / by James Foster, Suman Seth, Michael Lokshin, Zurab Sajaia.
    pages cm
  Includes bibliographical references and index.
  ISBN 978-0-8213-8461-9 — ISBN 978-0-8213-9864-7 (electronic)
  1. Poverty. 2. Equality. I. Title.
  HC79.P6F67 2013
  339.4'6—dc23

2012050221

Contents

Contents

Figures

Contents

Tables

Foreword

This book is an introduction to the theory and practice of measuring poverty and inequality, as well as a user's guide for readers wanting to analyze income or consumption distribution for any standard household dataset using the ADePT program—a free download from the World Bank's website.

In the prosaic world of official publications, *A Unified Approach to Measuring Poverty and Inequality: Theory and Practice* is sure to stand out. It is written with a flair and fluency that is rare. For readers with little interest in the underlying philosophical debates and a desire simply to use ADePT software for computations, this book is, of course, a must. But even for someone with no interest in actually computing numbers but, instead, wanting to learn the basic theory of poverty and inequality measurement, with its bewildering plurality of measures and axioms and complex philosophical debates in the background, this book is an excellent read.

But, of course, the full book is designed for analysts wishing to do hands-on work, converting raw data into meaningful indices and unearthing regularities in large and often chaotic statistical information. The presentation is comprehensive, with all relevant concepts defined and explained. On completing this book, the country expert will be in a position to generate the analyses needed for a Poverty Reduction Strategy Paper. Researchers can construct macrodata series suitable for empirical analyses. Students can replicate and check the robustness of published results.

Several recent initiatives have lowered the cost of accessing household datasets. The goal of this book, then, is to reduce the cost of analyzing data and sharing findings with interested parties.

This book has two unique aspects. First, the theoretical discussion is based on a highly accessible, unified treatment of inequality and poverty in terms of income standards or basic indicators of the overall size of the income distribution. Examples include the mean, median, and other traditional ways of summarizing a distribution with one or several representative indicators. The literature on the measurement of inequality has proliferated since the 1960s. This book provides an excellent overview of that extensive literature.

Most poverty measures are built on two pillars. First, the "poverty line" delineates the income levels that define a poor person, and second, various measures capture the depths of the incomes of those below the poverty line. The approach here considers income standards as the basic measurement building blocks and uses them to construct inequality and poverty measures. This unified approach provides advantages in interpreting and contrasting the measures and in understanding the way measures vary over time and space.

Second, the theoretical presentation is complemented by empirical examples that ground the discussion, and it provides a practical guide to the inequality and poverty modules of the ADePT software developed at the World Bank. By immediately applying the measurement tools, the reader develops a deeper understanding of what is being measured. A battery of exercises in chapter 2 also aids the learning process.

The ADePT software enables users to analyze microdata—from sources such as household surveys—and generate print-ready, standardized tables and charts. It can also be used to simulate the effect of economic shocks, farm subsidies, cash transfers, and other policy instruments on poverty, inequality, and labor. The software automates the analysis, helps minimize human error, and encourages development of new methods of economic analysis.

For each run, ADePT produces one output file—containing your selection of tables and graphs, an optional original data summary, and errors and notifications—in Microsoft Excel® format. Tables of standard errors and frequencies can be added to a report, if desired.

These two components—a unifying framework for measurement and the immediate application of measures facilitated by ADePT software—make this book a unique source for cutting-edge, practical income distribution analysis.

The book is bound to empower those already engaged in the analysis of poverty and inequality to do deeper research and plumb greater depths in searching for regularity in larger and larger datasets. But I am also hopeful that it will draw new researchers into this important field of inquiry. This book should also be of help in enriching the discussion and analysis relating to the World Bank's recent effort to define new targets and indicators for promoting work on eradicating poverty and enhancing shared prosperity.

The work on this project was facilitated by the proximity of two key institutions, the World Bank and the George Washington University. But as anyone who has contemplated the world knows, proximity does not necessarily lead to cooperation. It is a tribute to the authors that they made use of this natural advantage and, through their shared willingness to support collaborative research across institutional boundaries, managed to produce this very useful monograph. My expectation is that this will be the first of many such collaborations.

Kaushik Basu
Senior Vice President and Chief Economist
The World Bank

Preface

This book is made possible by financial support from the Research Support Budget of the World Bank, the Knowledge for Change Program (KCP), and the Rapid Social Response (RSR) Program. The KCP is designed to promote high-quality, cutting-edge research that creates knowledge to support policies for poverty reduction and sustainable development. KCP is funded by the generous contributions of Australia, Canada, China, Denmark, the European Commission, Finland, France, Japan, the Netherlands, Norway, Singapore, Sweden, Switzerland, the United Kingdom, ABN AMRO Bank, and the International Fund for Agricultural Development. RSR is a multidonor endeavor to help the world's poorest countries build effective social protection and labor systems that safeguard poor and vulnerable people against severe shocks and crises. RSR has been generously supported by Australia, Norway, the Russian Federation, Sweden, and the United Kingdom.

James Foster is grateful to the Elliott School of International Affairs and Dean Michael Brown for facilitating research on global poverty and international development. The Ultra-poverty Initiative of its Institute for International Economic Policy (IIEP), spearheaded by its former director, Stephen Smith, has been a focal point of these efforts. A major gift to the Elliott School from an anonymous donor significantly enhanced the research capacity of IIEP and helped make the present project a reality.

We are grateful to the Oxford Poverty and Human Development Initiative (OPHI) and its director, Sabina Alkire, for allowing Suman Seth time away from OPHI's core efforts on multidimensional measures of poverty and well-being to work on the unidimensional methods presented here. Streams of students have helped refine the ideas, and we are particularly grateful to Chrysanthi Hatzimasoura who organized the weekly Development Tea at the Elliott School in which many useful conversations have been held.

The authors thank Bill Creitz for his excellent editorial support and Denise Bergeron, Mark Ingebretsen, and Stephen McGroarty in the World Bank Office of the Publisher for managing the production and dissemination of this volume.

Elliott School of
International Affairs
THE GEORGE WASHINGTON UNIVERSITY

Institute for
International
Economic Policy
THE GEORGE WASHINGTON UNIVERSITY

RAPID SOCIAL RESPONSE

Chapter 1

Introduction

What is poverty? At its most general level, poverty is the absence of acceptable choices across a broad range of important life decisions—a severe lack of freedom to be or to do what one wants. The inevitable outcome of poverty is insufficiency and deprivation across many of the facets of a fulfilling life:

- Inadequate resources to buy the basic necessities of life
- Frequent bouts of illness and an early death
- Literacy and education levels that undermine adequate functioning and limit one's comprehension of the world and oneself
- Living conditions that imperil physical and mental health
- Jobs that are at best unfulfilling and at worst dangerous
- A pronounced absence of dignity, a lack of respect from others
- Exclusion from community affairs.

The presence of poverty commonly leads groups to undertake activities and policies designed to reduce poverty—responses that take many forms and that are seen at many levels. A family in India helps pay for the children of its housekeeper or *aiya*. Buddhists, Confucians, Christians, and Muslims work together in Jakarta, Indonesia, to deliver alms to the poor during the fasting month. The governments of Mexico and Brazil implement PROGRESA (Programa de Educación, Salud y Alimentación, now called Oportunidades) and Bolsa Família, conditional cash transfer programs to help the poorest families invest in their children's human capital and to break the cycle of poverty. A nongovernmental organization from Bangladesh offers microfinance loans and education to poor people in Uganda.

At the United Nations Millennium Forum in 2000, 193 countries agreed on the Millennium Development Goals, which, among other targets, aim to reduce the proportion of people living on $1.25 a day by half within 15 years. Following the Group of 8 (G-8) Summit in Gleneagles, Scotland, in 2005, the World Bank, the International Monetary Fund, and the African Development Bank agreed to a plan of debt relief for the poorest countries.

What reasons underlie efforts to alleviate poverty? Individuals often consider alleviating poverty a personal responsibility that arises from religious or philosophical convictions. Many see poverty as the outcome of an unfair system that privileges some and constrains opportunities for others—a fundamental injustice that can also lead to social conflict and violence if not addressed. Others view poverty as a denial of universal rights and human dignity that requires collective action at a global level.

Political leaders often portray poverty as the enemy of social stability and good governance. Economists focus on the waste and inefficiency of allowing a portion of the population to fall significantly below potential. Many countries include poverty alleviation as an essential component of their programs for sustainable growth and development. Business leaders are reevaluating the "bottom of the pyramid" as a substantial untapped market that can be bolstered through efforts to address poverty.

Measurement is an important tool for the many efforts that are addressing poverty. By identifying who the poor are and where they are located, poverty measurements can help direct resources and focus efforts more effectively. The measurements create a picture of the magnitude of the problem and the way it varies over space and time. Measurements can help identify programs that work well in addressing poverty. Civil society groups can use information on poverty as evidence of unaddressed needs and missing services. Governments can be held accountable for their policies. Analysts can explore the underlying relationships between poverty and other economic and social variables to obtain a deeper understanding of the phenomenon.

How can poverty be measured? The process has three main steps:

1. Choose the *space* in which poverty will be assessed. The traditional space has been income, consumption, or some other welfare indicator measured in monetary units. This book will focus on the traditional space (although attention is turning to other dimensions, such as opportunities and capabilities).

2. *Identify* the poor. This step involves selecting a poverty line that indicates the minimum acceptable level of income or consumption.

3. *Aggregate* the data into an overall poverty measure. Headcount ratio is the most basic measure. It simply calculates the share of the population that is poor. But following the work of Amartya Sen, other aggregation methods designed to evaluate the depth and severity of poverty have become part of the poverty analyst's standard toolkit.[1]

Applying and interpreting poverty measures require understanding the methods used to assess two other aspects of income distribution: its spread (as evaluated by an inequality measure like the Gini coefficient) and its size (as gauged by an "income standard" like the mean or median income). There are several links between income inequality, poverty, and income standards. For instance, inequality and poverty often move together—particularly when growth in the distribution is small and its size is relatively unchanged.

Other links exist for individual poverty measures. To gauge the depth of poverty, a poverty measure can assess the size of the income distribution among the poor—or a *poor income standard*. Other measures incorporate a special concern for the poorest of the poor and are sensitive to the income distribution among the poor. This sensitivity takes the form of including a measure of inequality among the poor within the measure of poverty. Thus, to measure and to understand the many dimensions of income poverty, one must have a clear understanding of income standards and inequality measures.

This chapter is a conceptual introduction to poverty measurement and the related distributional analysis tools. It begins with a brief discussion of the variable and data to be used in poverty assessment. It then discusses the various income standards commonly used in distributional analysis. Inequality measures are then introduced, and their meanings in income standards are presented. The final part of this introduction combines those elements to obtain the main tools for evaluating poverty.

The second chapter complements this introduction by providing a detailed outline and more formal analysis of the concepts introduced here, and follows the composition of this chapter closely. The third chapter and the appendix includes tables and figures that may be useful in understanding some of the concepts and examples in the first two chapters.

The Income Variable

Our discussion begins with the variable *income*, which may also represent consumption expenditure or some other single dimensional outcome variable. Data are typically collected at the household level. So to construct an income variable at the individual level, one must make certain assumptions about its allocation within the household. Using these assumptions, household data are converted into individual data that indicate the *equivalent* income level an individual commands, thereby taking account of household structure and other characteristics.

One simplification is to assume that overall income is spread evenly across each person in the household. However, many other *equivalence scales* can be used. This adjustment enables comparisons to be made symmetrically across people irrespective of household or other characteristics. This simplification justifies the assumption of *symmetry* invoked when evaluating income distributions—whereby switching the (equivalent) income levels of two people leaves the evaluation unchanged. Additionally, it is assumed that the resulting variable can be measured with a *cardinal* scale that allows comparison of income differences across people.

The Data

Income distribution data can be represented in a variety of ways. The simplest form is a vector of incomes, one for each person in the specified population. This format naturally arises when the data are derived from a population census. The population distribution may be proxied by an unweighted sample, which yields a vector of incomes, each of which represents an equal share of the population. It can also be represented by a weighted sample, which differentiates across observations in the vector in a prescribed way. For clarity, we will focus on the equal-weighted case here.

Of course, a sample carries less information than does a full census, but the extent of the loss can be gauged and accounted for via statistical analysis. One further assumption must be made at this point: the evaluation method is invariant to the population size, in that a replication of the vector (having, say, k copies of each observation for every original observation) is evaluated in the same way as the original sample vector. This *population invariance* assumption ensures that the method can be applied directly to a sample vector when attempting to evaluate a population. More generally, the method depends on a distribution function, which normalizes the population size to one.

The second way of representing an income distribution is with a *cumulative distribution function* (cdf), in which each level of income indicates the percentage of the population having that income level or lower. A cdf automatically treats incomes symmetrically or anonymously (in that it ignores who has what income) and is invariant with respect to the population size. It is straightforward to construct the cdf for a particular vector of incomes as a step function that jumps up by $1/N$ for each observation in the vector, where N is the number of observations. For large enough samples, the income distribution can be approximated by a continuous distribution having a density function whose integral up to an income level is the value of the cdf at that income level.

Whereas a cdf is a standard representation, one that is even more intuitive in the present context is the *quantile* function. The quantile function gives the minimum income necessary to capture a given percentage p of the population, so that, for example, the quantile at $p = 12.5$ percent is the income level above which 87.5 percent of the population lies. For the case of a strictly increasing and continuous cdf, the quantile function is the inverse of the cdf found by rotating the axes. If the cdf has flat portions or jumps up discontinuously, then certain alterations to the rotated function must be made to obtain the quantile function. Another version of the quantile function is Pen's Parade, which displays the distribution as an hour-long parade of incomes from lowest to highest.

Income Standards and Size

Given an income distribution, three separate but related aspects are of interest: the distribution's size, the distribution's spread, and the distribution's base. We will discuss the size issue here. Subsequent sections deal with the spread and base concepts.

Distribution size is most often indicated by the *mean* or per capita income. For the vector representation, the mean is obtained by dividing total income by the total number of people in the distribution. The mean can also be viewed as the average height (or, in mathematical terms, the integral) of the quantile function. It is the income level that all people would achieve if they were given an equal share of overall resources.

Another size indicator, *median income*, is the income at the midway point of the quantile function, with half the incomes below and half above. Most empirical income distributions are skewed so that the mean (which includes the largest incomes in the averaging process) exceeds the median income (which is unaffected by the values of the largest incomes). Still another measure of size is given by the mean income of the lowest fifth of the population, which focuses exclusively on the lower incomes in a distribution. Each of these indicators is an example of an *income standard*, which reduces the overall income distribution to a single income level indicating some aspect of the distribution's size.

What Is an Income Standard?

To understand what a measure or index means, explicitly stating a set of properties that it should satisfy is helpful. In the case of an income standard, there are several requirements that go beyond the basic symmetry and population invariance discussed above:

- *Normalization* states that if all incomes happen to be the same, then the income standard must be that commonly held level of income—a natural property indeed.
- *Linear homogeneity* requires that if all incomes are scaled up or down by a common factor, then the income standard must rise or fall by that same factor.
- *Weak monotonicity* requires the income standard to rise, or at least not fall, if any income rises and no other income changes.

These basic requirements ensure that the income standard measures the size of the income distribution as a "representative" income level that responds "in the right way" when incomes change (for example, these requirements rule out envy effects). It is easy to see that the size indicators discussed in the previous section—mean, median, and mean of the lowest fifth—conform to these general requirements.

Common Examples

Four types of income standards are in common use:

- First are the *quantile incomes*, such as the income at the 10th percentile, the income at the 90th percentile, and the median. Each is informative about a specific point in the distribution but ignores the values of the remaining points.

- Next are the (relative) *partial means* obtained by finding the mean of the incomes below a specific percentile cutoff (the *lower partial means*) or above the cutoff (the *upper partial means*), such as the mean of the lowest 20 percent and the mean of the highest 10 percent. Each of these income standards indicates the size of distribution by focusing on one or the other side of a given percentile and by measuring the average income of this range while ignoring the rest. As the cutoff varies between 0 percent and 100 percent, the lower partial mean varies between the lowest income and the mean income, whereas the upper partial mean varies between the mean income and the highest income.

  By focusing on a specific income or a range of incomes, the quantile incomes and the partial means ignore income changes outside that range. The remaining two forms of income standard, by contrast, are *monotonic* so that the increase in income causes the income standard to strictly rise.

- The *general means* take into account all incomes in the distribution, but emphasize lower or higher incomes depending on the value of parameter α (that can be any real number). When α is nonzero, the general mean is found by raising all incomes to the power α, then by averaging, and finally by taking the result to the power $1/\alpha$. This process of transforming incomes and then untransforming the average ensures that the income standard is, in fact, measured by income (or, in income space, as we might say).

  In the remaining case of $\alpha = 0$, the general mean is defined to be the *geometric mean*. It is obtained by raising all incomes to the power $1/N$, then taking the product. For $\alpha < 1$, incomes are effectively transformed by a concave function, thus placing greater emphasis on lower incomes. For $\alpha > 1$, the transformation is convex, and the general mean emphasizes higher incomes.

As α varies across all possible values, the general mean rises from minimum income (as α approaches $-\infty$), to the *harmonic mean* ($\alpha = -1$), the *geometric mean* ($\alpha = 0$), the mean ($\alpha = 1$), the *Euclidean mean* ($\alpha = 2$), up to the maximum income (as α approaches ∞). General means with $\alpha < 0$ are only defined for positive incomes.

- The final income standard is a step in the direction of a "maximin" approach, which evaluates a situation by the condition of the least advantaged person. The usual mean can be reinterpreted as the expected value of a single income drawn randomly from the population. Suppose that instead of a single income, we were to draw *two* incomes randomly from the population (with replacement). If we then evaluated the pair by the lower of the two incomes, this would lead to the *Sen mean*, defined as the expectation of the minimum of two randomly drawn incomes.

Because we are using the minimum of the two, this number can be no higher than the mean and is generally lower. Consequently, the Sen mean also emphasizes lower incomes but in a different way to the general means with $\alpha < 1$, the lower partial means, or the quantile incomes below the median.

Calculating the Sen mean for an income vector is straightforward. Create an $N \times N$ matrix that has a cell for every possible pair of incomes, and place the lower value of the two incomes in the cell. Add up all the entries and divide by the number of entries (N^2) to obtain their mean, which is the expected value of the lower income. This mean has close ties to the well-known Gini coefficient measure of inequality.

Welfare

The general means for $\alpha < 1$ and the Sen mean are also commonly interpreted as measures of welfare. The key additional property that allows this interpretation is the *transfer principle*, which requires an income transfer from one person to another who is richer (or equally rich) to lower the income standard. In other words, a regressive transfer that does not change the mean income should lower the income standard.

One way to justify this property begins with a utilitarian symmetric welfare function that views welfare derived from an income distribution to be the average level of (indirect) utility in society, where it is assumed that everyone's utility function is identical and strictly increasing. In this context, the intuitive assumption of diminishing marginal utility (each additional dollar leads to a higher level, but a lower increment, of utility) yields the transfer principle, because the loss to the giver is greater than the gain to the richer receiver.

This form of welfare function was considered by Atkinson (1970), who then defined a helpful transformation of the welfare function called the *equally distributed equivalent income* (ede). The ede is that income level which, if received by all people, would yield the same welfare level as an original income distribution. The particular ede he focused on was, in fact, the general mean for $\alpha < 1$. Sen suggested going beyond the utilitarian form. One key nonutilitarian example is the Sen mean, which can be viewed as both an ede and a general welfare function and also satisfies the transfer principle.

Applications

Income standards are used to assess a population's prosperity, the way it compares to other populations, and the way it progresses through time. The most common examples are country-level assessments of mean or per capita income and its associated growth rate. This is a mainstay of the growth literature, and many interesting economic questions about the determinants of growth and its effect on other variables of interest have been addressed. In the recent example of *The Growth Report: Strategies for Sustained Growth and Inclusive Development* (Commission on Growth and Development 2008), countries with high and sustained levels of growth in the mean income were evaluated to see if the factors that made this possible could be identified.

Imagine undertaking a similar study with a different income standard to focus on one part of the income distribution or, perhaps, even examining growth in a different underlying variable. Some studies use the median income, arguing that it corresponds more naturally to the middle of the income distribution (see, for example, the report by the Commission on the Measurement of Economic and Social Progress [2009], also known as the *Sarkozy Report*). Other authors have used the mean of the lowest fifth of the population, or a general mean (with $\alpha < 0$) as a low-income standard, to examine how growth in one income standard (the mean) relates to growth in the incomes of the poor. Because each income standard measures the distribution's size in a distinct way, examining several at once can clarify the quality of growth—including whether it is *shared* or *pro-poor* growth.

Subgroup Consistency

In certain empirical applications, there is a natural concern for certain identifiable subgroups of the population as well as for the overall population. For example, one might be interested in the achievements of the various states or subregions of a country to understand the spatial dimensions of growth. When population subgroups are tracked alongside the overall population value, there is a risk that the income standard could indicate contradictory or confusing trends.

A natural consistency property for an income standard might be that if subgroup population sizes are fixed but incomes vary, then when the income standard rises in one subgroup and does not fall in the rest, the overall population income standard must rise. This property is known as *subgroup consistency*; and using a measure that satisfies it avoids inconsistencies arising from this sort of multilevel analyses. In fact, several income standards discussed above do not survive this test and, hence, may need to be avoided when undertaking regional evaluations or other forms of subgroup analyses.

The mean of the lowest 20 percent is subject to this critique because a given policy could succeed in raising the mean of the lowest 20 percent in *every* region of a given country; yet the mean of the lowest 20 percent in the *overall* population could fall. The same is true of the Sen mean or the median. In contrast, every general mean satisfies the consistency requirement. In fact, it can be shown that the general means are the *only* income standards that are subgroup consistent while satisfying some additional basic properties.

Moreover, each of the general means has a simple formula that links regional levels of the income standard to the overall level. If one were to go further and specify an additive aggregation formula across subgroup standards—a requirement that might be called *additive decomposability*—the only general mean that would survive is the mean itself. The overall mean is just the population-weighted sum of subgroup means.

Dominance and Unanimity

One motivation for examining several income standards at the same time is *robustness*: Do conclusions about the direction of change in the distribution size using one income standard (say, the mean) hold for others (say, the nearby generalized means)? A second reason might be *focus* or an identified concern with different parts of the distribution: Has rapid growth at the top (say, the 90th percentile income) been matched by growth at the middle (say, the median) or the bottom (say, the 10th percentile income)?

We can answer questions of this sort by plotting an entire class of income standards against percentiles of income distribution. We can then use the curve to determine if a given comparison is unambiguous (one curve is above the other) or if it is contingent (the curves cross).

A first curve is given by the quantile function itself, which simultaneously depicts incomes from lowest to highest. As income standards, quantiles are somewhat partial and insensitive—yet when they all agree that one distribution is larger than another, this ensures that *every* other income standard must follow their collective judgment.

The quantile function represents *first-order stochastic dominance*, which also ensures higher welfare according to every utilitarian welfare function with identical, increasing utility functions. Thus, on the one hand, the robustness implied by an unambiguous comparison of quantile functions extends to *all* income standards and *all* symmetric welfare functions for which "more is better." On the other hand, if some quantiles rise and others fall, then the resulting curves will cross and the final judgment is contingent on which income standard is selected. In this case, the quantile function can be helpful in identifying winning and losing portions of the distribution.

A second curve of this sort is given by the *generalized Lorenz curve*, which graphs the area under the quantile function up to each percent p of the population. It can be shown that the height of the generalized Lorenz curve at any p is the lower partial mean times p itself. For example, if the lowest income of a four-person vector were 280, then the generalized Lorenz curve value (ordinate) at $p = 25$ percent would be 70.

A comparison of generalized Lorenz curves conveys information on lower partial means, with a higher generalized Lorenz curve indicating agreement among *all* lower partial means. As income standards, the lower partial means are insensitive to certain increments and income transfers. Yet when all these income standards are in agreement, it follows that *every* monotonic income standard satisfying the transfer principle would abide by their judgment.

Indeed, the generalized Lorenz curve represents *second-order stochastic dominance*, which signals higher welfare according to *every* utilitarian welfare function with identical and increasing utility function exhibiting diminishing marginal utility (Atkinson's general class of welfare functions).

However, if generalized Lorenz curves cross, then the final judgment is contingent on which monotonic income standard satisfying the transfer principle is employed.

Notice that when quantile functions can rank two distributions, generalized Lorenz curves must rank them in the same way, because a higher quantile function ensures that the area beneath it is also greater. However, even when quantile functions cross, generalized Lorenz curves may be able to rank the two distributions. We will use these two curves and their stochastic dominance rankings later in discussing inequality and poverty measurement.

A final curve depicts the general mean levels as the parameter α varies. Given the properties of the general means, this curve is increasing in α and tends to the minimum income for very low α and rises through the harmonic, geometric, arithmetic, and Euclidean means, tending toward the maximum income as α becomes very large. A higher quantile function will raise the general mean curve. A higher generalized Lorenz curve will raise the general mean curve for $\alpha < 1$ or the general means that favor the low incomes. The curve is useful for determining whether a given comparison of general means is robust, and if not, which of the income standards are higher or lower. It will also be particularly relevant to discussions of inequality in later sections.

Growth Curves

Some analyses go beyond the question of which distribution is larger to consider the question of how much larger in percentage terms is one distribution than another. This question is especially salient when the two distributions are associated with the same population at two points in time. Then the next question becomes at what percentage rate did the income standard grow. Such growth is most often defined by income per capita, or the mean income. However, the defining properties of an income standard ensure that its rate of growth is a meaningful number that can be compared with the growth rates of other income standards, either for robustness purposes or for an understanding of the quality of growth.

A *growth curve* depicts the rate of growth across an entire class of income standards, where the standards are ordered from lowest to highest. Each of the dominance curves described above suggests an associated growth curve.

For the quantile function, the resulting growth curve is called the *growth incidence curve*. The height of the curve at $p = 50$ percent gives the growth rate of the median income. Varying p allows us to examine whether this growth rate is robust to the choice of income standard or whether the lower income standards grew at a different rate than the rest.

The *generalized Lorenz growth curve* indicates how the lower partial means are changing over time, so that the height of this curve at $p = 20$ percent is the rate at which the mean income of the lowest 20 percent of the population changed over time. Finally, the *general means growth curve* plots the rate of growth of each general mean against the parameter α. When $\alpha = 1$, the height of the curve is the usual growth rate of the mean income; $\alpha = 0$ yields the rate of growth for the geometric mean, and so forth. As we will see below, each of these growth curves can be of help in understanding the link between growth and the evolution of inequality over time.

Inequality Measures and Spread

The second aspect of the distribution—spread—is evaluated using a numerical inequality measure, which assigns each distribution a number that indicates its level of inequality. The Gini coefficient is the most commonly used measure of inequality. It measures the average or expected difference between pairs of incomes in the distribution, relative to the distribution size, and also is linked to the well-known Lorenz curve (discussed below). The *Kuznets ratio* measures inequality as the share of the income going to the top fifth divided by the income share of the bottom two-fifths of the population. Finally, the *90/10 ratio* is the income at the 90th percentile divided by the 10th percentile income. It is often used by labor economists as a measure of earnings inequality. These are just a few of the many inequality measures used to evaluate income distribution.

What Is an Inequality Measure?

There are two main ways to understand what an income inequality measure actually gauges. The first way is through the properties it satisfies. The second makes use of a fundamental link between inequality measures and income standards. We begin with the first approach.

There are four basic properties for inequality measures:

- The first two are *symmetry* and *population invariance* properties, which are analogous to those defined for income standards. They ensure that inequality depends entirely on income distribution and not on names or numbers of income recipients.
- The third is *scale invariance* (or *homogeneity of degree zero*), which requires the inequality measure to be unchanged if all incomes are scaled up or down by a common factor. This ensures that the inequality being measured is a purely relative concept and is independent of the distribution size. In contrast, doubling all incomes will double distribution size as measured by any income standard, thereby reflecting its respective property of linear homogeneity.
- The final property is the *weak transfer principle*, which in this context requires income transfer from one person to another who is richer (or equally rich) to raise inequality or leave it unchanged. In other words, a regressive transfer cannot decrease inequality. This is an intuitive property for inequality measures. It is often presented in a stronger form, known as the *transfer principle*, which requires a regressive transfer to (strictly) increase inequality.

The Gini coefficient and the Kuznets ratio satisfy all four basic properties for inequality measures. The 90/10 ratio satisfies the first three but violates the weak transfer principle: a regressive transfer between people at the 5th percentile and the 10th percentile can raise the 10th percentile income, thus lowering inequality as measured by the 90/10 ratio. Although this result does not rule out the use of the intuitive 90/10 ratio as an inequality measure, it does suggest that conclusions obtained with this measure should be scrutinized.

The four basic properties define the general requirements for inequality measures. Additional properties help to discern between acceptable measures. For example, *decomposability* and *subgroup consistency* (discussed in a later section) are helpful in certain applications. *Transfer sensitivity* ensures that an inequality measure is more sensitive to changes in the income distribution at the lower end of the distribution.

A second way of understanding inequality measures relies on an intuitive link between inequality measures and pairs of income standards. The basic structure is perhaps easiest to see in the extreme case where there are only two people and, hence, only two incomes. Letting *a* denote the smaller income of the two, and b denote the larger income, it is natural to measure inequality by the relative distance between a and b, such as $I = (b - a)/b$, or some other increasing function of the ratio b/a. Indeed, scale invariance and the weak transfer principle essentially require this form for the measure.

Suppose that instead of evaluating the inequality between two people, we want to measure the inequality between two equal-sized groups. A natural way of proceeding is to represent each group's income distribution using an income standard. This yields a pair of representative incomes—one for each group—that can then be compared. Where a denotes the smaller of these two incomes and b the larger, it is natural to measure inequality between the two groups as $I = (b - a)/b$, or some other increasing function of the ratio b/a. For example, if the distributions are the earnings of men and women and the income standard is the mean, then b/a would be the ratio of the average income for men to the average income for women—a common indicator of inequality between the two groups. As will be discussed below, this "between-group" approach is useful in decompositions of inequality by population subgroup and also in the measurement of inequality of opportunities.

The general idea that inequality depends on two income standards is also relevant when evaluating the overall inequality in a population's distribution of income. But instead of applying the *same* income standard to *two* distributions, we now apply *two* income standards to the *same* distribution. One of the income standards (the upper standard) places greater weight on higher incomes, and the second (the lower standard) emphasizes lower incomes; so for any given income distribution, the lower-income standard's value is never larger than the upper-income standard's value.

This is true, for example, when the lower standard is the geometric mean and the upper is the arithmetic mean or, alternatively, when the lower is the 10th percentile income and the upper is the 90th percentile income. Inequality is then seen as the extent to which the two income standards are spread apart: where a denotes the lower-income standard and b the upper-income standard, overall inequality is $I = (b - a)/b$, or some other increasing function of the ratio b/a.

Common Examples

Virtually all inequality measures in common use are based on twin income standards. This is easily seen in the case of the 90/10 ratio, and generalizes to any *quantile ratio* b/a, where a corresponds to the income at a percentile p of the distribution and b is the income at a higher percentile q of the distribution. The quantile incomes are relatively insensitive income standards, and hence they yield inequality measures that are somewhat crude and that disagree with the weak transfer property that is traditionally regarded as a basic property of inequality measures. Nonetheless, they succeed at conveying tangible information about the distribution—namely, the extent to which two quantile incomes differ from one another—and can be informative, if crude, measures of inequality.

The Kuznets ratio has as its twin income standards the mean of those from 40 percent downward and the mean of those from 80 percent upward, respectively. This can be generalized to any ratio of two standards of this form by varying the cutoffs. The resulting measure, which we call the *partial mean ratio*, is given by b/a, where a is the lower partial mean at p and b is the upper partial mean at q. The case where $p = 10$ percent and $q = 90$ percent is often called the *decile ratio*. Another related measure is the *income share of the top 1 percent*, which is a multiple of the partial mean ratio with $p = 100$ percent and $q = 99$ percent. Although each partial mean ratio satisfies four basic properties of an inequality measure, the component income standards are still rather crude and focus on only a limited range of incomes. Those falling outside the range are ignored entirely, while the income distribution within the range is also not considered. The resulting measure is thus insensitive to certain transfers. As before, though, the twin standards and their ratio convey tangible and easily understood information about the income distribution.

The Gini coefficient is defined as the expected (absolute) difference between two randomly drawn incomes divided by twice the mean. Calculating the Gini coefficient is therefore straightforward:

1. Create an $N \times N$ matrix having a cell for every possible pair of incomes, and place the absolute value of their difference in the cell.
2. Add all the entries and divide by the number of entries (N^2) to obtain the expected value of the absolute difference between two randomly drawn incomes.
3. Divide by two times the mean income of the distribution to obtain the Gini coefficient. It is a natural indicator of how "spread out" incomes are from one another.

The Gini coefficient has as its twin income standards the mean and the Sen mean and can be written as $I = (b - a)/b$, where b is the mean and a is the Sen mean. The expected (absolute) difference between two incomes can be written as $(a' - a)$, where a' is the expectation of their maximum and a is the expectation of their minimum. Because the mean b can be written as $(a' + a)/2$, the difference $(b - a)$ is half of the expected absolute difference between incomes, which confirms that $(b - a)/b$ is an equivalent definition of the Gini coefficient. In other words, the Gini coefficient is the extent to which the Sen mean falls below the mean as a percentage of the mean.

Atkinson's class of inequality measures also takes the form $I = (b - a)/b$, where the upper-income standard b is also the mean, but now the lower-income standard a is a general mean with parameter $\alpha < 1$. This income standard focuses on lower incomes by raising each income to the α power, averaging across all the transformed incomes, then converting back to income space by raising the result to the power $1/\alpha$. A lower value of the parameter α yields an income standard that is more sensitive to lower incomes and is lower in value. This will be reflected in a higher value for $(b - a)/b$, so the percentage loss from the mean is seen to be higher.

The final example is the family of *generalized entropy measures*, whose definition and properties vary with a parameter α. There are three distinct ranges for the parameter: a lower range where $\alpha < 1$, an upper range where $\alpha > 1$, and a limiting case where $\alpha = 1$.

When $\alpha < 1$, the generalized entropy measures evaluate inequality in the same way as the Atkinson class of inequality measures (and, in fact, are monotonic transformations). For example, when $\alpha = 0$, the measure is the *mean log deviation* or *Theil's second measure* given by $ln(b/a)$, where b is the arithmetic mean and a is the geometric mean. Atkinson's version is $(b - a)/b$.

Over the second range where $\alpha > 1$, the general mean places *greater* weight on higher incomes and yields a representative income that is typically higher than the mean. If all incomes were equal, the general mean and the mean would be equal. However, when incomes are unequal, the general mean will rise above the mean. The extent to which this occurs is used by the measure to evaluate inequality. For example, the inequality measure obtained when $\alpha = 2$ is *(half) the squared coefficient of variation*, that is, one-half of the variance over the squared mean. The general mean in this case is the Euclidean mean, which first squares all incomes, then averages the transformed incomes, and finally returns to income space by taking the square root. The Euclidean mean and the mean of the two-income distribution (4, 4) are both 4. Altering the distribution to (1, 7) raises the Euclidean mean to 5 but leaves its mean at 4.

The final case where $\alpha = 1$ leads to Theil's first measure, which is one of the few inequality measures without a natural twin standards representation, but is, in fact, a limit of such measures.

Inequality and Welfare

The Gini coefficient and Atkinson's family share a social welfare interpretation. Both are expressible as $I = (b - a)/b$, where b is the mean income of the distribution and a is an income standard that can be viewed as a welfare function (satisfying the weak transfer principle). Note that the distribution where everyone has the mean has a level of welfare that is highest among all distributions with the same total income, and its measured level of welfare is just the mean itself (by the normalization property of income standards).

The mean b is the maximum value that the welfare function can take over all income distributions of the same total income. When incomes are all equal, $a = b$ and inequality is zero. When the actual welfare level a falls below the maximum welfare level b, the percentage welfare loss $I = (b - a)/b$ is used as a measure of inequality. This is the welfare interpretation of both the Gini coefficient and the Atkinson class.

The simple structure of these measures allows us to express the welfare function by the mean income and the inequality measure. A quick rearrangement leads to $a = b(1 - I)$, which can be reinterpreted as the welfare function a viewed as an inequality-adjusted mean. If there is no inequality in the distribution, then $(1 - I) = 1$ and $a = b$. If the inequality level is $I > 0$, then the welfare level is obtained by discounting the mean income by $(1 - I) < 1$. For example, if we take I to be the Gini coefficient, the Sen mean (or Sen welfare function) can be obtained by multiplying the mean by $(1 - I)$. Similarly, if we take I to be the Atkinson measure with parameter $\alpha = 0$, then the welfare function is the geometric mean, and it can be obtained by multiplying the mean by $(1 - I)$.

Applications

Inequality measures are used to assess the extent to which incomes are spread apart in a country or region and the way this level changes over time and space. Of particular interest is the interplay between a population's average prosperity, as represented by the mean income, and the income distribution, as represented by an inequality measure. The positive achievement of a high per capita income can be viewed less favorably if inequality is high, too. The combined effect on welfare can be evaluated using an inequality-adjusted mean.

The Kuznets hypothesis postulates that growth in per capita income initially comes at a cost of a higher level of inequality, but eventually inequality falls with growth. The resulting Kuznets curve, which depicts per capita income on the horizontal axis and inequality on the vertical axis, has the shape of an inverted U. If the hypothesis were true, then a rapidly growing developing country could have only moderate welfare improvements, whereas a moderately growing developed country could experience rapid improvements in welfare, all because of the changing levels of inequality.

An alternative view takes the initial level of inequality as one of the determinants of income growth. For example, greater inequality might lead to a higher average savings rate if the richer groups have a greater propensity to save, and this can positively influence long-term growth. Conversely, high inequality might create political pressure to raise the marginal tax rate on the rich, which could diminish incentives to invest and grow. These applications of inequality measures view inequality as a valuable macro indicator of the health of a country's economy that influences and is affected by other macro variables.

Other applications try to assess the origins of inequality in the micro economy. Could inequality in earned incomes be due to (a) a high return to education, (b) a decline in union power, (c) increased competition from abroad, (d) discrimination, or (e) demographic changes such as increased female labor force participation? Mincer (1974) equations can help trace earnings inequality to the underlying characteristics of the labor force, including the level and distribution of human capital. Oaxaca decompositions (1973) test for the presence of discrimination by sex, race, or other characteristics and have been adapted to evaluate the contribution of demographic changes to observed earnings inequality.

Depending on the policy question, it may make sense to move from an overall inequality measure (that evaluates the spread across the entire distribution) to a group-based inequality measure (that compares the mean or other income standard across several groups). The latter, more limited, notion of inequality can often have greater significance, particularly if the underlying groups are easy to understand and have social or political salience. Examples include racial, sex, and ethnic inequality, or the inequality between urban and rural areas.

The techniques for evaluating *between-group* inequality involve *smoothing* incomes within each subgroup to the subgroup mean (or other income standard) and then applying an inequality measure to the resulting smoothed distribution. Because the inequality within groups is suppressed, all that is left is between-group inequality.

Similar techniques have recently been employed to evaluate the *inequality of opportunity* in a given country. This exercise begins by identifying *circumstances* or the characteristics of a person that are not under the direct control of that person and arguably should not be systematically linked to higher or lower levels of income. The population is then divided into subgroups of people sharing the same circumstances and the distribution is smoothed to suppress inequalities within subgroups. The inequality of the smoothed distribution then measures how much inequality is present across subgroups and, hence, how much is associated with circumstances. It can be viewed as a measure of the inequality of opportunity (given the posited circumstances).

The overall inequality in a country could be very high. But if the three main ethnic groups have more or less the same average levels of income, inequality of opportunity across the ethnic groups may not be such an important issue—much of the inequality arises from variations within ethnic groups. If the mean incomes vary greatly across ethnic groups so that the between-group inequality level is also quite high, then a concern for social stability may lead policy makers to address the high level of inequality of opportunity.

Analogous discussions might be made for other indicators besides income. For instance, if we are evaluating the distribution of health, then the way that health varies across subgroups defined by an indicator of *socioeconomic status* (SES)—such as occupation, income, education, or education of the parents—may be more salient than the overall distribution of health. The strength of the *gradient* or positive relationship between health and SES variables is often viewed as a key indicator of the *inequity* of health and is the target of policies to affect this particularly objectionable portion of health inequalities.

Different inequality measures have properties that make them well suited for certain applications. *Decomposability* is one such property discussed below. A second is *transfer sensitivity*, which ensures that a measure is especially sensitive to inequalities at the lower end of the distribution (in that a given transfer of income will have a greater effect the lower the incomes of the giver and the receiver). Transfer sensitive measures include the Atkinson family of measures, Theil's two measures, and the "lower half" of the generalized entropy measures with $\alpha < 2$.

Note that the coefficient of variation (a monotonic transformation of the generalized entropy measure with $\alpha = 2$) is transfer neutral in that a given transfer has the same equalizing effect up and down the distribution: a one-unit transfer of income between two rich people has the same effect on inequality as does a one-unit transfer of income between two poor people the same initial income distance apart. The upper half of the generalized entropy measures with $\alpha > 2$ focuses on inequality among upper incomes.

The Gini coefficient is often considered to be most sensitive to changes involving incomes at the middle, but this is not entirely accurate. The effect of a given-sized transfer on the Gini coefficient depends on the number of people between giver and receiver, not on their respective income levels. Because, empirically, there tend to be more observations bunched together in the middle of the distribution, the effect of a transfer near the middle tends to be larger.

Subgroup Consistency and Decomposability

Although the variance is not itself a measure of relative inequality (it violates scale invariance and focuses on absolute differences), the analysis of variance (ANOVA) provides a natural model for decomposition of inequality measures into a within-group and a between-group term. The motivating question here is given a collection of population subgroups, how much of the overall inequality can be attributed to inequality within the subgroups, and how much can be attributed to inequality across the subgroups.

Answers to this type of question become feasible when an inequality measure is *additively decomposable*, in which case the within-group inequality term is expressible as a weighted sum of the inequality levels within the groups, the between-group term is the inequality measure applied to the smoothed distribution, and the overall inequality level is just the sum of the within-group and between-group terms. The *contributions* of within-group and between-group inequality (within-group inequality divided by total inequality and between-group inequality divided by total inequality, respectively) will sum to one.

Decomposition analysis can help clarify the structure of income inequality across a population. It can identify regions or sectors of the economy that disproportionally contribute to inequality. And when the subgroups are defined with reference to an underlying variable such as schooling, the analysis can help identify the extent to which the variable explains inequality.

To analyze changes in inequality over time, one can separate the effect of changes in population sizes across subgroups (for example, arising from demographic factors) from the fundamental shifts in subgroup income distributions. This can be combined with regression analysis to model income changes and to pinpoint the variables that appear to be driving inequality.

The generalized entropy measures are the only inequality measures satisfying the usual form of additive decomposability, with the Theil measures ($\alpha = 0$ and $\alpha = 1$) and half the squared coefficient of variation ($\alpha = 2$) being most commonly used in empirical evaluations. The second Theil measure, also called the mean log deviation, has a particularly simple decomposition in which the within-group term is a population-share weighted average of subgroup inequality levels. This streamlined weighting structure can greatly simplify interpretation and application of decomposition analyses.

The allied property of *subgroup consistency* is helpful in ensuring that regional changes in inequality are appropriately reflected in overall inequality. Suppose there is no change in the population sizes and mean income levels of the subgroups. If inequality rose in one subgroup and was unchanged or rose in each of the other subgroups, it would be natural to expect that inequality overall would rise. For additively decomposable measures, this rise in inequality is assured: because the smoothed distribution is unchanged, the between-group term is unaffected. Because the weights on subgroup inequality levels are fixed (when subgroup means and population sizes do not change), the within-group term must rise.

Subgroup consistency is a more lenient requirement, because it does not specify the functional form that links subgroup inequality levels and overall inequality. Consequently, on the one hand we find that the Atkinson measures (which are transformations of the generalized entropy measures) are all subgroup consistent without being additively decomposable. On the other hand, the Gini coefficient is not subgroup consistent.

The problem with the Gini coefficient arises when the income ranges of the subgroup distributions overlap. In that case, the effect of a given distributional change on subgroup inequality can be opposite to its effect on overall inequality. The Gini coefficient can be broken into a within-group term, a between-group term, and an overlap term—and it is the overlap term that can override the within-group effect to generate subgroup inconsistencies.

Dominance and Unanimity

One alternative to numerical inequality measures for making inequality comparisons is the so-called *Lorenz curve* and its associated criterion of *Lorenz dominance*. The Lorenz curve graphs the share of income received by the lowest p percent of the population as p varies from 0 percent to 100 percent. A completely equal distribution yields a Lorenz curve where the lowest p percent receives p percent of the overall income, or the 45 degree line. Inequality results in a Lorenz curve that falls below this line in accordance with the extent and location of the inequality. When one compares two distributions, a higher Lorenz curve is associated with lower inequality. This is the case of Lorenz dominance in which one distribution is unambiguously less unequal than another. Alternatively, if the two Lorenz curves cross, no unambiguous determination can be made.

The Lorenz curve is a useful tool for locating pockets of inequality along the distribution. For example, if a portion of the curve is straight, then there is no inequality over that slice of the population. If it is very curved, then there is significant inequality over the relevant population range. It also can help determine if a given inequality comparison is robust to the choice of inequality measure.

Indeed, when the Lorenz curve of one distribution dominates the Lorenz curve of another distribution, it follows that every inequality measure satisfying the four basic properties (symmetry, replication invariance, scale invariance, and the weak transfer principle) will not go against this judgment, whereas the subsets of measures satisfying the transfer principle are in strict agreement with the Lorenz judgment (that the first has less inequality than the second). So these unambiguous judgments are also unanimous judgments across wide classes of inequality measures.

The Lorenz curve is also the generalized Lorenz curve divided by the mean. At $p = 0$ percent, both curves have the value 0 percent; at $p = 100$ percent, the Lorenz curve has the value 100 percent, whereas the generalized Lorenz curve takes the mean as its value. At any percentage of the population p, the generalized Lorenz curve is p times the associated lower partial mean at p, and the Lorenz curve is p times the lower partial mean *over the mean*.

If one recalls the link between second-order stochastic dominance and the generalized Lorenz curve, it follows that when the means of the two distributions under comparison are the same, a distribution has greater equality according to Lorenz dominance exactly when it has higher welfare for the general class of welfare functions considered by Atkinson. This is a very useful result called *Atkinson's Theorem*, which provides an interesting welfare basis for (fixed mean) Lorenz comparisons.

There is a useful link between the points along the Lorenz curve and a simple class of inequality measures. Consider the partial mean ratios obtained when p is variable and q is fixed at 100 percent. With $q = 100$ percent, the upper partial mean is the mean itself, and the partial mean ratio becomes a comparison between a lower partial mean (for example, a_p) and the overall mean b.

Now consider the Lorenz curve evaluated at the pth percentile. The vertical distance between the Lorenz curve and the 45-degree line of perfect equality is simply p times the inequality measure $I_p = (b - a_p)/b$ associated with the partial mean ratio b/a_p. Consequently, Lorenz dominance—which ensures that one of the vertical distances is larger and the rest are no smaller—is equivalent to the requirement that I_p is larger for some p and no smaller for every remaining p. The Lorenz curve can thus be viewed as the dominance curve associated with I_p or, equivalently, the associated partial mean ratios.

Although these measures are crude—evaluating inequality by comparing the mean of the lowest p of the population to the overall mean—they collectively imply Lorenz dominance and, hence, agreement for the entire set of inequality measures satisfying the four basic properties.

Each of the three curves generated by a class of income standards—the quantile curve, the generalized Lorenz curve, and the general means curve—provides a natural way of depicting a related twin-standard inequality measure. Identify the two income standards a and b of the measure, and draw a line segment connecting the associated points along the curve.

Note that the lower standard a is to the left and the higher standard b is to the right. The *relative slope* of this line (or the slope relative to the value of either a or b) is a proxy for the associated inequality level, with a higher relative slope implying a higher inequality level. For example, the relative slope of the line connecting the 10th and the 90th percentile incomes along the quantile curve represents the extent of inequality according to the 90/10 ratio.

Along the generalized Lorenz curve, the relative slope of the line from $p = 20$ percent to $q = 100$ percent is linked to the associated partial mean ratio discussed previously. Along the general mean curve, the relative slope of the line from the geometric mean ($\alpha = 0$) to the mean ($\alpha = 1$) corresponds to Theil's second measure, or the mean log deviation.

A similar discussion applies to all the generalized entropy measures, apart from Theil's first measure. It is interesting to note that although Theil's first measure is not a twin-standard measure, it is represented as the relative slope of the general mean curve at $\alpha = 1$. In the extreme case where all incomes are the same, the quantile and general means curves will be entirely flat, because all the income standards are the same and correspond to the income level of everyone. The generalized Lorenz curve is a straight line from 0 to the mean, and the inequality measure $(b - a)/b$ takes on the value 0 in this case.

Growth and Inequality

The twin-standard view of inequality offers fresh insights on the relationship between growth and inequality. For example, use the Gini coefficient, with its underlying income standards of the Sen mean a and the (arithmetic) mean b, to evaluate the distribution of income at two points in time. If inequality as measured by the Gini coefficient has risen, then this is equivalent to saying that b grew more between the two periods than a. But the growth rate of b is precisely the usual income growth rate.

Consequently, to evaluate whether the change in the income distribution from one period to the next has increased or decreased the Gini coefficient, one need only calculate the growth rate of the Sen mean and compare it to the usual growth rate. If the growth rate of the Sen mean is lower than the usual growth rate, then the Gini coefficient rises. If the Sen growth rate is larger than the usual growth rate, then the Gini coefficient falls.

An analogous discussion holds for Theil's second measure, except that now growth in the geometric mean is compared to the usual growth rate. In both cases, the mean is the higher income standard, and the same would be true for the generalized entropy measures below the first Theil measure (or the Atkinson measures) and for the partial mean ratios underlying the Lorenz curve.

In contrast, for the upper half of the generalized entropy measures, the mean is the lower income standard a whereas the general mean is the higher income standard b, so the growth criterion for inequality is reversed. For example, the income standards of the squared coefficient of variation are the mean income and the Euclidean mean. If the Euclidean mean growth rate exceeds the usual growth rate, then the inequality level, as measured by the squared coefficient of variation, rises.

The growth curves described above can be useful in understanding the attributes of growth and the effect on inequality. Each depicts growth rates for a class of income standards, starting with standards favoring lower incomes to the left and with standards favoring higher incomes to the right. In the proportional growth case where all incomes rise by the same percentage, the growth curves will be constant at that percentage level. If higher incomes tend to be rising more rapidly, then the growth curve will have a positive slope, thereby reflecting higher growth rates among the income standards that emphasize higher incomes. If lower incomes are growing more, then the growth curve will have a negative slope. The latter case might be viewed as one form of pro-poor or inclusive growth.

Each growth curve has implications for the inequality measures associated with its constituent income standards. The growth incidence curve reveals changes in inequality as measured by the quantile ratios (such as the 90/10 ratio). The generalized Lorenz growth curve provides information on inequality as measured by its partial mean ratios. And the general means growth curve reveals how inequality changes for virtually all generalized entropy measures and for the Atkinson measures.

Poverty Measures and the Base of the Distribution

The final aspect examined here is the base or the bottom of the income distribution and the main topic of this book: poverty. Evaluation of poverty begins with an identification step in which the people considered poor are specified and continues with an aggregation step in which the data of the poor are combined to obtain a numerical measure. These two steps make up a methodology for measuring poverty in an income distribution.

The identification step is usually accomplished by selecting a level of income, called the *poverty line*, below which a person in a given distribution is considered poor. In its most general formulation, a poverty line is specified for every possible income distribution, so that the set of poor people in a population depends on the prevailing living conditions. Finding a proper functional relation between poverty line and income distribution is, of course, a challenging problem, and one that is subject to much controversy. Most evaluations of poverty have settled on two very simple approaches: (a) an absolute approach that takes the poverty line to be a constant and

(b) a relative approach that takes the poverty line to be a constant fraction of an income standard.

Absolute Poverty Line

An *absolute poverty line* is a fixed cutoff that does not change as the distribution being evaluated changes. Examples include the following:

- The $1.25-per-day standard of the World Bank that is used to compare poverty across many poor and middle-income countries over time
- The domestic poverty lines in most developing countries that are used to compare poverty within the country over time
- The nearly $15-per-day standard in the United States (per person in a family of four in 2009 dollars) that has been used for almost 50 years.

An absolute poverty line is frequently used for evaluating poverty within a country over short-to-moderate spans of time or across two countries when they have roughly similar levels of development. The approach may be harder to justify over longer periods of time or in a comparison of countries with very different levels of development.

Absolute poverty lines are often held constant over many periods, then updated to reflect changing living standards. After updating of lines, comparisons are typically not made across the two standards. Instead, each distribution is evaluated at the new, updated poverty line. The U.S. poverty line has remained fixed (in real terms) since 1965; the nominal poverty line is adjusted for inflation. A 1995 National Academy of Sciences recommendation to update the line to reflect current living standards has yet to be implemented. The World Bank's main poverty standard was updated in 2005, and all income distributions back to 1981 were reevaluated at the new line.

Absolute poverty lines are by far the most commonly used approach for identifying the poor over time and space and are universally used in low- and middle-income countries. They allow transparent comparisons where the changes in measured poverty can be attributed purely to changes in the distribution rather than to a moving poverty cutoff.

However, there are some practical challenges associated with the construction of absolute poverty lines:

- Several competing methods are available for deriving an absolute poverty line from a reference set of observations, each of which can generate a different poverty income cutoff.
- The reference set of observations must be selected, and this reference set, too, can influence the cutoff.
- To a certain extent, then, the choice of absolute poverty line is arbitrary. This arbitrary quality tempers the interpretation of results but can be partially addressed with the help of variable line robustness techniques discussed below.
- There is the related question of how frequently to update an absolute poverty line. But here the trade-offs are clear: it must be fixed long enough to be able to discern the underlying changes in poverty, and it must be updated often enough so that the standard is reasonably consistent with prevailing circumstances.

Relative Poverty Line

A *relative poverty line* is an explicit function of the income distribution—namely, a constant fraction of some income standard. One example is the European Union's country-level poverty lines, which are set at 60 percent of a country's median (disposable) income. The nature of a relative poverty line dictates that the cutoff below which one is considered to be poor varies proportionally with its income standard. Indeed, a level of income that is above the poverty line in one distribution may lie below the poverty line of a second distribution having a higher income standard.

Relative poverty lines are most often used in countries with higher incomes, where there is less concern about achieving a minimum absolute level of living and greater interest in inclusion or relative achievements. Unlike absolute poverty lines, the endogenous determination of relative lines also automatically updates the standard over time and space. However, this determination is done by making a very strong assumption on the functional form of the link between poverty line and income standard and by choosing an income standard and a specific fractional cutoff. Those components are often selected without a great deal of scrutiny or exploration of alternatives.

Moreover, with a relative line, the analysis of a change in poverty over time (or space) is less transparent. There are now two sources of change: (a) the direct impact of the change in the distribution and (b) the indirect impact through the change in the underlying income standard and, hence, the poverty standard. This second component is quite important, yet depends on the assumed functional form of the relative poverty line.

The elasticity of a relative poverty line with respect to its income standard is 1. If the income standard rises by 1 percent, then the relative poverty line will rise by 1 percent. In contrast, with an absolute poverty line, there is no change in the poverty standard when there is a 1 percent increase in the same income standard; the elasticity is 0 for an absolute poverty line.

Intermediate poverty lines exist—hybrid or weak relative poverty lines. They offer a poverty line that is a function of the income distribution, but with fixed (or weakly rising) elasticity between 0 and 1. The intermediate poverty lines are a topic of continuing research.

No matter which of these approaches to setting a poverty line is chosen, the outcome for a given distribution is a specific income cutoff and a subset of the population identified as being poor. For simplicity and because of the greater prevalence of absolute lines, we will assume that a fixed poverty line is given. The next step is to determine how to aggregate the data to obtain an overall picture of poverty.

What Is a Poverty Measure?

A *poverty measure* is a way of combining information on income distribution—especially incomes of the poor—to obtain a number that represents the poverty level in the distribution given the poverty line. The most common measures are counting measures, which evaluate poverty by numbers of people. The best-known counting measure is the headcount ratio, defined as the percentage of the total population that is poor.

An easy way of expressing a counting measure is to construct the *deprivation vector*, which replaces each poor income with 1 and every nonpoor income with 0. The *headcount ratio* is simply the mean of the deprivation vector or distribution. The headcount ratio is linked to the cumulative distribution function, which for continuous distributions is simply the graph of the headcount ratio as the poverty line is varied.

Other measures evaluate poverty by the average gap or depth of poverty:

- The *normalized gap* vector is constructed by replacing income of each poor individual with the normalized gap (or the gap between the poverty line and the income expressed as a share of the poverty line) and income of every nonpoor individual with 0. The *poverty gap* measure is the mean of the normalized gap vector. It is sensitive to both the prevalence of poverty in a society and the extent to which the poor fall below the poverty line.
- Another measure is based on the *squared gap vector*, which uses the square of the normalized gap for each poor person. The squaring process emphasizes the larger gaps relative to the smaller gaps. The *squared gap* or Foster-Greer-Thorbecke (FGT) measure index is the mean of the squared gap vector. It is sensitive to the prevalence of the poor, the extent to which their incomes fall below the poverty line, and the distribution of their incomes or shortfalls.

All of those measures are members of a parametric family of indices: the FGT family of poverty indices is derived by taking the mean of an α-gap vector, which is obtained by raising each positive entry in the normalized gap vector by a power of $\alpha \geq 0$.

There are two main ways of interpreting what a poverty measure is actually measuring. One way is by examining the properties that the measure satisfies. The other makes use of income standards in interpreting the measure. We begin with the axiomatic approach.

Poverty Measure Properties

There are six basic properties for poverty measures:

- The first two are the *symmetry* and *population invariance* properties given above for income standards and inequality measures. They are important for ensuring that the measure is based on the anonymous distribution and not on the income recipients' names or the population size.
- The third basic property is the *focus axiom*, which requires the poverty measure to ignore changes in the distribution involving nonpoor incomes. This approach ensures that the measure focuses on poor incomes in evaluating poverty.

- The fourth property is *scale invariance*, which requires the poverty measure to be unchanged if all incomes and the poverty line are scaled up or down by the same factor. This approach makes sure that the measure is independent of the unit of measurement of income.

The first four properties are *invariance* properties, which indicate how various changes in the distribution should *not* be taken into account by the measure. The next two properties are *dominance* properties that require the measure to be consistent with certain basic changes in the distribution.

- The fifth property is *weak monotonicity*, which requires poverty to rise or be unchanged if the income of a poor person falls—in other words, a decrement in a poor income cannot decrease poverty. Weak monotonicity is a central property of a poverty measure and is often presented in a stronger form, known as *monotonicity*, which requires an increment in a poor income to (strictly) decrease poverty.
- The final property considers the effect of a transfer on poverty. The *weak transfer* property requires poverty to fall or be unchanged as a result of a progressive transfer (from richer to poorer) between two poor people. This property also has a stronger version, known as the transfer principle, which requires poverty to (strictly) increase as a result of a regressive transfer (from poorer to richer) between two poor people.

Notice that both the monotonicity axiom and the transfer principle allow the number of poor to be altered in the process, whereas the weaker versions do not.

The headcount ratio, the poverty gap measure, and the FGT index satisfy all six basic axioms. The headcount ratio satisfies weak monotonicity and the weak transfer principle (because it is unaffected by the distributional changes specified in the two properties), but it violates the two stronger versions. The poverty gap measure satisfies the monotonicity axiom, but it violates the transfer principle (because it is unaffected by a small regressive transfer). The FGT index satisfies both stronger axioms.

Some additional properties can also be helpful in evaluating poverty measures. *Transfer sensitivity* requires a decrement in the income of a poor person, when combined with an equal-sized increment in the income of a richer poor person, to raise poverty. It ensures that a given-sized transfer has a larger poverty-reducing effect at lower poor incomes. *Decomposability* and *subgroup consistency* have proved to be very important for regional evaluations of poverty and for targeting. They are discussed below.

Income Standards

Another way of understanding poverty measures makes use of our previous insights from income standards. Like inequality measures, most poverty measures are based on a comparison of two income levels. In this case, however, one of them is the fixed poverty line z, whereas the other is an income standard applied to a modified distribution that focuses on the poor.

Two forms of modification are employed, leading to two general forms of poverty measures. The first makes use of a censoring process that ignores the portion of any income lying above the poverty line z. The *censored distribution* x^* for a given distribution x replaces all incomes above z with z itself. Applying an income standard to the censored distribution yields a *poor income standard*, which reflects the size of the censored distribution and is clearly bounded above by z (the maximum value achieved when no one is poor).

Many poverty measures take the form $P = (b - a)/b$, or some monotonic transformation, where a is some poor income standard and b is the poverty line z. P measures poverty as the shortfall of the poor income standard from the poverty line as a percentage of the poverty line. For example, if a were the mean censored income $\mu(x^*)$, then the resulting poverty measure would be $(z - \mu(x^*))/z$, which is another way of expressing the poverty gap. Below we will see other poverty measures that share this general structure but employ different income standards.

The second form of modification changes the focus from incomes to income gaps. The *gap distribution* g^* is found by replacing the income x_i^* in x^* with the income gap $z - x_i^*$. The gap will be 0 for anyone who is nonpoor, and it increases in size as the income of a poor person falls further below z.

Applying an income standard to the gap distribution yields a *gap standard*, which measures the overall departure of incomes in x^* from z. Many poverty measures take the form $P = a/b$, or some monotonic transformation, where a is some gap standard and b is the poverty line z. P measures poverty using a gap standard taken as a percentage of the poverty line. For example, if a were the mean gap $\mu(g^*)$, then the resulting poverty measure would be $\mu(g^*)/z$, which is another way of defining the poverty gap. Below we will discuss several other poverty measures that share this structure but use different income standards in constructing the gap standard.

Common Examples

The first general form of poverty measures uses an income standard applied to the censored distribution. An income standard that puts progressively greater weight on lower incomes will yield a poverty measure that is sensitive to the distribution of income among the poor. The *Sen-Shorrocks-Thon* (SST) index is given by $(b - a)/b$, where a is the Sen mean applied to x^* and b is the poverty line. This measure inherits its characteristics from the Sen mean: it satisfies all six basic properties and monotonicity and the transfer property. Increments and progressive transfers among the poor are reflected in a strictly higher poor income standard a, and hence a lower poverty level.

The next measure is based on another income standard that emphasizes lower incomes. The *Watts index* is defined as $\ln(b/a)$, where a is the geometric mean applied to the censored distribution and b is the poverty line z. It likewise satisfies the six basic axioms and the strict forms of monotonicity and the transfer principle. Additionally, the geometric mean has the property that a given-sized transfer among the poor has a greater effect at lower income levels, so the poverty measure satisfies *transfer sensitivity*.

The Watts index can be expanded to an entire class of measures, each of which uses a general mean to evaluate the censored distribution. The *Clark-Hemming-Ulph-Chakravarty* (CHUC) family of indices compares the poor income standard $a = \mu_\alpha(x^*)$ for $\alpha \le 1$ and the poverty line $b = z$. There are two forms of the measure: the original form $(b - a)/b$ and a decomposable form obtained by a simple transformation. The measure becomes the poverty gap at $\alpha = 1$ and the Watts index (or a transformation) at $\alpha = 0$. The properties of the general means ensure that the CHUC measures satisfy all six basic properties for poverty measures, for monotonicity, and for $\alpha < 1$ the transfer principle as well as transfer sensitivity.

The second general form of poverty measures uses an income standard applied to the gap distribution. The key family of measures has a traditional decomposable version and an alternative version that is only subgroup consistent.

The FGT family of decomposable poverty indices was defined above as the mean of the α-gap distribution and includes the headcount ratio for

$\alpha = 0$, the poverty gap measure for $\alpha = 1$, and the FGT or squared gap measure for $\alpha = 2$. Alternatively, we can transform each of the measures in the range $\alpha > 0$ by raising it to the power $1/\alpha$. This yields a subgroup-consistent measure that compares a gap standard $a = \mu_\alpha(g^*)$ to the poverty line $b = z$ via the formula $P = a/b$.

The properties for the FGT measures in this range follow from the properties of the associated general means. The first five properties and monotonicity are immediately satisfied for all $\alpha > 0$. For the transfer principles, note that the general means with $\alpha < 1$ emphasize the smaller entries, those with $\alpha > 1$ emphasize the larger entries, and $\alpha = 1$ ignores the distribution altogether. Thus, the FGT measures satisfy the weak transfer principle for $\alpha \geq 1$ and the transfer principle for $\alpha > 1$. In an analogous way, the FGT index for $\alpha = 2$ is *transfer neutral* in that a given-sized progressive transfer among the poor has the same effect at lower incomes, whereas the FGT measures with $\alpha > 2$ satisfy transfer sensitivity.

The above discussion excludes the case $\alpha = 0$, which corresponds to the headcount ratio. The simple structure of this poverty measure does not admit an interpretation of an income standard applied to the censored or gap distribution. Instead, a second censoring must be applied to obtain a distribution in which all nonpoor incomes are replaced by z and all poor incomes are replaced by 0. Let x^{**} denote the resulting *doubly censored* distribution. The headcount ratio can be represented as $(b - a)/b$, where $a = \mu(x^{**})$ and $b = z$. In other words, it is the poverty gap of the doubly censored distribution that converts nonpoor incomes to z *and* poor incomes to 0.

The first censoring ensures that the measure focuses on incomes of the poor. The second censoring forces the headcount ratio to ignore the actual income levels of poor people and violate monotonicity. The headcount ratio suppresses information that is relevant to poverty (the actual incomes of the poor) in order to capture one key aspect of poverty (the prevalence of poverty). Replacing x^{**} with x^* in this representation would recover this information and yield the poverty gap measure.

Poverty, Inequality, and Welfare

Poverty measures satisfying the transfer principle are called *distribution sensitive* because they account for the inequality of poor incomes in ways that the headcount ratio or the poverty gap cannot. In fact, each of the above distribution-sensitive poverty indices is built on a specific income or gap standard that is closely linked to an inequality measure. For the SST index, it is the Gini coefficient. For the CHUC indices, the Atkinson measures are used. For the Watts index, the mean log deviation is the inequality measure. In each case, the inequality measure is applied to the censored distribution x^* with greater *censored inequality* being reflected in a higher level of poverty (for a given poverty gap level).

The FGT measures (for $\alpha > 1$) use generalized entropy measures applied to the gap distribution g^* with greater *gap inequality* leading to a higher level of poverty (for a given level of the poverty gap). The *focused inequality* measures underlying these distribution-sensitive poverty indices ignore variations in incomes above the poverty line. Trends in focused inequality may well be very different from trends in overall inequality.

Certain income standards can be viewed as welfare functions, and this link can provide yet another lens for interpreting poverty measures. The Sen mean underlying the SST index and the general means for $\alpha \leq 1$ that are behind the CHUC indices can be interpreted as welfare functions. In each case, the welfare function is applied to the censored distribution to obtain the poor income standard a, which is now seen to be a *censored welfare function* that takes into account the incomes of the poor and only part of the incomes of the nonpoor (up to the poverty line).

For these measures, poverty and censored welfare are inversely related. Every increase in poverty is seen as a decrease in censored welfare. Of course, the trends in censored welfare may be very different from the trends in overall welfare, as the latter take into account the actual incomes of the nonpoor. We will see below another link between welfare and poverty when we consider poverty comparisons over a range of lines.

Applications

A poverty methodology can be used to identify the poor (through its identification step) and to evaluate the extent of poverty (through the aggregation step). The first step by itself allows many interesting analyses to be conducted, given appropriately rich data. Consider, for example, the following questions:

- Who are the poor and how do they differ from the nonpoor? A range of characteristics can be examined—including location, household size, ethnicity, education indicators, health indicators, housing, and ownership of certain assets—to see what it means to be poor. This is part of a countrywide *poverty profile* that relies purely on the identification step.

- What drives the dynamics of poverty? If panel data are available, one can explore the factors that seem to be forcing people into poverty or allowing them to escape. Even if two periods of data are not part of a panel (and hence not linked at the personal level), one can investigate how other general factors, such as food prices or economic conditions, affect the likelihood of being in poverty.
- Is a given poverty program reaching its intended recipients? The leakage or coverage of poverty programs can be evaluated to gauge the likelihood that a recipient is not poor or that a poor person is a nonrecipient.
- What affects and is affected by the condition of being poor? In some studies, the deprivation vector, or indicator function for poverty, is a key outcome variable. In other studies, it is an important dependent variable.

The aggregation step goes beyond a simple identification of the poor and provides a quantitative measure of the extent of poverty for any given population group. A poverty measure can be used to monitor poverty in a country over time and space. Poverty profiles evaluate the structure of poverty in a country by considering how poverty varies across an array of population subgroups.

Other applications include using a poverty measure as a basis for targeting social programs or for assessing their poverty impact. It is often thought that *chronic* poverty is qualitatively different from *transient* poverty. Panel data can allow the two to be evaluated in order to discern whether the poverty in a given region tends to be of one form or the other. Some people currently not in poverty may, nonetheless, be vulnerable to becoming poor. Poverty measures can be adapted to create measures of *vulnerability* to poverty.

Optimal taxation exercises use a welfare function as the objective function with which to evaluate the competing objectives of a larger pie versus a more equitable distribution. For many policy exercises, it may make sense to focus on the poor by using a censored welfare function or a poverty measure: Are food subsidies more effective in improving poverty than income transfers? This and other questions can be addressed in theory or practice once a poverty measure has been chosen. The choice of poverty measure will affect the answers obtained.

Subgroup Consistency and Decomposability

Many programs designed to address the needs of the poor are implemented at the local level. Suppose we are evaluating such a program in a country with two equal-sized regions. We find that poverty has fallen significantly in each region, yet when poverty is measured at the country level, it has increased. This possibility could present significant challenges to the analyst and could prove rather difficult to explain to policy makers. It turns out that the inconsistency between regional and national poverty outcomes may be due entirely to the way poverty is measured.

To ensure that this possibility does not arise, one can require the poverty measure to satisfy *subgroup consistency*. This property requires that if poverty falls in one subgroup and is unchanged in another and both have fixed population sizes, then the overall poverty level must likewise fall. The SST index is not subgroup consistent because of its use of the Sen mean. The FGT and CHUC measures, which depend on general means, are subgroup consistent and thus would not be subject to the regional-national dilemma.

Subgroup consistency requires overall poverty to move in the same direction as an unambiguous change in subgroup poverty levels. A stronger property provides an explicit formula that makes the link between overall and subgroup poverty. A poverty measure is said to be *(additively) decomposable* if overall poverty is a population-share weighted average of subgroup poverty levels. Unlike the case of inequality measures, there is no between-group term in this decomposition. The reason is that the standard against which subgroup poverty is evaluated is a fixed poverty line. In contrast, an inequality measure typically evaluates subgroup inequality relative to subgroup means, then takes the variation of subgroup means into account as another source of inequality.

Additively decomposable poverty measures transparently link subgroup poverty to overall poverty. This approach can be particularly useful in generating a coherent poverty profile in which a broad array of population subgroups and their poverty levels can be broken down or reassembled as needed. Consider these questions:

- Is a given change in overall poverty caused by changes in subgroup poverty levels, by population shifts across subgroups, or by a combination of the two effects? A counterfactual approach, which constructs an artificial intermediate distribution to separate the two, can help quantify the relative impacts of demographic changes and the changes in subgroup poverty on the overall poverty level.

- What share of overall poverty can be attributed to a particular population group? We can define a subgroup's *contribution* to overall poverty to be the population share of a subgroup times the poverty level of the subgroup divided by the overall poverty level. Some subgroups with low levels of poverty may have large contributions as a result of their population sizes. Others may have smaller population shares, but still have large contribution shares because subgroup poverty levels are high.

For decomposable poverty measures, subgroup contributions must sum to one.

Dominance and Unanimity

The above discussion assumes that it is possible to select a correct poverty line to separate the poor from the nonpoor. Yet it is clear that any cutoff selected is bound to be arbitrary and that alternative poverty lines could be chosen with equal justification. Conclusions obtained at the original poverty line may be reversed at some other reasonable standard. They also could be robust to a change in the poverty line.

To help discern which of these possibilities is true—a reversal or unanimity for all poverty lines—we can construct a *poverty (value) curve* which graphs the poverty measure as a function of the poverty line over the relevant range of poverty lines. If the original comparison continues to hold at all poverty lines in the range, then the comparison is robust. This gives rise to a *(variable line) poverty ordering*, which ranks one distribution as having less poverty than another when its poverty curve is not above (and is somewhere below) the poverty curve of the other distribution. The range of poverty lines usually begins at 0 and ends at some highest value z^*, although it is instructive to consider the case where there is no upper bound. Our discussion begins with the latter case.

Although the general approach can be used with any poverty measure, it is standard to focus on the three main measures from the FGT family: the headcount ratio, the poverty gap measure, and the FGT squared gap measure. The headcount ratio for a given poverty line is the share of the population having incomes below the poverty line. Consequently, the poverty curve for the headcount ratio traces the cumulative distribution function associated with the distribution (except that it takes its limits from the left rather than the right when it has jumps), so the poverty ordering is first-order stochastic dominance.

If one recalls the above discussion of stochastic dominance, this poverty ordering is equivalent to having a higher quantile function and also to having greater welfare according to every utilitarian welfare function with identical, increasing utility functions. The poverty curve associated with the headcount ratio is often called the *poverty incidence curve*.

The poverty curve for the poverty gap measure is closely linked to the area beneath (or the integral of) the poverty incidence curve (or the cdf), which is another way of representing second-order stochastic dominance. Hence, the poverty ordering for the poverty gap measure is simply second-order stochastic dominance. By the previous discussion, this means that the poverty ordering can also be represented by the generalized Lorenz curve, with a higher generalized Lorenz curve indicating unambiguously lower (or no higher) poverty according to the poverty gap measure.

In addition, there is a useful welfare interpretation of this poverty ordering: it indicates higher welfare according to every utilitarian welfare function with identical and increasing utility function exhibiting diminishing marginal utility (Atkinson's general class of welfare functions). The curve found by plotting the area beneath the poverty incidence curve for each income level z is often called the *poverty deficit curve*.

The FGT index has a poverty curve that is closely linked with the area beneath the poverty deficit curve (or the double integral of the cdf), and hence its poverty ordering is linked to a refinement of second-order stochastic dominance called *third-order stochastic dominance*. This poverty ordering also has a welfare interpretation: higher welfare according to every utilitarian welfare function with identical and increasing utility function exhibiting diminishing and *convex* marginal utility.

The final condition on the convexity of marginal utility ensures that the welfare function is more sensitive to transfers at the lower end of the distribution—a welfare version of the *transfer sensitivity* axiom. The curve found by plotting the area beneath the poverty deficit curve for each income level z is often called the *poverty severity curve*.

Notice that the poverty orderings for the three FGT measures are nested in that if the headcount ratio's ordering ranks two distributions, then the poverty gap's ordering also ranks the distributions in the same way (but not vice versa). Further, the poverty gap's ordering implies (but is not implied by) the FGT index's ordering. Because the poverty deficit curve is found by taking the area under the poverty incidence curve, a higher poverty incidence curve leads to a higher poverty deficit curve. The same is true for the poverty deficit and poverty severity curves.

The poverty orderings of the Watts and CHUC indices can also be easily constructed and lead to another nested set starting with second-order dominance for the poverty gap measure. The poverty ordering for the Watts index, for example, is simply generalized Lorenz (or second-order stochastic) dominance applied to the distributions of log incomes. Each CHUC poverty ordering likewise applies generalized Lorenz dominance to distributions of transformed incomes (see Foster and Jin 1998).

Placing an upper limit z^* on the range of poverty lines is equivalent to comparing poverty curves (or the poverty incidence, deficit, or severity curves) over this limited range or to using censored distributions associated with z^*. For example, the limited range poverty ordering for the poverty gap is equivalent to comparing the generalized Lorenz curves of the censored distributions or to comparing censored welfare levels across all utilitarian welfare functions with identical and increasing utility functions that have diminishing marginal utility.

In the above example, we varied the poverty line while holding the poverty measure fixed. We can also vary the poverty measure for a given poverty line to examine robustness to the choice of measure. For example, using a five-dimensional vector, one can depict the poverty levels of the FGT measures for $\alpha = 0$, 1, and 2; the Watts index; and the SST index. Vector dominance would then be interpreted as a *variable measure* poverty ordering that ranks distributions when all five measures unanimously agree.

An analogous approach using poverty curves can be employed when using poverty measures indexed by a parameter. Consider a poverty curve that depicts the CHUC indices $(z - \mu_\alpha(x^*))/z$ for $\alpha \leq 1$ and the FGT indices $\mu_\alpha(g^*))/z$ for $\alpha \geq 1$. We are using the income standard version of each measure (rather than the decomposable version) because of its nice interpretation as a normalized average gap. The poverty measure at $\alpha = 1$ is the usual poverty gap measure. As α rises, the FGT values progressively rise because the measures with higher α use a general mean that focuses on the higher gaps in the gap vector g^*.

The extent to which poverty rises as $\alpha > 1$ rises depends on the generalized entropy inequality in g^* for α. To the left, the CHUC values progressively rise as the measures with lower α use a general mean that focuses on lower incomes in the censored vector x^*. The extent to which poverty rises as $\alpha < 1$ falls depends on the generalized entropy inequality in x^* for α. A higher curve would then be interpreted as the variable measure poverty ordering that ranks distributions when all these poverty measures agree.

The above approaches to varying the poverty line and the poverty measure can be combined to examine the robustness of comparisons to changing both simultaneously. Interestingly, though, in certain cases it is enough to examine a variable line poverty ordering. For example, if two distributions can be ranked by the poverty ordering of the headcount ratio, then they will also be ranked in the same way by the poverty ordering associated with *any* given poverty measure satisfying the basic axioms and monotonicity. This is also true for certain limited range poverty orderings.

Even in cases lacking a clear ranking for the relevant set of poverty lines (or measures), a poverty curve can be very useful in identifying ranges of poverty lines (and measures) where the ranking is unchanged and where the ranking reverses. This general methodology for checking the robustness of poverty comparisons is quite powerful.

Growth and Poverty

It is sometimes helpful to determine how fast poverty is falling or rising over time and to explore the extent to which the growth rate of poverty is robust to a change in the poverty line or measure. Associated with each of the above poverty curves is a *poverty growth curve* that gives the growth rate of poverty for each poverty line or measure. For example, the variable line poverty growth curves for the three standard FGT measures are the same as the growth curves of the poverty incidence, deficit, and severity curves.

Negative rates of growth throughout would indicate that poverty has fallen, and this conclusion is robust to changing the poverty line. If growth rates are similar across an entire range of poverty lines, then this suggests the percentage change in poverty is robust to changing the poverty line. Note, though, that poverty measures like the CHUC and the FGT measures have two versions—the decomposable version and the income standard version, which are monotonic but not direct (proportional) transformations of one another. Although the two versions will always agree on whether poverty has risen or fallen (for a given poverty line), the growth rates will, in general, be different.

We have seen above how the trend in inequality can be evaluated by comparing the growth rates of the two income standards underlying the inequality measure. The trend in poverty can likewise be evaluated by comparing the growth rate of the poverty line to the growth rate of the poor income standard (or gap standard) associated with the poverty measure. An absolute poverty line has a growth rate of zero, so poverty will decrease over time when the poor income standard has a positive growth rate (or the gap standard has a negative growth rate). If a relative poverty line is used, the growth rate in the poverty line is the same as the growth rate in the income standard underlying the relative poverty line.

Relative poverty will thus decrease over time when the overall income standard grows more slowly than the poor income standard, or more quickly than the gap standard. For example, suppose the relative poverty line is half the mean income and the poverty measure is the poverty gap. Then poverty will decrease over time if the mean income grows more slowly than the mean censored income. Alternatively, relative poverty will decrease if the mean income grows faster than the mean gap.

By plotting the growth rates for a range of income standards or gap standards and comparing them to the economywide growth rate, one can make robust comparisons of relative poverty. An analogous exercise is possible for the hybrid or weakly relative poverty lines whose elasticity with respect to the underlying income standard (called the *income elasticity of the poverty line*) falls between 0 (as with absolute lines) and 1 (as with relative lines). The growth rates of the poor income standards or gap standards are compared to the overall growth rate of the economy times the income elasticity of the poverty line to determine whether poverty of this form unambiguously decreases or increases.

A key question related to growth and poverty is whether general economic growth translates into elevated incomes for the poor. Is growth "shared" among all strata of society or are the poor excluded from growth? To address this question, various approaches to evaluating shared or pro-poor growth have been advanced.

A first approach compares the growth in the mean income to the growth in a lower or higher income standard. If the growth rate of a lower income standard exceeds the general growth rate so that the *growth elasticity* of the low-income standard is greater than one, then this rate is seen as evidence of pro-poor growth. If the growth rate for a high-income standard is lower than the general growth rate—so that the growth elasticity of the high-income standard is less than one—then this is also evidence of pro-poor growth.

If one uses the twin-standards interpretation of inequality, then this approach is equivalent to requiring an associated inequality measure to fall. Let a and b be the two income standards, with $a \leq b$, where one of the two is the mean, and let I be an inequality measure based on these twin standards (so that I is a monotonic transformation of b/a). Growth is pro-poor if a grows faster than b, which is equivalent to a falling ratio b/a and, hence, to a decrease in the associated inequality measure I. For example, one might describe growth as pro-poor if the Sen mean grew faster than the mean, and hence the Gini coefficient decreased. Or we could note that the Euclidean mean grew slower than the mean, and hence the coefficient of variation declined. This is basically the inequality-based approach to pro-poor growth we have discussed above.

A second poverty-based approach compares the actual change in poverty to the level that might be expected along a counterfactual growth path. Suppose that the distribution of income changes from x to x' and that this leads to a change in measured poverty from P to P'. Construct a counterfactual income distribution x'' that has the same mean as x' and the same relative distribution as x, and let P'' be its level of poverty. The growth from x to x' is then said to be pro-poor if the resulting change in poverty $P' - P$ exceeds the counterfactual change $P'' - P$; in other words, the rate of poverty reduction from actual growth is faster than the counterfactual rate from perfectly balanced growth. Of course, the relevance of this conclusion depends on the choice of counterfactual distribution and its assumption that the relative income distribution should not change.

A related technique is often used to analyze the extent to which a given change in poverty is primarily due to changes in the mean (the *growth effect*) or changes in the relative distribution (the *distribution effect*). As before, let x'' be the counterfactual distribution having the same relative distribution as the initial distribution x and the same mean as the final distribution x'. The overall difference in poverty $P' - P$ can be expressed as the sum of the growth effect $P''- P$ and the distribution effect $P' - P''$.

This breakdown first scales up the distribution x to the mean income of x' to explore how the uniform growth in all incomes alters poverty. Then it redistributes the income to obtain x', and explores how the distributional change alters poverty. Other breakdowns are possible using a different counterfactual distribution or, indeed, a different order of events (redistribute first, then grow). However, this version has the advantage of being easy to interpret and can be expressed as the sum of two component terms without a troublesome residual term.

Note

1. The third step may have two substeps, depending on the type of poverty measure selected: (a) evaluation of individual poverty and (b) selection of a method to aggregate individual poverty to obtain overall poverty.

References

Atkinson, A. B. 1970. "On the Measurement of Inequality." *Journal of Economic Theory* 2 (1970): 244–63.

Commission on Growth and Development. 2008. *The Growth Report: Strategies for Sustained Growth and Inclusive Development.* Washington, DC: World Bank and International Bank for Reconstruction and Development.

Commission on the Measurement of Economic and Social Progress. 2009. "Report by the Commission on the Measurement of Economic and Social Progress." Commission on the Measurement of Economic and Social Progress, Paris. http://www.stiglitz-sen-fitoussi.fr/en/index.htm.

Foster, J. E., and Y. Jin. 1998. "Poverty Orderings for the Dalton Utility-Gap Measures." In *The Distribution of Welfare and Household Production: International Perspectives*, edited by S. Jenkins, A. Kapteyn, and B. van Praag, 268–85. New York: Cambridge University Press.

Mincer, J. 1974. *Schooling, Experience, and Earnings.* New York: Columbia University Press.

Oaxaca, R. 1973. "Male-Female Wage Differentials in Urban Labor Markets." *International Economic Review* 14 (3): 693–709.

Chapter 2

Income Standards, Inequality, and Poverty

This chapter complements the introductory chapter by providing a detailed discussion and more formal analysis of the concepts involved in measuring income standards, inequality, and poverty. This chapter follows closely the introduction's organization. It is divided into four sections. The first section introduces notations and basic concepts that will be used throughout the rest of this chapter. The second and third sections discuss tools and instruments related to income standards and inequality measures. The fourth section uses the tools from the second and third sections to construct poverty measures.

According to Sen's seminal work (1976a), evaluating poverty within a society (which may be a country or other geographic region) involves two steps:

1. *Identification*, in which individuals are identified as poor or nonpoor
2. *Aggregation*, in which data about the poor are combined to evaluate poverty within the society.

However, to identify individuals as poor or nonpoor, we need to select a *space* on which their *welfare level* is to be assessed. The *welfare indicator* is the variable for assessing an individual's welfare level. Thus, evaluating poverty within a society involves three steps:

1. *Space selection*, which is described below
2. *Identification*, in which individuals with welfare levels below the threshold are classified as poor and individuals with welfare levels above the threshold are classified as nonpoor
3. *Aggregation*, our focus, which requires choosing an appropriate aggregation method to *measure* the poverty level in a society.

In this book, we define the space for evaluating poverty as money metric and single dimensional. The welfare indicator is either consumption expenditure or income:

- An individual's *consumption* is the destruction of goods and services through use by that individual. *Consumption expenditure* is the overall consumption of goods and services valued at current prices, regardless of whether an actual transaction has taken place.
- An individual's *income*, in contrast, is the maximum possible expenditure the individual is able to spend on consumption of goods and services, without depleting the assets held.

Whether it is income or consumption expenditure, welfare indicators are constructed by aggregating various components. For example, an individual's consumption expenditure is constructed by aggregating the commodities and services consumed by the individual using the prices paid. Consumption expenditure as a welfare indicator is more commonly used for assessing developing countries in Asia and Africa (Deaton and Zaidi 2002). In contrast, using income as a welfare indicator is common when assessing Latin American countries.

Although both income and consumption expenditure are used as welfare indicators, consumption expenditure has certain advantages. Income data, for example, may not lead to an accurate assessment of welfare when incomes fluctuate significantly. Furthermore, in developing countries, income data may be difficult to collect, and data accuracy is difficult to verify because most of the population may be employed in the informal sector.

To work around these problems, many developing countries collect consumer expenditure survey data, which include detailed information on goods and services consumed by individuals. Then they use the market prices to compute the overall consumption expenditure. The surveys ask about food consumption for several items over a specific reference period, which may be a month or any longer period of time. If the reference period is short (for example, one month), seasonality concerns may be overcome, but a shorter reference period may also lead to more noise in the expenditure data. Noise can be avoided by using a longer reference period, but difficulties in recollection may bias expenditures downward.[1]

A person may consume many private and public goods from the long list of commodities in a consumer expenditure survey. For a private good, total expenditure is the amount of commodity consumed times that commodity's price. Consumption expenditure for two individuals having the same consumption patterns and requirements, therefore, should be twice the consumption expenditure for either of the two.

This straightforward expenditure computation may not be possible when the consumed commodities are, instead, public goods. Given that public goods are nonrival and nonexcludable, the same amount of public goods may be consumed by multiple individuals without additional cost. Multiple individuals living together and sharing public goods enjoy *economies of scale*. Examples of public goods include a radio, a water pump, bulk purchase discounts of food items, and food preparation efficiencies (which may lower the cost of fuel and time).

Although the goal is to construct a money-metric wealth indicator for each person, fulfilling that goal may not be straightforward. Most of the time, data for commodities and services consumed are collected at the household level. A household typically consists of members with different characteristics, such as age, sex, and employment status. Usually, an individual's welfare indicator is calculated by dividing total household expenditures by the number of people residing in that household. The result is called the *per capita expenditure*.

Analyzing poverty on the basis of per capita expenditure, however, ignores the fact that different individuals may have different needs. The cost per person to reach a certain welfare level may be lower in large households, because large households enjoy certain economies of scale. For example, a child may not need the same share of income as an adult member, or the food consumption expenditure may not be the same across men and women within a household. The minimum income needed to meet the subsistence needs of a household with four adults may be much more than the subsistence income needed for a household with two adults and two children. This intrahousehold allocation can be adjusted using an *equivalence scale* tool.

There are various types of equivalence scales and economies of scale. Also, there are different ways of determining these scales, such as evaluating nutritional needs and behavioral needs. Differences in nutritional needs are derived from various health studies. Data on behavioral needs are obtained from econometric estimates that are based on observed commodity allocations.

However, the observed allocation is suspect because what is observed may not necessarily be what is actually needed. For example, if female children are observed to consume less, does this mean that they need less, or are they just discriminated against? There is no straightforward answer to this question, unfortunately, because it is beyond the scope of most consumer expenditure surveys.

Two adult equivalence (AE) scales are more commonly used than others. The first is used by the Organisation for Economic Co-operation and Development (OECD), which we denote by AE_{OECD}. It is defined as

$$AE_{OECD} = 1 + 0.7(N_A - 1) + 0.5N_C, \qquad (2.1)$$

where N_A is the number of adults in the household, and N_C is the number of children in the household.

This scale actually serves as both an equivalence scale and an economy of scale. Note that when there is only one adult member in the household, $AE_{OECD} = 1$. For a household with two adult members, $AE_{OECD} = 1.7$ ($AE_{OECD} = 2$ is incorrect because two adults sharing the same household are assumed to enjoy economy of scale). For instance, if the actual total income of a two-member household is Rs 17,000, then the per capita real income of the household is equivalent to Rs 17,000/1.7 = Rs 10,000 and not Rs 8,500, as it would be in the per capita case. This is an example of adjusting for economy of scale. For a single parent household with two children, however, the actual total income of Rs 17,000 is equivalent to a per capita real income of Rs 8,500 because $AE_{OECD} = 1 + 2 \times 0.5 = 2$.

The second adult equivalent scale is used by the Living Standards Measurement Study (LSMS), which we denote by AE_{LSMS}. It is defined as

$$AE_{LSMS} = (N_A + \varrho N_C)^\vartheta, \qquad (2.2)$$

where N_A is the number of adults in the household, and N_C is the number of children in the household.

In this scale, parameter ϱ measures the cost of a child compared to an adult. Parameter ϑ captures the effect of economy of scale. Both parameters are positive but not larger than one. When $\varrho = 1$, then the cost of a child is equal to the cost of an adult. The lower the value of ϱ, the lower the cost of each child compared to an adult. Similarly, when $\vartheta = 1$, no economy of scale is assumed. The lower the value of ϑ, the larger the economy of scale is assumed to be.

For example, suppose there are five members in a household: three adults and two children. If a child is assumed to be half as costly as an adult, then $\varrho = 0.5$ and $\vartheta = 0.5$. Then $AE_{LSMS} = (3 + 0.5 \times 2)^{0.5} = 2$. Therefore, if the actual total income of the household is Rs 20,000, then the real per capita income of the household is equivalent to Rs 10,000. However, if no economy of scale is assumed and each child is considered as equally expensive as an adult, then the household's per capita income is only Rs 4,000.

In the subsequent analysis in this chapter, we assume that we are using a dataset having all the information required for constructing a welfare indicator either at the individual level or at the household level. The dataset may cover the entire population or may just be a collection of samples from the population. There are other important issues one should take into account regarding a dataset (such as its survey design, sample coverage, sample variability, and so on), which are not covered in this chapter.[2]

To keep explanations and mathematical formulas simple, we make two fundamental assumptions. First, we use income as the welfare indicator and assume that information on income is available for every person in our dataset. Second, we assume that every household contains only one adult member. As a result of the second assumption, we do not need to make any adjustment for the economy of scale and equivalent scale because each member is an adult and lives in a single-member household. However, the tools and techniques introduced in this chapter can be easily extended to situations when the welfare indicator is consumption expenditure and more than one person lives in a household.

Basic Concepts

Suppose our reference society X consists of N people, where the income of person n is denoted by x_n for all $n = 1, 2, \ldots, N$. Thus, the income distribution data for society X has N incomes. For the sake of simplicity, we assume these incomes are ordered so that $x_1 \leq x_2 \leq \ldots \leq x_N$.

There are two different ways to represent an income distribution:

- The simplest income distribution is a vector of incomes. We denote the society's vector of incomes as $X = (x_1, x_2, \ldots, x_N)$.
- The second way is to represent the income distribution in terms of a cumulative distribution function (cdf) in which x is designated an income distribution. We denote the average, or mean, of all elements in x by $\bar{x} = (x_1 + \cdots + x_N)/N$. For a large enough sample, the cdf may be approximated by a density function.

Another, more intuitive, presentation of the cdf is the quantile function, which is more suitable to our needs. Before moving into the discussion on measurement, we will discuss these three concepts and examine their significance in describing various aspects of an income distribution.

Density Function

An income distribution's *density function* reports the percentage of the population that falls within an income range. Suppose incomes in distribution x range from \$100 to \$100,000, and we want to know what percentage of the population earns income between \$10,000 and \$20,000. The answer can be easily obtained by calculating the area underneath the density function between \$10,000 and \$20,000.

Notice that the total area underneath the density function between \$100 and \$100,000 is 100 percent because incomes of the entire population fall within this range. Thus, the density function is a frequency distribution that is normalized by the total population in the distribution.

Figure 2.1 depicts the probability density function of income distribution x. Recall that the minimum and maximum incomes in distribution x are x_1 and x_N, respectively. The horizontal axis reports the income and the vertical axis reports the density. We denote the density function of distribution x by f_x, which is a bell-shaped curve in figure 2.1. The total area between x_1 and x_N underneath the density function f_x is 100 percent. The share of the population with incomes between b' and b'' is the shaded area.

Two interesting statistics may be found in figure 2.1:

- The *median* is the income in the distribution that divides the entire population into two equal shares. In the figure, x_M is the median of

Figure 2.1: Probability Density Function

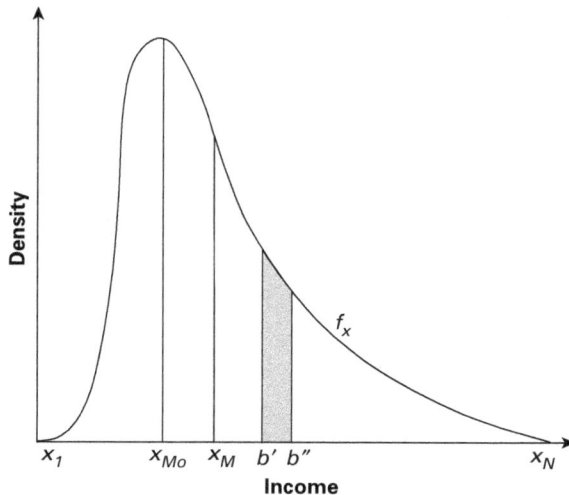

distribution x. Hence, 50 percent of the area underneath f_x lies to the right of x_M, and the remaining 50 percent lies to the left of x_M.

- The *mode* is the income in the distribution that corresponds to the largest density (locally). In figure 2.1, the distribution's mode is denoted by x_{Mo}.

Commonly, income distributions have one mode, but there can be distributions with more than one mode. A density with two modes is called *bimodal* and that with many modes is called *multimodal*. When there is more than one mode, a society is understood to be polarized in different groups according to their achievements. A polarized society may produce social tensions among different groups, which increases the chance of social unrest. These issues are discussed in more detail in chapter 3.

In addition, a density function can be a useful tool for understanding the *skewness* of an income distribution. Skewness is a measure of asymmetry in the distribution of incomes. It arises when most incomes lie on any one side of the mean of the distribution. If more observations are located to the left of the distribution's mean, then the distribution is *positively skewed*. If more observations lie to the right of the mean, then the distribution is *negatively skewed.* If there is an equal number of observations on both sides of the mean, then there is no skewness, and the distribution is *symmetric* around the mean. Income distributions are usually positively skewed.

Cumulative Distribution Function

A cdf, or cumulative distribution function, denotes the *proportion* of the population whose income falls below a given level. A cdf may be easily obtained from a density function and vice versa. For every income reported on the horizontal axis of figure 2.1, a distribution function reports the area to the left of the income underneath f_x. Because the total area underneath f_x is 100 percent, the highest value that a distribution function can take is 100 percent. We denote the distribution function of x by F_x, and $F_x(b)$ denotes the percentage of the population whose income is no greater than b.

For example, if the number of people in society X having incomes less than b is q, then $F_x(b) = 100 \times q/N$. For any two incomes b' and b'', $F_x(b') \leq F_x(b'')$ when $b' \leq b''$ because having income less than b' must also imply having income less than b''. Therefore, a distribution function should not decrease as income increases.

As seen in figure 2.2, the horizontal axis denotes income and the vertical axis denotes the value of the cumulative distribution function. For x_N, which is the largest income in distribution x, the value of the distribution function is $F_x(x_N) = 100$ percent because no one in distribution x has an income above x_N.

Figure 2.2: Cumulative Distribution Function

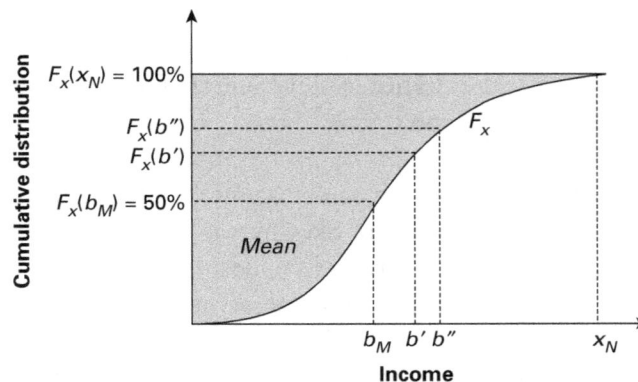

At median b_M, the distribution function's value is $F_x(b_M) = 50$ percent, which implies that half the population has an income less than b_M. In figure 2.1, the share of the population with income ranging between b' and b'' is represented by the shaded area, which, in figure 2.2, is denoted by the difference $F_x(b'') - F_x(b')$. A distribution function provides another important statistic: the *mean* of the distribution. In figure 2.2, the shaded area to the left of F_x is the mean $\bar{x}$ of distribution x.

Quantile Function

A *quantile function* is the inverse of a cdf. Recall that a distribution function shows the percentage of the population whose income falls below a *given* level of income. The quantile function, however, reports the level of *income* below which incomes of a *given* percentage of the population fall.

We denote the quantile function of distribution x by Q_x and by construction $Q_x = F_x^{-1}$, where F_x^{-1} is the inverse of the cdf F_x. For example, the level of income below which incomes of 25 percent of the population lie is $Q_x(25)$. If 25 percent of Georgia's population has income below GEL 2,000, then $Q_{GEO}(25) = GEL\ 2,000$.

Figure 2.3 describes the quantile function corresponding to distribution x. The horizontal axis denotes the population share, or the percentage of

Figure 2.3: Quantile Function

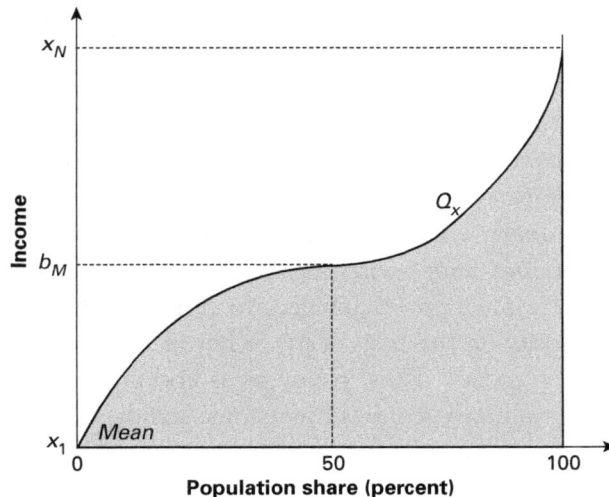

population. The vertical axis denotes the corresponding value of a quantile function in terms of income. Of course, no one in the society can have any income above $Q_x(100)$. Half of the population has an income less than the median b_M, so $Q_x(50) = b_M$. The shaded area underneath the quantile function is the mean $\bar{x}$ of the distribution x.

Having introduced these basic concepts, we discuss income standards in the next section.

Income Standards

An *income standard* gauges the size of a distribution by summarizing the entire distribution in a single income level. Some income standards can be viewed as stylized measures of a society's overall level of well-being. Others focus more narrowly on one part of the distribution or have no general welfare interpretation. We begin this section by introducing common properties that an income standard should satisfy. We denote any income standard by W and use subscripts to indicate specific measures or indices.

Desirable Properties

An income standard can satisfy several basic properties. We refer to the first two properties—*symmetry* and *population invariance*—as *invariance properties* because they describe changes in the distribution that leave the income standard unaltered. The second pair of properties—*weak monotonicity* and the *weak transfer principle*—are called *dominance properties* because they require the income standard to rise (or not fall) when the income distribution changes in a particular way. Finally, *normalization* and *linear homogeneity* are *calibration properties* that ensure the income standard is measured by income. The additional property of *subgroup consistency* is not a part of the basic properties, but it is desirable when evaluating income standards of subpopulations.

Symmetry requires that switching two people's incomes leaves the income standard evaluation unchanged. In other words, a person should not be given priority on the basis of his or her identity when calculating a society's income standard. Thus, symmetry is also known as *anonymity*. In technical terms, symmetry requires the income standard of distribution x to be equal to the income standard of distribution x', if x' is obtained from x by a permutation of incomes.

What is a permutation of income? An example will explain. Consider the three-person income vector $x = (\$10k, \$20k, \$30k)$ so that the first, second, and the third person receive incomes $10k, $20k, and $30k, respectively. If the incomes of the first and second persons are switched, then the new income vector becomes $x' = (\$20k, \$10k, \$30k)$. This new vector x' is said to be obtained from vector x' by a permutation of incomes. The symmetry property thus can be stated as follows:

> *Symmetry:* If distribution x' is obtained from distribution x by a permutation of incomes, then $W(x') = W(x)$.

The second property is *population invariance*. This property requires that the income standard not depend on population size. That is, a replication of an income vector results in the same income standard as the original sample vector. Consider the income vector of society X to be $x = (\$10k, \$20k, \$30k)$. Now suppose three more people join the society with the same income distribution. The new income vector of society X is $x' = (\$10k, \$10k, \$20k, \$20k, \$30k, \$30k)$. Society X now has more overall income, but population invariance requires that the income standard of society X remain unaltered.

What is the implication of population invariance? It allows us to compare income standards across countries and across time with varying population sizes. Furthermore, when combined with symmetry, population invariance allows the income standard to depend only on information found in a distribution function, which does not include the population size and the identities of income receivers.

> *Population Invariance:* If vector x' is obtained by replicating vector x at least once, then $W(x') = W(x)$.

The third property requires that if the income of any person in a society increases, then the income standard should register an increase, or at least should not fall. Implicitly, this property assumes that increasing someone's income is not harmful to the entire society.

There are two versions of this property. One is *weak monotonicity*, which requires that the income standard not fall because of an increase in anyone's income. The other version is *monotonicity*, the stronger version, which requires that the income standard register an increase if anyone's income in the society increases.

For vectors x and x', the notation $x' > x$ implies that at least one element in x' is strictly greater than that in x, and all other elements in x' are no less than the corresponding elements in x. For example, if $x' = (\$20k, \$10k, \$30k)$ and $x = (\$25k, \$10k, \$30k)$, then $x' > x$. However, if $x' = (\$20k, \$10k, \$30k)$ and $x = (\$25k, \$10k, \$25k)$, then $x' \not> x$ because the income of the third person is lower in x than that in x'.

> *Weak Monotonicity*: If distribution x' is obtained from distribution x such that $x' > x$, then $W(x') \geq W(x)$.
>
> *Monotonicity*: If distribution x' is obtained from distribution x such that $x' > x$, then $W(x') > W(x)$.

Some income standards are occasionally interpreted as social welfare measures. The fourth property, known as the *transfer principle*, is the key property that enables this interpretation. A *regressive transfer* occurs when income is transferred from a poorer person to a richer person. The transfer principle requires that a regressive transfer between two people in a society should lower the income standard. Conversely, a *progressive transfer* occurs when income is transferred from a richer person to a poorer person. The transfer principle requires that a progressive transfer between two people raise the income standard.

Here is a formal definition of these two kinds of transfers using vector x. We have already assumed that incomes in x are ordered so that $x_1 \leq x_2 \leq \ldots \leq x_N$. Let income δ be transferred from person n to person m, where $n < m$ and $0 < \delta < (x_m - x_n)/2$. Denote the post-transfer income vector by x', where all incomes except those for people n and m are the same as in x, but $x'_n = x_n - \delta$ and $x'_m = x_m + \delta$. Then x' is said to be obtained from x by a regressive transfer.

Now, let income $\delta > 0$ be transferred from person m to person n. Denote the post-transfer income vector by x'', where all incomes except those for people n and m are the same as in x, but $x''_n = x_n + \delta$ and $x''_m = x_m - \delta$ such that $x''_m > x''_n$. Then x'' is said to be obtained from x by a progressive transfer.

Consider the following example. Let the two income vectors of society X at two different points in time be $x = (\$10k, \$20k, \$30k)$ and $x' = (\$15k, \$20k, \$25k)$, where x' has been obtained from x by transferring $\$5k$ from the third person to the first person. This is a progressive transfer.

Below is the formal statement of the transfer principle property. This principle is also known as the Pigou-Dalton transfer principle after the English economists Arthur Cecil Pigou and Hugh Dalton.[3]

> *Transfer Principle:* If distribution x' is obtained from distribution x by a regressive transfer, then $W(x') < W(x)$. If distribution x'' is obtained from distribution x by a progressive transfer, then $W(x'') > W(x)$.

One justification of the transfer principle invokes a utilitarian form of welfare function that takes welfare to be the average level of (indirect) utility in society and assumes that all utility functions are identical and strictly increasing (see Atkinson 1970). In this context, the intuitive assumption of *diminishing marginal utility* yields the transfer principle. Diminishing marginal utility requires that the loss to the poorer giver is greater than the gain to the richer receiver because of a regressive transfer. Hence, overall welfare falls, or, equivalently, the gain to the poorer receiver is greater than the loss to the richer giver because of a progressive transfer—hence, welfare rises.

The fifth property is *normalization.* This property requires that if incomes are the same across all people in a society, then the income standard should be represented by that commonly held income. This property is intuitive. For example, let the income vector of a three-person society be ($20k, $20k, $20k). Then the income standard should be $20k.

> *Normalization:* For the income distribution, $x = (b, b, \ldots, b)$, $W(x) = b$.

The sixth property is *linear homogeneity.* This property requires that if an income distribution is obtained from another income distribution by changing the incomes by some proportion, then the income standard should also change by the same proportion. For example, if everyone's income in a society doubles, then the society's income standard doubles. If everyone's income is halved, then the society's income standard is halved.

> *Linear Homogeneity:* If distribution x' is obtained from distribution x such that $x' = cx$ where $c > 0$, then $W(x') = cW(x)$.

Subgroup consistency is the final property presented here. In some empirical applications, there is a natural concern for certain identifiable population subgroups as well as for the overall population. We might be interested, for instance, in the performances of various states or subregions of a country to understand how the overall improvement in income standard is distributed across those regions.

When population subgroups are tracked alongside the overall population value, there is a risk that the income standard could indicate contradictory or confusing trends. For example, it may be possible that the income standards of some regions within a country improve while the income standards of the rest of the country remain the same, but the income standard of the country as a whole deteriorates. This type of result may cause confusion because following the regional performances, one would expect the country's overall performance to improve.

Thus, a natural consistency property for an income standard might be that if subgroup population sizes are fixed but incomes are varying, when the income standard rises in one subgroup and does not fall in the rest, the overall population income standard must rise. This property, known as *subgroup consistency*, avoids inconsistencies arising from multilevel analyses of this sort.

As an example, suppose the income vector x with population size N is divided into two subgroup vectors x' with population size N' and x'' with population size N'' such that $N' + N'' = N$. Let a new vector y be obtained from x with the same population size N and its corresponding two subgroups be y' with population size N' and y'' with population size N''. The subgroup consistency property can be stated as follows:[4]

> *Subgroup Consistency:* Given that the overall population size and the subgroup population sizes remain unchanged, if $W(y') > W(x')$ and $W(y'') \geq W(x'')$, then $W(y) > W(x)$.

Having discussed the properties of the income standards, we now discuss the commonly used income standards. We outline these income standards and analyze their usefulness in terms of the properties they satisfy.

Commonly Used Income Standards

Four kinds of income standards are in common use: quantile incomes, partial means, general means, and means based on the maximin approach. (Among the maximin means, we discuss only the Sen mean in this book.) We now describe each kind in greater detail.

Quantile Income

Quantile incomes provide information about a specific point on the distribution. They can be directly calculated from a quantile function or a cdf.

The quantile income at the pth percentile is the income below which the incomes of p percent of the population fall. For the income distribution x with N people, the quantile income at the pth percentile is the income that is larger than the incomes of the poorest $pN/100$ people.

We denote the quantile income at the pth percentile of distribution x by $W_{QI}(x; p)$. For example, if $p = 50$ percent, then the quantile income at the pth percentile of distribution x is denoted by $W_{QI}(x; 50)$. If $W_{QI}(x; 50) = \$200$, then it should be read as *50 percent of the population in society X earns less than* $200. Similarly, if $W_{QI}(x; 90) = \$1,000$, then 90 percent of its population earns less than $1,000.

Commonly reported quantile incomes used when gauging societies' standard of living are the quantile incomes at the 10th percentile, 20th percentile, 50th percentile, 80th percentile, and 90th percentile. A close look at the quantile income at the 50th percentile reveals that this is the *income* below which half of the population of a distribution lies. Therefore, the quantile at the pth percentile income is just the *median* of a distribution. For a particular income distribution where each and every person earns equal income, the quantile incomes at all percentiles are equal to each other, ensuring that the quantile incomes satisfy the normalization property.

A *quantile function* is the most helpful tool for visualizing quantile incomes. Figure 2.4 shows the quantile function for income distribution x.

Figure 2.4: Quantile Function and the Quantile Incomes

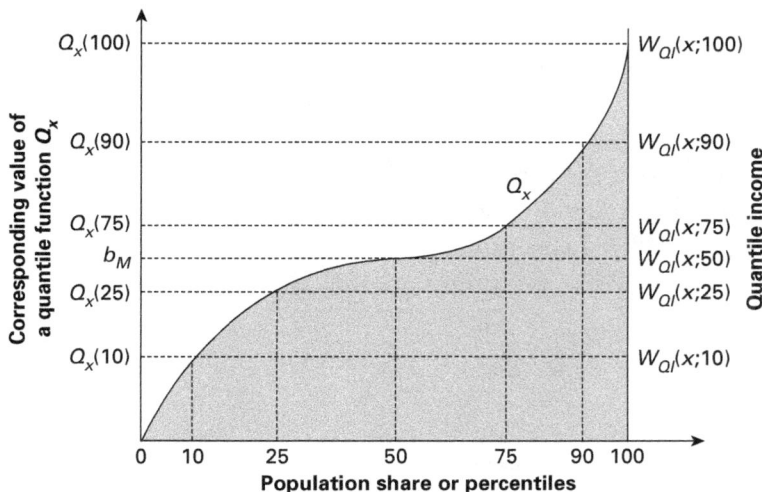

As in figure 2.3, the horizontal axis in figure 2.4 denotes the population share in percentage, which lies between 0 and 100. The left-hand vertical axis denotes the corresponding value of a quantile function Q_x and the right-hand vertical axis reports the quantile incomes.

By definition, the quantile income for a certain percentile is the value of the quantile function at that percentile, so $W_{QI}(x; p) = Q_x(p)$. In the figure, $W_{QI}(x; 50) = b_M$ is the median of distribution x. Likewise, $W_{QI}(x; 25)$ and $W_{QI}(x; 75)$ are the first and the third quartiles of distribution x. The well-known 10th and 90th percentiles of distribution x are $W_{QI}(x; 10) = Q_x(10)$ and $W_{QI}(x; 90) = Q_x(90)$, respectively. Given that a cdf is an inverse of a quantile function, quantile incomes can also be graphically portrayed and calculated using a cdf.

What properties do quantile incomes satisfy? It is straightforward to verify that any quantile income satisfies *symmetry*, *normalization*, *population invariance*, *linear homogeneity*, and *weak monotonicity*. However, no quantile income satisfies the other dominance properties: monotonicity, transfer principle, and subgroup consistency. Quantile incomes do not satisfy monotonicity because a person's income may increase, but as long as it does not surpass a certain quantile, that quantile income remains unaltered. Similarly, quantile incomes do not satisfy the transfer principle because they do not change to a transfer that takes place at a nonrelevant part of the distribution.

The income standards are not subgroup consistent because the quantile incomes of the subregions may increase, but the overall quantile income may fall. Consider the following example. Suppose the income vector of society X is $x = (\$10k, \$20k, \$30k, \$50k, \$60k, \$80k)$ and the income vector of two subgroups is $x' = (\$10k, \$20k, \$30k)$ and $x'' = (\$50k, \$60k, \$80k)$. The 67th quantile of the three distributions is $W_{QI}(x'; 67) = \$20k$, $W_{QI}(x''; 67) = \$60k$, and $W_{QI}(x; 67) = \$50k$. Now, suppose the subgroup income vectors over time become $y' = (\$10k, \$20k, \$30k)$ and $y'' = (\$45k, \$65k, \$80k)$. Apparently, the quantile income at the 67th percentile of the first group does not change, but that of the second does. In fact, $W_{QI}(x'; 67) = W_{QI}(y'; 67)$ but $W_{QI}(y''; 67) > W_{QI}(x''; 67)$. What happens to the quantile income at the 67th percentile of the overall distribution? It turns out that $W_{QI}(y; 67) = 45 < W_{QI}(x; 67)$.

Partial Mean

The next set of commonly used means is the *partial means*. There are two types of partial means: *lower partial means* and *upper partial means*. A lower partial mean is obtained by finding the mean of the incomes below a specific percentile cutoff. An upper partial mean is obtained by finding the mean of incomes above a specific percentile cutoff. Lower partial means are more commonly used than upper partial means.

The lower partial mean of the pth percentile is the average or mean income of the bottom p percent of the population. The upper partial mean of the pth percentile, in contrast, is the average or mean income of the top $(1 - p)$ percent of the population. We denote the lower partial mean and upper partial mean of distribution x for percentile p by $W_{LPM}(x; p)$ and $W_{UPM}(x; p)$, respectively. For example, if $p = 50$ percent, then the lower partial mean of the pth percentile of distribution x is denoted by $W_{LPM}(x; 50)$.

If $W_{LPM}(x; 50) = \$100$ and $W_{UPM}(x; 50) = \$10,000$, then together they should be read as *the mean income of the bottom 50 percent of the population is $100, and the mean income of the top 50 percent of the population is $10,000* (see example 2.1).

Example 2.1: Consider the income vector $x = (\$2k, \$4k, \$8k, \$10k)$. The lower partial mean of the 50th percentile of the distribution is $(\$2k + \$4k)/2 = \$3k$, and that of the 75th percentile of the distribution is $(\$2k + \$4k + \$8k)/3 = \$4.7k$. In contrast, the upper partial mean of the 50th percentile of the distribution is $(\$8k + \$10k)/2 = \$9k$ and that of the 75th percentile of the distribution is $\$10k$.

The following is a graphical description of how partial means can be calculated using quantile function Q_x. The vertical axis of figure 2.5 denotes income, and the horizontal axis denotes population share. There are two percentiles, p' and p'', for describing the lower and upper partial means. The lower partial mean of the p' percentile population is the shaded area underneath the quantile function Q_x to the left of p' divided by p'. The lower partial mean is the average income of all people in society X whose income is less than $Q_x(p')$. Similarly, the upper partial mean of the p'' percentile population is the shaded area underneath the quantile function Q_x to the right of p'' divided by $(100 - p'')$. This upper partial mean is the average income of all people in society X whose income is larger than $Q_x(p'')$.

Like the quantile incomes, any partial mean satisfies *symmetry, normalization, population invariance, linear homogeneity,* and *weak monotonicity,* but no partial mean satisfies monotonicity, transfer principle, and subgroup

Figure 2.5: Quantile Function and the Partial Means

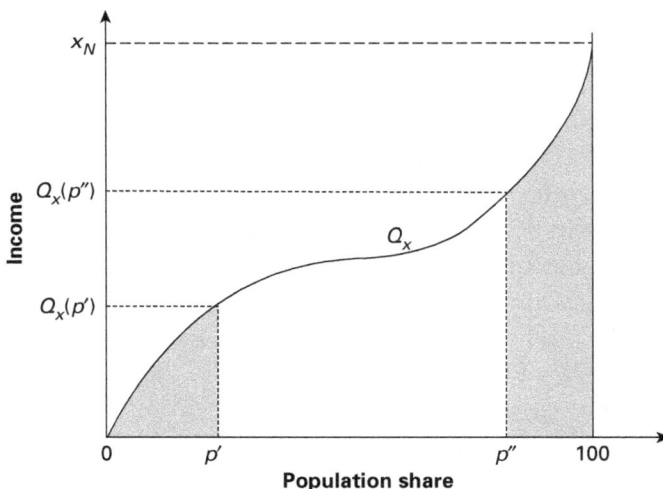

consistency. Like the quantile incomes, one can easily show using a simple example that partial means do not satisfy subgroup consistency.

Quantile incomes and partial means are crude income standards because they do not depend on the entire income distribution. Yet they are highly informative and easy to understand. Especially when income data are missing for certain parts of the income distribution, these crude income standards are useful tools for understanding a society's performance.

In contrast, when rich datasets are available, a study based on quantile incomes and partial means may be limited because they do not reflect changes in every part of the distribution. For example, if the income of a person below the median increases—but not by enough to surpass the median income—then the distribution *median* does not reflect any change.

The following income standards are designed to consider the entire distribution. These income standards will, in most cases, reflect a change in any part of the distribution.

General Mean

General means are a family of normative income standards. Standards in this family are normative because the formulation of each measure depends on a parameter denoted by α, which can take any value between $-\infty$ and $+\infty$. Unlike the quantile means and the partial means, general means take into account the entire income distribution, but emphasize lower or higher incomes depending on the value of α. Parameter α is familiar in the literature as the order of general means.

For income distribution x, we denote the general mean of order α by $W_{GM}(x; \alpha)$. It is defined as

$$W_{GM}(x;\alpha) = \begin{cases} \left(\dfrac{x_1^{\alpha} + x_2^{\alpha} + \ldots + x_N^{\alpha}}{N} \right)^{1/\alpha} & \text{if } \alpha \neq 0 \\ (x_1 \times x_2 \times \ldots \times x_N)^{1/N} & \text{if } \alpha = 0 \end{cases} \tag{2.3}$$

Although α may take any value between $-\infty$ and $+\infty$, four means in this family are more well known than others: *arithmetic mean*, *geometric mean*, *harmonic mean*, and *Euclidean mean*.

- For $\alpha = 1$, W_{GM} is known as the arithmetic mean (denoted by W_A) or the average $\bar{x}$ of all elements in x and can be written as[5]

$$W_A(x) = \frac{x_1 + x_2 + \cdots + x_N}{N}. \tag{2.4}$$

- For $\alpha = 0$, W_{GM} becomes the geometric mean (denoted by W_G) of all elements in distribution x and can be expressed as

$$W_G(x) = (x_1 \times x_2 \times \ldots \times x_N)^{1/N}. \tag{2.5}$$

If we take a natural logarithm on both sides of equation (2.5), we find

$$W_L(x) = \ln W_G(x) = \frac{\ln x_1 + \ln x_2 + \cdots + \ln x_N}{N}. \tag{2.6}$$

$W_L(x)$ is the average of the logarithm of all incomes in distribution x. The logarithm of incomes is frequently used for various analyses by labor economists.

- For $\alpha = -1$, W_{GM} becomes the harmonic mean (W_H) of distribution x and can be expressed as

$$W_H(x) = \left(\frac{x_1^{-1} + x_2^{-1} + \cdots + x_N^{-1}}{N} \right)^{-1}. \tag{2.7}$$

- Finally, another well-known mean is the Euclidean mean (W_E), obtained when $\alpha = 2$. The Euclidean mean formula is

$$W_E(x) = \left(\frac{x_1^2 + x_2^2 + \cdots + x_N^2}{N} \right)^{1/2}. \qquad (2.8)$$

Example 2.2 shows the results of calculating these means for a given income vector.

Example 2.2: Consider the income vector $x = (\$2k, \$4k, \$8k, \$10k)$.

- The arithmetic mean of x is $(\$2k + \$4k + \$8k + \$10k)/4 = \$6k$.
- The geometric mean of x is $(\$2k \times \$4k \times \$8k \times \$10k)^{1/4}$ $= \$5.03k$.
- The harmonic mean of x is $[(\$2k^{-1} + \$4k^{-1} + \$8k^{-1} + \$10k^{-1})/4]^{-1} = \$4.10k$.
- The Euclidean mean of x is $[(\$2k^2 + \$4k^2 + \$8k^2 + \$10k^2)/4]^{1/2}$ $= \$6.78k$.

Having been introduced to the family, one can now understand the properties of general means and the way they depend on parameter α. All means in this family satisfy *symmetry, normalization, population invariance, linear homogeneity, monotonicity,* and *subgroup consistency.* Furthermore, for $\alpha < 1$, general means satisfy the *transfer principle.* Thus, the general means satisfy all the dominance properties introduced earlier. One reason is that, unlike the quantile means and the partial means, general means consider all incomes in the distribution.

It is straightforward to show that general means satisfy symmetry, normalization, population invariance, linear homogeneity, and monotonicity. That general means satisfy subgroup consistency may be verified as follows: if vector x is divided into subgroup vectors x' and x'', then the general mean of x can be expressed as

$$W_{GM}(x; a) = W_{GM}((W_{GM}(x'; a), W_{GM}(x''; a)); a). \qquad (2.9)$$

In other words, the general mean of x is the general mean of the general means of x' and x''. Then the monotonicity property ensures that subgroup consistency is satisfied.

Another interesting property of W_{GM} is its monotonic relationship with parameter α, which requires that the value of W_{GM} increase as α rises and decrease as α falls. A lower α gives more emphasis to lower values within a distribution and thus causes W_{GM} to fall. Conversely, a higher α gives more emphasis to higher values within a distribution, causing the value of W_{GM} to rise. Technically speaking, $W_{GM}(x; \alpha) < W_{GM}(x; \alpha')$ for any $\alpha < \alpha'$. We refer to this property of general means as *increasingness to* α. It follows from this property that $W_E(x) \geq W_A(x) \geq W_G(x) \geq W_H(x)$.

There is an exception, however, when the values of general means do not change as α changes, and this happens when a distribution is degenerate. A society's income distribution is *degenerate* if all people in that society have equal incomes. For a degenerate income distribution, all general means are equal; that is, $W_{GM}(x; \alpha) = W_{GM}(x; \alpha')$ for all $\alpha \neq \alpha'$. Invariance of general means to degenerate distribution is another way of ensuring that they satisfy the *normalization* property.

Given that α ranges from $-\infty$ to $+\infty$, what is the range of W_{GM}? Unlike the value of α, however, W_{GM} is not unbounded. Rather, it has a lower bound and an upper bound. When α decreases and approaches $-\infty$, $W_{GM}(x; \alpha)$ converges to the minimum element in x. The society's income standard in this case is nothing, but the poorest person's income is x_1. In contrast, when α increases and approaches $+\infty$, $W_{GM}(x; \alpha)$ converges toward the maximum element in x, and the society's income standard equals the income of the richest person, x_N. Notice, however, that unlike the other general means, these two extreme income standards—$W_{GM}(x; -\infty)$ and $W_{GM}(x; +\infty)$ —are not sensitive to the entire distribution. That is, if any element in x other than x_1 and x_N changes, these two income standards do not reflect that change.

Figure 2.6 describes the relationship between the family of generalized means and parameter α. As already discussed, the general mean is the arithmetic mean at $\alpha = 1$, the geometric mean at $\alpha = 0$, the harmonic mean at $\alpha = -1$, and the Euclidean mean at $\alpha = 2$. Values of general means increase with parameter α. They are bounded below by $x_1 = \min\{x\}$ and are bounded above by $x_N = \max\{x\}$.

One feature we should note carefully is that the general means are undefined for $\alpha < 0$ when there is at least one nonpositive element in an income vector. For example, if an element of x is 0, then for $\alpha = -1$, we have $(0)^{-1} = 1/0$. Therefore, one requirement for any measure in this family with $\alpha < 0$ is that all elements in x be strictly positive.

Figure 2.6: Generalized Means and Parameter α

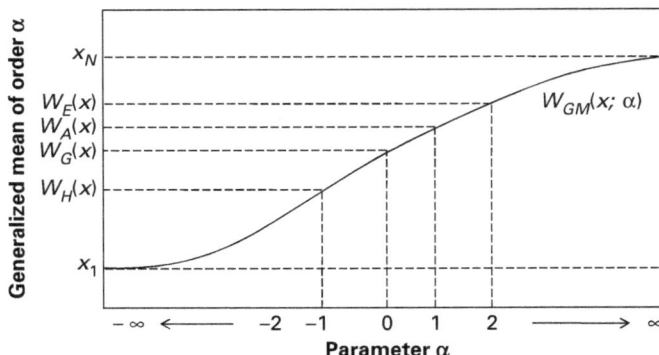

General Means as Welfare Measures

The transfer principle ensures that the general means may be interpreted as social welfare measures. Actually, the general means for $\alpha < 1$ are commonly interpreted as measures of social welfare. This form of welfare function was considered by Atkinson (1970), who then defined a helpful transformation of the function called the equally distributed equivalent income (ede). The utility function that Atkinson assumed to obtain his particular ede was $U(x_n) = \dfrac{1}{\alpha}(x_n)^{\frac{1}{\alpha}}$ for $\alpha < 1$ and $\alpha \neq 0$ and $U(x_n) = \ln x_n$ for $\alpha = 0$ for all n. The ede represents the level of income x_{ede}^{α}, which, if received by all people in a society, yields the same welfare level as that of the original income distribution. Thus, like the general mean itself, the value of ede depends on the parameter α, and for vector x, the ede of order α is $EDE(x; \alpha) = W_{GM}(x; \alpha)$.

Sen Mean

The usual mean can be reinterpreted as the expected value of a single income drawn randomly from the population. Now, suppose that instead of a single income, we were to draw *two* incomes randomly from the population (with replacement). If we then evaluated the pair in terms of the lower of the two incomes, this would lead to the *Sen mean*, which is defined as the expectation of the minimum of two randomly drawn incomes.[6] These two random incomes are drawn with replacement, which means that these two incomes may belong to the same person in a society. If every income in distribution x

is compared with every other income in x with replacement, then there are N^2 possible comparisons. Thus, the Sen mean can be defined as

$$W_S(x) = \frac{1}{N^2} \sum_{n=1}^{N} \sum_{n'=1}^{N} \min\{x_n, x_{n'}\}. \qquad (2.10)$$

Because we are using the minimum of the two incomes, this number can be no higher than the mean, and is generally lower. The Sen mean also emphasizes the lower incomes but in a way that differs from the general means with $\alpha < 1$, the lower partial means, or the quantile incomes below the median.

There is a straightforward way of calculating the Sen mean for an income vector—by creating an $N \times N$ matrix that has a cell for every possible pair of incomes and placing the lower value of the two incomes in the cell. Adding all the entries and dividing by the number of entries (N^2) to obtain their mean provides the Sen mean. Consider example 2.3 to better understand this way of calculating the Sen mean.

Example 2.3: Consider the income vector $x = (\$2k, \$4k, \$8k, \$10k)$. First, we construct the following matrix:

x	$2k	$4k	$8k	$10k
$2k	$2k	$2k	$2k	$2k
$4k	$2k	$4k	$4k	$4k
$8k	$2k	$4k	$8k	$8k
$10k	$2k	$4k	$8k	$10k

Each cell in this 4×4 matrix is the minimum of the top row and the left column, both of which represent the ordered income vector x. The Sen mean is the average of all elements in the matrix. Thus,

$$W_S(x) = \frac{1}{4^2}(7 \times \$2k + 5 \times \$4k + 3 \times \$8k + 1 \times \$10k) = \$4.25k.$$

The Sen mean of x is lower than the arithmetic mean of x, which is $6k.

There is another interesting way of understanding the Sen mean—the weighted average of all elements of an income distribution—where the weight on each element depends on the rank of the corresponding element. Recall that we assumed $x_1 \leq x_2 \leq \ldots \leq x_N$ for distribution x so that the Nth person has the highest income and the first person has the lowest income. Thus, element x_N receives the highest rank and element x_1 receives the lowest rank. The Sen mean attaches the highest weight to the lowest income, the second-highest weight to the second-lowest income, and the lowest weight to the highest income.

For distribution x, the Sen mean can be expressed as $W_S(x) = a_1 x_1 + \ldots + a_N x_N$, where $a_N = (2(N - n) + 1)/N^2$ for all n. Thus, the weight attached to the highest income x_N is $a_N = 1/N^2$; the weight attached to the second-highest income x_{N-1} is $a_{N-1} = 3/N^2$; and the weight attached to the lowest income x_1 is $a_1 = (2N - 1)/N^2$. The weight attached to the richest income in the example above ($10k) is 1/16, whereas the weight attached to the poorest income ($2k) is 7/16. Notice that the weights sum to one, that is,

$$a_1 + a_2 + \ldots + a_N = \frac{1}{N^2}(1 + 3 + 5 + \ldots + (2N - 1)) = \frac{N^2}{N^2} = 1. \quad (2.11)$$

Thus, the Sen mean can also be expressed as

$$W_S(x) = \frac{1}{N^2}((2N - 1)x_1 + (2N - 3)x_2 + \cdots + 3x_{N-1} + x_N). \quad (2.12)$$

The Sen mean satisfies *symmetry, normalization, population invariance, linear homogeneity, monotonicity,* and the *transfer principle.* It does not, however, satisfy subgroup consistency, which means it is possible that the Sen mean of one region increases while the Sen mean for the other regions remains the same and the overall Sen mean falls.

This failure to satisfy subgroup consistency can be shown using a simple example. Suppose the income vector of society X is $x = ($4k, $5k, $6k, $7k, $14k, $16k)$ and the income vectors of two subregions are $x' = ($4k, $5k, $7k)$ and $x'' = ($6k, $14k, $16k)$. The Sen means of these three income vectors are $W_S(x) = $6.22k$, $W_S(x') = $4.67k$, and $W_S(x'') = $9.78k$. Now, suppose the income vector of society X changes to $y = ($3.4k, $6.1k, $6k, $6.5k, $14k, $16k)$ so that the income vector of the first subgroup changes to $y' = ($3.4k, $6.1k, $6.5k)$, whereas that of the other subgroup remains unaltered such that $y'' = x''$. Note that the overall mean income and the mean income of both groups remain unchanged. The Sen means of the three income vectors become $W_S(y) = $6.24k$, $W_S(y') = $4.64k$, and $W_S(y'') = $9.78k$. Clearly, the Sen mean of the first subgroup decreases while that of the second subgroup remains the same; yet the overall Sen mean goes up. This feature of the Sen mean is inherited by the inequality and poverty measures that are based on the Sen mean—the famous Gini coefficient and the Sen-Shorrocks-Thon index of poverty.

Finally, unlike Atkinson, Sen suggested going beyond the utilitarian form. His key nonutilitarian example, the Sen mean, can be viewed as both an ede and a general welfare function, because it satisfies the transfer principle. If we denote the Sen ede as $EDE_S(x)$, then $EDE_S(x) = W_S(x)$.

During our subsequent discussion in this chapter, we will see that these five means (arithmetic, geometric, harmonic, Euclidean, and Sen) and their various functional forms are often used in the measurement of welfare, inequality, and poverty.

Dominance and Unanimity

An income standard provides a point estimate of the evaluation of a certain income distribution. We might ask one obvious question: Does the direction of comparison between distributions in a given point in time, or even across time, using one income standard continue to hold for other income standards? Let us clarify this concern with a few examples.

Consider two income vectors $x = (\$4k, \$5k, \$6k, \$7k, \$14k, \$16k)$ and $y = (\$3k, \$5k, \$6k, \$9k, \$14k, \$16k)$. If we use arithmetic mean W_A as an income standard, then $W_A(x) = 8.7$ and $W_A(y) = 8.8$. Clearly, distribution y has higher mean income than distribution x. What if we, instead, use the Sen mean? We get $W_S(x) = 6.22$ and $W_S(y) = 6.19$. Thus, according to the Sen mean, distribution x has higher welfare than distribution y.

How do the geometric mean and the Euclidean mean of these two vectors compare? According to the geometric mean, distribution x has higher welfare than distribution y because $W_G(x) = 7.57$ and $W_G(y) = 7.52$. According to the Euclidean mean, distribution y has higher welfare than distribution x because $W_E(x) = 9.81$ and $W_E(y) = 10.02$. What we see from these comparisons is that different income standards rank two distributions differently.

Are there situations when the various income standards agree with each other? This question leads to a discussion of dominance and unanimity. If there is a situation where we find a dominance relation holding between two distributions, then there is no need to use different income standards to evaluate that situation because all income standards would agree. If there is no unanimous relation, then certain curves may help in understanding the source of ambiguity. Thus, conducting a dominance analysis that is based on these curves should be the first step in welfare comparison.

A second important motivation for dominance analysis might be *focus*, or an identified concern with different parts of the distribution. Has the rapid growth for the higher-income group been matched by growth of the middle-income group or the lower-income group? We spend some time in this subsection finding answers to these questions by plotting entire classes of income standards using the various curves to be defined next. If one curve always remains above another curve, then all income standards in that class agree in ranking—for example, two income distributions. However, if the curves cross, then situations may arise in which different income standards in the same class disagree with each other.

A first such curve is the quantile function itself, which simultaneously depicts incomes from lowest to highest. When all income quantiles are the same, then one income distribution always lies above another income distribution. When two distributions never cross, the situation is known as first-order stochastic dominance (FSD). An income distribution x first order stochastically dominates another distribution y, denoted by x *FSD* y, if and only if (a) no portion of x's quantile function lies below y's quantile function and (b) at least some part of x's quantile function lies above y's quantile function. Let us denote quantile function using the notations introduced earlier. So x's quantile function is denoted by Q_x and that of y is denoted by Q_y. Then, the definition of FSD is as follows:

First-Order Stochastic Dominance: Distribution x first order stochastically dominates another distribution y if and only if $Q_x(p) \geq Q_y(p)$ for all p in the range [0,100] and $Q_x(p) > Q_y(p)$ for some p.

The concept of FSD may also be understood in terms of cumulative distribution functions. Recall that a quantile function is just an inverse of a cdf. Using the notations introduced earlier, we denote the cdf of x by F_x and that of y by F_y. The formal definition of FSD in terms of cdfs is as follows:

First-Order Stochastic Dominance: Distribution x first order stochastically dominates another distribution y if and only if $F_x(b) \leq F_y(b)$ for all b in the range [0, ∞] and $F_x(b) < F_y(b)$ for some b.

FSD ensures higher welfare according to every utilitarian welfare function with identical, increasing utility functions. The robustness implied by an unambiguous comparison of quantile functions extends to *all* income standards and *all* symmetric welfare functions for which "more is better." However, if the resulting curves cross, the final judgment is contingent on which income standard is selected. Even in this case, the quantile function can be helpful in identifying the winning and losing portions of the distribution.

Figure 2.7 depicts the situation where x FSD y. Panel a shows the FSD by quantile functions, and panel b shows the FSD by cdfs. In panel a, the quantile function of x lies completely above that of y, which means that every quantile income of distribution x is larger than the corresponding quantile income of distribution y, so x FSD y. The same argument applies to the cdfs in panel b, where the cdf of x lies to the right of y. Later, we will find the concept of FSD that is based on cdfs useful, especially in poverty analysis.

The *generalized Lorenz* (GL) *curve* is a second curve that is useful for dominance analysis. The generalized Lorenz curve graphs the area under the quantile function up to each percent p of the population. Thus, any point on a generalized Lorenz curve is the cumulative mean income held by the bottom p percent of the population. We denote the generalized Lorenz function of distribution x by GL_x, and that for the p percent of the population by $GL_x(p)$. By construction, for income distribution x, $GL_x(100) = W_A(x)$ and $GL_x(0) = 0$.

Figure 2.7: First-Order Stochastic Dominance Using Quantile Functions and Cumulative Distribution Functions

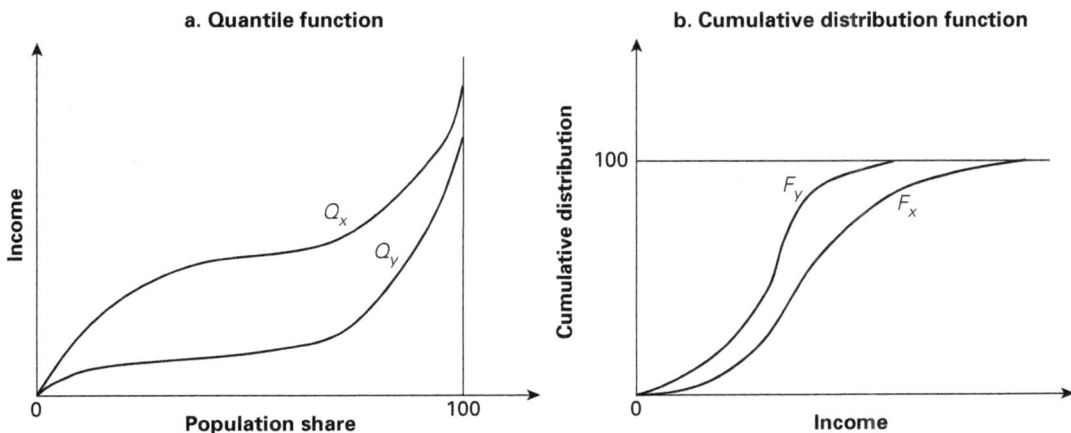

a. Quantile function

b. Cumulative distribution function

Figure 2.8 describes the construction of a generalized Lorenz curve from a quantile function of a five-person income vector x = ($10k, $15k, $20k, $25k, $30k). There are five percentiles: 20th, 40th, 60th, 80th, and 100th. In panel a, we outline the quantile function of x, Q_x. In panel b, we report the generalized Lorenz curve of x, GL_x. The mean of distribution x is $W_A(x) = 20$. A point on the generalized Lorenz curve denotes the area underneath the quantile function for the corresponding percentile of the population. Up to the 20th percentile of the population, the area under Q_x is the area A.

In panel b, the corresponding value of GL_x for the 20th percentile of the population is denoted by point I. Thus, the value at point I is A/100 = 10 × 20/100 = 2. Similarly, the value of GL_x for the 40th percentile of the population is denoted by point II, and the value at point II is (A+B)/100 = (10+15) × 20/100 = 5. Repeating this approach, we find that the value of GL_x for the 100th percentile of the population is denoted by point V, and the value at point V is (A + B + C + D + E)/100 = (10 + 15 + 20 + 25 + 30) × 20/100 = 20. Note that the value at point V is the same as the mean of distribution x, $W_A(x)$.

The generalized Lorenz curve is closely linked with *lower partial means* (see Shorrocks 1983). Recall from our earlier discussion that the lower partial mean for a certain percentile of population p is the area underneath

Figure 2.8: Quantile Function and Generalized Lorenz Curve

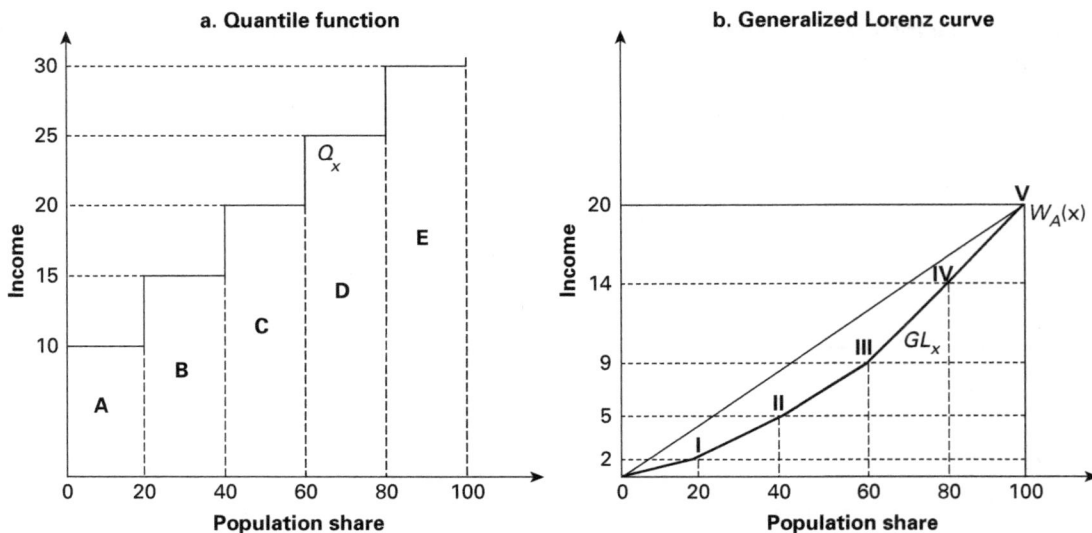

72

the quantile function divided by the percentile itself. Thus, the height of the generalized Lorenz curve at any percentile of population p is the lower partial mean times p itself, because the height of the generalized mean is the area underneath the quantile function at corresponding percentile p, that is, $GL_x(p) = pW_{LPM}(x; p)$. If income distribution x has a large enough sample size, the generalized Lorenz curve takes a form similar to the one described in figure 2.9.

The horizontal axis in figure 2.9 shows the population share, and the vertical axis denotes the height of the generalized Lorenz curve by income. The generalized Lorenz curve for distribution x is denoted by GL_x. The maximum height of GL_x is $W_A(x)$. The height of GL_x for the 50th percentile of the population is $GL_x(0.5)$.

If the total income in distribution x is distributed equally across all people in the society and distribution y is obtained, then the generalized Lorenz curve GL_y becomes a straight line. The maximum height of GL_y is also $W_A(x)$, because redistribution of incomes does not change the mean income. Notice that the height of GL_y is higher than the height of GL_x for every percentile p. This implies that every partial mean of distribution y is larger than the corresponding partial mean of distribution x. Thus, two generalized Lorenz curves of this sort show a *dominance* relation between two distributions in terms of partial means.

Figure 2.9: Generalized Lorenz Curve

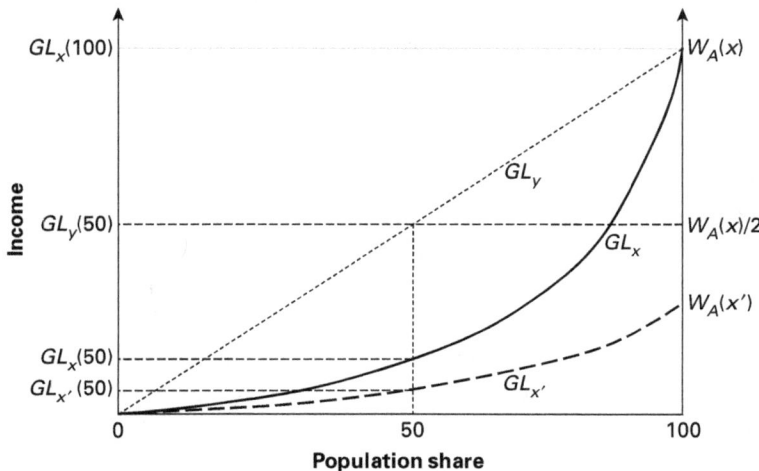

All partial means agree that distribution y has higher welfare than distribution x. Similarly, if there is another distribution x' whose generalized Lorenz curve, $GL_{x'}$, lies completely below GL_x (also shown in figure 2.9), then all partial means agree that distribution x has higher welfare than distribution x'. The heights of the generalized Lorenz curves for distributions y, x, and x' at the 50th percentile are $GL_y(50)$, $GL_x(50)$, and $GL_{y'}(50)$, respectively. The generalized Lorenz curve represents *second-order stochastic dominance*, which signals higher welfare according to *every* utilitarian welfare function with identical and increasing utility function exhibiting diminishing marginal utility. Example 2.4 provides a practical illustration of generalized Lorenz calculations. The generalized Lorenz curve is also closely related to the Sen mean. For distribution x, the Sen mean, $W_S(x)$, is twice the area underneath GL_x.

Example 2.4: Suppose per capita income in India is Rs 25,000. If only 3 percent of this mean income is received by the poorest 20 percent of the population, then $GL_{Ind}(20) = $ Rs 750.

Suppose incomes in India were redistributed, thereby keeping the average income unaltered so that everyone in India has identical income. Let us denote this income distribution by y. Then the cumulative average income received by the poorest 20 percent of the population is 20 percent and $GL_y(20) = $ Rs 5,000. Thus, $GL_y(20) - GL_{Ind}(20) = $ Rs 5,000 − Rs 750 = Rs 4,250. The loss of welfare because of unequal distribution of income for the poorest 20 percent of the population is Rs 4,250. In relative terms, the loss of welfare is 4,250/5,000 = 85 percent.

However, note that the loss presented in terms of the height of the generalized Lorenz curve is not the potential loss in the mean income of the poorest 20 percent of the population. The mean income of the poorest 20 percent of the population is $GL_{Ind}(20)/0.2 = $ Rs 3,750.

Had income been equally distributed, the mean income of the poorest 20 percent would have been Rs 25,000. In that scenario, the potential loss of mean income is Rs 21,250. But in a relative sense, the percentage loss in mean income is 25,205/25,000 = 85 percent, which is the same as the percentage loss in terms of the height of the generalized Lorenz curve. In fact, the percentage loss of welfare using the height of the generalized Lorenz curve is always the same as the percentage loss of mean income of that percentile.

Finally, a third curve depicts the general mean levels as parameter α varies. We call this curve a *general mean curve*. This curve has already been outlined in figure 2.6, where it is increasing in α; tends to the minimum income for very low α; rises through the harmonic, geometric, arithmetic, and Euclidean means; and tends toward the maximum income as α becomes very large.

Why is this curve useful? At the beginning of this subsection, an example showed that different generalized means may rank an income distribution differently. So the general mean curve is useful for determining (a) whether a given comparison of general means is robust to the choice of any income standard from the entire class of general means, and, if not, (b) which of the income standards is higher or lower.

General mean curves are also related to the quantile function and the generalized Lorenz curve. A higher quantile function will always yield a higher general mean curve, and a higher generalized Lorenz curve will raise the general mean curve for $\alpha < 1$, or the general means that favor the low incomes. The general mean curve concept will be particularly relevant to our later discussions of Atkinson's inequality measure.

Growth Curves

Some analyses go beyond the ordinal question (Which distribution is larger?) to consider the cardinal question: How much larger in percentage terms is one distribution than another? This question is especially salient when the two distributions are associated with the same population at two points in time. Thus, the second question follows: At what percentage rate did the income standard grow?

The most common and well-known way of understanding *growth* is by the growth of per capita income or mean income. The arithmetic mean is the income standard involved in this case. However, the defining properties of an income standard ensure that its rate of growth is a meaningful number that can be compared with the growth rates of other income standards, either for robustness purposes or for an understanding of the quality of growth.

As in our use of various curves in dominance analysis, we may also use different growth curves to understand how robust the growth of an income standard is and to understand whether the growth is of meaningful quality. A *growth curve* depicts the rates of growth across an entire class of income standards, in which the standards are ordered from lowest to highest.

In fact, each of the three dominance curves presented earlier suggests an associated growth curve. First, the *growth incidence curve* assesses how the quantile incomes are changing over time. Second, the *generalized Lorenz growth curve* indicates how the lower partial means are changing over time. Finally, the *general mean growth curve* plots the rate of growth of each general mean over time against parameter α. In the remainder of this section, we discuss the concepts of these different growth curves in greater detail.

Growth Incidence Curve

We start with the *growth incidence curve*. Consider two income distributions, x and y, at two different periods of time, where x is the initial income distribution. The quantile incomes of distribution x and distribution y at percentile p are denoted by $W_{QI}(x; p)$ and $W_{QI}(y; p)$, respectively. The growth of quantile income at percentile p is denoted by

$$g_{QI}(x,y;p) = \frac{W_{QI}(y;p) - W_{QI}(x;p)}{W_{QI}(x;p)} \times 100\%. \tag{2.13}$$

If every quantile registers an increase over time, then $g_{QI}(x, y; p) >$ for all p. The curve's height at $p = 50$ percent gives the median income's growth rate. Note that no part of this growth curve provides any information about the growth of mean income. Varying p allows us to examine whether this growth rate is robust to the choice of income standard, or whether the low-income standards grew at a different rate than the rest.

Figure 2.10 depicts the growth curves of quantile incomes. The vertical axis denotes the *growth rate of quantile income* and the horizontal axis denotes the *cumulative population share*. Suppose there are two societies, X and X'. The income distributions of society X at two different points in time are x and y, while those of society X' are x' and y'. The dashed growth curve $g_{QI}(x, y)$ denotes the quantile income growth rates of society X over time, whereas the dotted growth curve $g_{QI}(x', y')$ denotes the quantile income growth rates of society X' over time.

Suppose the growth rates of mean income across these two distributions are the same and are denoted by $\bar{g} > 0$. Thus, the solid horizontal line at $\bar{g}$ denotes the growth rate if the growth rate had been the same for all percentiles or the cumulative population share.

Figure 2.10: Growth Incidence Curves

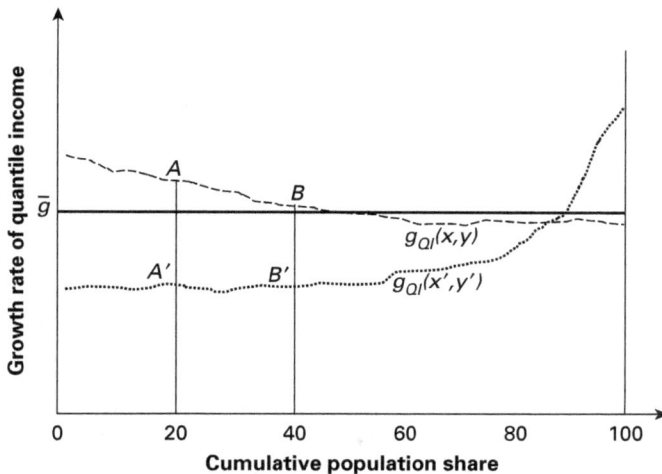

What information do these two growth curves provide? Growth between *x* and *y* is pro-poor in the sense that lower quantile incomes have positive growth, whereas the upper quantile incomes have negative growth. Growth between *x'* and *y'*, in contrast, is not pro-poor because lower quantile incomes have negative income growth, whereas upper quantile incomes have positive income growth. In society X, the growth rate of income for the 20th percentile is much higher than that of the 40th percentile, as denoted by point A and point B, respectively. Note that the growths are higher than the mean growth rates. In society X', however, the income growth rate for the 20th percentile is almost the same as that of the 40th percentile, as denoted by point A' and point B', respectively. We will discuss pro-poor growth in greater detail in the poverty section of this chapter.

Generalized Lorenz Growth Curve

The next growth curve is the *generalized Lorenz growth curve*. Consider the two income distributions, *x* and *y*, used previously. The lower partial means of distribution *x* and distribution *y* at percentile *p* are denoted by $W_{LPM}(x; p)$ and $W_{LPM}(y; p)$, respectively. The growth of partial means at percentile *p* is denoted by

A Unified Approach to Measuring Poverty and Inequality

$$g_{LPM}(x,y;p) = \frac{W_{LPM}(y;p) - W_{LPM}(x;p)}{W_{LPM}(x;p)} \times 100\%. \qquad (2.14)$$

If every quantile income registers an increase over time, then $g_{LPM}(x, y; p) > 0$ for all p. Given that $GL_x(p) = pW_{LPM}(x; p)$, the growth of the lower partial mean at a certain percentile is equal to the growth of the generalized Lorenz curve at that percentile. So the height of the generalized Lorenz growth curve at $p = 20$ percent is the rate at which the mean income of the lowest 20 percent of the population changed over time.

Unlike the growth incidence curve, this curve provides information about the growth rate of mean income, which is the height of the curve at $p = 100$ percent. Again, varying p allows us to examine whether this growth rate is robust to the choice of income standard, or whether the low-income standards grew at a different rate than that of the rest. If the growth rates of the lower-income standards are found to be lower than the mean income, then overall growth, indeed, has not been pro-poor. However, if all lesser "lower partial means" grow at a faster rate than the higher "lower partial means," then growth is assumed to be pro-poor.

Figure 2.11 depicts the growth curves of lower partial mean incomes. The vertical axis denotes the *growth rate of lower partial mean income*, and the horizontal axis denotes the *cumulative population share*. Following the same notations as the growth incidence curve, suppose that there are two

Figure 2.11: Growth Rate of Lower Partial Mean Income

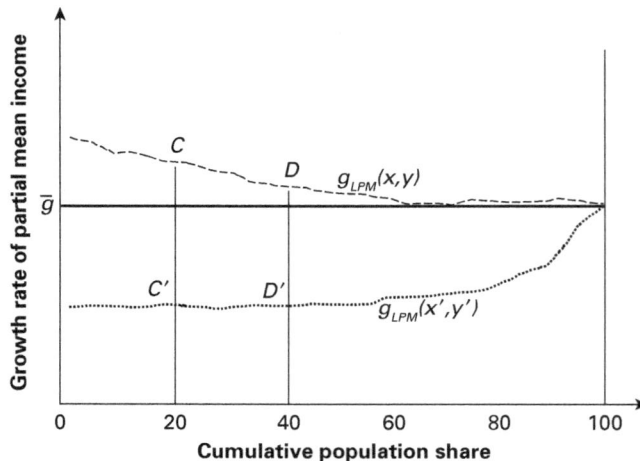

societies, X and X'. The income distributions of society X at two different points in time are x and y, whereas those of society X' are x' and y'. The dashed growth curve $g_{LPM}(x, y)$ denotes growth rates of lower partial mean income of society X over time, whereas the dotted growth curve $g_{LPM}(x', y')$ denotes growth rates of lower partial mean income of society X' over time.

Suppose the growth rates of mean income across these two distributions are the same and are denoted by $\bar{g} > 0$. Thus, the solid horizontal line at $\bar{g}$ denotes the growth rate if the growth rate had been the same for all percentiles or the cumulative population share.

What information do these two growth curves provide? Growth between x and y is pro-poor in the sense that mean incomes of the population's bottom percentiles have positive growth, whereas mean incomes of the population's upper percentiles have negative growth. Growth between x' and y', in contrast, is not pro-poor because mean incomes of the population's bottom percentiles have negative income growth, whereas mean incomes of the population's upper percentiles have positive growth.

In society X, the growth rates of the mean income of the bottom 20th percentile of the population and that of the bottom 40th percentile of the population are denoted by point C and point D, respectively. In society X', however, the growth rate of mean income of the bottom 20th percentile of the population and that of the bottom 40th percentile of the population are denoted by point C' and point D', respectively. Note that growth of mean income is the growth at the 100th percentile income where the two growth curves meet because they have been assumed to have the same growth rate of mean income.

General Mean Growth Curve

The final of the three growth curves is the *general mean growth curve*. Considering the income distributions x and y discussed previously, we denote the general mean of order α of distribution x and distribution y by $W_{GM}(x;\ \alpha)$ and $W_{GM}(y;\ \alpha)$, respectively. The growth of general mean of order α is denoted by

$$g_{GM}(x,y;\alpha) = \frac{W_{GM}(y;\alpha) - W_{GM}(x;\alpha)}{W_{GM}(x;\alpha)} \times 100\%. \qquad (2.15)$$

When every general mean registers an increase over time, $g_{GM}(x,y; \alpha) > 0$. When $\alpha = 1$, the curve's height is the usual mean income growth rate. This rate is equal to the growth of the generalized Lorenz growth curve at $p = 100$ percent. At $\alpha = 0$ the curve shows the growth rate for the geometric mean, and so forth. As we will see later, each of these growth curves can help in understanding the link between growth and change in inequality over time.

Figure 2.12 shows the growth curves of general mean incomes. The vertical axis denotes the *growth rate of general mean income*, and the horizontal axis denotes the values of *parameter α*. Following the same notations as the previous two growth incidence curves, suppose that there are two societies, X and X'. Income distributions of society X at two different points in time are x and y, whereas those of society X' are x' and y'. The dashed growth curve $g_{GM}(x, y)$ denotes the growth rates of general mean income of society X over time, whereas the dotted growth curve $g_{GM}(x', y')$ denotes the growth rates of general mean income of society X' over time.

Suppose the growth rates of mean income across these two distributions are the same and are denoted by $\bar{g} > 0$. Thus, the solid horizontal line at $\bar{g}$ denotes the growth rate if the growth rate had been the same for all α.

What information do these two growth curves provide? Growth between x and y is pro-poor in the sense that general means for lower α, which focus more on the lower end of the distribution, have positive growth, whereas

Figure 2.12: General Mean Growth Curves

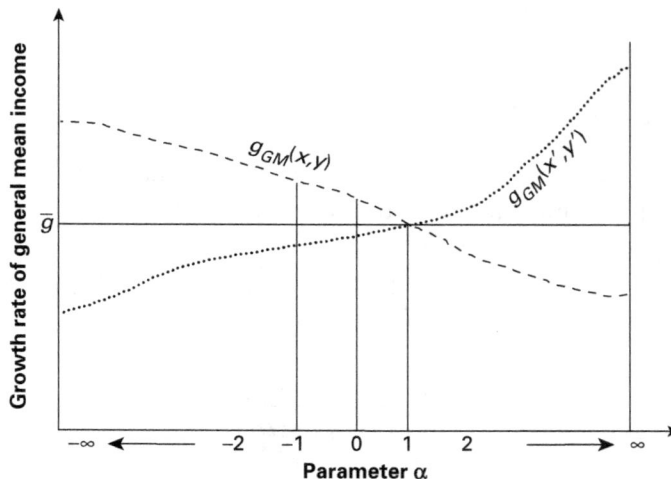

general means for larger α have negative growth. Growth between x' and y', in contrast, is not pro-poor because the general means for lower α have negative income growth whereas the general means for larger α have positive growth. The mean income growth rates are the heights of the two growth curves at $\alpha = 1$, which are equal by assumption for this example. Heights at $\alpha = 0$ and $\alpha = -1$ are growth rates of the geometric and harmonic means, respectively.

Inequality Measures

The second aspect of a distribution is *spread*, which is evaluated using a numerical inequality measure, assigning each distribution a number that indicates its inequality level. There are two ways of understanding and interpreting an income inequality measure. One way is through the properties it satisfies. The other way is by using a fundamental link between inequality measures and income standards. We begin with the first approach by outlining the desirable properties an inequality measure should satisfy. In this section, any inequality measure is denoted by the notation I. Specific indices are denoted by using corresponding subscripts.

Desirable Properties

An inequality measure should satisfy four basic properties: *symmetry*, *population invariance*, *scale invariance*, and the *transfer principle*. Like income standards, these properties may be classified into categories. Invariance properties leave the inequality measures invariant to certain changes in the dataset, and they include *symmetry*, *population invariance*, *scale invariance*, and *normalization*. The *normalization* property calibrates the measure's value when there is no inequality. Dominance properties cause inequality measures to change in a particular direction. Properties in this category include the *transfer principle* and *transfer sensitivity*. Other properties, such as *subgroup consistency* and *additive decomposability*, are compositional properties relating subgroups and overall inequality levels. Most of these properties are similar in interpretation to the corresponding properties of income standards.

The first property, *symmetry*, requires that switching the income levels of two people leaves the evaluation of a society's inequality unchanged. In other words, a person should not be given priority on the basis of his or her identity when evaluating a society's inequality. In more technical terms, it requires the inequality measure of distribution x to be equal to the inequality measure of another distribution x' if x' is obtained from x by a permutation of incomes.

For example, recall the three-person income vector $x = (\$10k, \$20k, \$30k)$ so that the first, second, and the third persons receive incomes $\$10k$, $\$20k$, and $\$30k$, respectively. If the incomes of the first and second persons are switched, then the new income vector becomes $x' = (\$20k, \$10k, \$30k)$. This new vector x' is said to be obtained from vector x by a permutation of incomes.

> *Symmetry*: If distribution x' is obtained from distribution x by permutation of incomes, then $I(x') = I(x)$.

The second property, *population invariance*, requires that the level of inequality within a society is invariant to population size, in the sense that a replication of an income vector results in the same inequality level as the original sample vector. What is the implication of this property? Consider the income vector of society X, $x = (\$10k, \$20k, \$30k)$. Now, suppose three more people join the society with the same income distribution so that the new income vector of society X is $x' = (\$10k, \$10k, \$20k, \$20k, \$30k, \$30k)$. The *population invariance* property requires that the inequality level in society X remain unaltered. This property allows us to compare the inequality level across countries and across time with varying population sizes. Furthermore, population invariance allows the inequality measure to depend on a distribution function, which normalizes the population size to one.

> *Population invariance*: If a vector x' is obtained by replicating vector x at least once, then $I(x') = I(x)$.

The third property, *scale invariance*, requires that if an income distribution is obtained from another distribution by scaling all incomes by the same factor, then the inequality level should remain unchanged. For example, if everyone's income in a society is doubled or halved, then the level of inequality of the society does not change. The scale invariance property ensures that the inequality being measured is a purely relative concept and is independent of the distribution's size.

Scale invariance is analogous to the linear homogeneity property for income standards, which ensures that the relative status of every person remains unchanged when compared to the income standard, even after all incomes are scaled up or down by the same factor. This similarity supports the idea that the relative inequality level remains unchanged.[7]

> *Scale Invariance:* If distribution x' is obtained from distribution x' such that $x' = cx$, where $c > 0$, then $I(x') = I(x)$.

The fourth property, *normalization*, requires that if incomes are the same across all people in a society, then no inequality exists within the society and the inequality measure should be zero. Normalization is a natural property. For example, if the income vector of a three-person society is ($20k$, $20k$, $20k$), then the inequality measure should be zero. Even if everyone's income increases 10-fold and the new income vector is ($200k$, $200k$, $200k$), the inequality measure should still be zero.

> *Normalization:* For the income distribution $x = (b, b, ..., b)$, $I(x) = 0$.

The fifth property is the *transfer principle*, which requires that a regressive transfer between two people in a society should increase inequality and a progressive transfer between two people should reduce inequality. Regressive and progressive transfers were defined earlier for income standards.

> *Transfer Principle:* If distribution x' is obtained from distribution x by a regressive transfer, then $I(x') > I(x)$. If distribution x'' is obtained from distribution x by a progressive transfer, then $I(x'') < I(x)$.

In inequality measurement, there is also a weaker version of the transfer principle, which requires that a regressive transfer between two people in a society not decrease inequality and that a progressive transfer between two people not increase inequality. Thus, the weaker principle allows the possibility that the level of inequality may remain unaltered because of progressive or regressive transfers.

> *Weak Transfer Principle:* If distribution x' is obtained from distribution x by a regressive transfer, then $I(x') \geq I(x)$. If distribution x'' is obtained from distribution x by a progressive transfer, then $I(x'') \leq I(x)$.

The transfer principle requires an inequality measure to decrease if the transfer is progressive. However, it does not specify the amount by which inequality should fall, and it is not concerned with the part of the distribution where the transfer is taking place. The same amount may be transferred between two poor people or between two rich people. Should the transfer have the same effect on the inequality measure no matter where it takes place? Consider the four-person income vector $x = (\$100, \$200, \$10,000, \$20,000)$. First, suppose \$20 is transferred from the second person to the first person. The post-transfer income vector is $x' = (\$120, \$180, \$10,000, \$20,000)$. Thus, transferring 10 percent of the second person's income has increased the first person's income by 20 percent.

Now, suppose instead that the same \$20 transfer takes place between the third and the fourth person. The post-transfer income vector is $x'' = (\$100, \$200, \$10,020, \$19,980)$, where transferring 0.1 percent of the fourth person's income has increased the third person's income by 0.2 percent. This transfer makes hardly any difference in the large incomes of the two richer people.

It may seem that a transfer of the same amount between two poor people and two rich people should not have the same effect on the overall inequality. However, the sixth property, *transfer sensitivity*, requires an inequality measure be more sensitive to transfers at the lower end of the distribution. In other words, this property requires that the inequality measure change more if a transfer takes place between two poor people than if the same amount of transfer takes place between two rich people the same distance apart.

Suppose the initial income distribution is $x = (x_1, x_2, x_3, x_4)$, where $x_1 < x_2 < x_3 < x_4$, $x_2 - x_1 = x_4 - x_3 > 0$. Note that the distance between x_1 and x_2 is the same as the distance between x_3 and x_4. Suppose distribution x' is obtained from distribution x by a progressive transfer of amount $\delta < (x_2 - x_1)/2$ between x_2 and x_1, that is, $x' = (x_1 + \delta, x_2 - \delta, x_3, x_4)$, and distribution x'' is obtained from distribution x by a progressive transfer of the same amount δ between x_3 and x_4, that is, $x'' = (x_1, x_2, x_3 + \delta, x_4 - \delta)$. Thus, the same amount of progressive transfer has been made between two poorer people and two richer people, who are equally distant from each other. Both x' and x'' are more equal than x according to the transfer principle, but can we compare x' and x''? The answer is yes. In fact, any transfer sensitive inequality measure should judge distribution x' as more equal than distribution x''. Shorrocks and Foster (1987) have reinterpreted the transfer sensitivity property in terms of *favorable composite transfer* (FACT). When a distribution is obtained from another distribution by a progressive transfer at the lower end of a distribution and simultaneously by a regressive transfer at the upper end of the same distribution, such that the variance remains unchanged, then the latter distribution is stated to be obtained from the former distribution by FACT. Thus, the transfer sensitivity property may be stated as follows:

> *Transfer Sensitivity:* If distribution x' is obtained from distribution x by FACT, then $I(x') < I(x')$.

When one distribution is obtained from another distribution by FACT, then the corresponding Lorenz curves intersect each other. In this case, the transfer principle cannot rank two distributions. However, if a Lorenz curve crosses the Lorenz curve of another distribution once from above, and the coefficient of variation (standard deviation divided by the mean) of the former distribution is no higher than that of the latter distribution, then all transfer sensitive measures agree that the former distribution has less inequality.[8]

The seventh property is *subgroup consistency*, which is conceptually the same as the corresponding property for income standards. This property requires that if the sizes and means of a subgroup population are fixed, then overall inequality must rise when the inequality level rises in one subgroup and does not fall in the rest of the subgroups.

For example, suppose that income vector x with population size N is divided into two subgroup vectors: x' with population size N' and x'' with population size N'' such that $N' + N'' = N$. Let a new vector, y, be obtained from x with the same population size N, and let its two subgroups be denoted by y' with population size N' and y'' with population size N''. The subgroup consistency property can be stated as follows:

> *Subgroup Consistency:* Given that subgroup population sizes and subgroup means remain unchanged, if $I(y') > I(x')$ and $I(y'') \geq I(x'')$, then $I(y) > I(x)$.

There is a closely related property that is often useful for understanding how much of the overall inequality can be attributed to inequality within subgroups and how much can be attributed to inequality across subgroups, given a collection of population subgroups. For example, the population of a country may be divided across various subgroups, such as across rural and urban areas, states, provinces, and other geographic regions; across ethnic and religious groups; across genders; or across age groups. One may want to evaluate the source of inequality, such as whether overall income inequality is due to unequal income distribution within sex or unequal income distribution across sex.

The eighth property is *additive decomposability*, which requires overall inequality to be expressed as a sum of *within-group inequality* and *between-group inequality*. *Within-group inequality* is a weighted sum of subgroup inequalities. *Between-group inequality* is the inequality level obtained when every person within each subgroup receives the subgroup's mean income. Kanbur (2006) discussed the policy significance of this type of inequality decomposition. It is often found that the contribution of the between-group term is much lower than the within-group term, and, thus, policy priority is directed toward ameliorating within-group rather than between-group inequality. These types of policy conclusions should be carefully drawn, because the lower between-group term may receive much larger social weight than its within-group counterpart. Also, the between-group term's share of overall inequality may increase as the number of groups increases. How to incorporate these issues into inequality measurement requires further research, and solving these issues is beyond the scope of this book. However, if the policy interest is in understanding how the between-group inequality as a share of total inequality has changed over time for a fixed number of groups, then the decomposability property is very useful.

To formally outline the additive decomposability property, we will use two groups to simplify the interpretation, but the definition can be extended to any number of groups. Suppose the income vector x with population size N is divided into two subgroup vectors: x' with population size N' and x'' with population size N'' such that $N' + N'' = N$. Let us denote the means of these three vectors by $\bar{x}$, $\bar{x}'$, and $\bar{x}''$. The additive decomposability property can be stated as follows:

> *Additive Decomposability:* If income distribution x is divided into two subgroup distributions x' and x'', then $I(x) = w'I(x') + w''I(x'') + I(\bar{x}', \bar{x}'')$, where w' and w'' are weights.

The between-group contribution is $I(\bar{x}', \bar{x}'')/I(x)$ and the within-group contribution is $[w' I(x') + w'' I(x'')]/I(x)$, as seen in example 2.5.

Example 2.5: Consider the five-person income vector $x = (\$10k, \$15k, \$20k, \$25k, \$30k)$, which is divided into two subgroups $x' = (\$10k, \$30k)$ and $x'' = (\$15k, \$20k, \$25k)$. The mean of x' is $\bar{x}' = \$20k$, and the mean of x'' is also $\bar{x}'' = \$20k$. Let an additively decomposable inequality index I be used to estimate the inequality level. The total within-group inequality is $w'I(x') + w''I(x'')$. However, there is no between-group inequality in this case, because the mean incomes of both groups are equal. So the between-group contribution $I(\bar{x}', \bar{x}'')/I(x)$ is 0.

Inequality and Income Standards

There is a second way of understanding inequality measures: through income standards. This, in fact, relies on an intuitive link between inequality measures and pairs of income standards: a and b. Let a be the smaller income standard, and let b be the larger income standard. It is natural to measure inequality in terms of the relative distance between a and b, such as $I = (b - a)/b$, or some other increasing function of the ratio b/a. Indeed, scale invariance and the weak transfer principle essentially require this form for the measure. We will find in our subsequent discussions that virtually all inequality measures in common use are based on twin income standards.

Commonly Used Inequality Measures

Commonly used inequality measures are mostly related to the five kinds of income standards we discussed earlier. The inequality measures that we discuss in this section are *quantile ratios*, *partial mean ratios*, *Gini coefficient*, *Atkinson's class of inequality measures*, and *generalized entropy measures*.

Quantile Ratio

A *quantile ratio* compares incomes of higher and lower quantile incomes. Inequality across quantile incomes provides a useful way to understand income dispersion across the distribution. Because no quantile ratio considers the entire distribution, this measure is a crude way of presenting inequality.

For income distribution x, let the quantile income at the pth percentile be denoted by $W_{QI}(x; p)$, and let the quantile income at the p'th percentile be denoted by $W_{QI}(x; p')$, such that $p > p'$. A quantile ratio is commonly reported as a ratio of the larger quantile income to the smaller quantile income. However, this view leads the values of inequality measures to range from one to ∞. This range is not comparable to other inequality measures, which commonly range from zero to one. In this book, we formulate the quantile ratio in such a way that it ranges from zero to one. The p/p' quantile ratio is represented by the following formula:

$$I_{QR}(x; p / p') = \frac{W_{QI}(x; p) - W_{QI}(x; p')}{W_{QI}(x; p)} = 1 - \frac{W_{QI}(x; p')}{W_{QI}(x; p)}. \qquad (2.16)$$

In this case, the quantile income at the pth percentile $W_{QI}(x; p)$ is the higher income standard, and the quantile income at the p'th percentile $W_{QI}(x; p')$ is the lower income standard.

The higher the quantile ratio, the higher the level of inequality across two percentiles of the population in the society. A quantile ratio is zero when both the upper and the lower quantile incomes are equal. A quantile ratio reaches its maximum value of one when the lower quantile income $W_{QI}(x; p')$ is zero. This means that no one in the lower percentile earns any income and that the upper quantile income is positive. Note that if all people in the society have equal incomes, then any quantile ratio is zero. However, a quantile ratio of zero does not necessarily mean that incomes are equally distributed across everyone in the society.

The quantile ratios used most often include the 90/10 ratio, 80/20 ratio, 50/10 ratio, and 90/50 ratio. The 90/10 ratio, for example, captures the distance between the quantile income at the 90th percentile and the quantile income at the pth percentile as a proportion of the quantile income at the 10th percentile. How should the number $I_{QR}(x; 90/10) = 0.9$ be interpreted? There are, in fact, several ways to interpret the number:

- The number may be directly read as the *gap* between the lowest income of the richest 10 percent and the highest income of the poorest 10 percent of the population, being 90 percent of the lowest income of the richest 10 percent of the population.
- The number may be seen as the highest income of the poorest 10 percent of the population, being 10 percent $(1 - 0.9 = 0.1)$ of the lowest income of the richest 10 percent of the population.

- The number can be interpreted as the lowest income of the richest 10 percent of the population, being 10 times $(1/(1-0.9))$ larger than the highest income of the poorest 10 percent of the population. Similarly, $I_{QR}(x; 90/50) = 0.75$ implies that the lowest income of the richest 10 percent of the population is $1/(1-0.75) = 4$ times larger than the highest income of the poorest 50 percent of the population.

Quantile ratios may be classified into three categories: *upper end quantile ratio*, *lower end quantile ratio*, and *mixed quantile ratio*. The first two categories capture inequality within any one side of the median, and the third category captures inequality in one side of the median versus that of the other side of the median. For example, $I_{QR}(x; 90/50)$ is an upper end quantile ratio, and $I_{QR}(x; 50/10)$ is a lower end quantile ratio, whereas $I_{QR}(x; 90/10)$ is a mixed quantile ratio.

What properties does a quantile ratio satisfy? A quantile ratio, as defined earlier, satisfies *symmetry*, *normalization*, *population invariance*, and *scale invariance*. Thus, a quantile ratio satisfies all four invariance properties. What about the dominance properties? It turns out that a quantile ratio satisfies none of the dominance properties.

The following example shows that a quantile ratio does not satisfy the weak transfer principle. Suppose the highest income of the poorest 10 percent of the population is $100 and the lowest income of the richest 10 percent of the population is $2,000. Then $I_{QR}(x; 90/10) = (\$2,000 - \$100)/\$2,000 = 0.95$. Now, suppose that a regressive transfer takes place between the poorest person in the society and the richest person among the poorest 10 percent of the population such that the highest income in that group increases to $120. Then the post-transfer quantile ratio is $I_{QR}(x; 90/10) = (\$2,000 - \$120)/\$2,000 = 0.94$.

Therefore, the quantile ratio shows a decrease in inequality even when a regressive transfer has taken place. If a quantile ratio does not satisfy the weak transfer principle, then it cannot satisfy its stronger version—the transfer principle, or transfer sensitivity. The quantile ratios are not additively decomposable and also do not satisfy subgroup consistency.

Partial Mean Ratio

A *partial mean ratio* is an inequality measure comparing an upper partial mean and a lower partial mean. Like quantile ratios, no partial mean ratio considers the entire income distribution; thus, it is also a crude way of understanding inequality.

For income distribution x, let the upper partial mean for percentile p be denoted by $W_{UPM}(x; p)$ and the lower partial mean for percentile p' be denoted by $W_{LPM}(x; p')$. A partial mean ratio is also commonly reported as a ratio of both partial means ranging from one to ∞. However, as with the quantile ratio, we formulate the partial mean ratio in such a way that it ranges from zero to one. The p/p' partial mean ratio is represented by the following formula:

$$I_{PMR}(x; p/p') = \frac{W_{UPM}(x; p) - W_{LPM}(x; p')}{W_{UPM}(x; p)} = 1 - \frac{W_{LPM}(x; p')}{W_{UPM}(x; p)}. \quad (2.17)$$

The higher the partial mean ratio, the higher the level of inequality across two percentiles of a society's population. A partial mean ratio is zero when both upper and lower partial mean incomes are equal. A quantile ratio reaches its maximum value of one when the lower partial mean income $W_{LPM}(x; p')$ is zero and the upper partial mean income is positive. Note that if all people in the society have equal incomes, then any partial mean ratio is zero. However, a partial mean ratio of zero does not necessarily imply that incomes are equally distributed across all people in the society.

The most well-known partial mean ratio was devised by Simon Kuznets and is known as the *Kuznets ratio*. It is based on two income standards: the mean of the poorest 20 percent of the population and the mean of the richest 40 percent of the population. Using our formulation, the Kuznets ratio equivalent inequality measure of distribution x is denoted by $I_{PMR}(x; 20/40)$. How should the number $I_{PMR}(x; 20/40) = 0.8$ be interpreted? Again, there are several ways to interpret this measure:

- The *difference* in mean income between the richest 20 percent of the population and the poorest 40 percent of the population is 80 percent of the mean income of the richest 20 percent of the population.
- The mean income of the poorest 40 percent of the population is $(1 - 0.8) = 0.2$ or 20 percent or one-fifth of the mean income of the richest 20 percent of the population.
- The mean income of the richest 20 percent of the population is $1/(1 - 0.8) = 5$ times larger than the mean income of the poorest 40 percent of the population.

What properties does a partial mean ratio satisfy? A partial mean ratio, as defined in equation (2.17), satisfies *symmetry*, *normalization*, *population invariance*, and *scale invariance*. Thus, a partial mean ratio satisfies all four invariance properties. What about the dominance properties? A quantile ratio satisfies the weak transfer principle but does not satisfy the transfer principle, transfer sensitivity, and subgroup consistency. It does not satisfy the transfer principle because some regressive and progressive transfers may leave the inequality measure unchanged, since a partial mean ratio does not consider the entire income distribution.

Atkinson's Class of Inequality Measures

Atkinson's class of inequality measures, developed by Sir Anthony Atkinson, is based on general means (see Atkinson 1970). All inequality measures in this family are constructed by comparing the arithmetic mean and another income standard from the family of general means. Recall that each measure's formulation in the general means family depends on a parameter denoted by α, which can take any value between $-\infty$ and $+\infty$.

In the Atkinson family of inequality measures, α is called the *inequality aversion parameter*. The lower the value of α, the higher a society's aversion toward inequality. In other words, the more averse a society is toward inequality across the population, the more emphasis it gives to lower incomes in the distribution by choosing a lower value of α. The Atkinson class of inequality measures for $\alpha < 1$ may be expressed as

$$I_A(x;\alpha) = \frac{W_A(x) - W_{GM}(x;\alpha)}{W_A(x)} = 1 - \frac{W_{GM}(x;\alpha)}{W_A(x)}. \qquad (2.18)$$

The Atkinson index of order α is the difference between the arithmetic mean and the general mean of order α divided by the arithmetic mean. Any Atkinson index lies between zero and one, and inequality increases as the index moves from zero to one. The minimum level of inequality, zero, is obtained when the total income is equally distributed across everyone in the society. Unlike the quantile ratios and the partial mean ratios, if $I_A(x;\alpha) = 0$ for any $\alpha < 1$, then, by implication, the total income in the society is equally distributed. This is because any inequality measure in this family is constructed by considering the entire distribution.

We already know from our discussion of income standards that the value of general means falls as α falls and vice versa. As α decreases, the distance between $W_A(x)$ and $W_{GM}(x; \alpha)$ increases, implying that I_A increases as α falls for a particular income distribution. Among the entire class of measures, three are used more frequently: $\alpha = 0$, $\alpha = -1$, and $\alpha = -2$. For $\alpha = 0$, the general mean takes the form of the geometric mean. The corresponding Atkinson's inequality measure for distribution x is expressed as

$$I_A(x;0) = \frac{W_A(x) - W_G(x)}{W_A(x)} = 1 - \frac{W_G(x)}{W_A(x)}. \qquad (2.19)$$

For $\alpha = -1$, the general mean is known as the harmonic mean. The corresponding Atkinson's inequality measure for distribution x is expressed as

$$I_A(x;-1) = \frac{W_A(x) - W_H(x)}{W_A(x)} = 1 - \frac{W_H(x)}{W_A(x)}. \qquad (2.20)$$

For $\alpha = -2$, the general mean has no such name, and we will call it simply $W_{GM}(x;-2)$. The corresponding Atkinson's inequality measure for distribution x is expressed as

$$I_A(x;-2) = \frac{W_A(x) - W_{GM}(x;-2)}{W_A(x)} = 1 - \frac{W_{GM}(x;-2)}{W_A(x)}. \qquad (2.21)$$

Following the relationship between the Atkinson's class of inequality measures and parameter α, we can state that $I_A(x;-2) < I_A(x;-1) < I_A(x;0)$ unless all incomes in distribution x are equal (see example 2.6).

Example 2.6: Consider the income vector $x = (\$2k, \$4k, \$8k, \$10k)$ used previously in the general means example. The arithmetic mean is $W_A(x) = \$6k$, the geometric mean is $W_G(x) = \$5.03k$, the harmonic mean is $W_H(x) = \$4.10k$, and $W_{GM}(x;-2) = \$3.44k$.

Thus,
$I_A(x;0) = (\$6k - \$5.03k)/\$6k = 0.162$.
$I_A(x;-1) = (\$6k - \$4.10k)/\$6k = 0.317$.
$I_A(x;-2) = (\$6k - \$3.44k)/\$6k = 0.427$.

What is the interpretation of the number $I_A(x;0) = 0.162$? First, note that $I_A(x;0)$ is based on two income standards: the arithmetic mean of x

and the geometric mean of x. The arithmetic mean represents the level of welfare obtained when the overall income is distributed equally across everyone in the society. This is an *ideal situation* when there is no inequality in the society.

The geometric mean, in contrast, is the equally distributed equivalent (ede) income, which, if received by everyone in the society, would yield the same welfare level as in x for the degree of inequality aversion $\alpha = 0$. So $I_A(x; 0) = 0.162$ implies that the loss of welfare because of inequality in distribution x is 16.2 percent of what the welfare level would be if the overall income had been equally distributed.

Suppose the society becomes more averse to inequality and α is reduced to -1. In this case, the equally distributed equivalent income is the harmonic mean of x. The loss of total welfare because of unequal distribution increases from 16.2 percent to 31.7 percent. Likewise, the percentage loss of welfare would increase to 42.7 percent if the society became even more averse to inequality and α fell to -2.

What properties does any index in this family satisfy? Any measure in this family satisfies all four invariance properties: *symmetry*, *population invariance*, *scale invariance*, and *normalization*. In addition, unlike the quantile ratios and the partial mean ratios, measures in this class satisfy the *transfer principle*, *transfer sensitivity*, and *subgroup consistency*.

If distribution x' is obtained from distribution x by at least one regressive transfer, then the level of inequality in x' is strictly higher than that in x. Furthermore, if transfers take place between poor people, then the inequality measure changes more than if the same amounts of transfers take place among rich people. Finally, because these measures satisfy subgroup consistency, they do not lead to any inconsistent results while decomposing across subgroups. If inequality in certain subgroups increases while inequality in the others does not fall, then overall inequality increases. However, measures in this class are not additively decomposable.

Gini Coefficient

The *Gini coefficient*, developed by Italian statistician Corrado Gini (1912), is the most commonly used inequality measure. It measures the average difference between pairs of incomes in a distribution, relative to the distribution's mean. The most common formulation of the Gini coefficient for the distribution x is

$$I_{Gini}(x) = \frac{1}{2N^2 \times W_A(x)} \sum_{n=1}^{N} \sum_{n'=1}^{N} |x_n - x_{n'}|. \qquad (2.22)$$

Note that equation (2.22) may be broken into two components: $W_A(x)$ (the mean of the distribution) and $(\sum_{n=1}^{N} \sum_{n'=1}^{N} |x_n - x_{n'}|)/2N^2$ (the average difference between pairs of incomes). The second component is divided by its number of elements, $2N^2$. There are $2N^2$ elements because each element in x is compared with another element in x including itself twice. This original Gini coefficient formula can be simplified further. The second component of the Gini coefficient can be written as

$$\frac{1}{2N^2} \sum_{n=1}^{N} \sum_{n'=1}^{N} |x_n - x_{n'}| = W_A(x) - \frac{1}{N^2} \sum_{n=1}^{N} \sum_{n'=1}^{N} \min\{x_n, x_{n'}\} = W_A(x) - W_s(x), \quad (2.23)$$

where $W_S(x)$ is the Sen mean of distribution x. Therefore, the Gini coefficient may be simply formulated by using the arithmetic mean and the Sen mean. Like any measure in Atkinson's class, the Gini coefficient can be expressed as

$$I_{Gini}(x) = \frac{W_A(x) - W_S(x)}{W_A(x)} = 1 - \frac{W_S(x)}{W_A(x)}. \qquad (2.24)$$

Thus, the Gini coefficient is the difference between the arithmetic mean and the Sen mean divided by the arithmetic mean. The coefficient lies between zero and one, and inequality increases as the index moves from zero to one. The minimum inequality level, zero, is obtained when income is equally distributed across everyone in the society. Like Atkinson's measures, if $I_{Gini}(x) = 0$, then, by implication, income in the society is equally distributed. Again, this is because any inequality measure in this family is constructed by considering the entire distribution (see example 2.7).

What is the interpretation of $I_{Gini}(x) = 0.292$? First, $I_{Gini}(x)$ is based on two income standards: the arithmetic mean of x and the Sen mean of x. The arithmetic mean represents the level of welfare obtained when the overall income is distributed equally across all people in the society. This is an *ideal situation* when there is no inequality in the society. The Sen mean, in contrast, is an ede income, which, if received by everyone in the society, would yield the same welfare level as in x. So $I_{Gini}(x) = 0.292$ implies that the loss of welfare because of inequality in distribution x is 29.2 percent of

Example 2.7: Consider the income vector $x = (\$2k, \$4k, \$8k, \$10k)$ that we used previously. First, we calculate the Gini coefficient using the formulation in equation (2.22). It can be easily verified that $W_A(x) = \$6k$. The second component is

$$\frac{1}{2 \times 4^2} (|2 - 2| + |2 - 4| + |2 - 8| + |2 - 10| + |4 - 2| + |4 - 4| + |4 - 8| + |4 - 10|$$
$$+ |8 - 2| + |8 - 4| + |8 - 8| + |8 - 10| + |10 - 2| + |10 - 4| + |10 - 8| + |10 - 10|)$$
$$= \frac{1}{32} (0 + 2 + 4 + 6 + 8 + 2 + 0 + 4 + 6 + 6 + 4 + 0 + 2 + 8 + 6 + 2 + 0)$$
$$= \frac{56}{32} = 1.75.$$

Thus, $I_{Gini}(x) = 1.75/6 = 0.292$.

Next, we calculate the Gini coefficient using equation (2.24). The Sen mean of distribution x is $W_S(x) = \$4.25k$. Thus, $I_{Gini}(x) = (\$6k - \$4.25k)/\$6k = 1.75/6 = 0.292$.

the welfare level if overall income had been equally distributed. We will see later that the Gini coefficient has an interesting relationship with the well-known Lorenz curve.

The Gini coefficient satisfies all invariance properties: *symmetry*, *population invariance*, *scale invariance*, and *normalization*. In addition, it satisfies the *transfer principle*. If distribution x' is obtained from distribution x by at least one regressive transfer, then the level of inequality in x' is strictly higher than that in x. However, the Gini coefficient is neither transfer sensitive nor subgroup consistent. It is not transfer sensitive because the Gini coefficient changes by the same amount whether transfers take place between poor people or between rich people. That the Gini coefficient is not subgroup consistent means that if the inequality in some subgroups increases while inequality in other subgroups does not fall, then the overall inequality may register a decrease.

The following is an example showing that the Gini coefficient is neither transfer sensitive nor subgroup consistent. Consider the vector $x = (\$4k, \$5k, \$6k, \$7k, \$14k, \$16k)$. If a progressive transfer of $\$0.5k$ takes place between the first person and the second person, then $x' = (\$4.5k, \$4.5k, \$6k, \$7k, \$14k, \$16k)$. If a progressive transfer of the same amount takes place between the two richer people, then $x'' = (\$4k, \$5k, \$6.5k, \$6.5k, \$14k, \$16k)$. As a result, $I_{Gini}(x') = I_{Gini}(x'') = 0.279$. Thus, the Gini coefficient cannot distinguish between these two transfers.

The next example shows that the Gini coefficient is not subgroup consistent. We use the same example that we used to show that the Sen mean does not satisfy subgroup consistency. The original income vector $x = (\$4k, \$5k, \$6k, \$7k, \$14k, \$16k)$ becomes, over time, $y = (\$3.4k, \$6.1k, \$6k, \$6.5k, \$14k, \$16k)$. The income vector of the first subgroup $x' = (\$4k, \$5k, \$7k)$ becomes $y' = (\$3.4k, \$6.1k, \$6.5k)$, whereas the income vector of the second subgroup remains unaltered. The Sen mean of the first group falls from $W_S(x') = \$4.67k$ to $W_S(y') = \$4.64k$, whereas the mean income remains unchanged at $W_A(x') = W_A(y') = \$5.33k$. So the inequality of the first group increases from $I_{Gini}(x') = 0.125$ to $I_{Gini}(y') = 0.129$. What happens to the overall inequality? It turns out that the overall Sen mean increases from $W_S(x) = \$6.22k$ to $W_S(y) = \$6.24k$, whereas the overall mean income remains unchanged at $W_A(x) = W_A(y) = \$8.67k$. The overall inequality decreases from $I_{Gini}(x) = 0.282$ to $I_{Gini}(y) = 0.280$.

However, unlike the Atkinson class of measures, the Gini coefficient is *additively decomposable*, but with an added residual term. If distribution x is divided into population subgroups x' with population size N' and x'' with population size N'', then the decomposition formula of the Gini coefficient is

$$I_{Gini}(x) = w'I_{Gini}(x') + w'' I_{Gini}(x'') + I_{Gini}(\bar{x}', \bar{x}'') - \text{residual}, \quad (2.25)$$

where the weights are $w' = (N'/N)^2(\bar{x}'/\bar{x})$ and $w'' = (N''/N)^2(\bar{x}''/\bar{x})$. Note, however, that the weights may not sum to one. The residual term is not zero if and only if the groups' income ranges overlap. If we consider the example above, where the income vector $x = (\$4k, \$5k, \$6k, \$7k, \$14k, \$16k)$ is divided into two subgroup vectors: $x' = (\$4k, \$5k, \$7k)$ and $x'' = (\$6k, \$14k, \$16k)$. These vectors overlap as $\$7k > \$6k$. Thus, the residual term will not vanish. However, if the two subgroups were $x' = (\$4k, \$5k, \$6k)$ and $x'' = (\$7k, \$14k, \$16k)$, then the residual term would be zero.[9]

Generalized Entropy Measures

The final inequality measures we consider are in the class of *generalized entropy measures*. Two well-known Theil measures are also in this class. The common formula for the generalized entropy measures of order α for any distribution x is

$$I_{GE}(x;\alpha) = \begin{cases} \dfrac{1}{\alpha(\alpha-1)}\left[\dfrac{1}{N}\sum_{n=1}^{N}\left(\dfrac{x_n}{\bar{x}}\right)^{\alpha}-1\right] & \text{if } \alpha \neq 0,1 \\[2ex] \dfrac{1}{N}\sum_{n=1}^{N}\dfrac{x_n}{\bar{x}}\ln\left(\dfrac{x_n}{\bar{x}}\right) & \text{if } \alpha = 1. \\[2ex] \dfrac{1}{N}\sum_{n=1}^{N}\ln\left(\dfrac{\bar{x}}{x_n}\right) & \text{if } \alpha = 0 \end{cases} \qquad (2.26)$$

At first glance, the formula above looks complicated. However, measures in this class are closely related to general means. Every index in this class, except one, can be expressed as a function of the arithmetic mean and the general mean of order α. For $\alpha \neq 0, 1$, the class of generalized entropy measures can be written as

$$I_{GE}(x;\alpha) = \frac{1}{\alpha(\alpha-1)}\left(\frac{\left[W_{GM}(x;\alpha')\right]^{\alpha}-\left[W_A(x)\right]^{\alpha}}{\left[W_A(x)\right]^{\alpha}}\right), \qquad (2.27)$$

where we replace the term $\bar{x}$ by $W_A(x)$ (the arithmetic mean), and where $W_{GM}(x;\alpha)$ denotes the general mean of order α. Thus, a generalized entropy measure for any $\alpha \neq 0,1$ may be easily calculated once we know the arithmetic mean and the general mean of order α.

For $\alpha = 1$, the generalized entropy is Theil's first measure of inequality and can be written as

$$I_{T1}(x) = \frac{1}{N}\sum_{n=1}^{N}\frac{x_n}{W_A(x)}\ln\left(\frac{x_n}{W_A(x)}\right). \qquad (2.28)$$

This is the only measure in this class that cannot be expressed as a function of general means and does not have a natural twin-standards representation.

For $\alpha = 0$, the generalized entropy index is Theil's second measure of inequality, which is also known as the *mean logarithmic deviation* and can be expressed as a function of the arithmetic mean, $W_A(x)$, and the geometric mean, $W_G(x)$, as follows:

$$I_{T2}(x) = \ln W_A(x) - \ln W_G(x) = \ln\frac{W_A(x)}{W_G(x)}. \qquad (2.29)$$

Besides the two Theil measures, the other commonly used measure in the entropy class is the index for $\alpha = 2$, which is closely related to the *coefficient of variation* (CV). The CV is the ratio of the standard deviation and mean. For $\alpha = 2$, the general entropy measure is half the CV squared and can be expressed as

$$I_{GE}(x;2) = \frac{1}{2}\frac{\left[W_E(x)\right]^2 - \left[W_A(x)\right]^2}{\left[W_A(x)\right]^2} = \frac{1}{2}\frac{Var(x)}{\left[W_A(x)\right]^2} = \frac{CV^2}{2}, \qquad (2.30)$$

where $Var(x)$ is the variance of the distribution x, which is the square of its standard deviation. In equation (2.29), $W_E(x)$ is the Euclidean mean, as in equation (2.8) and $[W_E(x)]^2 = \frac{1}{N}\sum_{n=1}^{N} x_n^2$. Clearly, $\left[W_E(x)\right]^2 - \left[W_A(x)\right]^2 = \frac{1}{N}\sum_{n=1}^{N} x_n^2 - \overline{x}^2$ is the variance of x (see example 2.8).

Example 2.8: Consider the income vector $x = (\$2k, \$4k, \$8k, \$10k)$ that we used in the general means example. The arithmetic mean is $W_A(x) = \$6k$, the geometric mean is $W_G(x) = \$5.03k$, and the Euclidean mean is $W_E(x) = \$6.78k$.

We now calculate the two Theil inequality measures and the squared coefficient of variation:

$$I_{GE}(x;2) = ([W_E(x)]^2 - [W_A(x)]^2)/(2[W_A(x)^2] = (6.78^2 - 6^2)/(2 \times 6^2)$$
$$= 0.279.$$

$$I_{T2}(x) = \ln[W_A(x)/W_G(x)] = \ln\,[\$6k/\$5.03k] = 0.176.$$

The calculation of Theil's first measure is not as straightforward as that of the previous two measures. However, it can be calculated using the following steps. First, create a new vector from vector x by dividing every element by the mean of x as $(2/6, 4/6, 8/6, 10/6)$. Then

$$I_{T1}(x) = \frac{1}{4}\left[\frac{2}{6}\ln\left(\frac{2}{6}\right) + \frac{4}{6}\ln\left(\frac{4}{6}\right) + \frac{8}{6}\ln\left(\frac{8}{6}\right) + \frac{10}{6}\ln\left(\frac{10}{6}\right)\right] = 0.15.$$

Having introduced the measures in the generalized entropy class, now we try to understand their behavior. First, what is the range of any measure in this class? The lower bound of any measure in this class is zero, which is obtained when incomes in a society are equally distributed across all people. However, unlike the Atkinson's measures and the Gini coefficient, generalized entropy measures may not necessarily be bounded above by one.

Next, how do the measures in this class relate to the parameter? There are, in fact, three distinct ranges: a lower range $\alpha < 1$, an upper range $\alpha > 1$, and a limiting case where $\alpha = 1$. For the lower range, $\alpha < 1$, measures in this class are monotonic transformations of the Atkinson's class of measures and can be written as

$$I_{GE}(x;\alpha) = \begin{cases} \dfrac{\left[1-I_A(x;\alpha-1)\right]^\alpha}{\alpha(\alpha-1)} & \text{if } \alpha \neq 0,\ \alpha<1 \\ \ln\dfrac{1}{1-I_A(x;0)} & \text{if } \alpha=0 \end{cases}, \qquad (2.31)$$

where $I_A(x;\alpha)$ is the Atkinson's inequality measure for parameter α. For the range $\alpha < 1$, the entropy measures behave the same way as the Atkinson's measures. Over the range $\alpha > 1$, the general mean places greater weight on higher incomes and yields a representative income that is typically higher than the mean income. An example is the squared coefficient of variation.

All measures in the generalized entropy class satisfy the invariance properties: *symmetry, normalization, population invariance,* and *scale invariance.* Furthermore, they all satisfy the *transfer principle* and *subgroup consistency.* However, transfer sensitivity is satisfied only by the measures in this class with $\alpha < 2$. Measure $I_{GE}(x;2)$ is, in fact, transfer neutral like the Gini coefficient. It turns out that the generalized entropy measures are the only inequality measures that satisfy the usual form of additive decomposability (see Shorrocks 1980). If distribution x is divided into two population subgroups, x' with population size N' and x'' with population size N'', then the decomposition formula of the generalized entropy measure for $\alpha \neq 0,1$ is

$$I_{GE}(x;\alpha) = w'I_{GE}(x';\alpha) + w''I_{GE}(x'';\alpha) + I_{GE}(\bar{x}',\bar{x}'';\alpha), \qquad (2.32)$$

where the weights are $w' = (N'/N)(\bar{x}'/\bar{x})^\alpha$ and $w'' = (N''/N)(\bar{x}''/\bar{x})^\alpha$. For example, when $\alpha = 2$, the weights are $w' = (N'/N)(\bar{x}'/\bar{x})^2$ and $w'' = (N''/N)(\bar{x}''/\bar{x})^2$.

Note that the weights may not always sum to one. However, for the two Theil measures, the weights do sum to one. The first Theil measure can be decomposed as

$$I_{T1}(x) = w'I_{T1}(x') + w''I_{T1}(x'') + I_{T1}(\bar{x}', \bar{x}''), \qquad (2.33)$$

where the weights are $w' = \bar{x}'/\bar{x}$ and $w'' = \bar{x}''/\bar{x}$. Although it is difficult to get an intuitive interpretation of the first Theil measure, the additive decomposability property makes the first Theil measure useful in understanding within-group and between-group inequalities. The second Theil measure can be decomposed as

$$I_{T2}(x) = w'I_{T2}(x') + w''I_{T2}(x'') + I_{T2}(\bar{x}', \bar{x}''),\qquad(2.34)$$

where the weights are $w' = (N'/N)$ and $w'' = (N''/N)$.

Inequality and Welfare

The Gini coefficient and the inequality measures in Atkinson's family share a social welfare interpretation. As we have already discussed, they can be expressed as $I = (\bar{x} - a)/\bar{x}$, where $\bar{x}$ is the mean income of the distribution x and a is an income standard that can be viewed as a welfare function (satisfying the weak transfer principle). Note that the distribution in which everyone has the mean income has the highest level of welfare among all distributions with the same total income, and the distribution's measured welfare level is just the mean itself. This finding results from the normalization property of income standards.

Thus, the mean $W_A(x) = \bar{x}$ is the maximum value that the welfare function can take over all income distributions of the same total income. When incomes are all equal, $a = W_A(x)$ and inequality is zero. When the actual welfare level a falls below the maximum welfare level $W_A(x)$, the percentage welfare loss $I = (W_A(x) - a)/W_A(x)$ is used as a measure of inequality. This is the welfare interpretation of both the Gini coefficient and the Atkinson's class of measures.

The simple structure of these measures allows us to express the welfare function in terms of the mean income and the inequality measure. A quick rearrangement leads to $a = W_A(x)(1 - I)$, which can be reinterpreted as saying that the welfare function a can be viewed as an inequality-adjusted mean. If there is no inequality in the distribution, then $(1 - I) = 1$ and $a = W_A(x)$. If the inequality level is $I > 0$, then the welfare level is obtained by discounting the mean income by $(1 - I) < 0$.

For example, if we take I to be the Gini coefficient, $I_{Gini}(x)$, then the Sen mean (or Sen welfare function) can be obtained by multiplying the mean by $[1 - I_{Gini}(x)]$, that is, $W_S(x) = W_A(x)[1 - I_{Gini}(x)]$. Similarly, if we take I to be the Atkinson's measure with parameter $a = 0$, $I_A(x; 0)$, then the welfare function is the geometric mean, and the geometric mean can be obtained by multiplying the mean by $[1 - I_A(x; 0)]$, that is, $W_G(x) = W_A(x)[1 - I_A(x; 0)]$.

Dominance and Unanimity

An inequality measure estimates, with a single number, the inequality level in a society. A question may naturally arise: Do all inequality measures compare two income distributions in the same way? In other words, if an inequality measure evaluates income distribution x to be more equal than distribution y, would another inequality measure evaluate distributions x and y in the same way? The answer depends on the two inequality measures we use for evaluation. Not all inequality measures evaluate various distributions in the same manner.

We can clarify this concern with an example. Consider the two income vectors $x = (\$4k, \$5k, \$6k, \$7k, \$14k, \$16k)$ and $y = (\$3.4k, \$6.1k, \$6k, \$6.5k, \$14k, \$16k)$. These two vectors have the same mean. The Gini coefficient indicates that the inequality level in x is 0.282, which is higher than the inequality in y (0.280). However, the Atkinson's measure that is based on the geometric mean shows that the inequality level in x is 0.127, which is lower than the level of inequality in y (0.132). Therefore, different inequality measures may disagree in different situations.

Is there any condition in which different inequality measures agree with each other? The answer is yes. Inequality measures that satisfy the four basic properties—symmetry, population invariance, scale invariance, and the weak transfer principle—agree with each other when *Lorenz dominance* holds between two distributions. To understand Lorenz dominance, we need to understand the Lorenz curve.

The Lorenz curve of an income distribution shows the proportion of total income held by the poorest p percent of the population.[10] We denote the Lorenz curve of distribution x by L_x. Then $L_x(p)$ is the share of total income held by the poorest p percent of the population. Indeed, $L_x(100) = 100$ percent and $L_x(0) = 0$ percent. Suppose the total income of Nigeria is ₦25 trillion and only ₦1 trillion is received by the poorest 20 percent of the population. Then $L_{Nig}(20) = 4$ percent. Suppose that income in Nigeria is redistributed, keeping the total income unaltered, so that everyone has identical income. Let us denote the equal income distribution by y. Then the percentage of total income enjoyed by the poorest 20 percent of the population is 20 percent, and $L_y(20) = 20$ percent.

In figure 2.13, the horizontal axis denotes the cumulative share of the population (p), and the vertical axis shows the share of total income. Note that the lowest and the highest values for both axes are 0 and 100,

Figure 2.13: Lorenz Curve

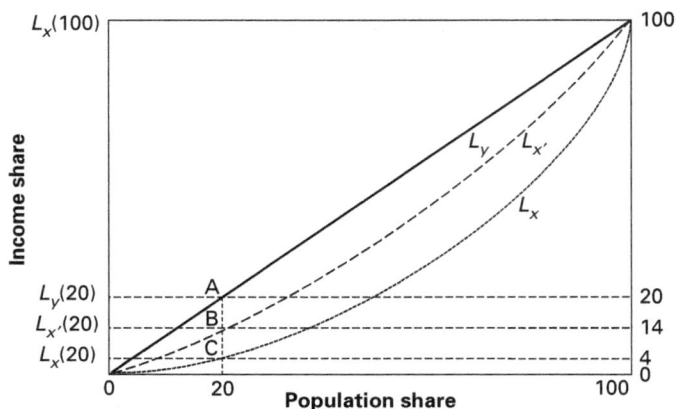

respectively. For income distribution x, L_x represents its Lorenz curve, denoted by the dotted curve. Following the example of Nigeria, $L_x(20) = 4$ percent, which is the height of the curve L_x at point C.

If distribution y is obtained from distribution x by distributing income equally across the population, then the Lorenz curve becomes a 45-degree straight line, L_y (the solid line in figure 2.13). In this case, the share of the population's bottom 20 percent in distribution y is $L_y(20) = 20$ percent. This is obtained at point A on Lorenz curve L_y.

Now, suppose the income distribution in Nigeria improves over time and the new income distribution is denoted by x'. The Lorenz curve for x' is denoted by the dashed curve $L_{x'}$ in figure 2.13. The share of the bottom 20 percent in the total income increases from 4 percent to 14 percent. This is shown at point B on the Lorenz curve $L_{x'}$.

Notice that every portion of Lorenz curve $L_{x'}$ lies above that of Lorenz curve L_x. This is what we mean by *Lorenz dominance*: the income share of every cumulative population share in x' is higher than that in x. Thus, distribution x' Lorenz dominates distribution x'. Similarly, distribution x Lorenz dominates both distributions x and x'.

Any inequality measure satisfying the four basic properties—symmetry, population invariance, scale invariance, and the weak transfer principle—would evaluate distribution y as more equal than distributions x and x' and distribution x' as more equal than distribution x. Thus, before comparing distributions using different inequality measures, the distributions' Lorenz curves should be compared. If one distribution's Lorenz curve dominates that of another distribution, then all inequality measures satisfying these four basic properties would consider the former distribution to be more equal than the latter.

Well-known inequality measures satisfying these four basic properties are the Gini coefficient, measures in the Atkinson's family, measures in the generalized entropy family, and partial mean ratios. What happens when two Lorenz curves cross? In this situation, Lorenz dominance does not hold, and the inequality level needs to be judged using inequality measures when different inequality measures may agree or disagree with each other. However, even in this case, the Lorenz curve can be helpful in identifying the winning and losing portions of the distribution.

The Lorenz curve also has interesting relationships with income standards and inequality measures. First, consider its relationship with the generalized Lorenz curve. A Lorenz curve may be obtained from a generalized Lorenz curve by dividing the latter by the mean. Thus, for distribution x, $L_x(p) = GL_x(p)/W_A(x)$. The construction of a Lorenz curve can be easily understood by following the construction of the generalized Lorenz curve in figure 2.8. Next, recall that the height of the generalized Lorenz curve at a certain percentile of population p is the lower partial mean times p itself, that is, $GL_x(p) = p \times W_{LPM}(x; p)$. Therefore, the height of the Lorenz curve at a certain percentile of population p is the *ratio of the lower partial mean to the overall mean* times p itself, that is, $L_x(p) = p \times [W_{LPM}(x; p)/W_A(x)]$. Note that the ratio of the lower partial mean to the overall mean itself may be used to construct a partial mean ratio, denoted by $I_{PMR}(x; 100/p)$.

Finally, an interesting relationship exists between the Lorenz curve and the Gini coefficient. The Gini coefficient of distribution x is twice the area between the Lorenz curves L_x and L_y in figure 2.13. Similarly, the Gini coefficient for distribution x'' is twice the area between the Lorenz curves $L_{x'}$ and L_y.

Inequality and Growth

The twin-standard view of inequality offers fresh insights into the relationship between growth and inequality. Almost all inequality measures are constructed in terms of a larger income standard b and a smaller income standard a, and these income standards are expressed as $1 - a/b$ or $b/a - 1$. Suppose income standard a changes to a' over time with growth rate $\bar{g}_a$, that is, $a' = (1 + \bar{g}_a)a$, and income standard b changes to b' over time with growth rate $\bar{g}_b$, that is, $b' = (1 + \bar{g}_b)b$. The inequality measure then changes from $I = 1 - a/b$ to $I' = 1 - a'/b'$. To have a fall in inequality, we require $I' < I$ or $1 - a'/b' < 1 - a/b$, which occurs when $\bar{g}_a > \bar{g}_b$. Therefore, for a reduction in inequality, the smaller income standard a needs to grow faster than the larger income standard b.

Consider the example of the Gini coefficient, which is constructed from two income standards. The larger income standard is the arithmetic mean W_A, and the smaller income standard is the Sen mean W_S. Let us denote the growth rate of the mean income by $\bar{g}$ and the growth rate of the Sen mean by $\bar{g}_S$. The Gini coefficient will register a fall in inequality when the growth rate of the Sen mean is larger than the growth rate of the arithmetic mean, that is, $\bar{g}_S > \bar{g}$. Similarly, inequality over time, in terms of the Gini coefficient, increases when $\bar{g}_S < \bar{g}$.

What about the Atkinson's measures and the generalized entropy measures? Measures in these classes, including Theil's second measure, are based on the arithmetic mean and on any income standard from the class of general means. For $\alpha < 1$, the arithmetic mean is the larger income standard, and the other general mean–based income standard is the smaller income standard. In this case, if the growth rate of the smaller income standard of order α is denoted by $\bar{g}_{GM}(\alpha)$, then inequality decreases when $\bar{g}_{GM}(\alpha) > \bar{g}$. If inequality is evaluated by Theil's second index, then inequality falls when the growth of geometric mean $\bar{g}_{GM}(0)$ is larger than that of the arithmetic mean, that is, $\bar{g}_{GM}(0) > \bar{g}$. For $\alpha > 1$ in the generalized entropy measure, the arithmetic mean is the smaller income standard, and the other general mean–based income standard is the larger one. Inequality falls, according to these indices, when the growth rate of the arithmetic mean $\bar{g}$ is higher.

Is there any way to tell if all inequality measures in the Atkinson family and the generalized entropy family have fallen? Yes, it is possible to do so just by looking at the general mean growth curve, as described in figure 2.12.

A generalized mean growth curve is the loci of the growth rates of all income standards in the class of general means. Comparing distributions x and y for the general mean growth curve $g_{GM}(x,y)$ in figure 2.12 shows that all inequality measures in Atkinson's class and the generalized entropy class agree that the inequality has fallen because the growth rates of the lower income standards are higher than $\bar{g}$. The growth rates of the larger income standards are lower than $\bar{g}$. However, for the general mean growth curve $g_{GM}(x',y')$ in the same figure, all inequality measures in Atkinson's class and the generalized entropy class agree that the inequality has risen because the growth rates of the lower income standards are lower than $\bar{g}$, whereas the growth rates of the larger income standards are higher than $\bar{g}$.

In a similar manner, the growth incidence curve may be used to understand the change in inequality using quantile ratios. If the growth rate of the upper quantile income is larger than the growth rate of a lower quantile income, then inequality has risen over time. In contrast, if the growth rate of a lower quantile income is larger than the growth rate of the higher quantile income, then inequality has fallen. For example, consider the growth incidence curve $g_{QI}(x,y)$ in figure 2.10. If inequality is measured by the 90/10 measure $I_{QR}(x;90/10)$, then inequality has fallen. Furthermore, for growth incidence curve $g_{QI}(x',y')$, the level of inequality has increased for the same inequality measure.

Poverty Measures

The third aspect of a distribution is *base*, which is evaluated using a numerical poverty measure, assigning each distribution a number reflecting its level of deprivation. In this section, before proceeding further, we introduce additional notations that are more specific to poverty measures than income standards and inequality measures. The income distribution of society X with N people can be summarized by the vector $x = (x_1,x_2, ..., x_N)$, where x_n is the income of person n. We also assume that the income distribution is ordered, that is, $x_1 \leq x_2 \leq ... x_N$.

Any poverty measure is constructed in two steps. The first step is *identification*, where each person is identified as poor or nonpoor by using a threshold called the *poverty line*, denoted by z. More specifically, a person is identified as poor if his or her income falls below the poverty line z and nonpoor if his or her income is greater than or equal to z. We denote the number of poor in our reference society X by q. So the number of nonpoor is $N - q$. Because elements in income distribution x are ordered, people 1,..., q are poor and people $q + 1$, ..., N are nonpoor.

Suppose society X consists of four people with the income vector $x = (\$1k,$ $\$2k, \$50k, \$70k)$. If the poverty line is set at $\$10k$, this means that a person must have $\$10k$ to meet the minimum necessities to lead a healthy life. This requirement would identify the first two people as poor with earnings $\$1k$ and $\$2k$, whereas the third person and the fourth person are identified as nonpoor. In this example, society X has two poor people and two nonpoor people. We summarize the incomes of the poor in vector x by the vector x^q.

Poverty analysis is concerned only with the poor or the distribution's base, which should be the group targeted for public assistance. It naturally ignores the incomes of nonpoor people in a society. In this way, the identification step allows us to construct a censored distribution or censored vector of incomes for society X, which we denote by $x^* = (x_1^*, x_2^*, \ldots, x_N^*)$ such that $x_n^* = x_n$ if income x_n is less than the poverty line z and $x_n^* = z$ if income x_n is greater than or equal to the poverty line z.

For the four-person income vector $x = (\$1k, \$2k, \$50k, \$70k)$ in the previous example, the censored vector is denoted by $x^* = (\$1k, \$2k, \$10k, \$10k)$. Notice that incomes of the two nonpoor people are replaced by the poverty line, and portions of their income above the poverty line are ignored. A policy maker's objective should be to include poor people at or above the poverty line. Including all poor people at or above the poverty line results in a *nonpoverty censored distribution* of income. We denote the nonpoverty censored distribution of society X corresponding to poverty line z by $\bar{x}_z^*$ such that $\bar{x}_z^* = (z, z, \ldots, z)$.

The second step for constructing a poverty measure is *aggregation*. In this step, incomes of individuals who are identified as poor using the poverty line in the identification stage are aggregated to obtain a poverty measure. Therefore, a poverty measure depends on both the incomes of the poor and the criterion that is used for identifying the poor—that is, the poverty line. In fact, it turns out that any poverty measure is obtained by aggregating elements in the censored distribution x^*.

In this section, we denote a poverty measure by P, where specific indices are denoted using corresponding subscripts. We denote the poverty measure of distribution x for poverty line z by $P(x; z)$. Alternatively, it may be denoted by $P(x^*)$. There are two different ways to understand a poverty measure: one is based on the properties it satisfies and the other is through its link with income standards. First, we discuss the properties that a poverty measure should satisfy.

Desirable Properties

A useful poverty measure should satisfy some desirable properties. Like income standards and inequality measures, poverty measure properties can fall into two categories:

- *Invariance properties* leave poverty measures invariant to certain changes in the dataset. Properties in the invariance category are *symmetry, normalization, population invariance, scale invariance,* and *focus.*
- *Dominance properties* cause a poverty measure to change in a particular direction. Properties in the dominance category are *monotonicity, transfer principle, transfer sensitivity,* and *subgroup consistency.*

Six of these properties—*symmetry, population invariance, scale invariance, focus, monotonicity,* and *transfer principle*—are called basic properties. Many of these properties are analogous to the corresponding properties of income standards and inequality measures.[11]

The first invariance property, *symmetry,* requires that switching the income levels of two people while the poverty line remains the same leaves poverty unchanged. In other words, a person should not be given priority on the basis of his or her identity when evaluating the level of poverty within a society. Formally, it requires that the poverty measure of distribution x be equal to the poverty measure of another distribution x′, if x′ is obtained from x by a permutation of incomes without changing the poverty line.

For example, recall the four-person income vector (1k$, 2k$, 50k$, 70k$). If the poverty line is $z = \$10k$, then the first two people are poor and the last two people are nonpoor. Now, if the income of the first and the fourth individuals are switched, the new income vector becomes $x' = ($70k, 2k$, 50k$, 1k$). This new vector x′ is said to be obtained from vector x by a permutation of incomes.

> *Symmetry:* If distribution x′ is obtained from distribution x by permutation of incomes and the poverty line z remains the same, then $P(x'; z) = P(x; z)$.

The second invariance property, *normalization,* requires that the poverty measure be zero if no one's income in the society is less than the poverty line. This is a natural property. For example, if the income vector of the four-person society is (1k$, 2k$, 50k$, 70k$), but the poverty line in this case is 1k$, then any poverty measure should be 0, reflecting that there are no poor in the society.

> *Normalization:* For any income distribution x and poverty line z, if $\min\{x\} \geq z$, then $P(x; z) = 0$.

The third invariance property, *population invariance*, requires that poverty be invariant to the population size, in the sense that a replication of an income vector results in the same level of poverty as the original sample vector if the poverty line does not change. The implication of this property is as follows. Consider the income vector of society X, $x = (\$1k, \$2k, \$50k, \$70k)$. Suppose four more people with the same income distribution join the society so that the new income vector is $x' = (\$1k, \$1k, \$2k, \$2k, \$50k, \$50k, \$70k, \$70k)$. The population invariance property requires that the poverty level in society x remains unaltered, at least if the poverty line does not change. This allows us to compare the extent of poverty across countries and across time with varying population sizes. Furthermore, this property allows any poverty measure to depend on a distribution function, which normalizes the population size to one.

Population Invariance: If vector x' is obtained by replicating vector x at least once and the poverty line remains unaltered, then $P(x'; z) = P(x; z)$.

The fourth invariance property, *scale invariance*, requires that if an income distribution is obtained from another income distribution by scaling all incomes and the poverty line by the same factor, then the poverty level should remain unchanged. For example, if everyone's income and the poverty line in a society are tripled or halved, then the level of deprivation of the society does not change. The scale invariance property ensures that the measure is independent of the unit of measurement for income. Consider the following example, where the income of each person in vector $x = (\$1k, \$2k, \$50k, \$70k)$ increases by three times and becomes $x' = (\$3k, \$6k, \$150k, \$210k)$ over time. If the poverty line also increases from, say, $6k$ to $18k$, then the level of deprivation should not change over time.[12]

Scale Invariance: If distribution x' is obtained from distribution x such that $x' = cx$ and $z' = cz$ where $c > 0$, then $P(x'; cz) = P(x; z)$.

The fifth and final axiom in the invariance properties is *focus*, which requires that if the income of a nonpoor person in a society changes but does not fall below the poverty line, then the level of poverty should not change. This property ensures that the measure focuses on the poor incomes in evaluating poverty. In fact, focus ensures that the income distribution is censored at the poverty line before evaluating a society's poverty. For example, suppose the initial income vector is x = ($1k, $2k, $50k, $70k) and the poverty line income is $6k. Thus, the third person and the fourth person are nonpoor. If the income of either the third or the fourth person increases, but the poverty line remains unaltered at $6k, then the society's poverty level does not change.

> *Focus:* If distribution x' is obtained from distribution x by increasing the income of a nonpoor person while the poverty line remains the same at z, then $P(x';z) = P(x;z)$.

The next group of properties are dominance properties. The first of these properties requires that if the income of a poor person in a society increases, then the poverty level should register a fall, or at least it should not increase. There are two versions of this property. One is *weak monotonicity*, which requires that poverty should not increase because of an increase in a poor person's income. The other is *monotonicity*, the stronger version, which requires that poverty should fall if a poor person's income in the society increases.

These two properties are the same as the two corresponding properties of income standards, except the ones introduced here are solely concerned with incomes of the poor. For example, suppose the initial income vector is $x = $($1k, $2k, $50k, $70k) and the poverty line income is $6k so that the first two people are identified as poor. If a new vector x' is obtained by increasing the income of either the first or the second person, while the poverty line remains unchanged, then according to the weak monotonicity property, poverty should not be higher in x', and, according to the monotonicity property, poverty should be lower in x'.

> *Weak Monotonicity:* If distribution x' is obtained from distribution x by increasing the income of a poor person while keeping the poverty line unchanged at z, then $P(x';z) \leq P(x;z)$.
>
> *Monotonicity:* If distribution x' is obtained from distribution x by increasing the income of a poor person while keeping the poverty line unchanged at z, then $P(x';z) < (x;z)$.

The second dominance property is the *transfer principle*, which requires that a regressive transfer between two poor people in a society increase poverty and a progressive transfer between two poor people reduce poverty.[13] (For definitions of regressive and progressive transfers, refer to the section discussing the transfer principle for income standards.) Suppose the initial income vector is $x = (\$1k, \$2k, \$50k, \$70k)$ and the poverty line income is $6k$, so the first two people are poor. If a new vector x' is obtained by a progressive transfer between the first and the second person such that $x'= (\$1.5k, \$1.5k, \$50k, \$70k)$ and the poverty line is still fixed at $6k, then poverty in x' should be lower. Note that the transfer principle property allows the number of poor to change as a result of a regressive transfer because the richer poor may become nonpoor because of a regressive transfer.[14]

> *Transfer Principle:* If distribution x' is obtained from distribution x by a regressive transfer between two poor people while the poverty line is fixed at z, then $P(x';z) > P(x;z)$. If distribution x'' is obtained from another distribution x by a progressive transfer between two poor people while the poverty line is fixed at z, then $P(x'';z) < P(x;z)$.

As in inequality measurement, we also define a weaker version of transfer principle in poverty measurement. It requires that a regressive transfer between two people in a society not decrease poverty and a progressive transfer between two people not increase poverty. Thus, the weaker principle allows the possibility that the poverty level may remain unchanged because of a progressive or a regressive transfer.

> *Weak Transfer Principle:* If distribution x' is obtained from distribution x by a regressive transfer between two poor people while the poverty line is fixed at z, then $P(x';z) \geq P(x;z)$. If distribution x'' is obtained from another distribution x by a progressive transfer between two poor people while the poverty line is fixed at z, then $P(x'';z) \leq P(x;z)$.

The transfer principle requires a poverty measure to decrease if the transfer is progressive. However, it is not concerned with which part of the distribution the transfer is taking place. A same amount of transfer may take place between two extremely poor people, who are further away from the poverty line, or between two moderately poor people, who are much closer to the poverty line.

Should the effect of transfer, no matter where it takes place, have the same effect on the poverty level? We elaborate this situation with an example. Consider the five-person income vector x = ($80, $100, $800, $50, 000, $70,000). Let the poverty line be set at $1,050. Then the first four people are identified as poor because their incomes are below the poverty line. First, suppose $10 is transferred from the second person to the first person. Then the post-transfer income vector is x' = ($90, $90, $800, $1,000, $50,000, $70,000). Transferring 10 percent of the second person's income has increased the first person's income by 12.5 percent.

Suppose, instead, that the same $10 transfer takes place between the third and the fourth persons, who are also poor. The post-transfer income vector is x'' = ($80, $100, $810, $990, $50,000, $70,000), where transferring 1 percent of the fourth person's income increases the third person's income by 1.25 percent. This transfer makes hardly any difference in the large pool of income of the two richer poor people. Therefore, one might feel that a transfer of the same amount between two extreme poor and two richer poor should not have the same effect on the society's overall poverty.

The third dominance property, *transfer sensitivity*, requires a poverty measure to be more sensitive to a transfer between poor people at the lower end of the income distribution of the poor. In other words, this property requires that a poverty measure should change more when a transfer takes place between two extremely poor people than between two richer poor people. In terms of the example above, the level of deprivation should be lower in x' than in x''.

Suppose the initial income distribution is x and distribution x'' is obtained from distribution x by a progressive (or regressive) transfer between two extremely poor people. Suppose further that distribution x'' is obtained from distribution x by a progressive (or regressive) transfer of the same amount between two richer poor people. The following is the transfer sensitivity property:

Transfer Sensitivity: A poverty measure that satisfies transfer sensitivity places greater emphasis on progressive (or regressive) transfers at the lower end of the distribution of the poor than at the upper end of the distribution of the poor; so $P(x'; z) < (>) P(x''; z)$.

The final dominance property is *subgroup consistency*, which is conceptually the same as the corresponding property for income standards and inequality measures. This property requires that if subgroup population sizes are fixed, then overall inequality must rise when poverty rises in one subgroup and does not fall in the rest of the subgroups. For example, suppose that income vector x with population size N is divided into two subgroup vectors: x' with population size N' and x'' with population size N'' such that $N' + N'' = N$. Let a new vector, y, be obtained from x with the same population size N, and let its two corresponding subgroups be denoted by y' with population size N' and y'' with population size N''. The subgroup consistency property can be stated as follows:

> *Subgroup Consistency*: Given that subgroup population sizes remain unchanged, if $P(y';z) > P(x';z)$ and $P(y'';z) \geq P(x'';z)$, then $P(y;z) > P(x;z)$.

There is a property closely related to subgroup consistency that is often useful for understanding how much of the overall poverty is attributed to the poverty of a particular group, given a collection of population subgroups. For example, a country's population may be divided into subgroups such as rural and urban areas, states, provinces, and other geographic regions; ethnic and religious groups; genders; or age groups. Often, one may want to evaluate a particular group's contribution. The *additive decomposability* property requires that overall poverty is expressed as a population-weighted average of subgroup poverty levels. This property is similar in spirit to the corresponding properties of income standards and inequality measures. However, it is more analogous to that of income standards in the sense that there are no within-group and between-group terms as we see for a decomposable inequality measure.

To formally outline the property, we will use two groups to simplify the interpretation, but the definition can be extended to any number of groups. Suppose income vector x with population size N is divided into two subgroup vectors: x' with population size N' and x'' with population size N'' such that $N' + N'' = N$. The additive decomposability property can be stated as follows (see example 2.9):

> *Additive Decomposability*: If income distribution x is divided into two subgroup distributions x' and x'', then $P(x';z) = \dfrac{N'}{N}P(x';z) + \dfrac{N'}{N}P(x'';z)$.

> *Example 2.9:* Consider the six-person income vector x = ($80, $100, $800, $1,000, $50,000, $70,000), which is divided into two subgroups x' = ($80, $100, $50,000) and x'' = ($800, $1,000, $70,000). Suppose the poverty line is z = $1,100, which is the same across both subgroups. Note that N' = 3, N'' = 3, and N = 6, and, thus, $N'/N = N''/N = 3/6$ = 0.5. Then any additively decomposable poverty index can be expressed as $P(x;\$1,100) = 0.5P(x';\$1,100) + 0.5P(x'';\$1,100)$.

Poverty and Income Standards

The second way of understanding poverty measures is through the income standards discussed earlier. Like inequality measures, most poverty measures are based on a comparison between two income standards: a higher income standard b and a lower income standard a. However, there is a crucial difference between inequality measures and poverty measures. In inequality measures, the higher and lower income standards are two different income standards applied to the same income vector. In poverty measures, the higher and lower income standards are the same income standards applied to two different income vectors: one is the *censored distribution* and the other is the *nonpoverty censored distribution*. Recall that a censored distribution is obtained from an original income distribution by replacing the income of the nonpoor by the poverty line. The nonpoverty censored distribution is that income distribution where all incomes are equal to the poverty line income.

It turns out that the higher income standard for poverty measures is the poverty line itself. Why is that so? This can be understood by the normalization property of income standards, which requires that if all incomes are equal in an income distribution, then an income standard of the distribution should be equal to that commonly held income. Because in a nonpoverty censored income distribution all incomes are equal to the poverty line, any income standard of the nonpoverty censored distribution should be equal to the poverty line itself, that is, $b = z$. Many well-known poverty measures take the form $P = (z - a)/z$ or the form $P = a/z$ or a monotonic transformation of either form.

Commonly Used Poverty Measures

In this section, we introduce various poverty measures that are in common use. We classify them into two categories. The first category lists basic poverty measures, and the second category lists advanced poverty measures. There are two basic poverty measures in common use: *headcount ratio* and *poverty gap measure*.

Headcount Ratio

The *headcount ratio* (P_H) is a crude measure of poverty that simply counts the number of people whose incomes are below the poverty line z and divides that number by the total number of people in the society. In society X with population size N, if there are q poor people, then the headcount ratio is simply q/N. It is obvious that the headcount ratio lies between zero and one. If all people are poor in a society, then the headcount ratio is one. When there are no poor, it is zero.

The headcount ratio can also be understood using income standards applied to the nonpoverty censored distribution and a *doubly censored* distribution. What is a doubly censored distribution, and how do we obtain it? A doubly censored distribution x^{**} is obtained from an original income distribution x by replacing nonpoor incomes with the poverty line income z and by replacing the poor incomes with zero. Therefore, income distribution x is censored upward at poverty line z for nonpoor and again censored at zero for the poor. The term *doubly censored* comes from the fact that distribution x_z^{**} is obtained by censoring distribution x twice.

The arithmetic mean is the income standard used to understand headcount ratio. The arithmetic mean of the nonpoverty censored distribution is poverty line z, and the arithmetic mean of the doubly censored distribution is called the *dichotomous mean*. If there are q poor people, or $N - q$ nonpoor people, in society X, then the dichotomous mean of the society is

$$W_A(x^{**}) = q \times 0 + \frac{N-q}{N} z = \frac{N-q}{N} z. \tag{2.35}$$

The headcount ratio of distribution x is a normalized shortfall of the dichotomous mean from the mean of the nonpoverty censored distribution (see example 2.10). Thus, the headcount ratio can be expressed as

$$P_H(x;z) = \frac{W_A(\bar{x}_z^*) - W_A(x_z^{**})}{W_D(\bar{x}_z^*)} = \frac{z - \frac{N-q}{N} z}{z} = \frac{q}{N}. \tag{2.36}$$

> *Example 2.10:* How is the headcount ratio calculated by different methods? Consider the four-person income vector $x =$ ($800, $1,000, $50,000, $70,000). If the poverty line is set at $z = \$1,100$, then two of the four people are poor. Thus, the headcount ratio is $P_H(x;z) = 2/4 = 0.5$ or 50 *percent*.
>
> How can the headcount ratio be calculated using the concept of *doubly censored distribution?*
>
> The doubly censored vector of x is $x_z^{**} = (0, 0, \$1,100, \$1,100)$ and the nonpoverty censored distribution is $\bar{x}_z^* = (\$1,100, \$1,100, \$1,100, \$1,100)$.
>
> Then $W_A(\bar{x}_z^*) = 4 \times \$1,100/4 = \$1,100$ and $W_A(x_z^{**}) = 2 \times \$1,100/4 = \$550$.
>
> Hence, $P_H(x;z) = (\$1,100 - \$550)/\$1,100 = 0.5$.

The headcount ratio is the most well-known and most widely used poverty measure because its interpretation is highly intuitive and simple. However, the effectiveness of the headcount ratio depends on which properties the headcount ratio satisfies. It satisfies all invariance properties: *symmetry, normalization, population invariance, scale invariance,* and *focus.* However, it does not satisfy any dominance property except *subgroup consistency.* The headcount ratio is not sensitive to changes in the income level of the poor as long as incomes do not cross the poverty line. This is why the headcount ratio does not satisfy the other dominance properties and monotonicity, which require poverty measures to change as the incomes of the poor change. The headcount ratio satisfies *subgroup consistency* because the headcount ratio is additively decomposable, as shown by example 2.11.

Poverty Gap Measure

The second basic poverty measure is the *poverty gap measure.* Like headcount ratio, it is also widely used. The poverty gap measure (P_G) is the average normalized shortfall with respect to the poverty line across the poor. In society X, the normalized income shortfall of a person, say, n, is calculated as $(z - x_n^*)/z$, which means that the normalized income shortfall of a nonpoor person is zero. The average normalized income shortfall is the average of all normalized income shortfalls within a society. We denote the normalized gap vector of x by $g^* = ((z - x_1^*)/z,\ldots,(z - x_N^*)/z)$. Then the poverty gap measure is

> *Example 2.11*: Consider the six-person income vector $x = (\$80, \$100, \$800, \$1,000, \$50,000, \$70,000)$, which is divided into two subgroups $x' = (\$80, \$100, \$800)$ and $x'' = (\$1,000, \$50,000, \$70,000)$.
>
> Suppose the poverty line, $z = \$1,100$, is the same across both subgroups.
>
> Note that $N' = 3, N'' = 3,$ and $N = 6$; thus, $N'/N = N''/N = 3/6 = 0.5$ is the population share of each group.
>
> The headcount ratio of x is $P_H(x;z) = 4/6 = 2/3$; the headcount ratio of x' is $P_H(x';z) = 3/3 = 1$; and the headcount ratio of x'' is $P_H(x'';z) = 1/3$.
>
> Thus, the overall headcount ratio may be obtained from the subgroup headcount ratios. The population-weighted average headcount ratio of the subgroups is $0.5P(x';z) + 0.5P(x'';z) = 0.5 \times 1 + 0.5 \times 1/3 = 2/3$.

$$P_G(x;z) = W_A(g^*) = \frac{1}{N}\sum_{n=1}^{N}\frac{z - x_n^*}{z}. \qquad (2.37)$$

The poverty gap measure may also be understood and interpreted by using two income standards. The higher income standard is the poverty line z itself, obtained by taking an arithmetic mean of the nonpoverty censored distribution $\bar{x}_z^*$. The lower income standard is obtained by applying the arithmetic mean to the censored income distribution x^*. Thus, the poverty gap measure can be expressed as

$$P_G(x;z) = \frac{W_A(\bar{x}_z^*) - W_A(x^*)}{W_A(\bar{x}_z^*)} = \frac{z - W_A(x^*)}{z} = \frac{1}{N}\sum_{n=1}^{N}\frac{z - x_n^*}{z}. \qquad (2.38)$$

There is a third way to interpret the poverty gap measure, which is as a product of the headcount ratio and the average normalized income shortfall among the poor. The average normalized income shortfall among the poor is $P_{IG}(x;z) = \frac{1}{q}\sum_{n=1}^{q}(z - x_n)/z$. The poverty gap measure can be expressed as

$$P_G(x;z) = \frac{N-q}{N}\times 0 + \frac{q}{N}\times\frac{1}{q}\sum_{n=1}^{q}\frac{z - x_n}{z} = P_H \times P_{IG}(x;z). \qquad (2.39)$$

The poverty gap measure lies between zero and one. Zero is obtained when there are no poor in the society. A value of one is obtained when everyone in the society is poor and has zero income. When everyone in a society is poor, then the poverty gap measure is the average normalized income shortfall among the poor, P_{IG}, because the headcount ratio is one in this situation, that is, $P_H = 1$ (see example 2.12).

Example 2.12: How is the poverty gap measure calculated by different methods? Consider the four-person income vector x = ($800, $1,000, $50,000, $70,000). The poverty line is set at $z = \$1,100$. The censored income vector is x^* = ($800, $1,000, $1,100, $1,100).

- Use the method in equation (2.37) to calculate the poverty gap measure. The poverty gap vector is $g^* = (300/1100, 100/1100, 0, 0)$. Then the poverty gap measure is $P_G(x;z) = W_A(g^*) = 0.09$.
- The method in equation (2.38) uses two income standards. The mean of the censored distribution is $W_A(x^*) = 1,000$. The nonpoverty censored distribution is $\bar{x}_z^* = (\$1,100, \$1,100, \$1,100, \$1,100)$. Thus, the mean of the nonpoverty censored distribution is $W_A(x^*) = 1,100$. Hence, the poverty gap measure is $P_G(x;z) = (1,100 - 1,000) / 1,100 = 0.09$.
- The method in equation (2.39) uses the headcount ratio and the income gap ratio to calculate the poverty gap measure. We already know that the headcount ratio of x is 0.5. The income gap ratio of x may be obtained by taking the mean of the first two elements of G_x and so $P_{IG}(x;z) = 2/11$. Thus, the poverty gap measure is $P_G(x;z) = 0.5 \times 2/11 = 0.09$.

What properties does the poverty gap measure satisfy? It satisfies all invariance properties: *symmetry, normalization, population invariance, scale invariance,* and *focus.* Among dominance properties, it satisfies only *monotonicity* and *subgroup consistency* and does not satisfy the transfer principle and transfer sensitivity. Although it does not satisfy the transfer principle, it satisfies the weak transfer principle, which means that the poverty gap measure does not increase (or decrease) because of a regressive (or progressive) transfer but also does not fall (or increase). The poverty gap measure satisfies the monotonicity property, meaning that if the income of a poor person increases, then (unlike the headcount ratio) the poverty gap increases. The poverty gap measure satisfies subgroup consistency because, like the headcount ratio, it is additively decomposable.

There is a long list of advanced poverty measures. These measures may not necessarily be as intuitive and as easy to understand as the two basic measures, but they are capable of moderating the limitations of the two basic measures. The advanced measures discussed in this book include the *Watts index*, the *Sen-Shorrocks-Thon index*, the *squared gap measure*, the *Foster-Greer-Thorbecke indices*, the *mean gap measure*, and the *Clark-Hemming-Ulph-Chakravarty indices*.

Watts Index

The *Watts index* was proposed by Watts (1968), and it is the average difference between the logarithm of the poverty line and the logarithm of incomes. For income distribution x with population size N and poverty line z, the Watts index can be written as

$$P_W(x;z) = \frac{1}{N} \sum_{n=1}^{N} (\ln z - \ln x_n^*). \tag{2.40}$$

The lowest value the Watts index can take is zero, which is obtained when no one is poor in the society. However, unlike the headcount ratio and the poverty gap measure, the Watts index has no maximum value.

Like the two basic measures, the Watts index can also be expressed as a difference between two income standards. The income standard used for the headcount ratio and the poverty gap measure is the arithmetic mean, whereas the income standard for the Watts index is the geometric mean. The higher income standard is obtained by applying the geometric mean to the nonpoverty censored distribution $\bar{x}_z^*$. Because the geometric mean satisfies normalization, the higher income standard is equal to the common element in x^*, which is the poverty line z itself. The lower income standard is obtained by applying the geometric mean to the censored income distribution x^*. The Watts index is the logarithm of the ratio of the higher and the lower income standards.

The other way of interpreting the measure is by calculating the difference of their logarithms (see example 2.13). The formulation of the Watts index in terms of income standards is

$$P_W(x;z) = \ln\left[\frac{W_G(\bar{x}_z^*)}{W_G(x^*)}\right] = \ln\left[\frac{z}{W_G(x^*)}\right] = \ln z - \ln\left[W_G(x^*)\right]. \tag{2.41}$$

> *Example 2.13:* How is the Watts index calculated by different methods? Consider the four-person income vector $x = (\$800, \$1,000, \$50,000, \$70,000)$, with the poverty line set at $z = \$1,100$. The censored vector is $x^* = (\$800, \$1,000, \$1,100, \$1,100)$. The logarithm of the poverty line is $lnz = ln1,000 = 7$.
>
> - Use the method in equation (2.40) to calculate the Watts index. The logarithmic differences between the poverty line and the censored incomes are $(7 - ln800, 7 - ln1,000, 0, 0) = (0.3, 0.1, 0, 0)$, the mean of which is 0.103. Thus, $P_W(x;z) = 0.1$.
> - Calculate the Watts index using the income standards. The geometric mean of x^* is $W_G(x^*) = 991.9$ and $ln[W_G(x^*)] = 6.9$. Therefore, by equation 2.41, $P_W(x;z) = 7 - 6.9 = 0.1$. Thus, both calculation and understanding of the Watts index are much easier in terms of income standards.

The Watts index satisfies all invariance properties: *symmetry, normalization, population invariance, scale invariance,* and *focus,* as well as all dominance properties: *monotonicity, transfer principle, transfer sensitivity,* and *subgroup consistency.* It satisfies the transfer principle because poverty falls when income is transferred from a richer poor person to a poorer poor person. It satisfies transfer sensitivity because it is more sensitive to a transfer at the lower end of the distribution than at the upper end of the income distribution of the poor. It satisfies the subgroup consistency property because, like the two basic measures, it is additively decomposable.

Sen-Shorrocks-Thon Index

The *Sen-Shorrocks-Thon (SST) poverty index* was originally formulated in terms of a basic poverty measure and an inequality measure. The poverty gap measure is the basic poverty measure used for constructing the SST, and the Gini coefficient is the inequality measure. Thus, the SST index can be expressed as

$$P_{SST}(x;z) = P_G(x;z) + [1 - P_G(x;z)]I_{Gini}(x^*). \qquad (2.42)$$

Note that the Gini coefficient is applied to the censored income distribution x^*.[15] This measure is sensitive to inequality among the poor, which is evident from its formulation in equation (2.42). If there is no inequality among the poor, then $P_{SST}(x;z)$ reaches its minimum. As inequality increases, the values of $P_{SST}(x;z)$ increase because $1 - P_G(x;z) > 0$, which results from the fact that $P_G(x;z)$ lies between zero and one. The Gini coefficient lies between zero and one. When there are no poor in a society, the SST index is zero. The maximum value of one is obtained when everyone in the society is poor and has zero income.

The SST index has an interesting relationship with the average normalized income shortfall among the poor, P_{IG}. When everyone is poor in a society, but has equal income, then the SST index is equal to the average normalized income shortfall among the poor, that is, $P_{SST}(x;z) = P_{IG}(x;z)$. This is because in this situation $I_{Gini}(x^*)$ is zero and $P_H = 1$. When the inequality level among the poor increases while the average normalized income shortfall remains the same, the SST index becomes larger than the average normalized income shortfall.

The SST index can also be interpreted by an income standard. The income standard in this case would be the Sen mean. The SST index is the normalized difference between the Sen mean of the nonpoverty censored distribution and the Sen mean of the censored distribution. The Sen mean satisfies the normalization property of income standards. Thus, the Sen mean of the nonpoverty censored distribution is the poverty line itself, that is, $W_S(\bar{x}^*) = z$. The Sen mean of the censored distribution x^* is denoted by $W_S(x^*)$. The SST index[16] can be presented as

$$P_{SST}(x;z) = \frac{W_S(\bar{x}^*_z) - W_S(x^*)}{W_S(\bar{x}^*_z)} = \frac{z - W_S(x^*)}{z}. \quad (2.43)$$

Given a censored distribution, once the Sen mean is calculated using the procedure discussed in the income standard section, the SST index can easily be obtained by applying equation (2.43). How do equations (2.42) and (2.43) give the same result? That question can easily be answered as

$$\frac{z - W_S(x^*)}{z} = \frac{z - W_A(x^*)}{z} + \frac{W_A(x^*)}{z} I_{Gini}(x^*) = P_G + (1 - P_G) I_{Gini}(x^*). \quad (2.44)$$

In the previous section, when discussing dominance and ambiguity results for income standards, we mentioned that the Sen mean is related to the generalized Lorenz curve. The SST index is based on the Sen mean and thus is naturally related to the generalized Lorenz curve, which has been graphically depicted in Zheng (2000). Example 2.14 shows how to calculate the SST index.

Example 2.14: How is the Sen-Shorrocks-Thon index calculated by different methods? Consider the four-person income vector $x = (\$800, \$1,000, \$50,000, \$70,000)$; the poverty line is set at $z = \$1,100$. The censored vector is $x^* = (\$800, \$1,000, \$1,100, \$1,100)$.

- Calculate the SST index using equation (2.42). The poverty gap measure, as we already know, is 0.09. The Gini coefficient of x^* is 0.062. Then $P_{SST}(x;z) = 0.09 + (1 - 0.09) \times 0.062 = 0.15$.
- Calculate the SST index using equation (2.43). The Sen mean of x^* is 937.5. Thus, the SST index is $P_{SST}(x;z) = (1,100 - 937.5)/1,100 = 0.15$.

What properties does the SST index satisfy? It satisfies all invariance properties: *symmetry, normalization, population invariance, scale invariance,* and *focus.* However, it does not satisfy all dominance properties because it is based on the poverty gap measure and the Gini coefficient. It inherits the *monotonicity* property from the poverty gap measure, and it inherits the *transfer principle* from the Gini coefficient. However, neither the Gini coefficient nor the poverty gap ratio satisfies transfer sensitivity; consequently, the SST index does not satisfy transfer sensitivity. Furthermore, the Gini coefficient is neither subgroup consistent nor additively decomposable in the usual way. This shortcoming is also inherited by the SST index.

Despite these shortcomings, the SST index is useful because it can be broken down into the poverty gap measure and the Gini coefficient. In fact, the poverty gap measure can be further broken down into the headcount ratio (P_H) and the average income gap of the poor (P_{IG}).

Squared Gap Measure

The next poverty measure in the advanced measures category is the *squared gap measure.* This measure is calculated by averaging the square of the normalized income shortfalls and is denoted by

$$P_{SG}(x;z) = \frac{1}{N}\sum_{n=1}^{N}\left(\frac{z - x_n^*}{z}\right)^2. \qquad (2.45)$$

One way of interpreting the squared gap measure is as the weighted average of normalized income shortfalls, where each normalized income shortfall is weighted by itself. This method of weighting puts greater emphasis on larger shortfalls during aggregation. Thus, a transfer of income from a richer poor person to a poorer poor person should reduce poverty. Like the SST index, the squared gap measure can also be expressed as a function of the headcount ratio (P_H), the average normalized income shortfall (P_{IG}), and the generalized entropy measure for $\alpha = 2$ of the incomes of the poor (denoted by the vector x^q), such that

$$P_{SG}(x;z) = P_H[P_{IG}^2 + 2(1 - P_{IG})^2 I_{GE}(x^q;2)]. \qquad (2.46)$$

The squared gap measure lies between zero and one (see example 2.15). A zero value is obtained when there are no poor people in the society because the headcount ratio is zero. The maximum value of one is reached when everyone in the society is poor and has zero income.

Example 2.15: How is the squared gap measure calculated by different methods? Consider the four-person income vector $x = (\$800, \$1,000, \$50,000, \$70,000)$. The poverty line is set at $z = \$1,100$. The censored vector is $x^* = (\$800, \$1,000, \$1,100, \$1,100)$.

- Use the method in equation (2.45) to calculate the squared gap measure. The squared gap vector is $sg^* = ([300/1100]^2, [100/1100]^2, 0, 0)$. Then the squared gap measure is $P_{SG}(x;z) = W_A(sg^*) = 0.02$.
- The method in equation (2.46) uses the headcount ratio, average normalized income shortfall, and generalized entropy measure to calculate the squared gap measure. We already know that the headcount ratio of x^* is 0.5 and that the poverty gap measure is 0.18. The inequality measure $I_{GE}(x^q;2)$ among the poor is 0.006. Then the squared gap measure is $P_{SG}(x;z) = 0.5[0.18^2 + 2 \times (1 - 0.18)^2 \times 0.006] = 0.02$.

What properties does the squared gap measure satisfy? It satisfies all invariance properties: *symmetry, normalization, population invariance, scale invariance,* and *focus.* However, among the dominance properties, it satisfies *monotonicity,* the *transfer principle,* and *subgroup consistency,* but it does not satisfy transfer sensitivity because the headcount ratio, the income gap ratio, and the generalized entropy of order 2 do not satisfy this property. Hence, like the basic poverty measures and the SST index, the squared income gap measure is *transfer neutral*. However, unlike the SST index, it satisfies subgroup consistency because it is additively decomposable.

Foster-Greer-Thorbecke (FGT) Family of Indices

This family of measures was proposed by Foster, Greer, and Thorbecke (1984). The FGT family of measures has the following formulation:

$$P_{FGT} = (x;z,\alpha) = \frac{1}{N} \sum_{n=1}^{N} \left(\frac{z - x_j^*}{z} \right)^{\alpha}, \qquad (2.47)$$

where $\alpha \geq 0$. The parameter α can be interpreted as the inequality aversion parameter among the poor, which is conceptually the same as that for Atkinson's class of inequality measures. As α increases, a society's aversion toward inequality among the poor increases.

Notice that there is a minor difference between parameter α in this case and parameter α in Atkinson's class of inequality measures, where a lower value of α leads to greater aversion toward inequality. This difference exists because inequality is measured in the income space and poverty is measured in the normalized gap space, where large gaps imply worse situations.

Measures in the FGT family take the form of various well-known poverty measures introduced earlier for different values of α. For example, for $\alpha = 0$, the formulation in equation (2.45) becomes the headcount ratio because $(z - x_n^*/z)^0 = 1$ when $x_n < z$ and because $(z - x_n^*/z)^0 = 0$ when $x_n \geq z$. Thus, $P_{FGT}(x;z,0) = q/N = P_H(x;z)$. For $\alpha = 1$, the formula becomes the poverty gap measure, which is the average of all normalized income shortfalls. For $\alpha = 2$, the formula is the squared gap measure, which is the average of the square of all normalized income shortfalls.

As α increases and becomes very large, P_{FGT} approaches a Rawlsian measure[17] placing more emphasis on the largest normalized income gap of the poorest person. However, note that the value of P_{FGT} for any distribution decreases as α increases, and, for a very large α, the overall value of P_{FGT} may be infinitesimally small. This occurrence can be verified by expressing the FGT formulation in equation (2.47) in general mean form using equation (2.3) as follows:

$$P_{FGT}(x;z,\alpha) = [W_{GM}(g^*; \alpha)]^{\alpha} \text{ for } \alpha > 0. \qquad (2.48)$$

Recall that the general mean of a distribution converges toward the maximum or largest element in a vector or distribution. The largest element in the gap vector g^* belongs to the poorest person in the society.

We have already discussed the properties that the headcount ratio, the poverty gap measure, and the squared gap measure satisfy. Thus, we know what properties the FGT family of indices satisfies when $\alpha = 0$, 1, and 2. The additional property that the measures in this family satisfy is transfer sensitivity when $\alpha > 2$, which implies that if a similar amount of transfer takes place between two poorer poor people and two richer poor people, then this measure is able to distinguish between these two situations.

An aspect that is not so intuitive in this family of measures is interpretation of the inequality aversion parameter. A larger value of α implies greater aversion to inequality among the poor. However, when there is no inequality in the society, should the poverty measure alter because of a change in α? For example, suppose that in a society of 100 people, everyone is poor and all people have an equal income of $500. If the poverty line is $z = \$1,000$, then the normalized income gap of each person is one-half in this society. Given that there is no inequality in the society, it should not matter how averse the society is to inequality because there is no inequality.

However, the FGT family of measures may not remain the same for all α. For the simple example considered above, $P_{FGT}(x;z,1) = P_G(x;z) = 1/2$ and $P_{FGT}(x;z,2) = P_{SG}(x;z) = 1/4$. However, this problem can be easily solved by calculating a monotonic transformation of the original FGT family of measures as

$$P'_{FGT}(x;z,\alpha) = [P_{FGT}(x;z,\alpha)]^{1/\alpha} = W_{GM}(g^*; \alpha) \text{ for } \alpha > 0. \quad (2.49)$$

Note that this formula is not valid for the headcount ratio when $\alpha = 0$. For the example above, $P'_{FGT}(x;z,\alpha) = 1/2$ for all $\alpha > 0$ because the general mean satisfies the normalization property of income standards.

Mean Gap Measure

The *mean gap measure* of poverty can be obtained by taking the Euclidean mean (W_E) of the normalized income shortfalls. This is a monotonic transformation of the squared gap measure. More specifically, the mean gap measure is the square root of the squared gap measure. The mean gap measure can be expressed as

$$P_{MG}(x;z) = W_E(g^*) = P_{SG}^{\frac{1}{2}} = \left(\frac{1}{N} \sum_{n=1}^{N} \left(\frac{z - x_n^*}{z} \right)^2 \right)^{\frac{1}{2}}. \qquad (2.50)$$

There is another interpretation of the mean gap measure: $P'_{FGT}(x;z,2)$. Because the mean poverty gap is a monotonic transformation of the squared gap measure, it satisfies all the properties that are satisfied by the squared gap measure except the additive decomposability. One advantage of the mean gap measure compared with the squared gap measure is that the values of the mean gap measure are commensurate with the values of the poverty gap measure as discussed using equation (2.49). Values of the squared gap measure tend to be much smaller than the poverty gap measure, and these numbers are not comparable to each other.

Unlike the squared gap measure, values of the mean gap measure tend to be higher than those of the poverty gap measure, because it uses the Euclidean mean instead of the arithmetic mean. For example, for the four-person income vector $x = (\$800, \$1,000, \$50,000, \$70,000)$ and poverty line $z = \$1,100$, the poverty gap measure is 0.09, whereas the mean gap measure is $(0.02)^{1/2} = 0.14$. However, had the income of the poor been equally distributed, the income vector would have been $x' = (\$800, \$1,000, \$50,000, \$70,000)$, and the poverty gap measure would remain the same as that of x (that is, 0.09), but the mean gap measure would be 0.13.

Like the squared gap measure, the mean gap measure also lies between zero and one. Moreover, this measure has an interesting relationship with the average normalized income shortfall. When everyone in a society is poor, but there is no inequality, then the squared gap measure is equal to the average normalized income shortfall among the poor because $CV = 0$ and $P_H = 1$. Thus,

$$P_{MG} = \sqrt{P_{SG}} = \sqrt{P_H \left[P_{1G}^2 + z(1 - P_{1G})^2 I_{GE}(x^a; z) \right]} = \sqrt{P_{1G}^2} = P_{1G}. \qquad (2.51)$$

Clark-Hemming-Ulph-Chakravarty (CHUC) Family of Indices

The final measure in our discussion of poverty measures is the Clark-Hemming-Ulph-Chakravarty (CHUC) family of indices (see Clark, Hemming, and Ulph 1981; Chakravarty 1983). This family is an extension of the Watts index. The CHUC index is based on the generalized mean and is the normalized shortfall of the generalized mean of the observed censored income distribution x^* from the generalized mean of the nonpoverty censored income distribution $\bar{x}^*$. Again, the generalized mean satisfies the normalization property of income standards; thus, the generalized mean of the nonpoverty censored income distribution is the poverty line itself. The CHUC index for $\alpha \le 1$ can be expressed as

$$P_{CHUC}(x;z) = \frac{W_{GM}(\bar{x}_z^*;\alpha) - W_{GM}(x^*;\alpha)}{W_{GM}(\bar{x}_z^*;\alpha)} = \frac{z - W_{GM}(x^*;\alpha)}{z}. \qquad (2.52)$$

The CHUC index lies between zero and one. The minimum value of zero is obtained when there are no poor people in a society. However, the maximum value of the CHUC index cannot be larger than one. When everyone in a society is poor, having equal income, this measure is equal to the average normalized income shortfall. It satisfies all invariance and dominance properties. However, not all measures in this class are additively decomposable. For $\alpha = 1$, the CHUC index is the poverty gap measure, and for $\alpha = 0$, the CHUC index is a monotonic transformation of the Watts index.

Advantages and Disadvantages of Each Measure

We have shown that the two basic measures—the headcount ratio and the poverty gap measure—do not satisfy transfer-related properties and so are not sensitive to inequality across the poor. Besides not being sensitive to inequality, the headcount ratio does not satisfy monotonicity, which, if it is used as a target for public policy, may cause inefficiency in public spending. All of the subsequent advanced poverty measures, in contrast, are sensitive to inequality across the poor. The SST index and the mean gap measure are both equal to the poverty gap measure when everyone in a society is poor and no inequality exists among them. These two measures become larger than the poverty gap measure when the income gap remains the same, but inequality among the poor increases.

Each advanced measure, however, has its own pros and cons. Let us begin with the SST measure. We know from our previous discussion that this measure is not subgroup consistent, which means that it may lead to inconsistent outcomes when group-level analysis is of interest. This measure is also not transfer sensitive, which means that if a similar amount of transfer takes place between two poorer poor people and two richer poor people, then this measure cannot distinguish between the two situations.

What, then, are the SST index's advantages? The first is that it can be neatly broken down into the headcount ratio, the average normalized income shortfall among the poor, and the well-known Gini coefficient. If one is not interested in group-level analysis, then this measure can be broken down into these three components to understand the source of change in poverty. In fact, the Gini coefficient can be broken down further into a within-group and a between-group component using the Gini decomposition formula introduced earlier. The within-group component assesses inequality among the poor, and the between-group component measures inequality between the average income of the poor and the poverty line.

This decomposition reveals whether the change in the measure's inequality component is caused by the change in inequality among the poor or due to a change in the average income of the poor compared to the poverty line. Note that there is no within-group inequality among the nonpoor because they all have the same income equal to the poverty line. Furthermore, there is no residual term, which is commonly seen in the Gini decomposition, because there is no income overlap between the poor and the nonpoor.

Second, consider the squared gap measure. This measure has many positive features, such as it is additively decomposable and subgroup consistent. Furthermore, like the SST index, it can be broken down into the headcount ratio, the average normalized income shortfall among the poor, and the generalized entropy measure order of 2 among the poor to understand the poverty composition. However, like the SST index, this measure is not transfer sensitive, which means that if a similar amount of transfer takes place between two poorer poor people and two richer poor people, then this measure cannot distinguish between these two situations.

Also, the generalized entropy measure order of 2 may be a bit unintuitive in the sense that it may range from zero to infinity, unlike the Gini coefficient that ranges from zero to one. The same pros and cons apply to the mean gap measure, which is just a monotonic transformation of the squared gap measure.

Third, consider the Watts index. This measure appears to be a perfect measure of poverty in the sense that it satisfies all the properties that we discussed earlier: it is additively decomposable, is transfer sensitive, and satisfies the transfer principle and all other properties. However, this measure has two shortcomings. One is that it is not applicable when there are zero incomes because the logarithm of zero is undefined. The second shortcoming is that it does not have an intuitive interpretation like the two basic measures, the SST index and the squared gap measure and its monotonic transformation (the mean gap measure). Also, like these other measures, it does not have an upper bound of one. Finally, the CHUC class of indices is a generalization of the Watts index. Like the Watts index, its members satisfy all the properties discussed earlier and also lie between zero and one. However, measures in this class are not defined for zero incomes when $\alpha \leq 0$.

Policy Relevance of Poverty Measures

Besides gauging the level of deprivation in a society, a poverty measure can have crucial policy relevance. In fact, different measures may have different policy implications. We discuss three policy implications below with certain examples. First is the influence of poverty measures as targeting tools. Second is the relevance of poverty measures in guiding public policies. Third is the use of the additive decomposability property for geographic targeting.

How Do Different Poverty Measures Influence the Targeting Exercise?

Besides gauging the level of deprivation in a society, a poverty measure is a useful tool that can influence a policy maker's targeting exercise. An important question that is often asked is the following: if a policy maker has allotted a certain amount of the budget that he or she can spend on the welfare program for the poor, how should that budget be allocated among the poor? For instance, consider the following six-person society with income vector $x = (\$80, \$100, \$800, \$1,000, \$50,000, \$70,000)$. The poverty line is set at $1,100 so that four people are poor and two people are nonpoor.

It is evident that the society's policy maker requires at least $2,420 so that he or she can drive all four poor people out of poverty. Suppose that the policy maker can allot only $1,000 toward the welfare program for the poor. Then how should that budget of $1,000 be allocated among the poor? The answer depends on which poverty measure is used to assess the society's deprivation. Different poverty measures provide different answers for this targeting exercise.

We begin this analysis when the society's poverty is assessed by the headcount ratio. The easiest way for a policy maker to reduce the headcount ratio is to bring as many poor people as possible up to the poverty line. Therefore, the first $100 of the allotted budget would be spent on the richest poor person (with an income of $1,000). The next $300 would be spent on the second-richest poor person (with an income of $800).

After bringing these two poor people out of poverty, the policy maker still has $600 in his or her budget that remains unused. How and whom should this amount assist? Given that the headcount ratio does not satisfy the monotonicity property, because even if this entire amount is transferred to either of the two remaining poor people, the poorest people still remain under the poverty line and do not add to the headcount ratio. The policy maker in this situation would have no incentive to spend the remaining budget. This lack of incentive creates inefficiency in public spending. Although poverty is reduced by 50 percent, the poverty status of the two severely deprived people remains unchanged.

What if the society's poverty is assessed by the poverty gap measure? Recall that, unlike the headcount ratio, the poverty gap measure satisfies monotonicity; but, like the headcount ratio, it does not satisfy the transfer principle or transfer sensitivity. Thus, it is not sensitive to inequality among the poor. What implication does it have on the targeting exercise? In this case, the policy maker will be inclined to spend his or her entire budget because the poverty gap measure satisfies monotonicity. An increase in a poor person's income, even when he or she is not driven out of poverty, reduces the poverty gap measure. Therefore, unlike the headcount ratio, inefficiency in public spending does not arise.

Then how should the budget of $1,000 be allocated among the poor? The straightforward way is to spend the budget on any of the four poor people as long as they do not surpass the poverty line income. Given that the poverty gap measure is not sensitive to inequality among the poor, it does not matter who among the poor receives the assistance. For example, in one case, out of the budget of $1,000, the richest poor person, with an income of $1,000, may receive $100; the second-richest poor person may receive $300; and the third-richest poor person may receive the rest, or, in another case, the poorest person, with an income of $80, may receive the entire amount. In both cases, the improvements in the poverty gap measure are the same. Thus, the poverty gap measure is insensitive to whoever receives the assistance. The poorest section of a society may perpetually remain poor in spite of showing decent progress in terms of the poverty gap measure.

How would this policy exercise be affected when the society's poverty is gauged by a distribution-sensitive poverty measure? A distribution-sensitive measure requires that assistance should go to the poorest of the poor first. Thus, out of the $1,000 budget allotted for the poor, the first $20 should go to the poorest person whose income is $80 so that the incomes of the two poorest poor people are made equal. Then the rest of the budget should be equally divided between the two poorest people so that, after allocating the entire budget, the income distribution becomes $x' = (\$590, \$590, \$800, \$1,000, \$50,000, \$70,000)$.

What if, instead of $1,000, there was $1,600 allotted to the welfare of the poor? Then the first $20 would be transferred to the poorest person. Next, out of $1,580, $1,400 would be divided equally between the two poorest people so that the incomes of all three of the poorest people would be equalized at $800. Finally, the rest of the budget of $180 is equally divided among the three poorest poor so that the post-allocation income vector is $x'' = (\$860, \$860, \$860, \$1,000, \$50,000, \$70,000)$. All distribution-sensitive poverty measures support this type of targeting. However, not all measures reflect similar amounts of decrease in poverty, which depends on how these measures weight different people.

Can Poverty Measures Influence Public Policy?

Like the targeting exercise, can a poverty measure influence public policy? Consider an example of a developing country where the major staple food is rice. As with other agricultural producers, rice producers are poor and their incomes are scattered around the country's poverty line income. Some rice producers earn enough income to live just above the poverty line, but many rice producers are unfortunate enough to live below the poverty line.

There are other poor people in the country, such as those whose major occupation is agricultural labor, plantation labor, or other unskilled jobs. These poor people are the poorest in the country, and their major source of energy and nutrition is the staple food, rice. Rice is, in fact, a necessary commodity in that country, and the government controls its price.

Being benevolent, the government wants to see a reduction in poverty by adjusting the price of rice. Which of the following two policy options would reduce poverty?

- Option 1: *Reduce* the price of rice.
- Option 2: *Increase* the price of rice.

Suppose poverty in the country is assessed by the headcount ratio. If the government decides to choose option 1 and reduce the price, then rice producers would be adversely affected because their income would fall, and rice consumers would benefit because their real incomes would increase. Given that most rice consumers are poorer than rice producers, one does not know whether more or fewer people would become poor. Thus, the impact on the headcount ratio is *uncertain*.

However, if the price of rice increases, then producers gain, but the poorer consumers lose because their real incomes fall. Given that the already poor consumers become poorer, this is not taken into account by the headcount ratio because it does not satisfy monotonicity. Therefore, the number of poor people would most likely *fall*, thereby leading to a fall in the country's headcount ratio. Thus, the potential assessment of poverty using the headcount ratio would incline the government to choose option 2 and *increase* the price because *poverty*, according to the headcount ratio, would *fall*.

Note, however, that the decrease in the headcount ratio has ignored the change in inequality among the poor. The marginally poor producers would become better off because of the price increase, but the severely poor people would be worse off for the same reason. This occurrence is very similar to the idea of regressive transfer. The higher price paid by the poorer consumers is obtained by the lesser poor producers as profit.

Any inequality-sensitive poverty measure, such as the squared gap, the Watts index, or the SST index, would be sensitive to such inequality among the poor. Suppose the poverty level in that country is now assessed with one such measure that is sensitive to inequality among the poor. If the government now chooses option 1 and *reduces* the price of rice, then the poorer consumers benefit at the cost of a reduction in the producers' income. The result is uncertain. If some producers become poorer than some consumers, then the poverty measure may increase. But if the producers remain less poor than the consumers, then the poverty measure may fall.

However, if option 2 is chosen and the rice price rises, then inequality among the poor increases and, most certainly, the poverty measure would increase. Hence, the potential assessment of poverty using any inequality-sensitive poverty measure would incline the government to *not raise* the price because *poverty*, according to any inequality-sensitive measure, would *increase*. The conclusion is that different poverty measures would incline the government to choose different policies.

Additive Decomposability and Geographic Targeting

A poverty measure of a population subgroup reflects the level of deprivation for that subgroup. A higher value of a population subgroup's poverty measure reflects a higher level of deprivation. The poverty measures we have discussed in this chapter satisfy population replication invariance to be able to compare the poverty levels of different population sizes, so these measures are invariant to population size. However, a population subgroup with a higher level of poverty does not necessarily imply that the subgroup has a larger contribution to overall poverty.

A subgroup's contribution to overall poverty also depends on the population distribution across subgroups. Therefore, targeting a region or a group based on only a poverty measure may not be completely accurate. We also need to take the population distribution into account. If P is an additively decomposable poverty measure and the income distribution x with total population size N is divided into M subgroups—x_1 with population size N_1, x_2 with population size N_2, ..., x_M with population size N_M—then the contribution of group m to total poverty is $N_m P(x_m; z)/NP(x; z)$, where z is the poverty line.

Consider the situation when poverty is assessed by the headcount ratio. A population subgroup's headcount ratio denotes the population percentage identified as poor. Interpreting a population subgroup's contribution to overall poverty in terms of the headcount ratio is intuitive. If the total number of poor is q, and q_m is the number of poor in subgroup m, then the overall headcount ratio is q/N and that of subgroup m is q_m/N_m for all $m = 1, ..., M$. Then subgroup m's share of overall poverty is $N_m[q_m/N_m]/N[q/N] = q_m/q$. Thus, the contribution of the subgroup's poverty to overall poverty in terms of the headcount ratio is just the share of overall poor in that subgroup.

For example, consider table 3.9 in chapter 3, which shows the distribution of the poor across Georgian subnational regions for years 2003 and 2006. Suppose that, in 2003, the headcount ratio of the subnational region Kvemo Kartli is 44.4 percent, which is more than twice the headcount ratio of 20.9 percent in Tbilisi. However, the share of total poor living in Tbilisi is, in fact, slightly larger than that living in Kvemo Kartli, because the population size of Tbilisi is more than twice that of Kvemo Kartli. In 2006, the headcount ratio of Kvemo Kartli decreased to 35.1 percent, which is still 10 percent higher than the headcount ratio of Tbilisi, but the share of the poor living in Tbilisi increased to 20.4 percent alongside only 12.2 percent in Kvemo Kartli. Therefore, the Georgian government needs to understand that, despite having a lower headcount ratio, a massive number of poor people reside in Tbilisi.

The share of subgroup poverty in overall poverty also has an intuitive interpretation that can be relevant for geographic targeting. Using the same notations as in the previous paragraph, we can express the poverty gap measure as

$$[\Sigma_{i=1}^{q}(z - x_i)]/Nz,$$

where $[\Sigma_{i=1}^{q}(z - x_i)]$ is the total sum of financial assistance required to bring all poor people just to the poverty line to eradicate poverty. If the distribution x is divided into M subgroups as earlier, then the poverty gap measure of subgroup m is

$$[\Sigma_{i=1}^{qm}(z - x_i)]/N_m z,$$

where $[\Sigma_{i=1}^{qm}(z - x_i)]$ is the total amount of financial assistance required to eradicate poverty in subgroup m. The contribution of subgroup m's poverty gap measure to the overall poverty gap ratio is

$$[N_m\Sigma_{i=1}^{qm}(z - x_i)]/N_m z]/N[\Sigma_{i=1}^{q}(z - x_i)]/Nz = \Sigma_{i=1}^{qm}(z - x_i)/\Sigma_{i=1}^{q}(z - x_i). \quad (2.53)$$

Therefore, a subgroup's contribution is nothing but the share of total financial assistance that should be received by that subgroup to eradicate poverty. Thus, the contribution in terms of the poverty gap measure may be used to understand the requirement for fund allocation across geographic regions.

The subgroup contribution of other additively decomposable poverty measures that are sensitive to inequality, such as the squared gap or the Watts index, may not have such an intuitive implication for targeting. However, their additively decomposable property enables us to understand the subgroup's contribution to overall poverty and monitor the targeting exercise. Although for these examples we have considered only the population subgroups in terms of subnational regions, the population may well be grouped alternatively by gender, occupation, or household head characteristics, as depicted in chapter 3.

Poverty, Inequality, and Welfare

Poverty measures that satisfy the transfer principle are called distribution-sensitive poverty measures. The distribution-sensitive poverty measures introduced earlier were the Watts index, the SST index, the FGT family of measures for $\alpha > 1$, and the CHUC family of indices. Each of these distribution-sensitive poverty measures is built on a specific income or gap standard that is closely linked to an inequality measure. For example, the Watts index is closely linked with Theil's second measure of inequality, the SST index is closely linked with the Gini coefficient, the FGT family of indices for $\alpha > 1$ is linked with the generalized entropy measures, and the CHUC family of indices is linked with Atkinson's family of measures.

For the Watts index, SST index, and CHUC family of indices, the inequality measure is applied to the censored distribution x^*, with greater *censored inequality* being reflected in a higher level of poverty for a given poverty gap level. The FGT indices for $\alpha > 1$, however, use generalized entropy measures applied to the gap distribution g^*, with greater *gap inequality* leading to a higher level of poverty for a given poverty gap level.

Recall from our earlier discussion in the income standard section that certain income standards can be viewed as welfare functions, and this link provides yet another lens for interpreting poverty measures. The Sen mean used in the SST index and the general means for $\alpha \leq 1$ that are behind the CHUC indices can be interpreted as welfare functions. In each poverty measure, the welfare function is applied to the censored distribution to obtain the censored income standard, which is now seen to be a *censored welfare function* that takes into account poor incomes and only part of non-poor incomes up to the poverty line. For these measures, poverty and censored welfare are inversely related—every increase in poverty can be seen as a decrease in censored welfare.

Dominance and Unanimity

A poverty measure assesses the level of poverty within a society by a single number for a given poverty line. Two obvious questions arise: (a) Does a single poverty measure evaluate two distributions in the same way for all poverty lines? and (b) Do all poverty measures evaluate two income distributions in the same way? More specifically, according to the first question, if one distribution has more poverty than another distribution for a particular poverty line, is there any certainty that the former distribution would have more poverty than the latter for any other poverty line?

Consider the following example with two four-person income distributions $x = (\$800, \$900, \$5,000, \$70,000)$ and $x' = (\$200, \$1,200, \$1,600,$

$70,000). Let poverty be measured by the headcount ratio. If the poverty line is $1,000, then distribution x has more poverty than distribution x'. What happens if the policy maker decides that the correct poverty line should be $800? Then distribution x has no poor people, but distribution x'' has one poor person. Similarly, if the poverty line is $2,000, then, again, distribution x has less poverty than distribution x''. Hence, the choice of poverty line affects the poverty comparison.

According to the second question, if one poverty measure determines income distribution x to have more poverty than distribution x', would other poverty measures compare these two distributions in the same way? This situation is analogous to our discussion of dominance and ambiguity for inequality and income standards. The answer is not too optimistic and depends on the poverty measure used—not all poverty measures evaluate different distributions in the same manner.

Consider the same two four-person income vectors used above: $x = ($800, $900, $5,000, $70,000) and $x' = ($200, $1,200, $1,600, $70,000). Let the poverty line be $z = $1,000. We have already seen that the headcount ratio reflects more poverty in distribution x than in distribution x'. How does the poverty gap measure P_G compare these two distributions? It turns out that $P_G(x; z) = 0.08 < P_G(x'; z) = 0.18$. Distribution x has less poverty than distribution x'. Thus, these two basic measures disagree with each other.

Is there any way we can devise situations where we have unanimous results? To start, we try to answer the first question using a concept introduced at the beginning of this chapter: the *cumulative distribution function*, or cdf.[18] Recall that the cdf of distribution x denotes the *proportion* of people in the distribution whose income falls below a given income level. In the poverty analysis context, if that income level is the poverty line z, then the value of the cdf at z is nothing but the headcount ratio at poverty line z (see figure 2.14 below).

Poverty Incidence Curve

The horizontal axis of figure 2.14 denotes income, and the vertical axis denotes the values of a cumulative distribution function. If the poverty line is set at z, then the headcount ratio is $P_H(x; z)$, which is the percentage of people in distribution x who have incomes less than z. Similarly, $P_H(x; z')$ and $P_H(x; z'')$ are the headcount ratios of distribution x corresponding to poverty lines z' and z'', respectively.

A Unified Approach to Measuring Poverty and Inequality

Figure 2.14: Poverty Incidence Curve and Headcount Ratio

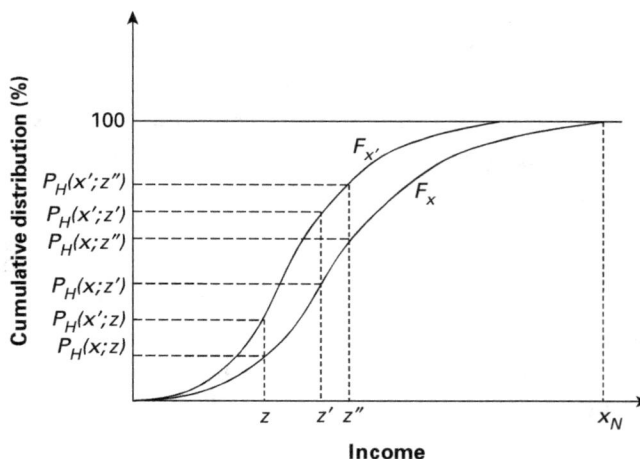

Suppose there is another distribution x'. One can see in figure 2.14 that the headcount ratios corresponding to poverty lines z, z', and z'' lie above the respective headcount ratios for distribution x. Is there any other poverty line that reflects a higher headcount ratio in x than in x'? The answer is no. The cdf of x lies to the right of the cdf of x', which means that the headcount ratio for x' for no poverty line can be lower than the headcount ratio for x. When a cdf lies to the right of another cdf, *first-order stochastic dominance* (introduced earlier) occurs. When such dominance relation holds between two cdfs, not only do the headcount ratios agree for all poverty lines, but the poverty gap measure, the squared gap measure, the mean gap measure, the Watts index, and the CHUC indices also agree for all poverty lines.

This approach also answers the second question, which asks when all poverty measures agree. Therefore, if the first-order stochastic dominance holds, then there is no need to compare any two distributions by any poverty measure introduced earlier with respect to varying the poverty line. The choice of poverty measure and the choice of poverty line simply do not matter when the first-order dominance condition holds. The cdf in the context of poverty measurement is also known as the *poverty incidence curve*.

Poverty Deficit Curve

What if two poverty incidence curves cross? Then a unanimous relationship in terms of the headcount ratio does not hold. However, there are two other poverty-value curves that lead to a unanimous relationship in terms of the poverty gap measure and the squared gap measure. These two curves are known as the *poverty deficit curve* and the *poverty severity curve*.

When the poverty deficit curve of one distribution lies above the poverty deficit curve of another distribution, then the former distribution has higher poverty—in terms of the poverty gap measure for all poverty lines—than the latter distribution. Similarly, if the poverty severity curve of a distribution lies above the poverty severity curve of another distribution, then the former distribution has higher poverty in terms of the squared gap measure for all poverty lines. We now elaborate these two concepts.

Figure 2.15 outlines the poverty deficit curve concept. We use the poverty incidence curve (panel a) to construct the poverty deficit curve (panel b). The poverty incidence curve of distribution x is denoted by F_x. The height of a poverty deficit curve at a poverty line is the area underneath the poverty incidence curve to the left of the poverty line. In figure 2.15, the height of the poverty incidence curve at poverty line z is denoted by height B, which is the shaded area below the poverty incidence curve F_x to the left of z. For instance, for the poverty line z, if q people are identified as poor, then $F_x(z) = q/N$ percent, which is the percentage of the poor population.

What does the area underneath the incidence curve denoted by B mean? To understand, first note that the lightly shaded area denoted by A is the average income of the q poor people times the share of the poor.

Figure 2.15: Poverty Deficit Curve and the Poverty Gap Measure

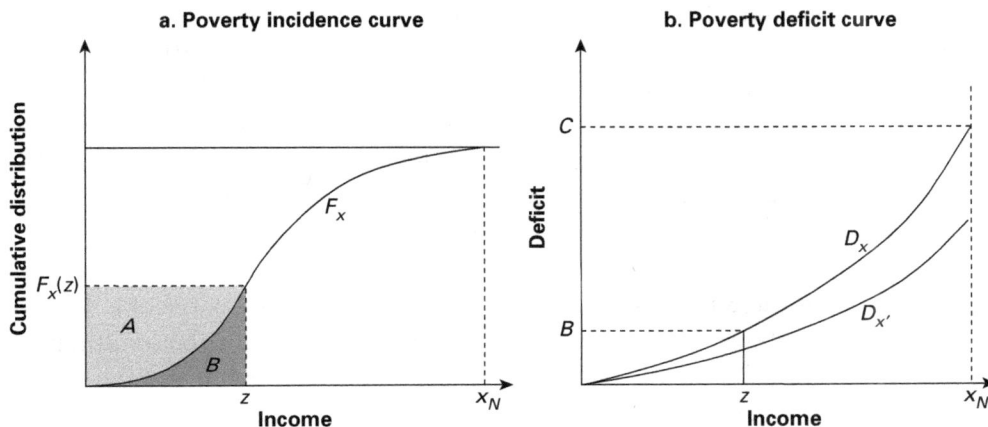

a. Poverty incidence curve

b. Poverty deficit curve

This can be easily verified from the quantile function as described earlier in figure 2.5.

Recall that an income distribution's cdf is just the inverse of the relevant distribution's quantile function. Thus, A is $W_A(x_A)(x^q)q/N = (x_1 + \ldots + x_q)/N$. Another interpretation of area A is that it is the per capita income of an average poor person in the society. The combined area $A + B$ denotes the society's per capita income, which, if held by each poor person, means that the poor will not be poor anymore.

This per capita income is qz/N. Thus, area B, which is also the height of the poverty deficit curve D_x at poverty line z, is the difference between the area $A + B$ and the area A, or the average income shortfall or the deficit, that is, $[z - W_A(x^q)]q/N$. This deficit is the minimum per capita income of the society, which, if transferred to the poor, will lift the poor out of poverty. Area B is also $zP_G(x; z)$. The maximum height of the poverty deficit curve is denoted by C, which is $x_N - W_A(x)$.

Example 2.16: Suppose in a country of 100 million (m) people with a per capita income of $20,000, 30 million people are poor. The average income of these poor people is $400. So the per capita income held by an average poor person is ($1,000 − $400) × 30m ÷ 180m.

If the poverty line is $1,000, then the deficit is ($1,000 − $400) × 30m ÷ 100m = $180.

Thus, $180 per capita, which is only 0.9 percent of the per capita income of the country, is the minimum amount required to bring all 30 million poor people out of poverty.

Note that the larger height of the poverty deficit curve D_x compared to the poverty deficit curve $D_{x'}$ at z reflects a larger poverty gap measure in distribution x than in distribution x' at poverty line z. It is evident from figure 2.15 that the poverty deficit curve D_x lies above the poverty deficit curve $D_{x'}$ for all poverty lines. Hence, distribution x has higher poverty than distribution x' for all poverty lines in terms of the poverty gap measure.

This type of unanimity result, however, fails to hold when two poverty deficit curves cross each other. We should then check the poverty severity curve of these two distributions. If the poverty severity curve of a distribution lies above the poverty severity curve of another distribution, then the former distribution has higher poverty than the latter in terms of the squared gap measure or the mean gap measure for all poverty lines.

Poverty Severity Curve

Panel a of figure 2.16 displays the poverty deficit curve that we will use to show how a poverty severity curve is constructed. As explained earlier, the height B of a poverty deficit curve is proportional to the poverty gap measure and is the poverty gap measure times the poverty line. As shown in panel b, the height of the poverty severity curve S_x at poverty line z is D, which is the area underneath the poverty deficit curve D_x. Area D is proportional to the squared gap measure. Therefore, the larger the height of the poverty severity curve S_x than the poverty severity curve Sx at z, the larger the squared gap measure in distribution x than in distribution x' at poverty line z. It turns out that the poverty severity curve S_x lies above the poverty severity curve $S_{x'}$ for all poverty lines. Hence, distribution x has higher poverty than distribution x' for all poverty lines.

Note that the dominance by the poverty deficit curve is equivalent to the second-order stochastic dominance, and the dominance by the poverty severity curve is equivalent to the third-order stochastic dominance.[19]

When there is dominance in terms of poverty incidence curves, all poverty measures satisfying the invariance properties and monotonicity agree with each other when ordering distributions according to the level of poverty for any poverty line. Such dominance relationships do not always hold. When two poverty incidence curves cross, one distribution has higher or lower poverty only for a part of the entire range of incomes. In fact, different poverty measures may order two distributions differently.

Figure 2.16: Poverty Severity Curve and the Squared Gap Measure

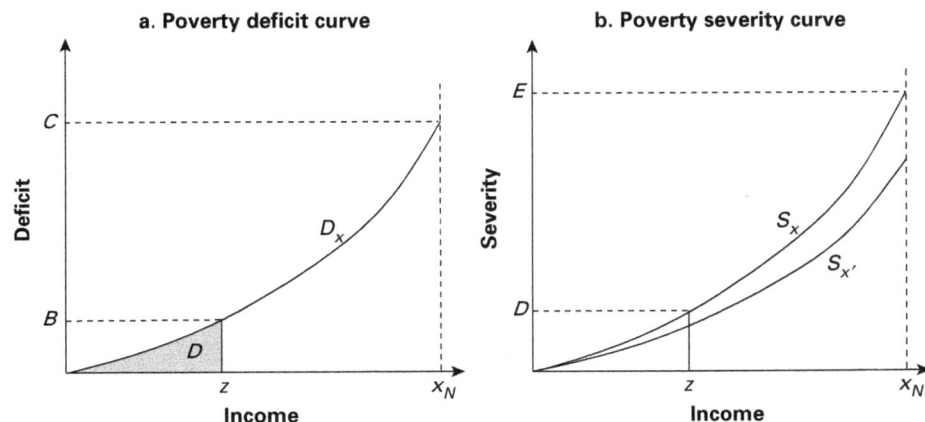

a. Poverty deficit curve   b. Poverty severity curve

One way of examining the robustness of poverty comparisons is by calculating the vector of poverty levels of different measures for a fixed poverty line. For instance, the headcount ratio, the poverty gap measure, the squared gap measure, the Watts index, and the SST index can be depicted in a five-dimensional vector. If there are two distributions x and x', then the five-dimensional vector of x for poverty line z is

$$(P_H(x;z), P_G(x;z), P_{SG}(x;z), P_W(x;z), P_{SST}(x;z)),$$

and the five-dimensional vector of x' for poverty line z is

$$(P_H(x';z), P_G(x';z), P_{SG}(x';z), P_W(x';z), P_{SST}(x';z)).$$

Vector dominance between these two vectors would then be interpreted as a *variable measure* poverty ordering that ranks distributions when all five measures unanimously agree. If each element in the vector x is greater than each corresponding element in the vector x', then distribution x has unanimously more poverty than distribution x' for poverty line z.

Sensitivity Analysis with Respect to the Poverty Line

The dominance analysis discussed earlier helps us understand whether one distribution has more or less poverty than another distribution. It is not concerned about the level of poverty, which is often of particular policy interest. The number of poor people in a country or the fact that many poor people have been moved out of poverty over a particular time period are always matters of great concern. These data, of course, depend on the particular poverty line chosen.

As discussed in the introductory chapter, there are three different types of poverty lines:

- An *absolute poverty line* may be adjusted with the rate of inflation over time, but it is not adjusted with income growth over time.
- A *relative poverty line* is not fixed over time, and it changes with income growth. For example, if a poverty line is set at 50 percent of the median income, then the poverty line changes as the median income changes over time. Or the poverty line may be set at 50 percent of mean income. In this case, the growth rate of the poverty line over time is the same as the growth rate of per capita income over time.
- A *hybrid poverty line* is created by taking a weighted average of an absolute poverty line and a relative poverty line.

No matter how a poverty line is chosen, one can argue that it is arbitrary. It is possible to propose a feasible alternative, which may change the perspective of poverty significantly. Thus, one must examine the sensitivity of poverty with respect to the poverty line. One way of conducting the sensitivity analysis is to change the poverty by certain percentages, then estimate how much the poverty level has changed.

For example, suppose the headcount ratio of society x is 25 percent for poverty line $z = \$10,000$. Let this figure increase to 30 percent when the poverty line is increased to $10,200. This means that a 2 percent increase in the poverty line increases the headcount ratio by 5 percent. The lower the change in the poverty estimate because of change in the poverty line, the more reliable the point estimate based on a particular poverty line. If there is too much variation, then the poverty estimate may not be considered reliable.

Growth and Poverty

When a country is rapidly growing, one must evaluate the quality of the growth. By *growth*, we generally mean a country or society's growth in *mean income*, and, by merely looking at the growth, there is no way of knowing who has benefited from this growth. This growth may result from a rise in incomes of the richer part of the distribution or from a rise in incomes of the poorer part of the distribution.

There are various ways of understanding if the growth is pro-poor or anti-poor. First, we may be interested in knowing directly if poverty has increased or decreased because of the growth. Second, we may want to know if the growth has *relatively* benefited or hurt the population with lower incomes. In this case, it is not enough just to understand if poverty has increased or decreased; it is also important to understand whether the situation of the poor has changed in comparison to others in the distribution. Third, we may be interested in knowing if the growth has lowered poverty more than a counterfactual-balanced growth path would. In this case, one may be interested in knowing how much of the change in poverty is due to growth and how much is due to the redistribution.

Consider some examples to clarify these various ways of understanding pro-poor growth. Suppose the society consists of four people and the income vector is $x = (\$80, \$100, \$200, \$260)$. The society's mean income is $160. First, if the poverty line income is $120, then two people are poor. Suppose that, over time, incomes of these four people change to

$x' = (\$100, \$125, \$160, \$575)$. The society's mean income has grown by 50 percent to $240. If the poverty line remains unchanged at $120, then the headcount ratio goes down. In fact, poverty goes down for any poverty measure that satisfies the monotonicity property. Thus, if one is merely interested in knowing if poverty has decreased because of growth, then the growth has been pro-poor for a fixed poverty line. If, instead of $120, the poverty line is set at $180, then the change in poverty may not appear to be pro-poor by all measures. For example, despite growth of 50 percent, the headcount ratio deteriorates. Thus, in terms of the headcount ratio, the growth in the distribution appears to be anti-poor.[20]

Given that a fixed poverty line is difficult to defend, we must understand the change in poverty for a variable poverty line. The approach is analogous to the dominance analysis. If one poverty curve (incidence, deficit, or severity) dominates another poverty curve, then poverty has improved unambiguously in the dominant distribution because of growth. Besides merely knowing the direction of change in poverty, we may be interested in the magnitude of the reduction in poverty relative to the growth in mean—the *growth elasticity of poverty*. The growth elasticity of poverty is defined as the percentage change in poverty resulting from a 1 percent change in the mean income. If the elasticity is greater than one, then the percentage change in poverty has been larger than the percentage change in mean income, or the growth of mean income. For an application of the growth elasticity of poverty using the headcount ratio, see Bourguignon (2003). To understand the change in the growth or elasticity of poverty for a variable poverty line, various *poverty growth curves* can be constructed (similar to the various growth curves discussed in the income standard section).

A second way of understanding a change in poverty as pro-poor is by looking at the gain of the poor *relative* to the gain in the mean. Reconsider the two income vectors in the previous example. The growth rate of the mean was 50 percent. Have the incomes of individuals at the bottom of the distribution improved enough to catch up with the growth in mean? The answer is no. The growth of the poorest person's income was 25 percent. The income growth of the two poorest people also totaled 25.0 percent, and the growth of the three poorest people totaled 1.3 percent. Then how was the 50 percent growth achieved? It was achieved because the richest person's income grew by about 121 percent. Thus, this second way understands the relationship between poverty and growth from an inequality perspective and may be referred to as an *inequality-based approach*, as discussed in chapter 1.

The tools we used to understand the relationship between growth and inequality can also be used here. Comparing the growth rates of two income standards may provide some insight. If a lower income standard grows faster than the mean, then incomes of the poorer section of the distribution must have grown faster than the mean. In contrast, if an upper income standard grows faster than the mean, then incomes of the richer section of the distribution must have grown faster than the mean. For example, one may compare the growth rate of the Sen mean (emphasizing lower incomes) vis-à-vis the growth of the average. Indeed, the growth in the Sen mean is only 24 percent compared to 50 percent growth in mean income.

One can also use other income standards, such as the general means, for this exercise. For example, Foster and Székely (2008) computed the growth in general means for different α to show that although the growth rate mean incomes in Mexico and Costa Rica were the same, the growth of general means was starkly different. In Mexico, the growth in mean income was mostly driven by the increase in the income of the richer section of the population. In Costa Rica, the growth in mean was driven by the increase in the income of the poorer section. The same amount of growth may have improved the situation of the poor in Costa Rica, but it may have deteriorated the situation of the Mexican poor.

One may also be interested in understanding the composition of change in poverty *because of growth* and *because of change in inequality*.[21] As discussed in chapter 1, pro-poor growth may be understood as a difference between the growth rate of an original distribution and a counterfactual distribution that has the same mean and relative distribution as the original distribution. Then the overall change in poverty can be split into a change because of growth and a change because of redistribution.

Consider the following simple example using the vectors above: $x = (\$80, \$100, \$200, \$260)$ and $x' = (\$100, \$125, \$160, \$575)$. The mean of x is \$160, whereas the mean of x' is \$240. We now rescale each element of vector x' in such a way that it has the same mean as x, and we denote the transformed vector by x''. Thus, $x'' = (66.7, 83.3, 106.7, 383.3)$.

Let us simply measure poverty by the headcount ratio (this exercise can be performed using any poverty measure). For the poverty line of \$120, the headcount ratio in x is 2/4, which decreases to 1/3 in x'.

How was this reduction obtained? Distribution x'' is obtained from x by redistribution while keeping the mean unchanged. The headcount ratio for x'', as a result, increases from two-fourths to three-fourths. Thus, poverty has increased because of redistribution. However, distribution x' may be seen as being obtained from distribution x'' by merely increasing everyone's income by the same proportion with balanced growth. As a result, the headcount ratio falls from three-fourths to one-fourth. Hence, the improvement in poverty in this case has resulted from growth rather than redistribution.[22]

Exercises

1. Consider the following table that enables you to construct a cumulative distribution function (cdf) from income data.

Category (i)	Income ($ x_i)	Number of people (n_i)	p_i	$F(x_i)$	$(p_i \times x_i)$
1	12,000	10			
2	13,000	15			
3	14,000	40			
4	15,000	20			
5	16,000	15			

There are five income categories (X_i) in the economy. Each category contains a certain number of people (n_i).

a. What is the total number of people (n) in the economy?

b. Let p_i denote the proportion of people in each category. Fill in the column corresponding to p_i for each i. The *probability mass function* is defined as a function that gives the probability of a discrete variable taking the same value. Now draw the probability mass function.
   Hint: Draw a diagram with x on the horizontal axis and p on the vertical axis.

c. Let $F(x_i)$ denote the proportion of people who have an income no higher than x_i. Fill in the column corresponding to $F(x_i)$ for each i. Now draw the cdf.
   Hint: Draw a diagram with x on the horizontal axis and $F(x)$ on the vertical axis.

d. What is the relationship between p_i and $F(x_i)$?

e. Calculate the proportion of people having an income less than $14,100. What is the proportion of people having an income more than $14,900?

f. What is the average income for the economy?

g. Fill in the last column, and find the sum of all cells in that column. What does the sum give you?

h. Use the cdf to calculate the area to the left of the cdf bounded by $x = 0$ and $F(x) = 1$. What do you get?

i. Calculate the median, the 95th percentile, and the 20th percentile using the cdf that you drew in 1c.

2. The Gini coefficient is probably the most commonly used index of relative inequality. What are some of the advantages and disadvantages of this measure?

3. The *variance of logarithm* (V_L) is an inequality measure that is computed as

$$V_L(x) = \frac{1}{N} \sum_{n=1}^{N} [\ln x_n - W_L(x)]^2,$$

where $W_L(x)$ is the mean of the logarithm of elements in x as defined in the chapter.

a. Verify that the variance of logarithms satisfies scale invariance. What property of the variance of logarithms ensures scale invariance?

b. Graph the Lorenz curves for the two distributions $x = (1,1,1,1,41)$ and $y = (1,1,1,21,21)$. Can the curves be ranked?

c. Find the variance of logarithms of the two distributions. What is wrong here?

d. Find the mean log deviation (the second Theil measure) of the two distributions. What is correct here?

4. Construct an inequality measure that violates replication invariance.

5. Are the following statements true, false, or uncertain? In each case, support your answer with a brief but precise explanation.

a. The Kuznets ratios satisfy the Pigou-Dalton transfer principle.

b. Distribution $y = (1,2,3,2,41)$ is more unequal than distribution $x = (1,8,4,1,36)$ in terms of the Lorenz criterion.

c. The four basic properties of inequality measurement are enough to compare any two income distributions in terms of relative inequality.

d. If everyone's income increases by a constant dollar amount, inequality must fall.

6. Consider the distribution $x = (1,3,6)$.

a. Draw the Lorenz curve, and calculate the area between the 45-degree line and the curve.

b. Calculate the Gini coefficient for x. What is the relationship between the Gini coefficient and the calculated area?

7. Consider the distribution $x = (3,6,9,12,24,36)$.
   a. Divide the distribution into the following two subgroups: $x_1 = (3,6,9)$ and $x_2 = (12,24,36)$. Calculate the Gini coefficient for x, x_1, and x_2. Using the traditional additive decomposability formula, check if the Gini coefficient is decomposable in this situation.
   b. Divide distribution x into the following two subgroups: $x_3 = (3,24,36)$ and $x_4 = (6,9,12)$. Again, using the traditional additive decomposability formula, check if the Gini coefficient is decomposable in this situation.
   c. What is the difference between these two circumstances? Explain.
   d. What is the residual for the Gini coefficient in these two circumstances?

8. For the two distributions $x = (2,100; 700; 1,100; 200)$ and $y = (3,410; 620; 2,170; 6,510)$, do the following:
   a. Calculate the $W_{GM}(.; \alpha)$ and use it to calculate the Atkinson measure $I_A(.; \alpha)$ for $\alpha = 0, -1$.
   b. Do you have the same $I_A(.; \alpha)$ for both distributions or not? What is going on here?

9. For the income distributions $x = (3,3,5,7)$ and $y = (2,4,6,6)$, do the following:
   a. Calculate the generalized entropy measure and $I_{GE}(x; \alpha)$ and $I_{GE}(y; \alpha)$ for $\alpha = 1,0,1,2,3,4$.
   b. Plot the values of α on the horizontal axis and the values of $I_{GE}(x; \alpha)$ and $I_{GE}(x; \alpha)$ on the vertical axis.
   c. Join the points, and check if they intersect. If they intersect, then report at what value of α they intersect, and explain why.

10. Are the following statements true, false, or uncertain?
    a. The second Theil measure is subgroup consistent.
    b. The arithmetic mean is higher than the harmonic mean but less than the geometric mean.
    c. The sum of the decomposition weights of the generalized entropy measure is always less than 1.

11. How is the generalized Lorenz curve $GL(p)$ derived from a cdf? Draw this process and explain. What value does the generalized Lorenz curve take at $p = 1$?

12. Suppose an inequality measure is given by $I(x) = (\bar{x} - e(x))/\bar{x}$, where $e(x)$ is one of the equally distributed equivalent income functions used by Atkinson (namely, a general mean with a parameter less than one).

a. Which equivalent income function is the lower income standard?

b. Show that if the lower income standard grows at a faster rate than the upper income standard, then inequality will fall.

c. Suppose the mean income grows at a rate of 3 percent. Under what circumstances will the Atkinson index fall? When will the Gini index fall?

13. Because of economic growth, the income distribution changes as follows over time: (1,1,1,1), (1,1,1,2), (1,1,2,2), (1,2,2,2), (2,2,2,2).

a. Explain the relevance of this example to the development literature.

b. Can unambiguous inequality comparisons be made between these distributions?

c. How does the Gini coefficient change over time in this example?

14. Provide an example illustrating that the Gini coefficient violates subgroup consistency. Explain why it does.

15. Country A has a more equal income distribution than Country B such that Country A's Lorenz curve dominates that of Country B.

a. What should be the relationship between these two countries in terms of generalized Lorenz?

b. What does this finding say about welfare and inequality?

16. Why should a poverty measure be sensitive to the distribution of income among the poor?

17. Suppose that the incomes in a population are given by $x = (4,2,10)$ and the poverty line is $z = 6$.

a. Find the number of people who are poor.

b. Find the headcount ratio P_H.

c. Find the (normalized) poverty gap measure P_G.

d. Find the squared poverty gap measure P_{SG}.

e. If the income of person 2 falls by one unit so that the new distribution is $y = (4,1,10)$, what happens to P_H, P_G, and P_{SG}?

f. If person 2 gives person 1 a unit of income, resulting in distribution $u = (5,1,10)$, what happens to P_H, P_G, and P_{SG}? Explain.

18. One of the big problems in evaluating poverty levels is arriving at a single poverty line that represents *the* cutoff level between the poor and the nonpoor. Many people believe that a poverty line must be arbitrary to some extent. But if this is so, and if changing the poverty line reverses poverty judgments, then all our conclusions about poverty might be ambiguous. To solve this problem, we might make

comparisons not only for a single poverty line but also for a range of poverty lines. Consider the three distributions from the previous example: $x = (4,2,10)$, $y = (4,1,10)$, $u = (5,1,10)$.

    a. If $z = 6$ is the poverty line, does x or y have more poverty according to the headcount ratio? Will this determination be reversed at some other poverty line? Explain. Does x or y have more poverty according to the poverty gap measure? Will this determination be reversed at some other poverty line? Explain.

    b. If $z = 6$ is the poverty line, does x or u have more poverty according to the headcount ratio? Will this determination be reversed at some other poverty line? Explain. Does x or u have more poverty according to the poverty gap measure? Will this determination be reversed at some other poverty line? Explain.

    c. Do you think unambiguous comparisons with variable poverty lines might be made in practice? If not, why not? If so, why?

19. Which inequality measure is the Sen-Shorrocks-Thon (SST) poverty index based on?

    a. Explain why the SST index is not subgroup consistent and provide a counterexample to illustrate your point.

    b. Which inequality measure is the Foster-Greer-Thorbecke (FGT) index $P_{SG}(x; z)$ based on? Show that the measure is subgroup consistent.

20. Why should a measure of poverty satisfy scale invariance (homogeneity of degree 0 in incomes and the poverty line)? Which poverty measures satisfy scale invariance?

21. Suppose instead of the $P_{SG}(x; z)$ measure one were to use the $P_{MG}(x; z)$ measure.

    a. What is the main constructive difference between these two measures?

    b. What would be the advantages and disadvantages of using the $P_{MG}(x; z)$ measure?

22. Why do inequality decompositions have a between-group term but poverty decompositions do not?

23. Suppose inequality decreases without growth of mean income. What may likely happen to poverty? Suppose growth of mean income occurs without a change in inequality. What may likely happen to poverty? Explain.

24. Suppose that the per capita poverty gap measure is used with a relative poverty line that sets $z = \alpha\mu$ for some $\alpha > 0$. When does one distribution have a lower level of relative poverty for all $\alpha > 0$? (*Hint:* Think Lorenz.)

25. We have already shown that the poverty measures are different from each other and differ in their sensitivity to a distribution. Please provide certain examples with illustrative distributions and poverty lines such that

   a. The SST index rises, but the three FGT indices fall.

   b. The headcount ratio rises, but the SST index, poverty gap measure, and squared gap measure fall.

   c. The poverty gap measure rises, but the headcount ratio, SST, and squared gap measures fall.

   d. The squared gap measure rises, but the headcount ratio, poverty gap measure, and SST measure fall.

Notes

1. For further discussion on the use of consumption expenditure data versus income data, see Atkinson and Micklewright (1983) and Grosh and Glewwe (2000).

2. For a more detailed discussion of some of these issues, see Deaton (1997).

3. For the concept and a more detailed discussion about the principle, see Pigou (1912, 24–25); Dalton (1920); Atkinson (1970); Dasgupta, Sen, and Starrett (1973); and Rothschild and Stiglitz (1973).

4. For further discussion of the concept, see Foster and Shorrocks (1991).

5. Going forward in this book, we will use the notation $W_A(x)$ and $\bar{x}$ interchangeably. They both denote the mean of distribution (x).

6. The measure was originally proposed by Sen (1976b) and thus we named the income standard after him. See also Foster and Sen (1997).

7. A related property has been developed by Zheng (2007a). Called *unit consistency*, it has a weaker requirement than the scale invariance property. The unit consistency property requires that if one distribution is more unequal than another distribution, then just changing the unit of measurement keeps the former distribution more unequal than the latter. The property can be formally stated as follows: for any two distributions x and x', if $I(x) < I(x')$, then $I(cx) < I(cx')$ for any $c > 0$.

For example, if the elements of two distributions are converted from Indian rupees to U.S. dollars, then the direction of inequality between any two distributions should not change if the inequality measure satisfies unit consistency. An inequality measure that satisfies scale invariance also satisfies unit consistency, but the converse is not necessarily true. A class of decomposable inequality measures satisfying unit consistency has been developed by Zheng (2007a). In this book, however, we focus on relative inequality measures satisfying the scale invariance.

8. For a more in-depth theoretical discussion of the transfer sensitivity property, see Shorrocks and Foster (1987).

9. A geographical interpretation of the residual term can be found in Lambert and Aronson (1993), where the residual term is shown to be an effect of the re-ranking effect. The inequality of a distribution is computed in three steps: (a) within-group inequalities are computed in each subgroup; (b) the groups are ranked by their mean incomes and a concentration curve representing between-group inequalities is constructed; and (c) the Lorenz curve is constructed. The difference between the Lorenz curve of the distribution in the third step and the concentration curve from the second step is known as the residual term.

10. The Lorenz curve was developed by Max Lorenz (1905).

11. Interested readers, who may desire to have further theoretical understanding of the properties and their interrelationship, should see Zheng (1997) and Chakravarty (2009).

12. A related but weaker property has been developed by Zheng (2007b). See note 8.

13. This axiom is also known in the literature as *strong transfer* (see Zheng 2000). However, to keep the terminologies comparable across sections, we prefer to use the term *transfer principle*.

14. A weaker version of this property exists that is known in the literature as *weak transfer* (see Chakravarty 1983), which can be stated as follows: if distribution x' is obtained from distribution x by a regressive transfer between two poor people while the poverty line is fixed at z and the number of poor does not change, then $P(x'; z) > P(x; z)$. If distribution x'' is obtained from another distribution x by a progressive transfer between two poor people while the poverty line is fixed at z and the number of poor does not change, then $P_S(x''; z) < P(x; z)$. Note that this property is different from the weak transfer principle that we define in this book.

15. Previously, Sen (1976b) proposed the index $P_S(x; z) = P_H[P_{IG} + (1 - P_{IG}) \cdot I_{Gini}(x^q)]$, where x^q is the income distribution of the poor only. This measure was modified later by Thon (1979) and Shorrocks (1995).

16. For a more elaborated discussion on various formulations of the SST index, see Xu and Osberg (2003).

17. Rawls's welfare function maximizes the welfare of society's worse-off member. "Social and economic inequalities are to be arranged ... to the greatest benefit of the least advantaged..." (Rawls 1971, 302).

18. For an in-depth discussion on poverty ordering, see Atkinson (1987), Foster and Shorrocks (1988), and Ravallion (1994).

19. Note that the poverty deficit curve and the generalized Lorenz curve have an interesting relationship. They are based on the area underneath the cdf and the quantile function, where a quantile function is an inverse of a cdf. See figure 2.7.

20. For various approaches to measuring pro-poor growth for a fixed poverty line, see Kakwani and Son (2008).

21. For a discussion on the poverty-growth-inequality triangle, see Bourguignon (2003).

22. The growth-redistribution decomposition becomes a bit more complicated when there is interregional migration. For such decomposition with change in population, see Huppi and Ravallion (1991). An application of their method can be found in table 30 of chapter 3.

References

Atkinson, A. B. 1970. "On the Measurement of Inequality." *Journal of Economic Theory* 2 (1970): 244–63.

———. 1987. "On the Measurement of Poverty." *Econometrica* 55 (4): 749–64.

Atkinson, A. B., and J. Micklewright. 1983. "On the Reliability of Income Data in the Family Expenditure Survey 1970–1977." *Journal of the Royal Statistical Society*, Series A (146): 33–61.

Bourguignon, F. 2003. "The Growth Elasticity of Poverty Reduction: Explaining Heterogeneity across Countries and Time Periods." In *Inequality and Growth: Theory and Policy Implications*, edited by T. Eicher and S. Turnovsky, 3–26. Cambridge, MA: Massachusetts Institute of Technology.

Chakravarty, S. R. 1983. "A New Index of Poverty." *Mathematical Social Sciences* 6: 307–13.

———. 2009. *Inequality, Polarization and Poverty: Advances in Distributional Analysis*. New York: Springer.

Clark, S., R. Hemming, and D. Ulph. 1981. "On Indices for the Measurement of Poverty." *The Economic Journal* 91 (362): 515–26.

Dalton, H. 1920. "The Measurement of the Inequality of Incomes." *The Economic Journal* 30: 348–61.

Dasgupta, P., A. Sen, and D. Starrett. 1973. "Notes on the Measurement of Inequality." *Journal of Economic Theory* 6 (2): 180–87.

Deaton, A. 1997. *The Analysis of Household Surveys: A Microeconometric Approach to Development Policy*. Baltimore: World Bank.

Deaton, A., and S. Zaidi. 2002. "Guidelines for Constructing Consumption Aggregates for Welfare Analysis." Living Standards Measurement Study Working Paper 135, World Bank, Washington, DC.

Foster, J. E., J. Greer, and E. Thorbecke. 1984. "A Class of Decomposable Poverty Measures." *Econometrica* 52 (3): 761–66.

Foster, J. E., and A. Sen. 1997. *On Economic Inequality*. 2nd ed. Oxford, U.K.: Oxford University Press.

Foster, J. E., and A. F. Shorrocks. 1988. "Poverty Orderings." *Econometrica* 56 (1): 173–77.

———. 1991. "Subgroup Consistent Poverty Indices." *Econometrica* 59 (3): 687–709.

Foster, J. E., and M. Székely. 2008. "Is Economic Growth Good for the Poor? Tracking Low Incomes Using General Means." *International Economic Review* 49 (4): 1143–72.

Gini, C. 1912. "Variabilità e mutabilità." Reprinted in *Memorie di metodologica statistica*, edited by E. Pizetti and T. Salvemini. Rome: Libreria Eredi Virgilio Veschi (1955).

Grosh, M., and P. Glewwe, eds. 2000. *Designing Household Survey Questionnaires for Developing Countries: Lessons from 15 Years of the Living Standards Measurement Study*. Washington, DC: World Bank.

Huppi, M., and M. Ravallion. 1991. "The Sectoral Structure of Poverty during an Adjustment Period: Evidence for Indonesia in the Mid-1980s." *World Development* 19 (12): 1653–78.

Kakwani N., and H. H. Son. 2008. "Poverty Equivalent Growth Rate." *Review of Income and Wealth* 54 (4): 643–55.

Kanbur, R. 2006. "The Policy Significance of Inequality Decompositions." *Journal of Economic Inequality* 4 (3): 367–74.

Lambert, P., and J. R. Aronson. 1993. "Inequality Decomposition Analysis and the Gini Coefficient Revisited." *The Economic Journal* 103 (420): 1221–27.

Lorenz, M. O. 1905. "Methods of Measuring the Concentration of Wealth." *Publications of the American Statistical Association* 9 (70): 209–19.

Pigou, A. C. 1912. *Wealth and Welfare*. London: Macmillan.

Ravallion, M. 1994. *Poverty Comparisons*. Chur, Switzerland: Harwood Academic Press.

Rawls, J. 1971. *A Theory of Justice*. Cambridge, MA: Harvard University Press.

Rothschild, M., and J. E. Stiglitz. 1973. "Some Further Results on the Measurement of Inequality." *Journal of Economic Theory* 6 (2): 188–204.

Sen, A. K. 1976a. "Poverty: An Ordinal Approach to Measurement." *Econometrica* 44 (2): 219–31.

———. 1976b. "Real National Income." *Review of Economic Studies* 43 (1): 19–39.

Shorrocks, A. F. 1980. "The Class of Additively Decomposable Inequality Measures." *Econometrica* 48 (3): 613–25.

———. 1983. "Ranking Income Distributions." *Economica* 50 (197): 3–17.

———. 1995. "Revisiting the Sen Poverty Index." *Econometrica* 63 (5): 1225–30.

Shorrocks, A. F., and J. E. Foster. 1987. "Transfer Sensitive Inequality Measures." *Review of Economic Studies* 54 (3): 485–97.

Thon, D. 1979. "On Measuring Poverty." *Review of Income and Wealth* 25 (4): 429–39.

Watts, H. W. 1968. "An Economic Definition of Poverty." Discussion paper, Institute for Research on Poverty, University of Wisconsin, Madison.

Xu, K. and L. Osberg. 2003. "The Social Welfare Implications, Decomposability, and Geometry of the Sen Family of Poverty Indices." *Canadian Journal of Economics* 35 (1): 138–52.

Zheng, B. 1997. "Aggregate Poverty Measures." *Journal of Economic Surveys* 11 (2): 123–62.

———. 2000. "Poverty Orderings." *Journal of Economic Surveys* 14 (4): 427–66.

———. 2007a. "Unit-Consistent Decomposable Inequality Measures." *Economica* 74 (293): 97–111.

———. 2007b. "Unit-Consistent Poverty Indices." *Economic Theory* 31 (1): 113–42.

Chapter 3

How to Interpret ADePT Results

In this chapter, we discuss how to interpret tables and graphs generated by the ADePT analysis program. The chapter is organized in six sections:

- In the first section, we discuss how to interpret results at the country level, decomposing across rural and urban areas.
- In the second and third sections, we move into analyses at a more disaggregated level: across subnational regions in the second section and across various population subgroups—such as household characteristics, employment situation, and so forth—in the third section.
- In the fourth and fifth sections, we perform sensitivity and dominance analyses. These are useful for policy evaluation, because results in the first two sections are based on many assumptions, such as choice of poverty line and selection of methodologies for measuring poverty and inequality.
- It is always important to check how robust these results are with respect to the assumptions. For example, we may assume the poverty line to be a certain level of income or per capita expenditure and find poverty decreasing over time. Then how can we be sure that poverty has not increased for other possible poverty lines?
- Insights revealed in the first five sections may be helpful when preparing any report on poverty and inequality.
- In the final section, we discuss some advanced analyses.

Tables and graphs in this chapter were generated by ADePT's Poverty and Inequality modules using the Integrated Household Survey of Georgia dataset for 2003 and 2006. Calculations assumed the equivalence scale parameter is 1, which implies that every household member is assumed to be adult equivalent. Hence, per capita expenditure was calculated by dividing the total expenditure by the number of household members regardless of their age and gender. Calculations assumed the economy-of-scale parameter is 1. This implies that no economies of scale exist when two or more individuals share a household. (Other scale choices are, of course, possible, and these parameters can be changed in ADePT.)

Consumption expenditures are in lari (or GEL, the Georgian national currency) per month. Many tables use one or two poverty lines of GEL 75.4 and GEL 45.2 per month. In the first case, if a household fails to meet a monthly consumption expenditure of GEL 75.4 for each member in that household, then the household (and each member in the household) is identified as poor. In the second case, a household is identified as poor if the household fails to meet a per capita expenditure of GEL 45.2 per month.

Tables may have an occasional small numerical inconsistency. To improve readability, ADePT displays data with a limited number of decimal places by rounding the underlying raw data. This process can result in values that appear incorrect, such as 29.9 + 1.0 = 31.0 (as opposed to 29.9 + 1.0 = 30.9, or 29.9 + 1.1 = 31.0). Spreadsheets generated by ADePT (the sources for tables in this chapter) include raw data, which are visible in the formula bar when a cell is selected.

Rounding numbers also affects how we present some of the results. Certain poverty and inequality measures are traditionally reported in decimals. However, this presentation does not provide us enough power to differentiate between numbers. For example, the Gini coefficient of 0.26 and the Gini coefficient of 0.34 both may read as 0.3. Similarly, the FGT2 poverty index, or the squared poverty gap index, may take reasonable low values in decimals such as 0.019 or 0.024. Again, these numbers may be significantly different. Therefore, to improve readability, we normalize all poverty and inequality figures in a 0–100 scale.

The text in this chapter has numerous references to table cells. To help you quickly find data in tables, numbers and letters in brackets reference table cells by row and column. For example, [3,E] refers to the cell in row 3, column E.

Analysis at the National Level and Rural/Urban Decomposition

While preparing a report on poverty and inequality, one would first be interested in results at the national level. This part of the chapter contains seven tables with results at the national level. We then decompose the results across urban and rural areas.

Income Distribution across the Population

Initially, understanding income distribution across the population is important. A distribution's *density function* is the percentage of population that falls within a range of per capita expenditure. Figure 3.1 graphs the per capita expenditure density function for urban Georgia. The vertical axis shows probability density function of consumption expenditures. The horizontal axis is per capita expenditure or any other equivalent achievement.

Figure 3.1: Probability Density Function of Urban Georgia

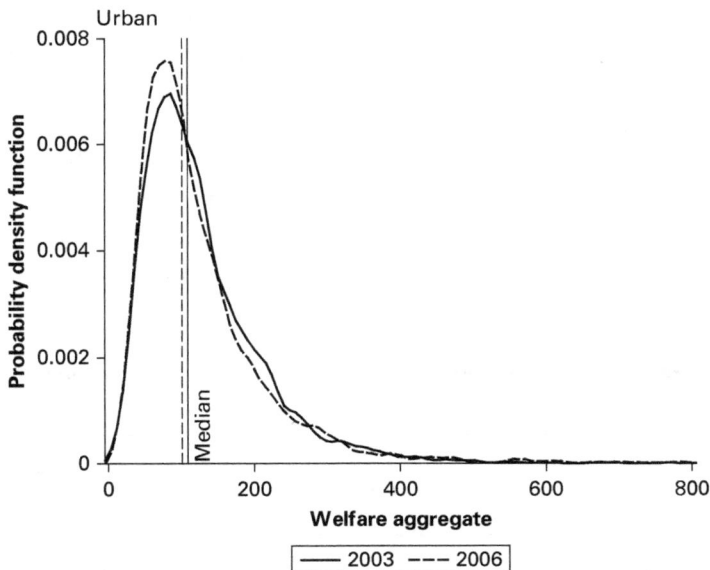

Source: Based on ADePT Poverty and Inequality modules using Integrated Household Survey of Georgia 2003 and 2006.

In figure 3.1, the solid curve is urban Georgia's density function for 2003, and the dotted curve is the density function of urban consumption expenditure distribution for 2006. The *median* is an important income standard that can be found in the diagram. It is indicated by the corresponding vertical lines: solid line for 2003 and dotted line for 2006.

A density function can also be useful for understanding a distribution's *skewness*. As can be seen from figure 3.1, the density functions for both years are positively skewed. However, an important change from 2003 to 2006 is that more people mass around the distribution's median in 2006. We can also see that the density functions for both years are unimodal. When more than one mode exists, a society is considered to be polarized by consumption expenditure or income.

Standard of Living and Inequality across the Population

Table 3.1 reports the mean and median per capita consumption expenditure and their growth over time, and the inequality across the population using the Gini coefficient. It also decomposes them across rural and urban areas and across two years: 2003 and 2006. Table rows denote three geographical regions: urban area, rural area, and all of Georgia (row 3). Per capita consumption expenditure is measured in lari per month.

Columns A and B report the mean per capita consumption expenditure for 2003 and 2006, respectively. Column C reports the percentage change or growth in per capita expenditure over the course of these three years. The average per capita expenditure of the urban area in 2003 is GEL 128.9 *[1,A]*, which is larger than the average rural per capita expenditure of GEL 123.5 *[2,A]*. The mean urban per capita expenditure in 2006 is GEL 127.3 *[1,B]*,

Table 3.1: Mean and Median Per Capita Consumption Expenditure, Growth, and the Gini Coefficient

		Mean			Median			Gini coefficient		
		2003 (GEL)	2006 (GEL)	Growth (%)	2003 (GEL)	2006 (GEL)	Growth (%)	2003	2006	Change (%)
	Region	A	B	C	D	E	F	G	H	I
1	Urban	128.9	127.3	−1.2	108.4	101.1	−6.8	33.5	35.6	2.2
2	Rural	123.5	124.8	1.0	101.5	105.3	3.7	35.3	35.1	−0.3
3	**Total**	**126.1**	**126.0**	**−0.1**	**104.7**	**103.3**	**−1.4**	**34.4**	**35.4**	**0.9**

Source: Based on ADePT Poverty and Inequality modules using Integrated Household Survey of Georgia 2003 and 2006.

which fell by 1.2 percent *[1,C]*. The mean rural per capita expenditure, in contrast, increased by 1.0 percent to GEL 124.8 in 2006 *[2,B]*. Georgia's overall per capita consumption expenditure in 2003 is GEL 126.1 *[3,A]*, which fell by 0.1 percent to GEL 126.0 in 2006 *[3,B]*.

Columns *D*, *E*, and *F* report the median per capita expenditures for 2003 and 2006 and their growth rates. The percentage changes in medians or median growths are much larger than the mean per capita expenditure growth. The rural median growth is 3.7 percent *[2,F]*, whereas the urban median "growth" is –6.8 percent *[1,F]*. The overall change in median is –1.4 percent *[3,F]*.

Columns *G*, *H*, and *I* use the Gini coefficient to capture inequality in the distribution. The rural Gini coefficient has marginally fallen from 35.3 *[2,G]* to 35.1 *[2,H]*, while the urban Gini coefficient over these three years increased from 33.5 in 2003 *[1,G]* to 35.6 in 2006 *[1,H]*. The overall Gini coefficient changed by 0.9 from 34.4 *[3,G]* to 35.4 *[3,H]*. (Gini coefficient is reported on a scale from 0 to 100 in this chapter, rather than from 0 to 1.)

Lessons for Policy Makers

Note that the mean and the median, two different measures of standard of living, are differently sensitive to the distribution of per capita consumption expenditure. Mean is more sensitive to extreme values, whereas median is more robust to extreme values. For example, if the only change in the distribution of per capita expenditure is at the highest quintile or the lowest quintile, the change would be reflected by the mean, but the median would not change. In contrast, in certain situations, when changes occur in the middle of the distribution, mean per capita expenditures may remain unaltered, but the median may reflect the change.

It is important to analyze and understand the growth in both these measures of central tendency. However, changes in different measures of central tendency do not provide enough information about the change in the overall distribution. They do not tell us how the spread or inequality within the distribution changes over time, which can be captured by an inequality measure. In the above exercise, rural mean and median per capita expenditure increased, but rural inequality marginally fell. On the contrary, the urban inequality has increased over these three years from 33.5 in 2003 *[1,G]* to 35.6 in 2006 *[1,H]*, while the mean and median have fallen.

Overall Poverty

Table 3.2 examines the performance of groups of people considered poor. It analyzes poverty in Georgia by decomposing across rural and urban areas using three different poverty measures: headcount ratio, poverty gap measure, and squared gap measure. These three poverty measures belong to the FGT (Foster-Greer-Thorbecke) family of poverty measures. Table rows denote three geographic regions: urban, rural, and all of Georgia (rows 3 and 6). The variable is monthly per capita consumption expenditure in lari. There are two poverty lines: GEL 75.4 per month and GEL 45.2 per month.

Columns A and B report headcount ratios for 2003 and 2006, respectively. A region's *headcount ratio* is the proportion of the population that is poor compared to that region's total population. When the poverty line is GEL 75.4 per month, then the urban headcount ratio in 2003 is 28.1 percent [1,A]. This means that 28.1 percent of the population in the urban area belongs to households that cannot afford the per capita consumption expenditure of GEL 75.4 per month. The urban headcount ratio for 2006 is 30.8 percent [1,B]. Column C reports the change in urban headcount ratios over the course of these three years, which is an increase of 2.7 percentage points [1,C].

In contrast, the rural headcount ratio decreased by 0.5 percentage point from 31.6 percent [2,A] in 2003 to 31.1 percent [2,B] in 2006. Overall, Georgia's poverty headcount has increased by 1.0 percentage point from 29.9 percent [3,A] to 31.0 percent [3,B]. Similarly, for the poverty line of

Table 3.2: Overall Poverty

percent

	Region	Headcount ratio			Poverty gap measure			Squared gap measure		
		2003	2006	Change	2003	2006	Change	2003	2006	Change
		A	B	C	D	E	F	G	H	I
	Poverty line = GEL 75.4									
1	Urban	28.1	30.8	2.7	8.6	9.3	0.7	3.9	4.0	0.1
2	Rural	31.6	31.1	−0.5	10.7	10.9	0.2	5.2	5.5	0.3
3	**Total**	**29.9**	**31.0**	**1.0**	**9.7**	**10.1**	**0.4**	**4.6**	**4.8**	**0.2**
	Poverty line = GEL 45.2									
4	Urban	8.9	9.3	0.4	2.4	2.4	0.0	1.0	1.0	−0.1
5	Rural	11.4	12.1	0.7	3.6	4.0	0.3	1.7	1.9	0.2
6	**Total**	**10.2**	**10.7**	**0.5**	**3.0**	**3.2**	**0.2**	**1.4**	**1.4**	**0.1**

Source: Based on ADePT Poverty and Inequality modules using Integrated Household Survey of Georgia 2003 and 2006.

GEL 45.2 per month, Georgia's headcount ratio increased from 10.2 percent in 2003 [6,A] to 10.7 percent in 2006 [6,B]. The rural headcount ratio in this case increased from 11.4 percent [5,A] to 12.1 percent [5,B]. This change implies that the proportion of extreme poor (per capita expenditure below GEL 45.2) in the rural area increased, but the proportion of nonextreme poor (per capita expenditure between GEL 45.2 and GEL 75.4) decreased.

Columns D, E, and F analyze the poverty gap measure in 2003 and 2006. The poverty gap measure lies between a minimum of 0 and a maximum of 100, where the minimum is when no one in a region is poor and the maximum is when everyone has zero consumption expenditure and the poverty line is positive. When the poverty line is GEL 75.4, the urban area's poverty gap measure is 8.6 in 2003 [1,D], which increases by 0.7 to 9.3 in 2006 [1,E]. Likewise, the rural area's poverty gap measure increases by 0.2 from 10.7 in 2003 [2,D] to 10.9 in 2006 [2,E]. The total increase in poverty gap measure is 0.4 from 9.7 [3,D] to 10.1 [3,E]. When the poverty line is GEL 45.2, the overall poverty gap measure increases by 0.2 from 3.0 in 2003 [6,D] to 3.2 in 2006 [6,E].

Columns G, H, and I analyze the squared gap measure. The squared gap measure also lies between a minimum of 0 and a maximum of 100, where the minimum is when no one in a region is poor and the maximum is when everyone has zero consumption expenditure and the poverty line is positive. This measure is sensitive to inequality across the poor. Column I shows that the rural area's squared gap measure when the poverty line is GEL 75.4 increased by 0.3 from 5.2 in 2003 [2,G] to 5.5 in 2006 [2,H]. For the rural area it increased by 0.1 point from 3.9 [1,G] to 4.0 [1,H]. A similar pattern of changes is visible for the lower poverty line.

Lessons for Policy Makers

Consider the situation when the poverty line is GEL 75.4. From column C, one can see that the headcount ratio increased in the urban area by 2.7 percentage points and it decreased in the rural area by 0.5 percentage point. In other words, the rural area performed better than the urban area in reducing the proportion of poor people.

However, when we look at the poverty gap numbers, we see a different scenario. It turns out, in fact, from column F that the poverty gaps for both regions have registered increases, with the urban area registering a larger increase (0.7 point increase in the urban area compared with 0.2 point increase in the rural area). Thus, although the number of poor in the rural area decreased, the same is not true when deprivation is measured in terms of the average relative shortfall. Column F still reflects that the increase in the rural poverty gap is lower than that of its urban counterpart. But column I shows that the increase in the squared gap measure is larger in the rural area (0.3) than in the urban area (0.2), which implies that inequality among the rural poor has been sufficiently high that despite a fall in the headcount ratio, the increase in the squared gap measure is larger than that in the urban area.

The change in the rural area's headcount ratio is quite different when the poverty line is GEL 45.2 per month. The increase in rural poverty is much higher than the increase in urban poverty by all three measures. In fact, the squared gap measure slightly decreases for the urban area. We conclude from this result that the situation for the rural area's extreme poor has actually worsened in 2006 compared with 2003.

Distribution of Poor across Rural and Urban Areas

Table 3.3 analyzes the distribution of population and poor people across rural and urban areas. Table rows denote three geographic regions: urban, rural, and all of Georgia (rows 3 and 6). The variable is per capita consumption expenditure in l per month. There are two poverty lines: GEL 75.4 per month and GEL 45.2 per month.

Columns A, B, and C analyze the headcount ratio, that is, the population percentage that is poor. Columns A and B report the headcount ratio

Table 3.3: Distribution of Poor in Urban and Rural Areas
percent

	Region	Headcount ratio			Distribution of the poor			Distribution of population		
		2003	2006	Change	2003	2006	Change	2003	2006	Change
		A	B	C	D	E	F	G	H	I
	Poverty Line = GEL 75.4									
1	Urban	28.1	30.8	2.7	45.6	48.6	3.0	48.5	48.9	0.3
2	Rural	31.6	31.1	−0.5	54.4	51.4	−3.0	51.5	51.1	−0.3
3	**Total**	**29.9**	**31.0**	**1.0**	**100.0**	**100.0**	**0.0**	**100.0**	**100.0**	**0.0**
	Poverty Line = GEL 45.2									
4	Urban	8.9	9.3	0.4	42.4	42.3	−0.1	48.5	48.9	0.3
5	Rural	11.4	12.1	0.7	57.6	57.7	0.1	51.5	51.1	−0.3
6	**Total**	**10.2**	**10.7**	**0.5**	**100.0**	**100.0**	**0.0**	**100.0**	**100.0**	**0.0**

Source: Based on ADePT Poverty and Inequality modules using Integrated Household Survey of Georgia 2003 and 2006.

for the years 2003 and 2006, respectively, while column C reports the difference across these two years. Columns D, E, and F report the distribution of poor people across rural and urban areas, with the number in the cell being the proportion of poor people located in that region. Another way of seeing this is as the region's percentage contribution to poverty, or the headcount ratio times the share of the region's overall population divided by the overall headcount ratio. Columns G, H, and I provide the population distribution across rural and urban areas, or the percentage of the overall population residing in that region.

The headcount ratio for the urban area's population in 2003 is 28.1 percent [1,A]. In other words, 28.1 percent of the urban area population is poor. The headcount ratio increased for urban Georgia in 2006 to 30.8 percent [1,B].

Of all poor people in Georgia in 2003, 45.6 percent [1,D] reside in urban areas. The share of all poor people living in urban areas increases to 48.6 percent in 2006 [1,E]. This represents an increase of 3.0 percentage points [1,F]. The shares of rural and urban area population do not change much over the course of the three years. But when the poverty line is GEL 75.4 per month, the share of poor in urban areas increases in 2006 because of the increase in headcount ratio.

Lessons for Policy Makers

This exercise has a very useful policy implication because the headcount ratio does not provide any information about where most poor people live. A region may have a lower headcount ratio, but if that region is highly populated, then the number of poor may be high. Thus, policies should focus on regions with high headcount ratios as well as regions with larger shares of poor.

Composition of the FGT Family of Indices

Table 3.4 analyzes the composition of poverty figures reported in table 3.2. Table rows denote three geographic regions: urban, rural, and all of Georgia (rows 3 and 6). The variable is per capita consumption expenditure in lari per month. There are two poverty lines: GEL 75.4 Lari per month and GEL 45.2 Lari per month.

A Unified Approach to Measuring Poverty and Inequality

Table 3.4: Composition of FGT Family of Indices by Geography

	Region	Headcount ratio (%)	Income gap ratio	Poverty gap measure	GE(2) among the poor	Squared gap measure
		A	B	C	D	E
	Poverty line = GEL 75.4					
				2003		
1	Urban	28.1	30.5	8.6	4.6	3.9
2	Rural	31.6	33.7	10.7	5.9	5.2
3	**Total**	**29.9**	**32.3**	**9.7**	**5.3**	**4.6**
				2006		
4	Urban	30.8	30.1	9.3	4.1	4.0
5	Rural	31.1	34.9	10.9	6.4	5.5
6	**Total**	**31.0**	**32.6**	**10.1**	**5.3**	**4.8**
	Poverty line = GEL 45.2					
				2003		
7	Urban	8.9	26.8	2.4	4.0	1.0
8	Rural	11.4	31.8	3.6	5.3	1.7
9	**Total**	**10.2**	**29.7**	**3.0**	**4.7**	**1.4**
				2006		
10	Urban	9.3	25.7	2.4	3.3	1.0
11	Rural	12.1	32.7	4.0	5.7	1.9
12	**Total**	**10.7**	**29.7**	**3.2**	**4.7**	**1.4**

Source: Based on ADePT Poverty and Inequality modules using Integrated Household Survey of Georgia 2003 and 2006.

The headcount ratio reports the proportion of people within a region who are poor. The poverty gap measure and the squared gap measure can be broken down as follows:

- The poverty gap measure is the headcount ratio multiplied by the income gap ratio divided by 100.
- The income gap ratio is the average per capita expenditure shortfall from the poverty line divided by the poverty line.

The squared gap (P_{SG}) can be decomposed into three factors: headcount ratio (P_H), income gap ratio (P_{IG}), and generalized entropy measure (G_E) for $\alpha = 2$ among the poor, such that $P_{SG} = P_H [P_{IG}^2 + 2(1 - P_{IG})^2 I_{GE} (x; 2)]$.

These measures make possible a richer set of information for policy analysis. An improvement in the poverty gap measure may result from a reduction in the number of poor or a reduction in the average normalized gap among the poor. Similarly, an improvement in the squared coefficient of variation may result from a decrease in the number of poor, a decrease in the average normalized gap among the poor, or a decrease in inequality among the poor in terms of the generalized entropy measure.

For the GEL 75.4 per month poverty line, the poverty gap measure for Georgia increased from 9.7 in 2003 [3,C] to 10.1 in 2006 [6,C]. This increase comes from both a headcount ratio increase from 29.9 percent [3,A] to 31.0 percent [6,A] and an income gap ratio increase from 32.3 [3,B] to 32.6 [6,B]. However, the urban poverty gap measure increase derives from an increase in the headcount ratio and a reduction in the income gap ratio. In contrast, the rural poverty gap measure increase was a result of an increase in the income gap ratio because the rural headcount ratio fell slightly between 2003 and 2006.

Some interesting results are also evident when the poverty line is set at GEL 45.2 per month. The urban poverty gap measure does not change because an increase in the number of poor has been offset by an income gap ratio decrease. In fact, the total poverty gap measure increase from 3.0 in 2003 [9,C] to 3.2 in 2006 [12,C] was caused solely by an increase in the headcount ratio from 10.2 percent [9,A] to 10.7 percent [12,A], because the income gap ratio remained unchanged at 29.7 [9,B] and [12,B].

Lessons for Policy Makers

The squared gap measure depends on another component: inequality among the poor. Surprisingly, inequality among the poor does not change between 2003 and 2006 for both the higher and the lower poverty lines. For both poverty lines and both years, inequality among the poor is higher in the rural area. Thus, not only does the number of rural poor increase when the poverty line is GEL 45.2, but also the average normalized shortfalls and inequality across the poor go up.

Quantile Incomes and Quantile Ratios

Besides analyzing poverty, one must understand the situation of the relatively poor population compared to the rest of the population. Table 3.5 reports five quantile per capita expenditures (PCEs) and certain quantile ratios of per capita consumption expenditure for Georgia and its rural and urban areas. It compares two different periods: 2003 and 2006. Table rows denote three geographic regions: urban, rural, and all of Georgia

Table 3.5: Quantile PCEs and Quantile Ratios of Per Capita Consumption Expenditure

		Percentile					Quantile ratio			
		10th (GEL)	20th (GEL)	50th (median, GEL)	80th (GEL)	90th (GEL)	90-10	80-20	90-50	50-10
	Region	A	B	C	D	E	F	G	H	I
					2003					
1	Urban	47.4	64.1	108.4	182.1	229.6	79.3	64.8	52.8	56.3
2	Rural	42.2	58.8	101.5	173.1	230.0	81.6	66.0	55.9	58.4
3	**Total**	**44.8**	**61.4**	**104.7**	**177.0**	**229.8**	**80.5**	**65.3**	**54.4**	**57.3**
					2006					
4	Urban	46.7	61.2	101.1	174.0	231.3	79.8	64.8	56.3	53.8
5	Rural	41.0	58.5	105.3	175.9	229.1	82.1	66.8	54.0	61.1
6	**Total**	**43.8**	**59.8**	**103.3**	**175.0**	**230.5**	**81.0**	**65.8**	**55.2**	**57.6**

Source: Based on ADePT Poverty and Inequality modules using Integrated Household Survey of Georgia 2003 and 2006.
Note: PCE = per capita expenditure.

(rows 3 and 6). Per capita consumption expenditure is measured in lari per month.

Columns A through E denote quantile PCE for five percentiles. Column A denotes the quantile PCE at the 10th percentile, column B denotes the quantile PCE at the 20th percentile, and so forth. Columns F through I report the quantile ratios based on the quantile PCE reported in the first five columns. Column F, for example, reports the 90/10 ratio, computed as (quantile PCE at the 90th percentile – quantile PCE at the 10th percentile) / quantile PCE at the 90th percentile. The larger the 90/10 ratio, the larger is the gap between these two percentiles.

In 2003, the quantile PCE at the 10th percentile of Georgia is GEL 44.8 [3,A], implying that 10 percent of the Georgian population lives with per capita consumption expenditure less than 44.8. Similarly, 20 percent of the Georgian population lives with per capita consumption expenditure less than 61.4 [3,B]. In contrast, 10 percent of the Georgian population lives with per capita expenditure more than GEL 229.8 [3,E], which is the 90th percentile.

The corresponding 90/10 quantile ratio using these two quantile PCEs is 80.5 [3,F], which means that the gap between the two percentiles is 80.5 percent of the quantile PCE at the 90th percentile. Stated another way, the quantile PCE at the 90th percentile is 100 / (100 – 80.5) = 5.1 times larger than the 10th percentile. Likewise, the quantile PCE at the 80th percentile of Georgia is GEL 177.0 [3,D], which is nearly three times larger than the quantile PCE at the 20th percentile [3,B]. The corresponding 80/20 measure is 65.3 [3,G]. Inequality between the quantile PCE at the 90th percentile per capita expenditure and the quantile PCE at the 10th percentile is larger in the rural area (81.6 [2,F]) than in the urban area (79.3 [1,F]) in 2003. The 90/10 measure increases for Georgia and both its urban and rural areas in 2006 [4,F] and [5,A].

Lessons for Policy Makers

This table is helpful in holistically understanding inequality across the per capita consumption expenditure distribution. The mean and median are measures of a distribution's central tendency and the distribution's size, while the Gini coefficient is a single measure of the overall distribution that does not provide any information about which part of the distribution changed.

The four additional quantile PCEs reported in table 3.5 provide information about different parts of the distribution. For example, the Gini coefficient analysis in table 3.1 shows that inequality in the rural area has decreased, whereas inequality in the urban area has increased. Which part of the distribution is responsible for such changes? The Gini coefficient does not provide an answer to this question. A decrease in inequality in the rural area has not been obtained by increasing the income of the poorest because the quantile PCE at the 10th percentile in the rural area fell to GEL 41.0 in 2006 [5,A] compared to GEL 42.2 in 2003 [2,A]. The quantile PCE at the 80th percentile increased from GEL 173.1 in 2003 [2,D] to GEL 175.9 in 2006 [5,D]. In other words, even though the Gini coefficient fell, inequality between the quantile PCEs at the 80th percentile and the 20th percentile increased in the rural area: from 66.0 in 2003 [2,G] to 66.8 in 2006 [5,G], according to the 80/20 measure.

Partial Means and Partial Mean Ratios

Table 3.6 reports two lower partial means, two upper partial means, and two partial mean ratios, based on the partial means between two periods: 2003 and 2006. Table rows denote three geographic regions: urban, rural, and all of Georgia (rows 3 and 6). Per capita consumption expenditure is measured in lari per month.

Columns A and B report two lower partial means (LPM), columns C and D report two upper partial means (UPM), and columns E and F report partial mean ratios. The first partial mean ratio, for example, reports the 90/10 partial mean ratio, computed as (90th percentile UPM – 10th percentile

A Unified Approach to Measuring Poverty and Inequality

Table 3.6: Partial Means and Partial Mean Ratios

		Lower partial mean		Upper partial mean		Partial mean ratio	
		10th percentile (GEL)	20th percentile (GEL)	90th percentile (GEL)	80th percentile (GEL)	90-10	80-20
	Region	A	B	C	D	E	F
				2003			
1	Urban	34.5	45.2	319.5	261.8	89.2	82.7
2	Rural	29.0	39.9	321.3	259.1	91.0	84.6
3	**Total**	**31.5**	**42.3**	**320.4**	**260.5**	**90.2**	**83.8**
				2006			
4	Urban	34.5	44.3	347.7	273.5	90.1	83.8
5	Rural	27.8	39.0	317.0	258.2	91.2	84.9
6	**Total**	**30.8**	**41.6**	**332.0**	**265.7**	**90.7**	**84.4**

Source: Based on ADePT Poverty and Inequality modules using Integrated Household Survey of Georgia 2003 and 2006.

LPM) / 90th percentile UPM). The larger the 90/10 ratio, the larger is the gap between these two partial means.

A lower partial mean is the average per capita expenditure of all people below a specific percentile cutoff. An upper partial mean is the mean per capita expenditure above a specific percentile. A partial mean ratio captures inequality between a lower partial mean and an upper partial mean.

It is evident from the table that the average per capita expenditure of the urban Georgian population's poorest 20 percent is only GEL 45.2 in 2003 [1,B], whereas the average income of the population's richest 20 percent is GEL 261.8 [1,D]. The corresponding 80/20 partial mean ratio is 82.7 [1,F], which means that the gap between the two partial means is 82.7 percent of the 80th upper partial mean. Stated another way, the mean per capita expenditure of the population's richest 20 percent is 100 / (100 − 82.7) = 5.8 times larger than the mean per capita expenditure of the population's poorest 20 percent. Likewise, in rural areas, the mean per capita expenditure of the population's richest 20 percent (GEL 259.1 [2,D]) is 6.5 times larger than the mean per capita expenditure of the population's poorest 20 percent (GEL 39.9 [2,B]) in 2003. The corresponding 80/20 partial mean ratio is 84.6 [2,F].

Lessons for Policy Makers

In table 3.5, we reported different percentiles of a distribution. For example, the 10th percentile for Georgia in 2003 is GEL 44.8 [3,A], meaning that

10 percent of the Georgian population lives with a per capita expenditure less than GEL 44.8. But what is the average income of these people? Similarly in table 3.5, 10 percent of the Georgian population has a per capita expenditure more than GEL 229.8 *[3,E]*, which is the 90th percentile for Georgia, but we do not know exactly how rich this group is. Partial means are useful for answering this question, and the partial mean ratios tell us the difference in the average per capita expenditures between a poorer and a richer group.

Distribution of Population across Quintiles

Table 3.7 analyzes the population distribution in Georgia and its rural and urban areas across five quintiles of per capita consumption expenditure. It compares two time periods: 2003 and 2006. Table rows denote three geographic regions: urban, rural, and all of Georgia (row *1*). Per capita consumption expenditure is measured in lari per month. Each of the five columns denotes a quintile. Column A denotes the lowest, or first, quintile, column B denotes the second quintile, and so forth.

All cells in row *1* have a value of 20, obtained by dividing Georgia's entire population into five equal groups in terms of per capita expenditure. Each group contains 20 percent of the population. The fifth quintile contains the richest 20 percent of the population, the fourth quintile consists of the second-richest 20 percent of the population, and so on, and the first quintile consists of the poorest 20 percent of the population.

Table 3.7: Distribution of Population across Quintiles
percent

		Quintile				
		First	*Second*	*Third*	*Fourth*	*Fifth*
	Region	A	B	C	D	E
1	Total	20.0	20.0	20.0	20.0	20.0
		2003				
2	Urban	18.1	19.6	20.4	20.8	21.1
3	Rural	21.8	20.4	19.6	19.2	19.0
		2006				
4	Urban	19.0	21.6	20.6	19.2	19.7
5	Rural	21.0	18.5	19.4	20.8	20.3

Source: Based on ADePT Poverty and Inequality modules using Integrated Household Survey of Georgia 2003 and 2006.

Rows 2 and 3 report the population distribution in urban and rural areas for 2003 using the national quintiles. Consider the value 18.1 [2,A] in the urban row. This value implies that 18.1 percent of the total urban population falls in the first quintile. The next cell is 19.6 [2,B], meaning that 19.6 percent of the total urban population falls in the second quintile. Similarly, 21.1 percent [2,E] of the total urban population falls in the fifth quintile.

The picture is slightly different for the rural area, where 19.0 percent [3,E] of the total rural population falls in the fifth quintile and 21.8 percent [3,A] falls in the lowest quintile. In 2006, the urban population share in the first two quintiles increased to 19.0 percent [4,A] and 21.6 percent [4,B], respectively, but the rural population share in the same two quintiles decreased to 21.0 percent [5,A] and 18.5 percent [5,B], respectively. In contrast, the rural population share in the two highest quintiles increased, [3,D] and [3,E] compared with [5,D] and [5,E], but the urban population share in the two highest quintiles decreased, [2,D] and [2,E] compared with [4,D] and [4,E].

Lessons for Policy Makers

This table is helpful in understanding the population's mobility across different consumption expenditure levels in different regions. A single welfare measure—inequality or poverty—cannot reflect this mobility.

Analysis at the Subnational Level

Analyses in the previous section concentrate at the national level and across rural and urban areas. For better policy implementation, we need to understand the results at a more disaggregated level, such as across subnational or geographic regions, or across population groups having different characteristics.

In this section, we conduct subnational analysis, and in the next section, we conduct analysis across other population subgroups. Some tables here are similar to tables discussed in the previous section, and we occasionally refer to those tables.

During the analysis across population subgroups, we assume the poverty line to be the same across all subgroups. However, in the ADePT program different poverty lines can be used for different subgroups in the analyses.

Standard of Living and Inequality

Table 3.8 results from calculating the mean and median per capita consumption expenditure, and the Gini coefficient, for Georgia's subnational regions. Columns A and B report the mean per capita consumption expenditure for years 2003 and 2006, respectively. Column C reports the percentage change or growth in per capita expenditure over the course of these three years.

The mean per capita expenditure decreases for some regions (such as Kakheti [1,C], Tbilisi [2,C], and Imereti [9,C]) and increases for others (such as Shida Kartli [3,C], Kvemo Kartli [4,C], and Samtskhe-Javakheti [5,C]). Imereti registers the steepest fall (7.0 percent [9,C]) in mean per capita consumption expenditure, from GEL 150.3 in 2003 [9,A] to GEL 139.9 in 2006 [9,B]. In contrast, Kvemo Kartli reflects the highest increase in mean per capita expenditure, 16.1 percent [4,C]. It increased from GEL 93.5 in 2003 [4,A] to GEL 108.5 in 2006 [4,B].

Columns D, E, and F report median per capita expenditures and their growth. Although the change in overall median is −1.4 percent [11,F] (much larger than the change in overall mean), changes in subnational regions are mixed. For Kvemo Kartli, the growths of mean and median are almost the same [4,C] and [4,F]. For Samtskhe-Javakheti, the growth in mean [5,C] is three times larger than the growth of median [5,F]. In contrast, the growth

Table 3.8: Mean and Median Per Capita Income, Growth, and the Gini Coefficient across Subnational Regions

	Region	Mean 2003 (GEL)	Mean 2006 (GEL)	Mean Growth (%)	Median 2003 (GEL)	Median 2006 (GEL)	Median Growth (%)	Gini 2003	Gini 2006	Gini Change (%)
		A	B	C	D	E	F	G	H	I
1	Kakheti	107.9	102.2	−5.2	92.7	80.4	−13.2	34.4	38.5	4.0
2	Tbilisi	144.5	143.1	−0.9	122.2	111.4	−8.8	32.1	36.4	4.3
3	Shida Kartli	122.9	125.6	2.3	98.7	101.7	3.0	36.6	35.9	−0.7
4	Kvemo Kartli	93.5	108.5	16.1	81.0	94.1	16.2	32.6	32.7	0.1
5	Samtskhe-Javakheti	116.5	121.5	4.3	98.8	100.3	1.5	32.9	31.1	−1.8
6	Ajara	107.8	101.8	−5.6	91.6	83.3	−9.0	33.9	34.4	0.4
7	Guria	134.3	125.6	−6.5	113.9	101.3	−11.1	33.9	35.0	1.1
8	Samegrelo	117.2	125.1	6.7	97.0	109.5	12.8	34.1	32.3	−1.9
9	Imereti	150.3	139.9	−7.0	128.6	122.4	−4.8	33.0	32.9	−0.1
10	Mtskheta-Mtianeti	113.0	123.6	9.3	103.7	96.7	−6.7	33.5	37.4	3.9
11	**Total**	**126.1**	**126.0**	**−0.1**	**104.7**	**103.3**	**−1.4**	**34.4**	**35.4**	**0.9**

Source: Based on ADePT Poverty and Inequality modules using Integrated Household Survey of Georgia 2003 and 2006.

of median in Samegrelo *[8,F]* is twice as large as the growth of mean per capita consumption expenditure *[8,C]*. The most interesting pattern can be seen for Mtskheta-Mtianeti, where the mean grows by 9.3 percent *[10,C]*, but the median falls by 6.7 percent *[10,F]*.

Columns *G*, *H*, and *I* analyze inequality within subnational regions using the Gini coefficient, which lies between 0 and 100. Although the overall Gini coefficient has increased by 0.9 *[11,I]*, a mixed picture is found across subnational regions. In Tbilisi and Kakheti, inequality rises by 4.3 percent *[2,I]* and 4.0 percent *[1,I]*, respectively. In Samtskhe-Javakheti, inequality falls by 1.8 percent *[5,I]*, while in Kvemo Kartli and Imereti, the Gini coefficient changes by a meager 0.1 *[5,I]* and *[9,I]*, going up and down, respectively.

Headcount Ratio and the Distribution of Poor

Table 3.9 analyzes the headcount ratio of Georgia by population subgroup, where each subgroup is classified by subnational regions—such as Kakheti, Ajara, and Imereti—which could be states or provinces. The poverty line for this table is GEL 75.4 per month (we use only one poverty line here, but the analysis could be conducted for any number of poverty lines).

Table 3.9: Headcount Ratio by Subnational Regions, 2003 and 2006
percent

		Headcount ratio			Distribution of the poor			Distribution of population		
		2003	*2006*	*Change*	*2003*	*2006*	*Change*	*2003*	*2006*	*Change*
	Region	A	B	C	D	E	F	G	H	I
	Poverty line = GEL 75.4									
1	Kakheti	38.9	46.2	7.3	12.6	13.8	1.3	9.7	9.3	−0.4
2	Tbilisi	20.9	25.2	4.3	17.1	20.4	3.3	24.6	25.2	0.6
3	Shida Kartli	35.2	30.8	−4.5	8.3	7.2	−1.1	7.0	7.2	0.2
4	Kvemo Kartli	44.4	35.1	−9.3	16.8	12.2	−4.6	11.3	10.8	−0.5
5	Samtskhe-Javakheti	30.0	24.4	−5.7	4.6	3.8	−0.8	4.6	4.8	0.2
6	Ajara	37.1	44.6	7.5	10.7	13.7	2.9	8.7	9.5	0.8
7	Guria	25.3	34.4	9.2	2.7	3.5	0.7	3.2	3.1	−0.1
8	Samegrelo	33.5	29.4	−4.1	11.8	9.0	−2.8	10.5	9.5	−1.1
9	Imereti	20.6	23.0	2.3	12.1	13.4	1.3	17.5	18.0	0.5
10	Mtskheta-Mtianeti	34.3	35.2	0.9	3.3	3.1	−0.2	2.9	2.7	−0.2
11	**Total**	**29.9**	**31.0**	**1.0**	**100.0**	**100.0**	**n.a.**	**100.0**	**100.0**	**n.a.**

Source: Based on ADePT Poverty and Inequality modules using Integrated Household Survey of Georgia 2003 and 2006.
Note: n.a. = not applicable.

Table rows list subnational regions. Columns A, B, and C analyze headcount ratios. Columns D, E, and F outline the distribution of poor people across the subgroups, with the number in the cell being the proportion of all poor people in the country that are included in that subgroup. Another way of seeing this is the percentage contribution of the subgroup to overall poverty, or the headcount ratio times the population share in that group, divided by the overall headcount ratio. Columns G, H, and I depict the population distribution in subnational regions, or the percentage of the population that resides in that region. Row 11 shows that the overall headcount ratio increases from 29.9 percent in 2003 [11,A] to 31.0 percent in 2006 [11,B], reflecting a 1.0 percentage point (rounded) increase.

In cell [1,A], we find that in 2003, 38.9 percent of the population in Kakheti is poor. In other words, the headcount ratio for this population subgroup is 38.9 percent. Cell [1,B] is 46.2, the headcount ratio for the same population subgroup in 2006. Thus, the headcount increased by 7.3 percentage points [1,C] over the course of these three years. In row 4, we see that Kvemo Kartli's headcount ratio decreased by 9.3 percentage points, from 44.4 percent [4,A] to 35.1 percent [4,B]. The headcount ratio also fell between 2003 and 2006 in other regions, such as Shida Kartli [3,C] and Samtskhe-Javakheti [5,C].

Cell [1,D] is 12.6, meaning that of all poor people in Georgia in 2003, 12.6 percent can be found in Kakheti. The share of all poor living in Kakheti increases to 13.8 percent in 2006 [1,E], an increase of 1.3 percentage points.

Now compare Kvemo Kartli and Imereti. Clearly, Kvemo Kartli's poverty headcount ratio (44.4 percent [4,A]) is more than twice as large as Imereti's poverty headcount ratio (20.6 percent [9,A]) in 2003. However, the share of all poor people is only around 40 percent larger in Kvemo Kartli (16.8 percent in Kvemo Kartli [4,D], compared with 12.1 percent in Imereti [9,D]). This is due to the different population shares of the two regions as given in the table's final columns. The population share living in Imereti in 2003 is 17.5 percent [9,G], while the Kvemo Kartli share is only 11.3 percent [4,G]. Therefore, a policy maker should take into account a region's population share in addition to the headcount ratio, because a region may have a lower headcount ratio because of a higher number of poor.

Poverty Gap Measure and Subnational Contribution to Overall Poverty

Table 3.10 analyzes Georgia's poverty gap measure across subnational regions. The poverty line is GEL 75.4 per month. Table rows list subnational regions. Columns A, B, and C analyze poverty gap measures for 2003, 2006, and the changes over time. Columns D, E, and F report the percentage contribution of the subnational regions to the overall poverty gap measure. Columns G, H, and I depict the population distribution of the subnational regions, or the percentage of the overall population that resides in each region.

The overall poverty gap measure increases from 9.7 in 2003 [11,A] to 10.1 in 2006 [11,B], reflecting a 0.4 point increase [11,C]. For Kakheti, the poverty gap measure in 2003 is 13.4 [1,A]. The poverty gap measure for the same population subgroup in 2006 is 17.8 [1,B]. Thus, the poverty gap measure increased by 4.4 points [1,C] over three years. The poverty gap measure in Kvemo Kartli decreased by 3.5 points, from 15.4 in 2003 [4,A] to 11.9 in 2006 [4,B]. The poverty gap measure also fell between 2003 and 2006 in other regions, such as Samegrelo [8,C] and Mtskheta-Mtianeti [10,C]. Kakheti's contribution to the overall poverty gap measure is 13.4 percent [1,D]. Its contribution increased to 16.3 percent in 2006 [1,E], an increase of 2.9 percentage points [1,F].

Table 3.10: Poverty Gap Measure by Subnational Regions

	Region	Poverty gap measure			Contribution to overall poverty (%)			Distribution of population (%)		
		2003	2006	Change	2003	2006	Change	2003	2006	Change
		A	B	C	D	E	F	G	H	I
	Poverty line = GEL 75.4									
1	Kakheti	13.4	17.8	4.4	13.4	16.3	2.9	9.7	9.3	−0.4
2	Tbilisi	5.5	7.3	1.8	14.0	18.2	4.2	24.6	25.2	0.6
3	Shida Kartli	11.7	10.9	−0.8	8.5	7.8	−0.7	7.0	7.2	0.2
4	Kvemo Kartli	15.4	11.9	−3.5	18.1	12.8	−5.3	11.3	10.8	−0.5
5	Samtskhe-Javakheti	10.0	6.6	−3.4	4.7	3.2	−1.6	4.6	4.8	0.2
6	Ajara	12.8	14.6	1.8	11.5	13.7	2.2	8.7	9.5	0.8
7	Guria	8.3	10.6	2.3	2.8	3.3	0.5	3.2	3.1	−0.1
8	Samegrelo	11.0	8.8	−2.2	12.0	8.2	−3.8	10.5	9.5	−1.1
9	Imereti	6.1	7.5	1.4	11.1	13.4	2.4	17.5	18.0	0.5
10	Mtskheta-Mtianeti	13.1	11.7	−1.4	3.9	3.1	−0.8	2.9	2.7	−0.2
11	**Total**	**9.7**	**10.1**	**0.4**	**100.0**	**100.0**	**n.a.**	**100.0**	**100.0**	**n.a.**

Source: Based on ADePT Poverty and Inequality modules using Integrated Household Survey of Georgia 2003 and 2006.
Note: n.a. = not applicable.

Now compare Guria and Imereti. Clearly, Guria's poverty gap measure (8.3 *[7,A]*) is larger than Imereti's poverty gap measure (6.1 *[9,A]*) in 2003. But Guria's contribution is only 2.8 percent *[7,D]*, whereas Imereti's contribution is 11.1 percent *[9,D]*. The contribution of subnational regions to the overall poverty gap and the share of poor in each region are quite different. The share of poor in each of Kakheti and Ajara is almost identical in 2006 (9.3 percent for Kakheti *[1,H]*, compared with 9.5 percent in Ajara *[6,H]*), but their contributions to the total poverty gap measure are quite different (16.3 percent in Kakheti *[1,E]*, compared with 13.7 percent in Ajara *[6,E]*). Thus, the average normalized shortfall of per capita expenditure from the poverty line is much higher in Kakheti, and that is not captured by the headcount ratio analysis.

Squared Gap Measure and Subnational Contribution to Overall Poverty

Table 3.11 analyzes Georgia's squared gap measure across subnational regions. The poverty line is GEL 75.4 per month. Table rows list subnational regions. Columns A, B, and C analyze the squared gap measure for 2003, 2006, and the difference over time. Columns *D, E,* and *F* report the

Table 3.11: Squared Gap Measure by Subnational Regions

Region	Squared gap measure			Contribution to overall poverty (%)			Distribution of population (%)		
	2003	2006	Change (%)	2003	2006	Change	2003	2006	Change
	A	B	C	D	E	F	G	H	I
Poverty line = GEL 75.4									
1 Kakheti	6.6	9.4	2.7	14.0	18.2	4.2	9.7	9.3	−0.4
2 Tbilisi	2.1	3.0	0.9	11.4	15.9	4.6	24.6	25.2	0.6
3 Shida Kartli	6.0	5.5	−0.6	9.3	8.2	−1.1	7.0	7.2	0.2
4 Kvemo Kartli	7.8	6.2	−1.7	19.4	13.9	−5.5	11.3	10.8	−0.5
5 Samtskhe-Javakheti	4.8	2.8	−2.0	4.8	2.9	−1.9	4.6	4.8	0.2
6 Ajara	6.4	6.8	0.5	12.1	13.6	1.5	8.7	9.5	0.8
7 Guria	3.7	4.6	0.9	2.6	3.0	0.4	3.2	3.1	−0.1
8 Samegrelo	5.2	3.7	−1.4	11.9	7.4	−4.5	10.5	9.5	−1.1
9 Imereti	2.7	3.6	0.9	10.3	13.6	3.3	17.5	18.0	0.5
10 Mtskheta-Mtianeti	6.8	5.9	−0.8	4.2	3.3	−0.9	2.9	2.7	−0.2
11 Total	4.6	4.8	0.2	100.0	100.0	n.a.	100.0	100.0	n.a.

Source: Based on ADePT Poverty and Inequality modules using Integrated Household Survey of Georgia 2003 and 2006.
Note: n.a. = not applicable.

percentage contribution of the subnational regions to the overall squared gap measure. Columns G, H, and I depict the population distribution of the subnational regions, or the percentage of the overall population that resides in each region. Row 11 shows that the overall squared gap measure increased from 4.6 in 2003 [11,A] to 4.8 in 2006 [11,B], reflecting a 0.2 point increase [11,C].

The squared gap measure for Kakheti is 6.6 in 2003 [1,A]. The squared gap measure for the same population subgroup is 9.4 in 2006 [1,B]. Thus, the squared gap measure increased by 2.7 points in three years [1,C]. The squared gap measure in Kvemo Kartli decreased by 1.7 points, from 7.8 in 2003 [4,A] to 6.2 in 2006 [4,B]. The squared gap measure also fell between 2003 and 2006 in other regions, such as Samegrelo [8,C] and Mtskheta-Mtianeti [10,C]. Kakheti's contribution to the overall squared gap measure in 2003 is 14.0 percent [1,D]. The contribution increased to 18.2 percent in 2006 [1,E], an increase of 4.2 percentage points [1,F].

Lessons for Policy Makers

Comparing the contribution of subnational regions to the overall squared gap measure to the contribution to the overall squared gap measure and the share of poor in each region, we see they are not necessarily the same. Tbilisi's contribution to overall poverty in 2006 is larger than Kakheti's contribution when poverty is measured by headcount ratio and poverty gap measure, but Tbilisi's contribution is lower in 2006 (3.0 [2,B]) than that of Kakheti (9.4 [1,B]) when poverty is measured using the squared gap measure. This finding may reflect that inequality across the poor, captured by the squared normalized shortfalls, is much higher in Kakheti, and that is not captured by the analysis based on headcount ratio or poverty gap measure.

Quantile Incomes and Quantile Ratios

In addition to analyzing poverty, understanding how a population's poor segment compares to the rest of the population is important. Table 3.12 reports quantile per capita expenditure for five percentiles and certain quantile ratios of per capita consumption expenditure for Georgia's subnational regions in 2003. Each of the first five columns denotes a quantile PCE. Column A denotes the quantile PCE at the 10th percentile, column

Table 3.12: Quantile PCE and Quantile Ratio of Per Capita Consumption Expenditure, 2003

		Quantile PCE					Quantile ratio			
		10th percentile (GEL)	20th percentile (GEL)	50th percentile (median, GEL)	80th percentile (GEL)	90th percentile (GEL)	90-10 (%)	80-20 (%)	90-50 (%)	50-10 (%)
	Region	A	B	C	D	E	F	G	H	I
1	Kakheti	37.8	52.6	92.7	150.4	191.1	80.2	65.0	51.5	59.2
2	Tbilisi	56.0	74.3	122.2	202.8	252.9	77.9	63.3	51.7	54.2
3	Shida Kartli	38.6	55.9	98.7	169.8	228.4	83.1	67.1	56.8	60.9
4	Kvemo Kartli	34.3	48.3	81.0	126.5	165.1	79.2	61.8	51.0	57.7
5	Samtskhe-Javakheti	43.0	61.2	98.8	160.5	190.2	77.4	61.9	48.0	56.5
6	Ajara	37.8	53.1	91.6	146.5	203.3	81.4	63.7	54.9	58.7
7	Guria	47.7	64.0	113.9	189.1	241.9	80.3	66.1	52.9	58.1
8	Samegrelo	41.2	56.2	97.0	160.7	208.5	80.2	65.0	53.5	57.5
9	Imereti	54.0	74.1	128.6	211.6	267.0	79.8	65.0	51.8	58.0
10	Mtskheta-Mtianeti	33.9	52.5	103.7	162.0	200.1	83.1	67.6	48.2	67.3
11	**Total**	**44.8**	**61.4**	**104.7**	**177.0**	**229.8**	**80.5**	**65.3**	**54.4**	**57.3**

Source: Based on ADePT Poverty and Inequality modules using Integrated Household Survey of Georgia 2003 and 2006.
Note: PCE = per capita expenditure.

B denotes the quantile PCE at the 20th percentile, column C denotes the median, column D denotes the quantile PCE at the 80th percentile, and column E denotes the quantile PCE at the 90th percentile.

Columns F through I report the quantile ratios based on the quantiles reported in the first five columns. Column G, for example, reports the 80/20 ratio, computed as (quantile PCE at the 80th percentile – quantile PCE at the 20th percentile) / quantile PCE at the 80th percentile. The larger the 80/20 ratio, the larger is the gap between these two percentiles.

In 2003, the quantile PCE at the 10th percentile of Kakheti is 37.8 [1,A], which implies that 10 percent of the population in Kakheti lives with per capita consumption expenditure less than GEL 37.8. Similarly, 20 percent of Kakheti's population lives with per capita consumption expenditure less than GEL 52.6 [1,B]. In contrast, 10 percent of people in Kakheti live with per capita expenditure more than GEL 191.1 [1,E], the quantile PCE at the 90th percentile. The corresponding 90/10 measure using these two quantile PCEs is 80.2 [1,F], meaning that the gap between the two quantile PCEs is 80.2 percent of the quantile PCE at the 90th percentile. Described another way, the quantile PCE at the 90th percentile is 100 / (100 – 80.2) = 5.1 times larger than the quantile PCE at the 10th percentile.

Likewise, the quantile PCE at the 80th percentile of Kakheti is GEL 150.4 [1,D], nearly three times larger than the quantile PCE at the

20th percentile per capita expenditure *[1,B]*. It is evident that Shida Kartli has a lower quantile PCE at the 10th percentile than Samegrelo but a larger quantile PCE at the 90th percentile. As a result, the 90/10 quantile ratio of Shida Kartli *[3,F]* is higher than the 90/10 quantile ratio of Samegrelo *[8,F]*.

Lessons for Policy Makers

This table is helpful in holistically understanding inequality across the per capita consumption expenditure distribution. The mean and median measure a distribution's central tendency and measure. The Gini coefficient is a single measure of the overall distribution, but it does not provide any information about which part of the distribution has changed. The four additional quantile PCEs reported in the table provide further information about different parts of the distribution.

Partial Means and Partial Mean Ratios

Table 3.13 reports two lower partial means, two upper partial means, and two partial mean ratios for Georgia's subnational regions in 2003. Columns *A* and *B* report the two lower partial means, columns *C* and *D* report the two upper partial means, and columns *E* and *F* report the partial mean ratios. The first of the partial mean ratios, for example, reports the 90/10 partial

Table 3.13: Partial Means and Partial Mean Ratios for Subnational Regions, 2003

		Lower partial mean		Upper partial mean		Partial mean ratio (%)	
		p10	p20	p20	p10	90-10	80-20
	Region	A	B	C	D	E	F
1	Kakheti	25.6	35.9	222.3	276.0	90.7	83.8
2	Tbilisi	44.1	54.9	286.7	348.8	87.3	80.9
3	Shida Kartli	26.2	37.1	263.3	331.0	92.1	85.9
4	Kvemo Kartli	23.9	32.3	186.7	230.9	89.6	82.7
5	Samtskhe-Javakheti	30.5	41.5	234.4	294.8	89.6	82.3
6	Ajara	26.2	36.5	222.4	273.4	90.4	83.6
7	Guria	35.9	45.8	275.3	337.2	89.4	83.4
8	Samegrelo	30.8	40.1	241.1	302.9	89.8	83.4
9	Imereti	39.8	52.4	299.1	362.1	89.0	82.5
10	Mtskheta-Mtianeti	25.0	34.7	222.7	265.7	90.6	84.4
11	**Total**	**31.5**	**42.3**	**260.5**	**320.4**	**90.2**	**83.8**

Source: Based on ADePT Poverty and Inequality modules using Integrated Household Survey of Georgia 2003 and 2006.

mean ratio, computed as (90th percentile UPM – 10th percentile LPM) / 90th percentile UPM. The larger the 90/10 partial mean ratio, the larger is the gap between these two partial means.

A *lower partial mean* is the average per capita expenditure of all people below a specific percentile cutoff. An upper partial mean is the mean per capita expenditure above a specific percentile. A partial mean ratio captures inequality between a lower partial mean and an upper partial mean. In table 3.5, we reported a distribution's different quantile PCEs. For example, the quantile PCE at the 10th percentile of Georgia in 2003 was GEL 44.8, meaning that 10 percent of the Georgian population lives with per capita expenditure less than GEL 44.8. However, that does not tell us the average income of these people. Similarly, 10 percent of the Georgian population has per capita expenditure more than GEL 229.8, Georgia's quantile PCE at the 90th percentile, but we do not know exactly how rich this group is. Partial means are useful for determining these values, and partial mean ratios tell us the difference in the average per capita expenditures between a poorer and a richer group.

It is evident from table 3.13 that the average per capita expenditure of the poorest 20 percent of people in Ajara is only GEL 36.5 in 2003 [6,B], whereas the average income of the richest 20 percent of the population is GEL 222.4 [6,C]. The corresponding 80/20 partial mean ratio is 83.6 [6,F], meaning that the gap between the two partial means is 83.6 percent of the 80th upper partial mean. Stated another way, the mean per capita expenditure of the population's richest 20 percent is 100 / (100 – 83.6) = 6.1 times larger than the mean per capita expenditure of the population's poorest 20 percent. Likewise, in Shida Kartli, the mean per capita expenditure of the population's richest 20 percent (GEL 263.3 [3,C]) is 7.1 times larger than the mean per capita expenditure of the population's poorest 20 percent (GEL 37.1 [3,B]) in 2003. The corresponding 80/20 partial mean ratio is 85.9 [3,F].

Lessons for Policy Makers

A larger inequality in terms of the quantile ratio does not necessarily translate into higher inequality in terms of the partial mean ratio. In table 3.12, we found that the 80/20 quantile ratio for Imereti (65.0) was larger than that of Ajara (63.7), but in table 3.13 Ajara's 80/20 partial mean ratio (83.6 [3,F]) is slightly larger than Imereti's (82.5 [9,F]).

Distribution of Population across Quintiles by Subnational Region

Table 3.14 analyzes the population distribution in subnational regions across five quintiles of per capita consumption expenditure. Column *1* denotes the lowest or the first quintile, column *2* denotes the second quintile, and so forth.

All cells in row *1* have a value of 20, obtained by dividing Georgia's entire population into five equal-sized groups in terms of per capita expenditure. Each group contains 20 percent of the population. The fifth quintile contains the richest 20 percent of the population; the fourth quintile consists of the second-richest 20 percent of the population, and so on, and the first quintile consists of the poorest 20 percent of the population.

For the subnational regions, table cells report population percentage in each quintile. Consider the value 27.6 for Kakheti *[2,A]*. This value implies that 27.6 percent of Kakheti's population lives with per capita expenditure less than the first quintile. The next cell to the right is 20.9 *[2,B]*, implying that 20.9 percent of Kakheti's population falls in the second quintile. Similarly, only 12.5 percent *[2,E]* of Kakheti's population falls in the fifth quintile.

The picture is slightly different for Imereti, where only 13.3 percent *[10,A]* and 15.3 percent *[10,B]* of its population fall in the first and second

Table 3.14: Distribution of Population across Quintiles by Subnational Region, 2003

percentage of population

		Quintile				
		First	*Second*	*Third*	*Fourth*	*Fifth*
	Region	*A*	*B*	*C*	*D*	*E*
1	**Total**	**20.0**	**20.0**	**20.0**	**20.0**	**20.0**
2	Kakheti	27.6	20.9	20.8	18.3	12.5
3	Tbilisi	12.4	17.9	19.9	22.5	27.2
4	Shida Kartli	23.0	21.7	17.0	19.7	18.5
5	Kvemo Kartli	30.0	27.5	21.2	13.5	7.9
6	Samtskhe-Javakheti	20.1	24.0	21.6	20.2	14.1
7	Ajara	25.9	22.9	21.7	15.6	13.8
8	Guria	17.4	17.7	20.7	20.4	23.8
9	Samegrelo	23.5	19.8	20.6	21.3	14.7
10	Imereti	13.3	15.3	18.2	22.9	30.3
11	Mtskheta-Mtianeti	25.5	17.5	20.2	21.2	15.6

Source: Based on ADePT Poverty and Inequality modules using Integrated Household Survey of Georgia 2003 and 2006.

quintiles, respectively, and 30.3 percent [10,E] of its population falls in the fifth or richest quintile. Kvemo Kartli appears to be the poorest among all subnational regions because 30.0 percent [5,A] of its population falls in the poorest quintile and only 7.9 percent [5,E] of its population falls in the richest quintile.

Lessons for Policy Makers

This table is helpful in understanding population mobility across different consumption expenditure levels in different regions, which a single measure of welfare, inequality, or poverty cannot reflect.

Subnational Decomposition of Headcount Ratio

Table 3.15 decomposes poverty to explore the factors that caused a change in headcount ratio. Table rows are divided into two categories. Rows 1 through 4 report the change in the overall poverty and three factors affecting this change: total intrasectoral effect, population-shift effect, and interaction effect. Rows 5 through 14 report the intrasectoral effects for various regions in Georgia.[1] Column A reports the absolute change in headcount

Table 3.15: Subnational Decomposition of Headcount Ratio, Changes between 2003 and 2006

		Absolute change	Percentage change
		A	B
	Poverty line = GEL 75.4		
1	Change in headcount ratio	1.04	100.00
2	Total intrasectoral effect	1.09	104.98
3	Population-shift effect	−0.18	−17.38
4	Interaction effect	0.13	12.40
	Intrasectoral effects by region		
5	Kakheti	0.70	67.93
6	Tbilisi	1.06	102.38
7	Shida Kartli	−0.31	−30.37
8	Kvemo Kartli	−1.05	−101.76
9	Samtskhe-Javakheti	−0.26	−25.06
10	Ajara	0.65	62.79
11	Guria	0.30	28.70
12	Samegrelo	−0.43	−41.25
13	Imereti	0.41	39.18
14	Mtskheta-Mtianeti	0.03	2.44

Source: Based on ADePT Poverty and Inequality modules using Integrated Household Survey of Georgia 2003 and 2006.

poverty and the size of the factors contributing to this change. Column B shows how these factors change the headcount ratio.

The change in overall headcount ratio between 2003 and 2006 is 1.04 [1,A]. This overall change of 1.04 percentage points is divided into three different effects. The first is the total intrasectoral effect, 1.09 [2,A]. The total population-shift effect is negative and amounts to –0.18 [3,A]. The interaction between the intrasectoral factor and the population shift factor is 0.13 [4,A]. If we sum these three effects, we get the overall absolute change in headcount ratio poverty: (1.09 – 0.18 + 0.13) = 1.04 [1,A].

The next column reports the proportion these effects have relative to the overall change. The proportion of the total intrasectoral effect on the overall change in poverty is 104.98 percent [2,B]. This number is calculated by dividing the total intrasectoral effect by the change in poverty: (100 × 1.09) / 1.04 = 104.98. The corresponding entries for the population-shift effect and the interaction effect are calculated by the same method. For example, (100 × –0.18) / 1.04 = –17.38 and (100 × 0.13) / 1.04 = 12.40 [4,B].

The next set of results decomposes the total intrasectoral effect across Georgia's regions. Column A reports the size of the intrasectoral effect, and column B reports the intrasectoral effect as a proportion of the total change in the overall headcount ratio. For example, the intrasectoral effect for Kakheti is 0.70 [5,A], and its proportion of the overall poverty change is 67.93 percent [5,B], calculated as (100 × 0.70) / 1.04 = 67.93.

The intrasectoral effect of Kakheti is calculated as the change in headcount ratio between 2003 and 2006, which is 7.3 percentage points (reported in column C of table 3.9), multiplied by its population share in 2003 (reported in column G of table 3.9). The intrasectoral effects are negative for regions such as Shida Kartli, Kvemo Kartli, Samtskhe-Javakheti, and Samegrelo, because the poverty headcount ratio fell in these regions. For the rest of the regions, the intrasectoral effects are positive. The contribution of this effect is highest for Tbilisi and lowest for Kvemo Kartli.

Lessons for Policy Makers

The total intrasectoral effect is even higher than the total change in the overall headcount ratio. Thus, if the region-wise population shares are kept constant, then the change in poverty is 1.09 percentage points [2,A]. However, if we keep the regional headcount ratios constant and consider only the changes in regional population shares, then the poverty rate would have fallen by 0.18 percentage point [3,A]. Thus, the intrasectoral effect dominates and the overall headcount ratio increases. Finally, the second set of results gives us an idea about the headcount ratio's regional contribution in terms of intrasectoral effect.

Poverty Analysis across Other Population Subgroups

In this section, we discuss the results when the population is divided in various ways: household head's characteristics, household member's employment status, education level, age group, demographic composition, and landownership.

Standard of Living and Inequality by Household Head's Characteristics

Table 3.16 reports the mean and median per capita consumption expenditure and their growth over time and inequality across the population using the Gini coefficient across various household characteristics. Table rows denote various household characteristics. Columns A and B report the mean per capita consumption expenditure for 2003 and 2006, respectively. Column C reports the percentage change in per capita expenditure over these three years. It is evident from rows 1 and 2 that the mean per capita expenditure goes up by 1.1 percent [2,C] for female household heads but decreases by 0.5 percent [1,C] for male household heads.

Columns D, E, and F report the median per capita expenditures for 2003 and 2006 and the growth rates between these years. Although the overall change in median is –1.4 percent [20,F] (much larger than the change in overall mean of –0.1 percent [20,C]), the changes in the groups with various household characteristics are mixed. For female household heads, the median increases by 1.5 percent [2,F], but it falls by 2.2 percent [1,F] for male household heads. We find a mixed picture for the other household characteristics.

Columns G, H, and I report inequality by household head's characteristics using the Gini coefficient, which lies between 0 and 100. Although the overall Gini coefficient increases by 0.9 [20,I] in 2006, changes for different household characteristics vary over a broad range.

183

Table 3.16: Mean and Median Per Capita Consumption Expenditure, Growth, and Gini Coefficient, by Household Characteristics

Characteristic of household head	Mean per capita consumption expenditure			Median per capita consumption expenditure			Gini coefficient		
	2003 (GEL)	2006 (GEL)	Change (%)	2003 (GEL)	2006 (GEL)	Change (%)	2003	2006	Change
	A	B	C	D	E	F	G	H	I
Poverty line = GEL 75.4									
Gender									
1 Male	127.2	126.6	−0.5	106.7	104.3	−2.2	33.7	34.8	1.1
2 Female	122.9	124.3	1.1	98.9	100.4	1.5	36.5	37.0	0.5
Age									
3 15–19	110.8	217.8	96.6	90.0	150.7	67.3	16.2	31.7	15.5
4 20–24	188.0	223.5	18.9	131.7	188.3	43.0	40.6	35.0	−5.6
5 25–29	121.1	153.9	27.1	114.8	121.9	6.2	32.1	33.8	1.7
6 30–34	130.1	121.7	−6.5	111.4	98.1	−12.0	33.2	38.1	4.8
7 35–39	121.3	124.2	2.4	103.9	105.1	1.2	32.7	34.3	1.6
8 40–44	127.9	128.5	0.5	109.7	105.1	−4.2	33.8	35.3	1.5
9 45–49	127.6	132.7	4.0	102.9	104.4	1.4	35.7	36.2	0.5
10 50–54	121.5	120.7	−0.6	100.9	105.0	4.1	34.4	32.6	−1.8
11 55–59	134.7	132.8	−1.4	117.0	104.2	−10.9	33.5	38.0	4.5
12 60–64	130.5	123.0	−5.7	109.4	102.5	−6.4	32.3	34.3	2.0
13 65+	122.8	121.8	−0.8	100.9	99.9	−1.0	35.1	34.8	−0.3
Education									
14 Elementary or less	101.3	101.6	0.4	80.9	84.6	4.5	36.5	37.5	1.0
15 Incomplete secondary	109.5	106.7	−2.6	90.8	90.3	−0.5	34.5	33.4	−1.0
16 Secondary	116.2	118.6	2.1	97.3	99.6	2.3	33.7	34.1	0.4
17 Vocational-technical	127.7	116.3	−8.9	107.1	97.5	−9.0	34.6	34.6	0.0
18 Special secondary	134.4	127.5	−5.2	113.1	106.1	−6.2	33.9	33.0	−1.0
19 Higher education	153.7	155.1	0.9	129.7	123.7	−4.7	31.9	36.0	4.1
20 Total	**126.1**	**126.0**	**−0.1**	**104.7**	**103.3**	**−1.4**	**34.4**	**35.4**	**0.9**

Source: Based on ADePT Poverty and Inequality modules using Integrated Household Survey of Georgia 2003 and 2006.

Headcount Ratio by Household Head's Characteristics

Table 3.17 analyzes poverty by population subgroup according to various household head characteristics. The poverty line is set at GEL 75.4 per month.

Table rows report categories for three household head characteristics: *gender, age,* and *education level.* Columns A, B, and C analyze the poverty headcount ratios for 2003, 2006, and the change between those years. Columns D, E, and F outline the distribution of poor people across the subgroups, with the number in the cell being the proportion of all poor people in the country contained in each subgroup. We can also call this the subgroup's percentage contribution to overall poverty, or the headcount ratio times the population share included in that group. Columns G, H, and

Table 3.17: Headcount Ratio by Household Head's Characteristics
percent

	Characteristic of household head	Poverty headcount ratio			Distribution of the poor			Distribution of population		
		2003	2006	Change	2003	2006	Change	2003	2006	Change
		A	B	C	D	E	F	G	H	I
	Poverty line = GEL 75.4									
	Gender									
1	Male	28.4	30.0	1.6	69.6	71.5	1.9	73.3	73.6	0.3
2	Female	34.1	33.5	−0.5	30.4	28.5	−1.9	26.7	26.4	−0.3
	Age									
3	15–19	0	0	0	0	0	0	0	0.1	0.1
4	20–24	18.5	8.2	−10.3	0.3	0.2	−0.2	0.5	0.6	0
5	25–29	33.4	18.4	−15.0	1.3	0.7	−0.7	1.2	1.1	−0.1
6	30–34	26.9	36.2	9.3	3.3	3.1	−0.2	3.7	2.7	−1.0
7	35–39	31.6	31	−0.6	5.7	4.8	−0.9	5.4	4.7	−0.6
8	40–44	28.5	29.9	1.4	9	8.2	−0.8	9.5	8.5	−1.0
9	45–49	30.1	28.2	−1.9	11.9	10.7	−1.3	11.9	11.7	−0.2
10	50–54	32.8	31.1	−1.7	12.7	12.2	−0.5	11.6	12.2	0.6
11	55–59	26.0	30.0	4.0	7.7	11.2	3.5	8.9	11.6	2.7
12	60–64	24.2	32.4	8.2	8.7	7.6	−1.1	10.8	7.3	−3.5
13	65+	32.1	32.4	0.2	39.2	41.4	2.2	36.5	39.6	3.1
	Education									
14	Elementary or less	44.2	43.1	−1.0	12.4	10.2	−2.2	8.4	7.3	−1.1
15	Incomplete secondary	38.4	38.7	0.3	12.7	10.0	−2.6	9.9	8.0	−1.9
16	Secondary	33.3	32.5	−0.7	42.9	40.1	−2.9	38.6	38.1	−0.5
17	Vocational-technical	30.2	36.5	6.3	8.4	11.7	3.4	8.3	9.9	1.7
18	Special secondary	26	26.9	0.9	9.9	11.2	1.3	11.4	12.8	1.5
19	Higher education	17.5	21.9	4.4	13.7	16.9	3.1	23.4	23.8	0.3
20	**Total**	**29.9**	**31.0**	**1.0**	**100**	**100**	**n.a.**	**100**	**100**	**n.a.**

Source: Based on ADePT Poverty and Inequality modules using Integrated Household Survey of Georgia 2003 and 2006.
Note: n.a. = not applicable.

I depict the subgroup population distributions, or the population percentage contained in each subgroup. Row *20* shows that overall headcount ratio increases from 29.9 percent in 2003 *[20,A]* to 31.0 percent in 2006 *[20,B]*, reflecting a 1.0 percentage point increase *[20,C]* in the headcount ratio.

We see that 28.4 percent of male household heads *[1,A]* are poor. In other words, the headcount ratio for this population's subgroup is 28.4 percent. The headcount ratio of the same group in 2006 is 30.0 percent *[1,B]*. So the headcount ratio for the population in the male-headed household increased by 1.6 percentage points *[1,C]* from 2003 to 2006.

In row 4, we find that 18.5 percent *[4,A]* of the population from households headed by someone in the 20–24 age group is poor. The headcount ratio for the same population subgroup in 2006 is 8.2 percent *[4,B]*, a change of –10.3 percentage points *[4,C]*. In fact, headcount ratios have also decreased for households with the head in the 25–29 age group *[5,C]*, 35–39 *[7,C]*, 45–49 *[9,C]*, and 50–54 *[10,C]*. When subgroups are divided according to household head's education, we find that the headcount ratio for the population living in the households where the head's education is elementary or less is 44.2 percent *[14,A]*. In both years, the population in this subgroup had the highest headcount ratio.

Of all people who were poor in Georgia in 2003, 69.6 percent *[1,D]* were from male-headed households. The share of all poor living in male-headed households increased to 71.5 percent in 2006 *[1,E]*, an increase of 1.9 percentage points *[1,F]*. In contrast, the share of poor in female-headed households fell by 1.9 percentage points from 30.4 percent *[2,D]* in 2003 to 28.5 percent *[2,E]* in 2006.

There was not a large change in the population share in either male- or female-headed households. For male-headed households, the proportion of population increased by 0.3 percentage point from 73.3 percent *[1,G]* to 73.6 percent *[1,H]*. For the female-headed households, the proportion of population decreased by 0.3 percentage point from 26.7 percent *[2,G]* to 26.4 percent *[2,H]*. Similarly, headcount ratios increased from 38.4 percent *[15,A]* to 38.7 percent *[15,B]* for the subgroup having household heads with incomplete secondary education. But the headcount ratio for the subgroup having household heads with secondary education fell from 33.3 percent *[16,A]* to 32.5 percent *[16,B]*. The shares of poor in both groups decreased over the course of these three years: from 12.7 percent *[15,D]* to 10.0 percent *[15,E]* for heads with incomplete secondary and from 42.9 percent *[16,D]* to 40.1 percent *[16,E]* for heads with secondary education.

One might wonder why the share of poor in households with heads having incomplete secondary education decreased despite the increase in the headcount ratio. The answer can be found if we look at columns G and H. Notice that the population share with heads having incomplete secondary or less decreased from 9.9 percent in 2003 *[15,G]* to 8.0 percent in 2006 *[15,H]*. At the same time, headcount ratios for other subgroups increased. For example, headcount ratios for the subgroups with household heads in vocational-technical education and higher education increased by 6.3 *[17,C]* and 4.4 *[19,C]* percentage points, respectively. Thus, despite an increase in headcount ratio, the shares of the poor population decreased for the subgroup with heads having incomplete secondary education.

Population Distribution across Quintiles by Household Head's Characteristics

Table 3.18 analyzes the distribution of population across five quintiles of per capita consumption expenditure by household head's characteristics. Column *1* denotes the lowest or first quintile, column *2* denotes the second quintile, and so forth.

All cells in row *1* have a value of 20, obtained by dividing Georgia's population into five equal-sized groups in terms of per capita expenditure. Each group consists of 20 percent of the population. The fifth quintile contains the richest 20 percent of the population, the fourth quintile consists of the second-richest 20 percent of the population, and so on, and the first quintile consists of the poorest 20 percent of the population.

Table 3.18: Distribution of Population across Quintiles by Household Head's Characteristics, 2003

percentage of per capita expenditure

		Quintile				
		First	Second	Third	Fourth	Fifth
	Characteristic of household head	A	B	C	D	E
1	Total	20.0	20.0	20.0	20.0	20.0
	Gender					
2	Male	18.6	20.2	20.1	20.7	20.3
3	Female	23.8	19.3	19.7	18.0	19.1
	Age (years)					
4	15–19	0.0	27.1	51.1	17.1	4.8
5	20–24	10.5	19.9	12.1	19.1	38.4
6	25–29	23.4	15.5	13.4	26.1	21.6
7	30–34	16.5	21.5	16.8	23.4	21.8
8	35–39	21.6	19.9	20.0	17.7	20.8
9	40–44	19.5	17.5	21.1	20.9	21.0
10	45–49	21.7	19.9	19.2	19.2	19.9
11	50–54	21.4	20.5	19.9	20.0	18.2
12	55–59	16.2	18.6	18.2	24.1	22.9
13	60–64	15.5	19.5	22.4	20.9	21.8
14	65+	21.5	21.1	20.3	18.6	18.5
	Education					
15	Elementary or less	32.5	23.8	16.5	15.9	11.3
16	Incomplete secondary	25.5	23.7	20.1	16.9	13.9
17	Secondary	22.3	22.4	20.3	18.5	16.5
18	Vocational-technical	20.1	18.9	20.1	21.0	19.9
19	Special secondary	17.4	18.1	19.9	22.7	21.8
20	Higher education	10.7	14.4	20.6	23.6	30.7

Source: Based on ADePT Poverty and Inequality modules using Integrated Household Survey of Georgia 2003 and 2006.

The rows below row *1* report the distribution of population by various household head characteristics for 2003 using the national quintiles. Consider the value 18.6 *[2,A]* for male household heads. This value implies that 18.6 percent of the total population in male-headed households lives with per capita expenditure less than the first quintile. The population living in male-headed households is 20.2 percent in the second quintile *[2,B]*. Similarly, 20.3 percent *[2,E]* of the population from the male-headed households falls in the fifth quintile. The population distribution is almost the same across all five quintiles.

The largest proportion of population living in the lowest quintile belongs to households headed by someone who has not acquired education beyond elementary level *[15,A]*. At the other extreme, the largest proportion of population living in the highest quintile belongs to the households headed by someone in the 20–24 age group *[5,E]*.

Lessons for Policy Makers

This table is helpful in understanding population mobility across different levels of consumption expenditure across different regions that a single welfare, inequality, or poverty measure cannot reflect.

Headcount Ratio by Employment Category

Table 3.19 analyzes Georgia's headcount ratio by population subgroups according to household members' employment category. The poverty line is set at GEL 75.4 per month. Table rows list employment sectors (agriculture, industry, government, and so on) as well as unemployed and inactive categories to account for those not working.

Columns *A*, *B*, and *C* analyze poverty headcount ratios for 2003, 2006, and the change over time. Columns *D*, *E*, and *F* outline the distribution of poor people across the subgroups, with the number in the cell being the percentage of all poor people in the country that are located in that subgroup. Stated another way, this is the percentage contribution of the subgroup to overall poverty, or the headcount ratio times the population share in that group. Columns *G*, *H*, and *I* depict subgroup population distribution, or the population percentage found in that subgroup. The last row shows that overall headcount ratio increases from 29.9 percent in 2003 *[15,A]* to 31.0 percent in 2006 *[15,B]*, reflecting a 1.0 percentage point increase in the headcount ratio.

Table 3.19: Headcount Ratio by Employment Category

percent

	Employment	Poverty headcount ratio 2003	2006	Change	Distribution of the poor 2003	2006	Change	Distribution of population 2003	2006	Change
		A	B	C	D	E	F	G	H	I
	Poverty line = GEL 75.4									
	Self-employed									
1	Agriculture	29.4	28.2	−1.3	23.2	20.2	−3.0	23.6	22.2	−1.4
2	Industry	20.5	32.2	11.7	0.4	0.5	0.1	0.5	0.5	−0.1
3	Trade	23.8	22.1	−1.6	2.5	1.8	−0.7	3.2	2.5	−0.7
4	Transport	19.2	28.9	9.7	0.4	0.7	0.3	0.7	0.7	0.1
5	Other services	20.7	27.8	7.2	0.7	0.9	0.2	1.0	1.0	−0.0
	Employed									
6	Industry	21.3	24.7	3.4	1.5	1.6	0.0	2.1	2.0	−0.2
7	Trade	19.5	24.1	4.6	1.1	1.1	0.1	1.6	1.5	−0.2
8	Transport	21.1	28.2	7.1	0.7	0.8	0.1	0.9	0.9	−0.1
9	Government	18.9	17.8	−1.1	1.4	1.1	−0.3	2.2	1.8	−0.4
10	Education	19.1	17.4	−1.7	2.1	1.7	−0.3	3.3	3.1	−0.2
11	Health care	16.7	19.1	2.5	0.6	0.7	0.1	1.1	1.2	0.0
12	Other	23.1	24.9	1.8	2.9	3.1	0.2	3.7	3.8	0.1
13	Unemployed	37.3	40.3	3.1	8.9	10.8	1.9	7.2	8.3	1.1
14	Inactive	32.9	33.7	0.8	53.6	55.1	1.5	48.8	50.7	1.8
15	**Total**	**29.9**	**31.0**	**1.0**	**100.0**	**100.0**	**n.a.**	**100.0**	**100.0**	**n.a.**

Source: Based on ADePT Poverty and Inequality modules using Integrated Household Survey of Georgia 2003 and 2006.
Note: n.a. = not applicable.

We find that 29.4 percent *[1,A]* of people engaged in the agricultural sector are poor in 2003. In other words, the headcount ratio for this population subgroup (with a household head employed in the agricultural sector) is 29.4 percent. The headcount ratio for the same population subgroup (with a household head in the agricultural sector) fell to 28.2 percent in 2006 *[1,B]*. Thus, a 1.3 percentage point decrease *[1,C]* occurred in the headcount ratio between the two years. We see that the headcount ratio among members in the other services sector increased by 7.2 percentage points *[5,C]*, from 20.7 percent *[5,A]* to 27.8 percent *[5,B]*. This headcount ratio increase from 2003 to 2006 is found in other sectors, such as employed industry *[6,C]*, trade *[7,C]*, and transport *[8,C]*.

Of all people who are poor in Georgia in 2003, 23.2 percent *[1,D]* are employed in agriculture. We find that the share of all poor employed in agriculture fell to 20.2 percent in 2006 *[1,E]*. This represents a decrease of 3.0 percentage points *[1,F]*.

Contrast those results with the figures for the unemployed population subgroup. Clearly, the poverty headcount ratio among this group in 2003

[13,A] is larger than the poverty headcount ratio in 2003 among the subgroup employed in the agricultural sector [1,A]. However, if we consider the share of all poor people who are found in these two subgroups in 2003, this number is nearly twice as large in the agricultural sector as that among the unemployed group. This is because of the different population shares of the two subgroups as given in the final columns. The population share in the agriculture subgroup in 2003 is 23.6 percent [1,G], while the share in the unemployed subgroup is only 7.2 percent [13,G].

In row 1, the agricultural subgroup's poverty headcount ratio falls 1.3 percentage points [1,C], while the share of poor in this subgroup falls by 3.0 percentage points [1,F]. For the other services subgroup, the headcount ratio increased 7.2 percentage points [5,C] between 2003 and 2006, while the share of poor in this subgroup increased by only 0.2 percentage point, from 0.7 percent [5,D] to 0.9 percent [5,E].

Lessons for Policy Makers

One might wonder why these two ways of evaluating changes are so different. Look at columns G and H. Notice that the population share employed in the agricultural sector is more than 20 percent of the total population in both 2003 [1,G] and 2006 [1,H]. In comparison, the population share engaged in other services is only 1.0 percent in 2003 [5,G] and 2006 [5,H]. Consequently, a change of smaller magnitude in the headcount ratio in the agricultural sector has a larger impact on its share of the poor and vice versa.

Headcount Ratio by Education Level

Table 3.20 analyzes poverty by education levels. The poverty line is set at GEL 75.4 per month. Columns A, B, and C analyze poverty headcount ratios for 2003, 2006, and the difference over time. Columns D, E, and F outline the distribution of poor people across the subgroups, with the number in the cell being the proportion of all poor people in the country located in that subgroup. This is the subgroup's percentage contribution to overall poverty, or the headcount ratio times the population share in that group. Columns G, H, and I depict subgroup population distribution, or the population percentage in that subgroup. Row 7 shows that the overall headcount

Table 3.20: Headcount Ratio by Education Level
percent

	Education level	Poverty headcount ratio			Distribution of the poor			Distribution of population		
		2003	2006	Change	2003	2006	Change	2003	2006	Change
		A	B	C	D	E	F	G	H	I
	Poverty line = GEL 75.4									
1	Elementary or less	40.4	35.9	−4.6	6.5	5.7	−0.7	4.6	4.1	−0.5
2	Incomplete secondary	36.1	38.2	2.1	14.3	13.9	−0.5	11.5	10.9	−0.6
3	Secondary	33.2	31.9	−1.3	46.8	44.1	−2.6	40.8	41.7	0.9
4	Vocational-technical	30.0	35.0	5.0	7.7	8.5	0.7	7.5	7.3	−0.2
5	Special secondary	25.2	27.7	2.5	10.1	11.2	1.2	11.6	12.2	0.6
6	Higher education	17.6	20.9	3.4	14.6	16.6	1.9	24.1	23.8	−0.3
7	**Total**	**29.9**	**31.0**	**1.0**	**100.0**	**100.0**	**n.a.**	**100.0**	**100.0**	**n.a.**

Source: Based on ADePT Poverty and Inequality modules using Integrated Household Survey of Georgia 2003 and 2006.
Note: n.a. = not applicable.

ratio increases from 29.9 percent in 2003 *[7,A]* to 31.0 percent in 2006 *[7,B]*, reflecting a 1.0 percentage point (rounded) increase in the headcount ratio.

We find that 40.4 percent *[1,A]* of the population who have elementary-level education or less are poor. In other words, the headcount ratio for this population subgroup is 40.4 percent. The headcount ratio for the same population subgroup fell to 35.9 percent in 2006 *[1,B]*. Thus, the headcount ratio fell by 4.6 percentage points *[1,C]* between these three years. At the other extreme, the headcount ratio for the subgroup with higher education increased by 3.4 percentage points, from 17.6 percent *[6,A]* to 20.9 percent *[6,B]*.

Of all people who are poor in Georgia in 2003, 6.5 percent *[1,D]* have elementary education or less. The share of all poor with elementary education or less decreased to 5.7 percent in 2006 *[1,E]*, a decrease of 0.7 percentage point *[1,F]*.

Clearly, the poverty headcount ratio among the population with incomplete secondary education in 2003 *[2,A]* is larger than the poverty headcount ratio in 2003 among the higher education subgroup *[6,A]*. However, if we consider the share of all poor people who are found in these two subgroups in 2003, the number is larger for the population with higher education because of the two subgroups' different population shares, as given in the table's final columns. The population share with higher education in 2003 is 24.1 percent *[6,G]*, whereas the population share with incomplete secondary education is only 11.5 percent *[2,G]*. The headcount ratios increased for the population with incomplete secondary education from

36.1 percent *[2,A]* to 38.2 percent *[2,B]*, for vocational-technical education from 30 percent *[4,A]* to 35 percent *[4,B]*, for special secondary education from 25.2 percent *[5,A]* to 27.7 percent *[5,B]*, and for higher education from 17.6 percent *[6,A]* to 20.9 percent *[6,B]*.

Headcount Ratio by Demographic Composition

Table 3.21 analyzes poverty by population subgroup, where each subgroup is based first on the number of children 0–6 years of age in the household, then on the household's size. The poverty line is set at GEL 75.4 per month. Columns *A*, *B*, and *C* analyze poverty headcount ratios for 2003, 2006, and the difference over time. Columns *D*, *E*, and *F* outline the distribution of poor people across the subgroups, with the number in the cell being the proportion of poor people in the country contained in that subgroup. This is the subgroup's percentage contribution to overall poverty, or the headcount ratio times the population share that falls in that group. Columns *G*, *H*, and *I* depict subgroup population distribution, or the percentage of the population in that subgroup. Row *12* shows that overall headcount ratio increased

Table 3.21: Headcount Ratio by Demographic Composition
percent

	Demographic characteristic	Poverty headcount ratio			Distribution of the poor			Distribution of population		
		2003	2006	Change	2003	2006	Change	2003	2006	Change
		A	B	C	D	E	F	G	H	I
	Poverty line = GEL 75.4									
	Number of children 0–6 years									
1	None	28.8	28.5	−0.4	69.6	66.1	−3.5	72.2	72.0	−0.2
2	1	31.2	36.2	5.0	20.5	22.2	1.7	19.7	19.0	−0.7
3	2	35.5	39.9	4.5	8.3	10.3	2.0	7.0	8.0	1.0
4	3 or more	43.7	40.6	−3.1	1.5	1.3	−0.2	1.0	1.0	−0.0
	Household size									
5	1	25.8	24.1	−1.7	2.6	2.6	−0.0	3.1	3.4	0.3
6	2	23.1	21.0	−2.1	6.7	5.9	−0.8	8.7	8.7	−0.0
7	3	25.0	23.2	−1.8	11.1	9.9	−1.2	13.3	13.2	−0.1
8	4	24.4	26.2	1.7	19.5	18.5	−1.1	23.9	21.8	−2.1
9	5	31.9	33.8	1.8	23.0	23.0	0.0	21.6	21.1	−0.5
10	6	36.2	35.4	−0.9	19.6	19.1	−0.4	16.2	16.7	0.6
11	7 or more	39.3	43.2	4.0	17.3	20.9	3.6	13.2	15.0	1.8
12	**Total**	**29.9**	**31.0**	**1.0**	**100.0**	**100.0**	**n.a.**	**100.0**	**100.0**	**n.a.**

Source: Based on ADePT Poverty and Inequality modules using Integrated Household Survey of Georgia 2003 and 2006.
Note: n.a. = not applicable.

from 29.9 percent in 2003 *[12,A]* to 31.0 percent in 2006 *[12,B]*, reflecting a 1.0 percentage point (rounded) increase in the headcount ratio.

First, consider the results based on the number of children in households. We find that 28.8 percent *[1,A]* of the population with no child in the household is poor in 2003. In other words, the headcount ratio for this population subgroup is 28.8 percent. The headcount ratio for the same population subgroup decreased to 28.5 percent in 2006 *[1,B]*. Thus, the headcount ratio decreased by 0.4 percentage point *[1,C]* over the course of these three years.

Headcount ratios also decreased for the population with three or more children in the household by 3.1 percentage points from 43.7 percent *[4,A]* in 2003 to 40.6 percent *[4,B]* in 2006. Similarly, consider the set of results corresponding to the household size. The headcount ratio among the population with only one member in the household in 2003 is 25.8 percent *[5,A]*, which falls by 1.7 percentage points to 24.1 percent in 2006 *[5,B]*. At the other extreme, the headcount ratio among the people living in households with seven or more members increased by 4.0 percentage points from 39.3 percent *[11,A]* to 43.2 percent *[11,B]*.

The next cell in row *1* is 69.6 *[1,D]*, meaning that of all people who are poor in Georgia in 2003, 69.6 percent of the population live in households with no child. In the next column, we find that the share of poor with no child decreased to 66.1 percent in 2006 *[1,E]*, a decrease of 3.5 percentage points *[1,F]*.

Compare those results with the subgroup having three or more children. It is evident that the headcount ratio among the subgroup with no child in both years (28.8 percent in 2003 *[1,A]* and 28.5 percent in 2006 *[1,B]*) is lower than the headcount ratio for the subgroup with three or more children (43.7 percent in 2003 *[4,A]* and 40.6 percent for 2006 *[4,B]*). Note that the share of the former subgroup to total poverty is 69.6 percent in 2003 *[1,D]*, which fell by 3.5 percentage points to 66.1 percent in 2006 *[1,E]*. The share of the latter to total poverty is 1.5 percent in 2003 *[4,D]*, which fell by 0.2 percentage point to 1.3 percent in 2006 *[4,E]*. However, in both years, the share of poor in the former subgroup is more than 40 times higher than that in the latter subgroup.

Lessons for Policy Makers

Note that the poverty rate among the subgroup with three or more children is higher than the subgroup with no child. However, the population share in the subgroup with no child is so large (72.2 percent in 2003 *[1,G]* and 72 percent in 2006 *[1,H]*), compared to the subgroup with three or more children (only 1.0 percent in both years *[4,G]* and *[4,H]*), that the share of the subgroup with no child in total poverty is high. The analysis in table 3.21 enables a policy maker to understand the origin of poverty at a more disaggregated level. A policy maker should also focus on households with no child, even though the headcount ratio is lowest in this subgroup. Similar intuition should hold for the next set of results where the subgroups are based on household size.

Headcount Ratio by Landownership

Table 3.22 analyzes poverty by population household landownership subgroups for 2003, 2006, and the change across those years. The poverty line is set at GEL 75.4 per month. Columns A, B, and C analyze the poverty headcount ratios. Columns A and B report the headcount ratio for 2003 and 2006, respectively, while column C reports the difference over time. Columns D, E, and F outline the distribution of poor people across the subgroups, with the number in the cell being the proportion of poor people in the country located in that subgroup. This is the subgroup's percentage contribution to overall poverty, or the headcount ratio times the population share that lies in that group. Columns G, H, and I depict the subgroups' population distribution, or the population percentage found in

Table 3.22: Headcount Ratio by Landownership
percent

	Size of landholding (hectares)	Poverty headcount ratio			Distribution of the poor			Distribution of population		
		2003	2006	Change	2003	2006	Change	2003	2006	Change
		A	B	C	D	E	F	G	H	I
	Poverty line = GEL 75.4									
1	0	29.4	32.7	3.3	39.0	46.4	7.3	39.7	43.9	4.2
2	Less than 0.2	39.4	36.2	−3.1	12.7	11.9	−0.7	9.6	10.2	0.6
3	0.2–0.5	33.9	36.9	2.9	17.2	18.4	1.1	15.2	15.4	0.2
4	0.5–1.0	25.1	24.3	−0.8	19.5	15.4	−4.1	23.2	19.6	−3.6
5	More than 1.0	28.2	22.4	−5.8	11.5	7.9	−3.6	12.2	10.9	−1.3
6	**Total**	**29.9**	**31.0**	**1.0**	**100.0**	**100.0**	**n.a.**	**100.0**	**100.0**	**n.a.**

Source: Based on ADePT Poverty and Inequality modules using Integrated Household Survey of Georgia 2003 and 2006.
Note: n.a. = not applicable.

each subgroup. Row 6 shows that the overall headcount ratio increases from 29.9 percent in 2003 [6,A] to 31.0 percent in 2006 [6,B], reflecting a 1.0 percentage point (rounded) increase in the headcount ratio.

We find that 29.4 percent [1,A] of people who belong to households with no landownership are poor in 2003. In other words, the headcount ratio for this population subgroup is 29.4 percent. The headcount ratio for the same population subgroup increases to 32.7 percent in 2006 [1,B]. Thus, the headcount ratio increased by 3.3 percentage points [1,C] over these three years. We see that the headcount ratio for the population in households with landownership of 0.5–1.0 hectare decreased by 0.8 percentage point, from 25.1 percent [4,A] to 24.3 percent [4,B].

Of all poor people in Georgia in 2003, 39 percent [1,D] lived in households with no landownership. The share of poor with no landownership increased to 46.4 percent in 2006 [1,E]. The headcount ratio among the subgroup with landownership of 0.5–1.0 hectare (25.1 percent in 2003 [4,A] and 24.3 percent in 2006 [4,B]) is lower than the headcount for the subgroup with a landownership of less than 0.2 hectare (39.4 percent in 2003 [2,A] and 36.2 percent for 2006 [2,B]). Note that the share of the former subgroup to total poverty is 19.5 percent in 2003 [4,D], which fell by 4.1 percentage points to 15.4 percent in 2006 [4,E]. The share of the latter to total poverty is 12.7 percent in 2003 [2,D], which fell by only 0.7 percentage point to 11.9 percent in 2006 [2,E]. Note that despite a larger fall in the poverty rate of 3.1 percentage points [2,C] for the subgroup with landownership of less than 0.2 hectare, the share of poor in that subgroup fell by only 0.7 percentage point [2,F]. One might wonder about the reason behind this phenomenon.

The answer can be found if we look at columns G and H. Notice that the population share with landownership of less than 0.2 hectare is 9.6 percent in 2003 [2,G], and it increased by 0.6 percentage point to 10.2 percent in 2006 [2,H]. In contrast, the population share with landownership of 0.5–1.0 hectare fell by 3.6 percentage points, from 23.2 percent [4,G] in 2003 to 19.6 percent [4,H] in 2006. Moreover, the population share in the latter subgroup is almost twice as high as that in the former subgroup in both years. Thus, despite a larger fall in headcount ratio for the subgroup with landownership of less than 0.2 hectare, its share in total number of poor did not decrease significantly compared to the subgroup with landownership of 0.5–1 hectare.

A Unified Approach to Measuring Poverty and Inequality

Headcount Ratio by Age Groups

Table 3.23 analyzes poverty by population subgroup according to individuals' ages. The poverty line is set at GEL 75.4 per month. Columns A, B, and C analyze poverty headcount ratios for 2003, 2006, and the difference over time, respectively. Columns D, E, and F outline the distribution of poor people across the subgroups, with the number in the cell being the proportion of poor people located in that subgroup. This is the subgroup's percentage contribution to overall poverty, or the headcount ratio times the overall population share that lies in that group. Columns G, H, and I depict the subgroups' population distribution, or the percentage of the population that can be found in that subgroup. Row 14 shows that the overall headcount ratio increased from 29.9 percent in 2003 [14,A] to 31.0 percent in 2006 [14,B], reflecting a 1.0 percentage point (rounded) increase in headcount ratio.

We see that 32.8 percent of the population in age group 0–5 years [1,A] is poor. In other words, the headcount ratio for this population subgroup is 32.8 percent. The headcount ratio for the same population subgroup increased to 34.9 percent in 2006 [1,B]. Thus, the headcount ratio increased by 2.1 percentage points [1,C] during these three years. In fact, the headcount ratio increased among all age groups except 50–54 and 65+ years.

Table 3.23: Headcount Ratio by Age Groups
percent

	Age group (years)	Poverty headcount ratio			Distribution of the poor			Distribution of population		
		2003	2006	Change	2003	2006	Change	2003	2006	Change
		A	B	C	D	E	F	G	H	I
	Poverty line = GEL 75.4									
1	0–5	32.8	34.9	2.1	5.9	6.2	0.2	5.4	5.5	0.1
2	6–14	33.3	34.5	1.2	14.4	12.6	−1.8	12.9	11.3	−1.7
3	15–19	33.3	33.7	0.4	9.6	9.5	−0.1	8.6	8.7	0.1
4	20–24	30.7	31.6	0.9	8.0	8.7	0.7	7.8	8.5	0.8
5	25–29	30.9	31.5	0.7	7.3	7.4	0.1	7.1	7.3	0.2
6	30–34	30.2	32.6	2.4	6.9	6.8	−0.2	6.9	6.4	−0.4
7	35–39	30.2	32.1	1.9	6.8	6.8	−0.0	6.7	6.5	−0.2
8	40–44	27.9	31.4	3.5	7.2	7.0	−0.2	7.7	7.0	−0.8
9	45–49	28.6	29.1	0.5	6.9	6.8	−0.1	7.2	7.2	−0.0
10	50–54	28.3	27.1	−1.1	5.6	5.4	−0.2	6.0	6.2	0.2
11	55–59	23.0	25.8	2.8	3.2	4.5	1.2	4.2	5.4	1.2
12	60–64	23.0	26.7	3.8	3.5	3.0	−0.5	4.5	3.4	−1.1
13	65+	29.3	28.8	−0.6	14.7	15.5	0.8	15.0	16.6	1.6
14	**Total**	**29.9**	**31.0**	**1.0**	**100.0**	**100.0**	**n.a.**	**100.0**	**100.0**	**n.a.**

Source: Based on ADePT Poverty and Inequality modules using Integrated Household Survey of Georgia 2003 and 2006.
Note: n.a. = not applicable.

Between 2003 and 2006, the headcount ratios decreased for age group 50–54 years by 1.1 percentage points, from 28.3 percent [10,A] to 27.1 percent [10,B], and for the age group 65+ years by 0.6 percentage point from 29.3 percent [13,A] to 28.8 percent [13,B]. In contrast, headcount ratios increased for all other groups by 0.4 to 3.8 percentage points. For example, the headcount ratio for age group 30–34 years increased by 2.4 percentage points from 30.2 percent [6,A] in 2003 to 32.6 percent [6,B] in 2006.

Of all poor people in Georgia in 2003, 5.9 percent are in the age group of 0–5 years [1,D]. The share of all poor in age group 0–5 years increased to 6.2 percent in 2006 [1,E], an increase of 0.2 percentage point. Now consider age groups 6–14 and 65+ years. The headcount ratio among the population in age group 6–14 years increased by 1.2 percentage points from 33.3 percent in 2003 [2,A] to 34.5 percent in 2006 [2,B], but the headcount fell by 0.6 percentage point for age group 65+ years [13,C]. However, if we consider the change in share of all poor people found in these two subgroups in 2003 (column F), this number went up for age group 65+ (0.8 [13,F]) and fell for age group 6–14 years (–1.8 [2,F]).

Lessons for Policy Makers

One might ask why the share of the poor has fallen in spite of an increase in headcount ratios. The answer can be found in columns G and H. Note that the share of people in the age group 6–14 years decreased by 1.7 percentage points from 12.9 percent in 2003 [2,G] to 11.3 percent in 2006 [2,H]. In contrast, the population share in age group 65+ years increased by 1.6 percentage points from 15.0 percent in 2003 [13,G] to 16.6 percent in 2006 [13,H]. Thus, despite a decrease in headcount ratio for age group 65+ years, its share of poor increased. A policy maker, therefore, should notice that a decrease in headcount among the 65+ years age group did not necessarily decrease the number of total poor in that age group.

Headcount Ratio and Age-Gender Pyramid

Until now, we have analyzed headcount ratios across individual population subgroups. We have not analyzed the headcount ratio across two different population subgroups simultaneously. Figure 3.2 presents one such example using a graph known as an age-gender pyramid. The age-gender pyramid analyzes the headcount ratios across gender and across different age groups

Figure 3.2: Age-Gender Poverty Pyramid

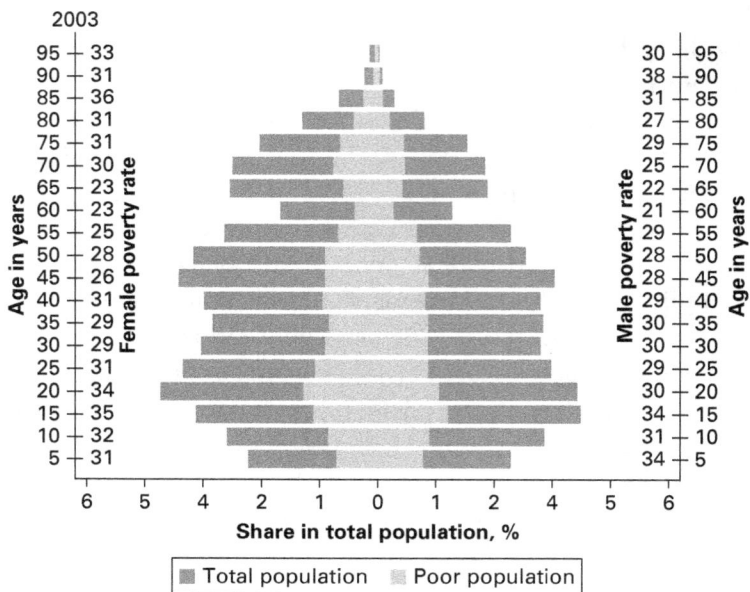

Source: Based on ADePT Poverty and Inequality modules using Integrated Household Survey of Georgia 2003 and 2006.

simultaneously. However, it can be used to analyze other subgroups with proper justification. As before, the variable for our analysis is per capita consumption expenditure in lari, and the poverty line is set at GEL 75.4 per month. The outside vertical axes denote the age of the members in years, and the horizontal axis presents the share of the population.

The figure is divided vertically by gender: the right-hand side represents males and the left-hand side represents females. The distance from the middle to each side in dark gray denotes the total population share in that age group. The distance in light gray is the proportion of poor people in that age group of the total number of poor, again for each gender. Data are aggregated in five-year increments, and each increment is displayed as a bar centered on the highest age in the increment. The data for ages 25 to 30 years, for example, are represented by the bar at 30 years. For those zero to five years of age, the shares of both males and females are 2.2 percent, and nearly 0.7 percent of both males and females in that age group reside in poor households. The headcount ratio among females in that age group is 32 percent and among males it is 31 percent. The headcount ratio is highest among male members in the 85–90 years age group: 38 percent of the males in that age group reside in poor households. The largest headcount ratio among females is seen in the 80–85 years age group.

Sensitivity Analyses

In this section, we perform sensitivity analysis of poverty line choice, poverty measures, and inequality measures, mostly at the national level and across urban and rural areas. In certain cases, the results are reported at the subnational levels or across geographic regions. However, all sensitivity analysis can be replicated at any disaggregated level.

Elasticity of FGT Poverty Indices to Per Capita Consumption

Table 3.24 provides a tool for checking the sensitivity of the three poverty measures to consumption expenditure. The table shows the result of increasing everyone's consumption expenditure by 1.0 percent and compares those values across two years, 2003 and 2006. There are two poverty lines: GEL 75.4 and GEL 45.2 per month.

The percentage change in poverty caused by a 1.0 percent change in the mean or average per capita consumption expenditure is referred to as the *elasticity of poverty with respect to per capita consumption*. The particular way

Table 3.24: Elasticity of FGT Poverty Indices to Per Capita Consumption Expenditure

		Headcount ratio			Poverty gap measure			Squared gap measure		
		2003	2006	Change	2003	2006	Change	2003	2006	Change
	Region	A	B	C	D	E	F	G	H	I
	Poverty line = GEL 75.4									
1	Urban	−1.89	−1.72	0.17	−1.95	−2.03	−0.09	−2.09	−2.23	−0.14
2	Rural	−1.66	−1.53	0.13	−1.71	−1.64	0.07	−1.82	−1.72	0.09
3	Total	−1.77	−1.62	0.15	−1.81	−1.82	0.00	−1.93	−1.93	0.00
	Poverty line = GEL 45.2									
4	Urban	−2.06	−2.35	−0.29	−2.36	−2.47	−0.12	−2.24	−2.50	−0.26
5	Rural	−1.87	−1.64	0.23	−1.86	−1.78	0.07	−1.94	−1.86	0.08
6	**Total**	**−1.95**	**−1.94**	**0.01**	**−2.05**	**−2.04**	**0.01**	**−2.05**	**−2.06**	**−0.02**

Source: Based on ADePT Poverty and Inequality modules using Integrated Household Survey of Georgia 2003 and 2006.
Note: FGT = Foster-Greer-Thorbecke.

in which we consider an increase in the average per capita consumption expenditure is by increasing everyone's consumption expenditure by the same percentage. This type of change is distribution neutral, because the relative inequality does not change.

The main columns denote three different sets of poverty measures: headcount ratio, poverty gap measure, and squared gap measure. The first two columns within each set report the elasticities for 2003 and 2006, respectively, while the third column reports the difference between these two years.

Let us start with the GEL 75.4 per month poverty line. The elasticity of poverty with respect to the mean consumption expenditure for the urban area in 2003 is −1.89 [1,A]. In other words, if the consumption expenditure increases by 1.0 percent for everyone, then the mean per capita consumption expenditure increases by 1.0 percent and the urban headcount ratio falls by −1.89 percent, or stated differently, 1.89 percent of the population who were living under the poverty line of GEL 75.4 will be out of poverty.

If the mean consumption expenditure is increased by 1.0 percent, then the headcount ratio for the urban area falls by 1.72 percent in 2006 [1,B]. A higher value implies higher sensitivity. The urban headcount ratio elasticity is less sensitive to consumption expenditure in 2006 than in 2003 by 0.17 [1,C]. Similarly, the elasticity of poverty gap to the per capita consumption expenditure for the urban area in 2003 is −1.95 [1,D], which increases by −0.09 (rounded) to −2.03 in 2006 [1,E]. The elasticity of squared gap measure in 2003 is −2.09 [1,G], which increases by −0.14 to −2.23 in 2006 [1,H].

Negative elasticities mean a fall in poverty caused by an increase in consumption expenditure. The higher magnitude implies higher elasticity even though the sign is negative. Note that both the poverty gap measure and the squared gap measure, unlike the headcount ratio, are more sensitive to consumption expenditure in 2006 than in 2003. A similar pattern is seen for the GEL 45.2 per month poverty line: the poverty gap measure and the squared gap measure are more sensitive to the per capita consumption expenditure.

All elasticities in the rural area are lower in magnitude compared to what we see in the urban area for both poverty lines. In other words, all rural poverty measures are less sensitive to the per capita consumption expenditure. The overall headcount ratio elasticity decreases slightly from −1.95 in 2003 [6,A] to −1.94 in 2006 [6,B] for the GEL 45.2 poverty line, but it decreases by 0.15 from −1.77 in 2003 [3,A] to −1.62 in 2006 [3,B] for the GEL 75.4 poverty line. The elasticities of the overall poverty gap and the squared gap measure did not change much between these two years for either poverty line.

Lessons for Policy Makers

Note that poverty lines are set normatively, which is difficult to justify exclusively. A slight change in per capita consumption expenditure may or may not change the poverty rates by significant margins. If the distribution is highly polarized or, in other words, if the society has two groups of people—one group consisting of rich people and the other group consisting of extreme poor—then a slight change in everyone's income by the same proportion may not affect the headcount ratio.

In contrast, if marginal poor are concentrated around the poverty line, then a slight change in everyone's income by the same proportion would have a huge impact on the poverty measures. For example, in the table the poverty measures are more sensitive to the lower GEL 45.2 per month poverty line than the higher GEL 75.4 per month poverty line. This is because the concentration of poor around the lower poverty line is much larger than that around the higher poverty line. Hence, this type of analysis may tell us about the impact of any policy on the poverty rate used by the policy maker.

Sensitivity of Poverty Measures to the Choice of Poverty Line

Table 3.25 presents a tool for checking the sensitivity of the headcount ratio with respect to the chosen poverty line. This exercise is similar to the exercise for checking the elasticity of poverty measures to per capita consumption expenditure, but it is more rigorous. It is always possible to find a certain percentage of decrease in the poverty line that matches the increase in the consumption expenditure for everyone by 1.0 percent. In this exercise, we check the sensitivity of the poverty measure by changing the poverty line in more than one direction. Thus, in the table, we ask how the actual headcount ratio changes as the poverty line changes from its initial value, whether it is GEL 75.4 per month or GEL 45.2 per month.

Rows denote the change in poverty line, both upward and downward. Columns report the change in three poverty measures: the headcount ratio, the poverty gap measure, and the squared gap measure, and their change from actual. The variable is per capita consumption expenditure, measured

Table 3.25: Sensitivity of Poverty Measures to the Choice of Poverty Line, 2003

		Headcount ratio	Change from actual (%)	Poverty gap measure	Change from actual (%)	Squared gap measure	Change from actual (%)
		A	B	C	D	E	F
	Poverty line = GEL 75.4						
1	Actual	29.9	0.0	9.7	0.0	4.6	0.0
2	+5 percent	32.6	9.0	10.7	10.7	5.1	11.4
3	+10 percent	35.3	18.0	11.7	21.7	5.6	23.3
4	+20 percent	40.5	35.2	13.9	44.3	6.8	48.5
5	−5 percent	26.9	−10.0	8.7	−10.2	4.1	−10.8
6	−10 percent	24.2	−19.1	7.7	−19.9	3.6	−21.1
7	−20 percent	19.4	−35.3	6.0	−38.1	2.7	−40.0
	Poverty line = GEL 45.2						
8	Actual	10.2	0.0	3.0	0.0	1.4	0.0
9	+5 percent	11.4	11.8	3.4	12.2	1.5	12.4
10	+10 percent	12.7	24.1	3.8	25.2	1.7	25.6
11	+20 percent	15.8	54.5	4.7	53.8	2.1	54.6
12	−5 percent	9.2	−9.9	2.7	−11.6	1.2	−11.6
13	−10 percent	8.0	−21.4	2.4	−22.4	1.1	−22.4
14	−20 percent	6.0	−40.9	1.8	−41.6	0.8	−41.4

Source: Based on ADePT Poverty and Inequality modules using Integrated Household Survey of Georgia 2003 and 2006.

in lari. In this table, we report the results only for 2003, but this analysis can be conducted for any year.

Column A reports the headcount ratios for different poverty lines, and column B reports the change in the headcount ratios from the actual poverty line, which can be either GEL 75.4 per month or GEL 45.2 per month. Rows 2 and 9, corresponding to +5 percent, denote the increase in poverty line by 5 percent. Thus, when the poverty line is GEL 75.4, then a 5 percent increase means the poverty line becomes GEL 79.2 and the headcount ratio increases by 3.7 percentage points from 29.9 percent [1,A] to 32.6 percent [2,A], or the headcount ratio increases by 9.0 percent [2,B] from its actual level of 29.9 percent.

Similarly, if the poverty line is decreased by 10 percent (−10 percent) from GEL 75.4, then the poverty headcount rate falls by 5.7 percentage points from 29.9 percent [1,A] to 24.2 percent [6,A], or the headcount ratio decreases by 19.1 percent from the actual level of 29.9 percent. The headcount ratio is more sensitive to the change in poverty line when the actual poverty line is GEL 45.2 than when the poverty line is GEL 75.4. In fact, the poverty gap measure and the squared gap measure are also more sensitive to change in poverty line when the actual poverty line is GEL 45.2 rather than GEL 75.4.

Lessons for Policy Makers

This table helps us understand the robustness of a particular poverty estimate. Selection of any poverty line is debatable, because it is set with normative judgment. If a change in the poverty line causes a drastic change in a poverty measure, then a cautious policy conclusion should be drawn from the analysis based on that particular poverty line. In contrast, if a poverty measure does not vary much because of a change in the poverty line, then a more robust conclusion can be drawn.

Other Poverty Measures

Table 3.26 analyzes the overall poverty for Georgia and decomposes it across rural and urban areas using three other poverty measures not in the FGT class. The table reports three different sets of poverty measures: the Watts index, Sen-Shorrocks-Thon (SST) index, and Clark-Hemming-Ulph-Chakravarty (CHUC) index (these measures are defined in chapter 2). This is a type of sensitivity analysis, but of the poverty measurement methodology. There are two poverty lines: GEL 75.4 per month and GEL 45.2 per month.

Columns *A* and *B* report the Watts index for both years. The Watts index is the mean log deviation relative to the poverty line. It is evident from row *1* that the urban Watts index increases from 12.0 in 2003 *[1,A]* to 12.7 in 2006 *[1,B]* when the poverty line is GEL 75.4 but falls slightly between the same years when the poverty line is GEL 45.2 *[4,A]* and *[4,B]*.

Table 3.26: Other Poverty Measures

		Watts index			Sen-Shorrocks-Thon index			CHUC index		
		2003	*2006*	*Change*	*2003*	*2006*	*Change*	*2003*	*2006*	*Change*
		A	*B*	*C*	*D*	*E*	*F*	*G*	*H*	*I*
	Poverty line = GEL 75.4									
1	Urban	12.0	12.7	0.7	15.7	16.8	1.1	16.6	16.5	0.0
2	Rural	15.6	16.2	0.5	19.2	19.6	0.4	22.2	22.8	0.6
3	Total	13.9	14.5	0.6	17.5	18.3	0.7	19.6	19.8	0.3
	Poverty line = GEL 45.2									
4	Urban	3.3	3.2	−0.1	4.7	4.6	0.0	5.1	4.5	−0.6
5	Rural	5.2	5.7	0.5	7.0	7.6	0.6	8.5	9.0	0.4
6	**Total**	**4.3**	**4.5**	**0.2**	**5.9**	**6.2**	**0.3**	**6.9**	**6.8**	**−0.1**

Source: Based on ADePT Poverty and Inequality modules using Integrated Household Survey of Georgia 2003 and 2006.
Note: CHUC = Clark-Hemming-Ulph-Chakravarty.

Columns *D* and *E* report the SST index, which is also based on the headcount ratio, the income gap ratio, and the Gini coefficient across the censored distribution of consumption expenditure. The last is obtained by replacing consumption expenditure of all nonpoor people by the poverty line. We see that when the poverty line is GEL 75.4, the SST index for the urban region in 2003 is 15.7 *[1,D]*, and it increases by 1.1 to 16.8 in 2006 *[1,E]*. Likewise, the rural region's SST index increased by 0.4, from 19.2 in 2003 *[2,D]* to 19.6 in 2006 *[2,E]*, for the same poverty line. The total increase in SST index is 0.7, from 17.5 in 2003 *[3,D]* to 18.3 in 2006 *[3,E]*.

The final three columns report the CHUC index and its changes across time. Unlike the SST index, the CHUC index does not reflect an increase in poverty across all regions. In fact, urban poverty falls marginally between 2003 *[1,G]* and 2006 *[1,H]* when the poverty line is GEL 75.4. Furthermore, when the poverty line is set at GEL 45.2, the CHUC index shows a fall in Georgia's overall poverty *[6,I]*.

Lessons for Policy Makers

If these three measures, capturing different aspects of poverty and inequality among the poor, agree with the results from the measures in the FGT class, then the poverty analysis is robust. In contrast, if these measures do not agree with each other, the policy conclusion should be drawn with more care. Comparing table 3.2 with table 3.26, we see that the three measures reported in table 3.2 do not always agree with the results based on the poverty gap measure and squared gap measure. Thus, any conclusion about whether poverty has increased or decreased should be made cautiously.

Other Inequality Measures

Table 3.27 reports the Atkinson inequality measures and generalized entropy measures for 2003, then decomposes them across different regions. This is a type of sensitivity analysis for inequality measurement methodology. We report the Gini coefficient only in the last two sections of this chapter. However, the Gini coefficient may not be subgroup consistent (subgroup consistency is defined in chapter 2). Rows denote results for urban and rural population subgroups and for different geographic regions, such as Kakheti, Tbilisi, and Shida Kartli.

Table 3.27: Atkinson Measures and Generalized Entropy Measures by Geographic Regions, 2003

		Atkinson measure			Generalized entropy measure		
		A(1/2)	A(0)	A(–1)	GE(0)	GE(1)	GE(2)
		A	B	C	D	E	F
1	Urban	9.1	17.7	34.3	19.4	18.8	22.8
2	Rural	10.1	19.8	38.9	22.0	21.0	25.6
	Subnational regions						
3	Kakheti	9.8	19.2	39.1	21.3	20.1	24.4
4	Tbilisi	8.3	15.9	29.8	17.3	17.3	20.8
5	Shida Kartli	11.0	21.6	44.8	24.4	22.8	28.2
6	Kvemo Kartli	8.9	17.3	33.9	19.0	18.6	24.0
7	Samtskhe-Javakheti	9.0	17.4	34.1	19.1	19.0	24.6
8	Ajara	9.4	18.5	36.5	20.4	19.2	22.6
9	Guria	9.4	18.2	35.7	20.1	19.9	27.2
10	Samegrelo	9.5	18.3	35.3	20.2	19.7	23.7
11	Imereti	8.8	17.3	33.8	19.0	18.0	20.8
12	Mtskheta-Mtianeti	9.3	18.6	36.7	20.6	18.5	20.2
13	**Total**	**9.6**	**18.8**	**36.8**	**20.8**	**20.0**	**24.2**

Source: Based on ADePT Poverty and Inequality modules using Integrated Household Survey of Georgia 2003 and 2006.
Note: GE = generalized entropy.

Columns A, B, and C report the Atkinson measures for $\alpha = 1/2$, 0, and –1, respectively, and columns D, E, and F report the generalized entropy measures for $\alpha = 0$, 1, and 2, respectively. (For a theoretical discussion on the Atkinson inequality measure and generalized entropy measures, please refer to chapter 2.) Intuitively, an Atkinson inequality measure of order α is the gap between the mean achievement and the generalized mean of achievements of order α divided by the mean achievement. Generalized mean is sensitive to inequality across the distribution, where a lower value of α reflects higher sensitivity to inequality across the distribution. In other words, a lower value of α reflects higher aversion toward inequality and, thus, it is also known as the *inequality aversion parameter*. When everyone has identical achievement, then it does not matter how sensitive one is toward inequality, so the generalized mean is equal to the arithmetic mean for all α. For the analysis in table 3.27, the inequality measures put more emphasis on the lower end of the distribution and thus assume $\alpha < 1$. The Atkinson measure lies between 0 and 1. Similarly, if a household has equal per capita expenditure in a region, then the generalized entropy measure is also 0 for all α.

The Atkinson measure for $\alpha = 1/2$, or A(1/2), for the urban area is 9.1 [1,A]. Intuitively, the number implies that the generalized mean of order 0.5 for urban Georgia is 9.1 percent lower than Georgia's mean per capita expenditure in 2003. The next two cells to the right report A(0) and A(–1) for urban Georgia, where A(0) = 17.7 [1,B] and A(–1) = 34.3 [1,C]. Therefore, A(0) is 17.7 percent lower than the mean per capita expenditure and A(–1) is 34.3 percent lower than the mean per capita expenditure. Columns D, E, and F report three generalized entropy measures for $\alpha = 0$, 1, and 2, denoted by GE(0), GE(1), and GE(2), respectively.

Row 2 reports the three Atkinson measures and three generalized entropy measures for rural Georgia. Each of these six measures shows that rural Georgia is more unequal than urban Georgia. For example, the A(1/2) for the rural area is 10.1 [2,A], compared with 9.1 in the urban area [1,A], and A(0) for the rural area is 19.8 [2,B], compared with 17.7 for the urban area [1,B]. However, the difference is much larger when the two regions are compared with respect to A(–1): 38.9 for the rural area [2,C] and 34.3 for the urban area [1,C].

Next, we consider the results across regions. The level of inequality of Ajara according to A(1/2) is 9.4 [8,A], which is higher than that of Samtskhe-Javakheti at 9.0 [7,A]. This means that Ajara has larger income inequality than Samtskhe-Javakheti. Even according to A(0), A(–1), GE(0), and GE(–1), Ajara has higher income inequality than Samtskhe-Javakheti. However, in terms of GE(2), which gives more weight to larger incomes across the population, Samtskhe-Javakheti [7,F] has higher income inequality than Ajara [8,F].

Lessons for Policy Makers

A region's income standards reflect that region's welfare level. However, higher welfare does not necessarily mean more equal distribution. A high level of inequality may be detrimental to a region's welfare. We already reported the Gini coefficient for that purpose. However, given that the Gini coefficient has certain limitations, we report three Atkinson inequality measures and three generalized entropy measures to check the inequality ranking for regions. These six inequality measures are commonly used separately from the Gini coefficient.

Also unlike the Gini coefficient, Atkinson and generalized entropy class inequality measures are normative measures, in which we may choose varying degrees of inequality aversion. If these six measures agree with the Gini coefficient, then a conclusion based on the Gini coefficient can be considered robust. However, if these six measures provide different rankings than the Gini coefficient, then a more cautious policy conclusion should be drawn based only on Gini.

Dominance Analyses

In the previous section, we conducted some dominance analysis with respect to the choice of poverty lines and measurement methodologies. In this section, we perform additional dominance analyses. Note that when we analyze sensitivity with respect to the poverty line, we do not compare the results for all poverty lines. Similarly, when we check the sensitivity of inequality using different Atkinson and generalized entropy measures, we do not conduct the analysis for all parameter values. The dominance tests in this part of the chapter go beyond the sensitivity analyses. For example, according to the dominance analyses in this section, we can say that poverty has unambiguously risen for all poverty lines, or inequality has risen, no matter which inequality measure is used to assess it.

Poverty Incidence Curve

A *poverty incidence curve* is the distribution function of the welfare indicator across the population. The poverty incidence curve is useful while performing a dominance analysis of the headcount ratio with respect to the poverty line. In this dominance exercise, the welfare indicator is per capita consumption expenditure, assessed by lari. The horizontal axis of figure 3.3 denotes per capita consumption expenditure. The height of the poverty incidence curve at any per capita consumption expenditure denotes the proportion of people having less than that per capita expenditure.

Therefore, the link between the poverty incidence curve and the headcount ratio is clear. The height of the poverty incidence curve is the headcount ratio when the poverty line is set at a particular per capita consumption expenditure. For a poverty line, a larger height denotes a larger headcount ratio or a larger share of the population having per capita expenditure below the poverty line. If the poverty incidence curve of a distribution lies to the right of the poverty incidence curve of another distribution, then the former distribution is understood to have an unambiguously lower headcount ratio or the former distribution has lower headcount ratios for all poverty lines.

Figure 3.3: Poverty Incidence Curves in Urban Georgia, 2003 and 2006

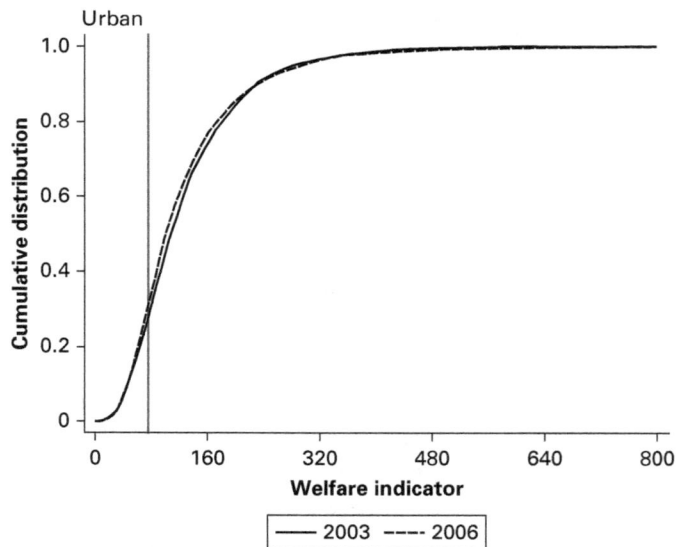

Source: Based on ADePT Poverty and Inequality modules using Integrated Household Survey of Georgia 2003 and 2006.
Note: The red vertical line is the poverty line.

Figure 3.3 graphs the poverty incidence curves for urban Georgia in 2003 and 2006. The vertical axis reports the headcount ratio. The solid line denotes the poverty incidence curve for 2003, while the dashed line denotes the poverty incidence curve for 2006. We saw earlier that the urban headcount ratio is higher in 2006 for both poverty lines: GEL 75.4 and GEL 45.2. What about other poverty lines? Can we say that poverty has unambiguously fallen for any poverty line? Figure 3.3 suggests that we may not be able to. If we set the hypothetical poverty line somewhere between GEL 320 and GEL 480, then the headcount ratio would have been lower in 2006 than that in 2003.

Lessons for Policy Makers

Although such a poverty line seems very high and unlikely to be set at that value, the main point of the exercise is clear. When two poverty incidence curves cross, then an unambiguous judgment cannot be made. The crossing may take place at a much lower level, as happened in the rural area. We have already seen that the headcount ratio showed an increase in 2006 when the poverty line is set at GEL 75.4 but showed a decrease when the poverty line is set at GEL 45.2. Given the infinite number of possible poverty lines, it would be cumbersome to check them all one by one. Instead, the poverty incidence curve is a convenient way of checking for dominance (if two poverty incidence curves never cross). If dominance does not hold, then the graph can tell us which part is responsible for the ambiguity.

Poverty Deficit Curve

A *poverty deficit curve* is useful while performing a dominance analysis of the poverty gap measure with respect to the poverty line. In this dominance exercise, the welfare indicator is per capita consumption expenditure, assessed by lari. In figure 3.4, the horizontal axis denotes the welfare indicator or per capita consumption expenditure. The height of the poverty density curve is proportional to the poverty gap measure, so that a larger height

Figure 3.4: Poverty Deficit Curves in Urban Georgia, 2003 and 2006

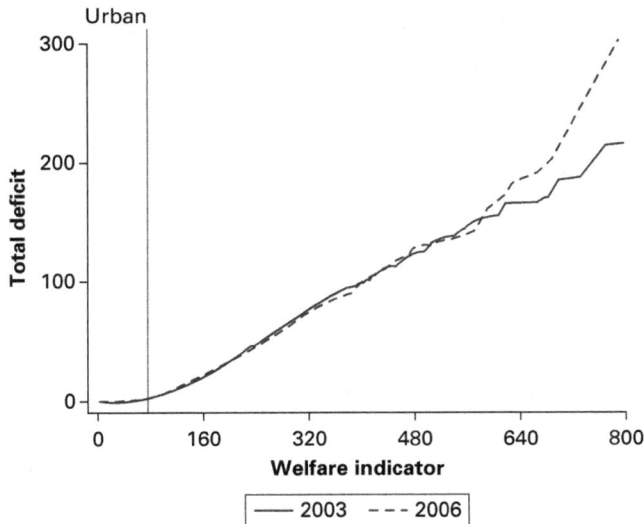

Source: Based on ADePT Poverty and Inequality modules using Integrated Household Survey of Georgia 2003 and 2006.
Note: The red vertical line is the poverty line.

for a poverty line denotes a larger poverty gap measure. If a distribution's poverty deficit curve lies to the right of another distribution's poverty deficit curve, then the former distribution is understood to have an unambiguously lower poverty gap measure, or the former distribution has lower poverty gap measures for all poverty lines.

Figure 3.4 graphs the poverty deficit curves of urban Georgia for 2003 and 2006. The vertical axis reports total deficit, which is directly proportional to the poverty gap measure for the corresponding poverty line. The solid line denotes the poverty deficit curve for 2003, while the dashed line denotes the poverty deficit curve for 2006. We saw earlier that the urban poverty gap measure is higher in 2006 for both poverty lines: GEL 75.4 and GEL 45.2. What about other poverty lines? Can we say that poverty has unambiguously fallen for any poverty line? The graph suggests that we may not be able to. If we set the hypothetical poverty line to about GEL 320, then the poverty gap measure would have been lower in 2006 than in 2003.

Lessons for Policy Makers

Although such a poverty line seems very high and unlikely to be set at that value, the main point of the exercise is clear. When two poverty deficit curves cross, then an unambiguous judgment cannot be made based on the poverty gap measure. Given the infinite number of possible poverty lines, it would be cumbersome to check them all one by one. Instead, the poverty deficit curve is a convenient way of checking for dominance (if two poverty deficit curves never cross). If dominance does not hold, then the graph can tell us which part is responsible for the ambiguity.

Poverty Severity Curve

A *poverty severity curve* is useful when performing a dominance analysis of the squared gap measure with respect to the poverty line. In this dominance exercise, the welfare indicator is the per capita consumption expenditure, assessed by lari. In figure 3.5, the horizontal axis denotes the welfare indicator or the per capita consumption expenditure. The height of the poverty severity curve is proportional to the squared gap measure, so that a larger height for a poverty line denotes a larger squared gap. If a distribution's poverty severity curve lies to the right of another distribution's poverty severity curve, then the former distribution is understood to have an unambiguously

Figure 3.5: Poverty Severity Curves in Rural Georgia, 2003 and 2006

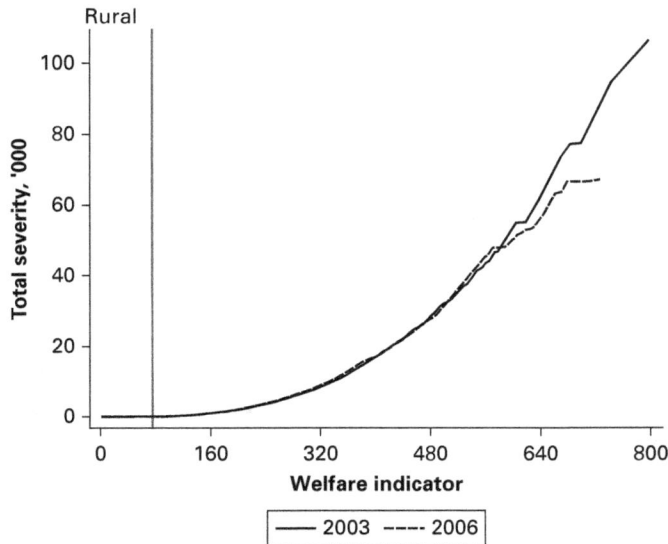

Source: Based on ADePT Poverty and Inequality modules using Integrated Household Survey of Georgia 2003 and 2006.
Note: The red vertical line is the poverty line.

lower squared gap, or the former distribution has a lower squared gap for all poverty lines.

Figure 3.5 graphs the poverty severity curves of rural Georgia for 2003 and 2006. The figure's vertical axis reports total severity, which is directly proportional to the squared gap measure of the corresponding poverty line. The solid line denotes the poverty severity curve for 2003, while the dashed line denotes the poverty severity curve for 2006. We saw earlier that the rural squared gap measure is higher in 2006 for both poverty lines: GEL 75.4 and GEL 45.2.

Lessons for Policy Makers

What about the other poverty lines? Can we say that poverty has unambiguously fallen for any poverty line? The figure suggests that we may not be able to. One of the poverty severity curves does not lie below another poverty severity curve for all poverty lines. When two poverty severity curves cross, then an unambiguous judgment cannot be made based on the squared gap measure. Given the infinite number of possible poverty lines, it would be cumbersome to check them all one by one. Instead, the poverty severity curve is a convenient way of checking for dominance (if two poverty severity curves never cross). If dominance does not hold, then the graph can tell us which part is responsible for the ambiguity.

Growth Incidence Curve

Figure 3.6 graphs the growth incidence curve of Georgia's per capita consumption expenditure. The vertical axis reports the growth rate of consumption expenditure between 2003 and 2006, and the horizontal axis reports the per capita consumption expenditure percentiles. We earlier reported the growth rate of mean per capita consumption expenditure and found that the overall growth rate was slightly negative. We also compared the median and four other quantile incomes.

Figure 3.6: Growth Incidence Curve of Georgia between 2003 and 2006

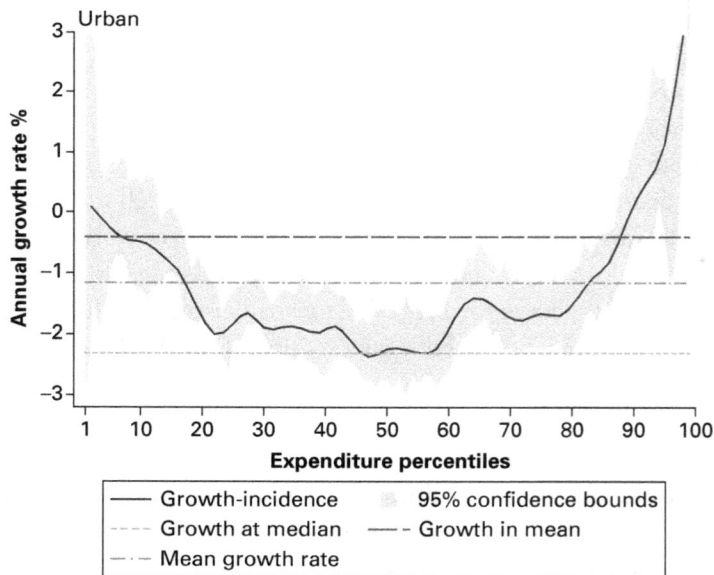

Source: Based on ADePT Poverty and Inequality modules using Integrated Household Survey of Georgia 2003 and 2006.

However, that analysis does not give us the entire picture, so we perform this dominance analysis through a growth incidence curve that graphs the growth rate of per capita consumption expenditure for each percentile of the population. The height of a growth incidence curve for a particular percentile of population is the per capita consumption expenditure growth of that percentile. In fact, a growth incidence curve assesses how the quantile incomes change over time. If the growth rates of the lower quintiles are larger than the growth rates of the upper quintiles, then the growth is said to be pro-poor.

The dotted-dashed straight line denotes the growth in mean per capita expenditure, which is negative in this case. It is not necessary that the entire population received an equal share of this growth. It is evident from the figure that the per capita expenditure growth rate for the population's higher percentiles between 2003 and 2006 is much larger and more positive than that for their lower percentile counterparts. Even though growth has been mixed throughout the quantile incomes, the lowest quantile income has a large negative growth. Given that the growth rate was negative, this means that the population's poorer section had a proportionally larger decrease in its per capita expenditure.

What we can state by looking at the figure is that the quantile ratios—such as 90/10, 80/20, or 90/50—increased between 2003 and 2006. The shaded area around the growth incidence curve reports the 95 percent confidence bounds. Can we say something about poverty? Yes, we can. For an absolute poverty line, the headcount ratio between 2003 and 2006 should not fall because the per capita expenditures of the population's lower percentile decreased. Thus, growth in Georgia between 2003 and 2006 was not pro-poor.

Lorenz Curve

Figure 3.7 graphs the Lorenz curve of urban Georgia's per capita expenditure for 2003 and 2006. The vertical axis reports the share of total consumption expenditure, and the horizontal axis reports the percentile of per capita expenditure. A Lorenz curve graphs the share of total consumption expenditure spent by each percentile of the population. Thus, the height of a Lorenz curve for a particular percentile is the share of total consumption expenditure spent by that percentile out of the region's total consumption expenditure. The Lorenz curve's height is 1 when the percentile is 1. In other words, the share of the total consumption expenditure spent by the entire population is

Figure 3.7: Lorenz Curves of Urban Georgia, 2003 and 2006

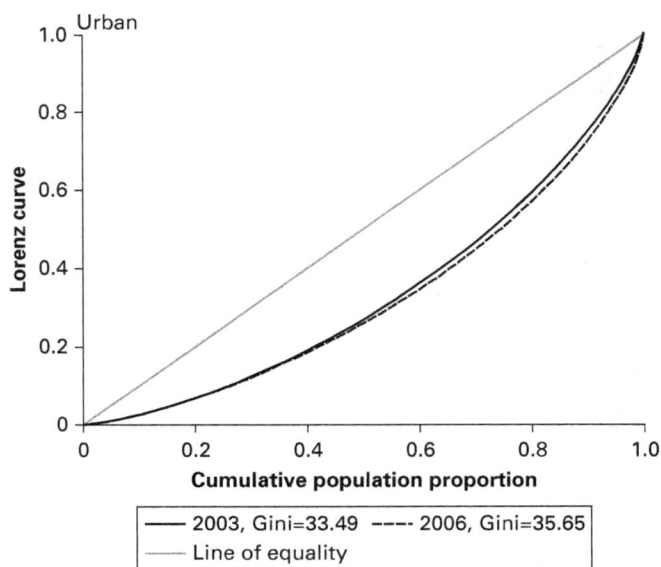

Source: Based on ADePT Poverty and Inequality modules using Integrated Household Survey of Georgia 2003 and 2006.

100 percent. The diagonal straight line denotes the situation of perfect equality: each person has the same per capita expenditure.

As inequality increases, the Lorenz curve bows out, and the area between the Lorenz curve and the line of perfect equality increases. The area between a Lorenz curve and the line of perfect equality is proportionally related to the Gini coefficient: it is twice the Gini coefficient. If a distribution's Lorenz curve lies completely to the right of another Lorenz curve, then the former distribution has unambiguously lower inequality, and any Lorenz-consistent measure—such as the Gini coefficient, the Atkinson class of indices, and the generalized entropy measures—ranks the former distribution as less unequal. If the Lorenz curves of two distributions cross, we cannot unambiguously rank those two distributions, even when one is ranked as more unequal than another by all the Lorenz-consistent measures we discussed earlier. Therefore, the Lorenz curve provides an opportunity to conduct a sensitivity analysis for the reported inequality measures.

The solid line represents the Lorenz curve for 2003, while the dotted line corresponds to 2006. It is evident that the dotted curve lies nowhere to the left of the solid curve. This implies that the inequality in urban Georgia unambiguously increased in 2006 compared with 2003. If these two curves had crossed, then the reported inequality measures would not have necessarily agreed with each other.

Standardized General Mean Curve

Dominance in terms of the Lorenz curves is not very common. Therefore, for inequality comparisons, we need to rely on various measures we covered earlier. We reported the Atkinson measures and generalized entropy measures in addition to the Gini coefficient. The Gini coefficient is not subgroup consistent, which means that if inequality in one region increases but remains the same in another region, the overall inequality may fall. We also showed in chapter 2 that each generalized entropy for $\alpha < 1$ is a monotonic transformation of the Atkinson inequality measures, and for $\alpha \neq 1$ it is a monotonic transformation of the general means. However, we report the Atkinson measures and the generalized entropy measures for only certain values of parameter α. This exercise should be understood as a dominance analysis of the Atkinson measures and the generalized entropy measures.

Figure 3.8 graphs the standardized general mean curve of Georgia's per capita expenditure for 2003 and 2006. The vertical axis reports the standardized general mean of per capita expenditure, where standardization is done by dividing the general mean of per capita expenditures by their mean. The horizontal axis reports parameter α, which is the degree of generalized mean and also known as the degree of a society's aversion toward inequality.

The general mean of a distribution tends toward the maximum and the minimum per capita expenditure in the distribution when α tends to ∞ and $-\infty$, respectively. Given that the largest per capita expenditure in any distribution is usually several times larger than the mean per capita expenditure, allowing α to be very large prevents meaningful analysis. Therefore, we restrict α to between -5 and 5, which we consider large enough. The height of a standardized general mean curve for a particular value of parameter α is the general mean per capita expenditure divided by the mean per capita expenditure. The height of any standardized general mean curve is 1 at $\alpha = 1$.

Figure 3.8: Standardized General Mean Curves of Georgia, 2003 and 2006

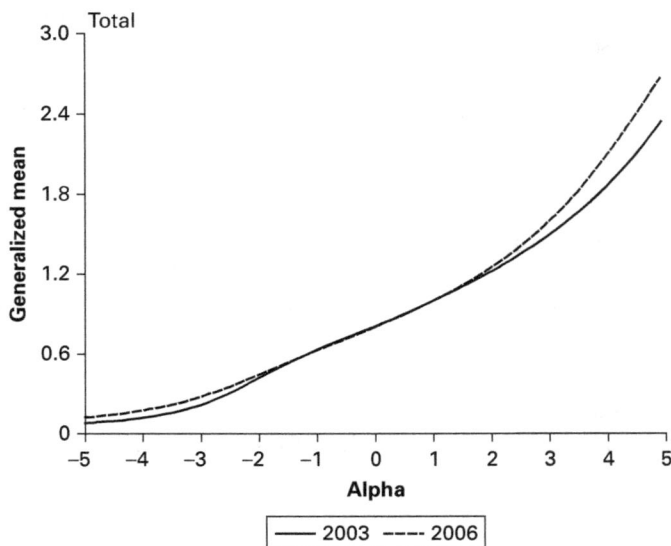

Source: Based on ADePT Poverty and Inequality modules using Integrated Household Survey of Georgia 2003 and 2006.

The solid line represents Georgia's standardized general mean curve in 2003, while the dashed line represents Georgia's standardized general mean curve in 2006. If a standardized general mean curve lies completely above another standardized general mean curve to the left of $\alpha = 1$ and completely below to the right of $\alpha = 1$, then every Atkinson inequality measure and generalized entropy measure for $\alpha \neq 1$ agree that the former distribution has lower inequality than the latter. It is evident from the figure that for larger values of parameter α, inequality in 2006 has worsened. However, for α less than 1, inequality has not significantly deteriorated. The standardized general mean curve is a convenient way of verifying the robustness of the Atkinson inequality measures and the generalized entropy measures.

Advanced Analysis

In this chapter's final section, we discuss certain advanced analysis methods. These techniques require knowledge of regression analysis. We assume readers have the required background.

Consumption Regression

Table 3.28 analyzes determinants of the variable used for measuring welfare (the per capita consumption expenditure in this case). Rows denote the set of regressors (such as logarithm of household size, share of children in the age group of 0–6 years, share of male adults, share of elderly) and a set of

Table 3.28: Consumption Regressions

		2003				2006			
		Urban		Rural		Urban		Rural	
		Coef	SE	Coef	SE	Coef	SE	Coef	SE
	Factors	A	B	C	D	E	F	G	H
	Household characteristics								
1	Log of household size	−0.093	0.06	−0.010	0.05	−0.001	0.06	0.051	0.05
2	Log of household size squared	−0.020	0.03	−0.078***	0.02	−0.102***	0.03	−0.114***	0.02
3	Share of children age 0–6 years	(dropped)		(dropped)		(dropped)		(dropped)	
4	Share of children age 7–16 years	−0.252***	0.09	0.223**	0.09	0.249**	0.10	0.076	0.09
5	Share of male adults	−0.064	0.10	0.254***	0.09	0.477***	0.11	0.251***	0.10
6	Share of female adults	−0.004	0.10	0.453***	0.10	0.592***	0.11	0.435***	0.10
7	Share of elderly (age ≥60 years)	−0.124	0.11	0.462***	0.10	0.488***	0.12	0.355***	0.10
	Characteristics of household head								
8	Log of household head's age	−0.063	0.05	0.076	0.05	−0.318***	0.05	0.210***	0.05
	Regions								
9	Kakheti	(dropped)		(dropped)		(dropped)		(dropped)	
10	Tbilisi	0.446***	0.05	(dropped)		0.258***	0.05	(dropped)	
11	Shida Kartli	0.182***	0.06	0.147***	0.03	−0.050	0.06	0.182***	0.03
12	Kvemo Kartli	0.061	0.06	0.075**	0.03	−0.023	0.06	0.183***	0.03
13	Samtskhe-Javakheti	−0.115*	0.06	0.185***	0.03	0.231***	0.07	0.163***	0.04
14	Ajara	0.226***	0.06	−0.035	0.04	0.103*	0.06	0.067*	0.04
15	Guria	−0.077	0.08	0.250***	0.03	0.030	0.08	0.131***	0.04
16	Samegrelo	0.112**	0.06	0.194***	0.03	−0.007	0.06	0.238***	0.03
17	Imereti	0.270***	0.05	0.529***	0.03	0.208***	0.05	0.381***	0.03
18	Mtskheta-Mtianeti	−0.060	0.07	0.164***	0.03	0.020	0.08	0.144***	0.04
	sland								
19	0 ha	(dropped)		(dropped)		(dropped)		(dropped)	
20	Less than 0.2 ha	0.121***	0.03	0.162***	0.05	0.104***	0.03	0.166***	0.04
21	0.2–0.5 ha	0.180***	0.04	0.356***	0.04	0.138***	0.05	0.193***	0.03
22	0.5–1.0 ha	0.255***	0.05	0.478***	0.04	0.125*	0.07	0.365***	0.03
23	More than 1.0 ha	0.021	0.09	0.565***	0.05	0.192**	0.08	0.484***	0.04
	Gender of household head								
24	Male	(dropped)		(dropped)		(dropped)		(dropped)	
25	Female	−0.073***	0.02	−0.002	0.02	−0.101***	0.02	−0.027	0.02
	Education of household head								
26	Elementary or less	(dropped)		(dropped)		(dropped)		(dropped)	
27	Incomplete secondary	−0.067	0.07	0.034	0.03	0.226***	0.07	0.086***	0.03
28	Secondary	0.021	0.06	0.105***	0.03	0.179***	0.06	0.196***	0.03
29	Vocational-technical	0.118*	0.06	0.147***	0.04	0.225***	0.07	0.255***	0.04
30	Special secondary	0.156***	0.06	0.217***	0.03	0.269***	0.06	0.322***	0.04
31	Higher education	0.289***	0.06	0.274***	0.03	0.441***	0.06	0.477***	0.04

(continued)

Table 3.28: Consumption Regressions (continued)

		2003				2006			
		Urban		Rural		Urban		Rural	
		Coef	SE	Coef	SE	Coef	SE	Coef	SE
	Factors	A	B	C	D	E	F	G	H
	Employment status of household head								
	Self-employed								
32	Agriculture	(dropped)		(dropped)		(dropped)		(dropped)	
33	Industry	−0.028	0.09	0.430***	0.09	−0.122	0.11	0.208*	0.11
34	Trade	0.082	0.05	0.275***	0.05	0.056	0.06	0.193***	0.06
35	Transport	0.026	0.08	0.311***	0.07	−0.039	0.08	0.311***	0.07
36	Other services	0.072	0.07	0.340***	0.08	−0.099	0.07	0.033	0.09
	Employed								
37	Industry	−0.043	0.06	0.127**	0.06	−0.036	0.06	0.140**	0.06
38	Trade	−0.094	0.06	0.144	0.09	−0.024	0.07	0.115	0.10
39	Transport	−0.021	0.06	0.212***	0.08	−0.174**	0.07	0.282***	0.08
40	Government	−0.041	0.06	0.227***	0.06	0.012	0.07	0.277***	0.08
41	Education	−0.037	0.06	0.054	0.06	−0.029	0.07	0.045	0.07
42	Health care	−0.041	0.06	0.085	0.15	−0.039	0.08	0.279*	0.15
43	Other	−0.120**	0.05	0.150***	0.04	−0.022	0.06	0.005	0.05
44	Unemployed	−0.376***	0.05	−0.138**	0.06	−0.325***	0.05	−0.066	0.06
45	Inactive	−0.219***	0.04	−0.117***	0.02	−0.169***	0.05	−0.067***	0.02
	Other								
46	Constant	4.851***	0.21	3.425***	0.19	5.328***	0.20	2.976***	0.20
47	Number of observations	4,525		7,106		4,112		6,773	
48	Adjusted R^2	0.18		0.20		0.17		0.16	

Source: Based on ADePT Poverty and Inequality modules using Integrated Household Survey of Georgia 2003 and 2006.
Note: Coef = coefficient. ha = hectare. SE = standard error, sland = area of land owned.
*** $p < 0.01$, ** $p < 0.05$, * $p < 0.1$.

dummy variables (such as regional dummies, gender dummies, dummies for household head education, and dummies for household head employment status). Columns report regression coefficients (Coef) and standard errors (SE) of four different ordinary least square regressions, where the *dependent variable*, or the regressand, is the logarithm of per capita consumption expenditure. The four regression results correspond to the urban and rural areas for 2003 and 2006.

Each regression result has two columns. The first column reports regression coefficients and the second reports standard errors of the coefficients. A regression coefficient of any regressor indicates the change in the regressand caused by a one-unit increase in that regressor. The standard error of a regressor indicates the reliability of its coefficient. Standard errors are always positive, and a higher standard error indicates lower reliability of the coefficient.

Rows *46, 47,* and *48* report the intercept term, number of observations, and adjusted R-squares (R^2), respectively. The *intercept term*, or constant term, denotes the level of the consumption expenditure logarithm not explained or determined by any regressors, or adjusted R-square denoted power of prediction of all regressors, or the model's goodness-of-fit. If the adjusted R-square is 1, then the regressors predict the regressand with complete accuracy. If a regressor's *p*-value is less than 0.01, then *** is added to the coefficient. If the *p*-value is less than 0.05, then ** is added to the coefficient. Finally, if the *p*-value is less than 0.1, then * is added to the coefficient. *P*-values denote regressors' significance level.

Note that all variables in the *regions, sland, gender of household head, education of household head,* and *employment status of household head* categories are dummy variables or binary variables. They take a value of only 0 or 1.

A binary variable coefficient denotes the change in regressand when the dummy variable's value changes from 0 to 1. For example, consider the coefficient of the regressor *Female* in the household head gender category for urban regression in 2003. The coefficient is –0.073 *[25,A]*, implying that the per capita expenditure logarithm for a member in a female-headed household is 0.073 units lower than that of a male-headed household. The regressor's standard error is 0.02 *[25,B]* with a *p*-value less than 0.01 (indicated by *** after the regressor), and thus the coefficient is highly significant. The coefficient of the same regressor for urban regression in 2006 is –0.101 *[25,E]* with a *p*-value of less than 0.01, implying that the per capita consumption expenditure gap between female- and male-headed households increased over the three-year period.

Lessons for Policy Makers

The table provides a detailed analysis of the determinants of per capita consumption expenditure. If we focus on column A, it is evident that variables such as the share of children age 7–16 years *[row 43]*, female-headed households *[row 25]*, and household head unemployed *[row 44]* and inactive employment *[row 45]* status have significant negative effects on per capita consumption expenditure for the urban area in 2003.

In contrast, the variables such as 0.5–1.0 hectare of landholding *[row 22]*, household head higher education *[row 31]*, and living in Imereti *[row 17]* have a significant positive impact on per capita expenditure for both urban and rural areas in both years. Hence, the analysis summarized in table 3.28

provides a tool to understand per capita consumption expenditure determinants and to develop appropriate poverty eradication policies.

Changes in the Probability of Being in Poverty

Table 3.29 analyzes changes in the probability of being in poverty using a probit regression model based on the consumption regression presented in table 3.28. Rows denote changes in values for various variables—such as change from having no children 0–6 years old to having one child, change

Table 3.29: Changes in the Probability of Being in Poverty
percent

		2003		2006	
		Urban	Rural	Urban	Rural
	Variables	A	B	C	D
	Demographic event, child born in the family				
1	Change from having no children 0–6 years old to having 1 child	2.0	18.0	31.5	17.8
2	Change from having no children 0–6 years old to having 2 children	4.7	33.1	57.9	33.5
	Land acquisition event				
3	Change from "0 ha" to "less than 0.2 ha"	−18.9	−15.3	−16.6	−18.0
4	Change from "0 ha" to "0.2–0.5 ha"	−27.4	−33.6	−21.8	−20.9
5	Change from "0 ha" to "0.5–1.0 ha"	−37.4	−44.5	−19.8	−38.5
6	Change from "0 ha" to "over 1.0 ha"	−3.5	−51.9	−29.5	−49.6
	Change of household head (following divorce, migration, and so forth)				
7	Change from "Male" to "Female"	13.0	0.2	18.4	3.9
	Education event: change in household head's education				
8	Change from "Elementary or less" to "Incomplete secondary"	10.5	−4.5	−28.0	−10.3
9	Change from "Elementary or less" to "Secondary"	−3.3	−13.6	−22.4	−23.0
10	Change from "Elementary or less" to "Vocational-technical"	−17.6	−18.8	−27.8	−29.5
11	Change from "Elementary or less" to "Special secondary"	−23.0	−27.2	−33.0	−36.7
12	Change from "Elementary or less" to "Higher education"	−40.3	−33.7	−51.4	−51.8
	Sector of employment event: household head's sector of employment				
13	Change from "Agriculture" to "Industry"	5.7	−53.1	25.3	−28.1
14	Change from "Agriculture" to "Trade"	−15.6	−36.5	−10.6	−26.2
15	Change from "Agriculture" to "Transport"	−5.2	−40.5	7.7	−40.3
16	Change from "Agriculture" to "Other Services"	−13.8	−43.8	20.3	−4.7
17	Change from "Agriculture" to "Industry"	8.8	−17.7	7.1	−19.4
18	Change from "Agriculture" to "Trade"	19.6	−20.0	4.8	−16.0
19	Change from "Agriculture" to "Transport"	4.2	−28.7	36.8	−37.0
20	Change from "Agriculture" to "Government"	8.4	−30.7	−2.3	−36.4
21	Change from "Agriculture" to "Education"	7.5	−7.8	5.7	−6.4
22	Change from "Agriculture" to "Health Care"	8.3	−12.0	7.8	−36.7
23	Change from "Agriculture" to "Other"	25.3	−20.9	4.3	−0.7
24	Change from "Agriculture" to "Unemployed"	87.4	20.7	72.1	9.7
25	Change from "Agriculture" to "Inactive"	48.2	17.4	35.6	9.8

Source: Based on consumption regression presented in table 3.28.

from owning 0 hectare of land to > 1 hectare of land, and change from male-headed household to female-headed household. Columns report the percentage changes in the probability of being in poverty for rural and urban areas and across 2003 and 2006.

Recall from our discussion about table 3.28 that the interpretation of dummy or binary variables is different from that of continuous variables. A dummy variable, unlike a continuous variable, may take only a value of either 0 or 1. Table 3.28 described how the probability of being in poverty changes as values of certain variables change.

The probability of being in poverty in 2003 increased by 2.0 percent [1,A] if an individual moved from an urban household with no children in the 0–6 years age group to an urban household with one child in the same age group, all other factors being identical. The probability of being in poverty in 2003 is increased by 18.0 percent [1,B] if an individual moved from a rural household with no children in the 0–6 years age group to a rural household with one child in the same age group, all else being identical. In the urban area, the increase in the probability of being in poverty in 2006 for the same reason is 31.5 percent [1,C].

Similarly, in 2003 if an individual moved from a male-headed urban household to a female-headed urban household, all else being identical, then the probability of being in poverty increased by 13.0 percent [7,A]. If an individual moved from a male-headed rural household to a female-headed rural household, all else being identical, then the probability of being in poverty increased by only 0.2 percent [7,B]. The largest increase in the probability of being in poverty in 2003 in the urban area occurred when an individual moved from a household where the head is employed in the agricultural sector to a household where the head is unemployed [24,A], all else being identical.

Lessons for Policy Makers

The table provides a detailed analysis of how the probability of being in poverty changes when some of the crucial determinants of poverty are adjusted. Note that if the household head's education in the urban area in 2006 increased from elementary education or less to secondary education, all else remaining equal, then the probability of a member in that household being in poverty fell by 22.4 percent [9,C]. Similarly, in rural Georgia for both years, if the household head transferred from the agricultural sector to any other employment sector, all else being equal, then the probability of being in poverty fell. Hence, this analysis provides a tool to better understand the source of poverty and what type of policy would be more efficient in terms of eradicating poverty.

Growth and Redistribution Decomposition of Poverty Changes

Table 3.30 decomposes the change in poverty into a change in the mean per capita consumption expenditure and a change in distribution of consumption expenditure around the mean, following Huppi and Ravallion (1991). Table rows denote three regions—urban, rural, and all of Georgia—for two different poverty lines. The per capita consumption expenditure is measured in lari per month. Poverty lines are set at GEL 75.4 (poor) and GEL 45.2 (extremely poor) for each household and household member. For simplicity in this table, we present the decomposition for headcount ratio only, but the technique is equally applicable to other poverty measures in the FGT class.

Columns A and B report the headcount ratio of the three regions for years 2003 and 2006, respectively, and column C reports the changes over time. Columns D, E, and F decompose the change in the headcount ratio between 2003 and 2006 into three different terms. Column D reports the effect of growth on poverty, referred to as the *growth effect*. Column E reports the effect of redistribution on poverty and is called the *redistribution effect*. Column F reports the interaction term and is referred to as the *interaction effect*, following Huppi and Ravallion (1991).

Table 3.30: Growth and Redistribution Decomposition of Poverty Changes, Headcount Ratio

percent

Region	2003	2006	Actual change	Growth	Redistribution	Interaction
	A	B	C	D	E	F
Poverty line = GEL 75.4						
1 Urban	28.1	30.8	2.7	0.6	1.9	0.1
2 Rural	31.6	31.1	−0.5	−0.7	−0.1	0.3
3 **Total**	**29.9**	**31.0**	**1.0**	**0.0**	**1.0**	**0.0**
Poverty line = GEL 45.2						
4 Urban	8.9	9.3	0.4	0.3	0.0	0.1
5 Rural	11.4	12.1	0.7	−0.2	1.0	0.0
6 **Total**	**10.2**	**10.7**	**0.5**	**0.0**	**0.5**	**0.0**

Source: Based on ADePT Poverty and Inequality modules using Integrated Household Survey of Georgia 2003 and 2006.

It is evident from the table that the overall headcount ratio in 2003 is 29.9 percent [3,A], which increased to 31.0 percent in 2006 [3,B]. These numbers can be verified from table 3.2. The actual change in the overall headcount ratio is 1.0 percentage point (rounded) [3,C]. The actual change is broken down into three components: growth effect, redistribution effect, and interaction effect. By looking at the corresponding figures in columns D, E, and F, we see that the change is caused mainly by redistribution rather than growth. We can verify from table 3.1 that growth in mean is negligible compared to change in inequality in terms of the Gini coefficient.

The picture is slightly different for the urban and rural areas. The urban headcount ratio rose by 2.7 percentage points from 28.1 percent [1,A] to 30.8 percent [1,B], with both growth effect and redistribution effect being positive. The urban redistribution effect [1,E] is more than three times larger than the urban growth effect [1,D]. For the rural area, the headcount ratio fell from 31.6 percent [2,A] to 31.1 percent [2,B]. In this case, both the growth effect [2,D] and the redistribution effect [2,E] are negative.

The appendix contains additional tables and figures that may be helpful in understanding concepts and results in terms of the data for Georgia in 2003 and 2006.

Note

1. For technical details, see Huppi and Ravallion (1991).

Reference

Huppi, M., and M. Ravallion. 1991. "The Sectoral Structure of Poverty during an Adjustment Period: Evidence for Indonesia in the Mid-1980s." *World Development* 19 (12): 1653–78.

Chapter 4

Frontiers of Poverty Measurement

As conditions change and policy concerns evolve, there is a steady demand from countries and institutions for new tools to evaluate poverty. In this chapter, we briefly discuss frontier technologies that are, at the time of this writing, in various stages of being implemented in the ADePT software. Most are refinements of the traditional approach to poverty measurement, but some elaborate on related concepts of inequality and income standards.

Ultra-Poverty

Our first enhancement builds on a theme that originally led to the construction of poverty measures beyond the headcount ratio, namely, that within the poor population important differences exist in the nature of poverty. The headcount ratio P_0 ignores these differences by valuing each poor person equally without regard to the depth of poverty. Measures like the poverty gap P_1 reflect the depth of poverty among the poor, while others like the FGT (Foster-Greer-Thorbecke) index P_2 take into account its distribution by emphasizing those with the largest gaps. The measurement of *ultra-poverty* carries this differentiation one step further by focusing on the poorest of the poor.

People who are most impoverished according to some well-defined criterion are often the subject of special concern. The poverty experienced by this group is often called "extreme" or "acute." Here we use the term *ultra-poverty* to describe the condition of poorest poor. Who are the ultra-poor and how can their poverty be measured? The answer depends on the underlying concept of poverty and the availability of data. The traditional monetary approach to poverty would suggest focusing on people more *deeply* income deprived. A second chronic poverty approach might define the ultra-poor as those who are more *persistently* deprived. If many different achievements are being measured, those who are more *multiply* deprived may be the ultra-poor. Alternatively, deprivation that is more spatially *concentrated* might be associated with ultra-poverty. The discussion here focuses on the first of these: ultra-poverty as deep deprivation in income.

In addition to the usual poverty line z that signifies the minimum acceptable level for the population under consideration, we now assume that an even lower *ultra-poverty line* $z_u < z$ is used to identify a more deeply deprived group called the *ultra-poor*. One method of evaluating ultra-poverty is to apply a traditional poverty measure P to the income distribution x given the lower line z_u. The resulting level $P(x;z_u)$ could then be used to evaluate ultra-poverty in a way entirely analogous to the way poverty is evaluated using $P(x;z)$ at the usual poverty line. Indeed, the pair $P(x;z)$ and $P(x;z_u)$ could be used in concert to gauge the extent to which poverty and ultra-poverty change across time and space.

A difficulty with this approach is that, aside from the special case of the headcount ratio, the levels of ultra-poverty and poverty obtained are not directly related to each other. For example, $P_1(x;z_u)$ identifies fewer people than $P_1(x;z)$, but because z_u is smaller than z, the normalized gaps of the ultra-poor are also reduced in $P(x;z_u)$. The ultra-poverty line z_u is playing two roles here: the cutoff by which the set of ultra-poor people is identified and the standard against which shortfalls are evaluated in the aggregation. An alternative would be to use the ultra-poverty line z_u in the first role and the standard poverty line z in the second. Ultra-poverty would be measured commensurate with overall poverty figures and would allow a straightforward calculation of the importance of the ultra-poor in a country's overall poverty.

Hybrid Poverty Lines

It was argued above that an absolute poverty line z_u may not be sustainable when a large change occurs in the size of the income distribution. A similar observation applies when comparing two countries at very different levels of development using an absolute line. The problem is that when the income standard varies a great deal, it seems reasonable that the poverty line should reflect this change, at least to some extent. Yet an absolute poverty line, by definition, is fixed and independent of any changes in the income standard. Stated differently, when an income standard (such as the mean) changes by 1 percent, an absolute poverty line changes by 0 percent, so that the *income elasticity of the poverty line* is zero.

An alternative approach uses a relative poverty line z_r, defined as a fixed proportion of a given income standard. For example, 60 percent of median income is a relative poverty line used in the European Union. For relative poverty lines, if a country's income standard changes by 1 percent, then the poverty line also changes by 1 percent, implying that the poverty line's income elasticity is one. An argument against this approach is that it makes the poverty line too sensitive to changes in the income standard.

Several approaches have been explored to negotiate the landscape between the extremes of absolute and relative poverty lines. Foster (1998) suggests a hybrid poverty line that is a weighted geometric mean of relative and absolute poverty lines. In symbols, the poverty line is $z = z_r^\rho z_a^{1-\rho}$, where $0 \leq \rho \leq 1$. Note that ρ can be interpreted as the income elasticity of the hybrid poverty line, because when z_r's income standard rises by 1 percent, the relative component z_r rises by 1 percent, which, in turn, increases the hybrid poverty line z by ρ percent.

On the one hand, if parameter ρ is set to zero so the entire weight is given to the absolute component, then the hybrid poverty line becomes the absolute poverty line where the elasticity is zero. On the other hand, if ρ is one so the full weight is on the relative component, then the hybrid poverty line becomes the relative poverty line and the elasticity is one. If $0 < \rho < 1$, then the hybrid poverty line will lie between the absolute and relative lines and have an elasticity between zero and one.

How is the elasticity to be set? One approach is to estimate the parameter using data on existing poverty lines and income levels. Foster and Székely (2006) regress poverty lines on private consumption per capita for 92 household surveys across 18 countries and find an elasticity of 0.36. A second approach is to select "reasonable" values and check for robustness. Madden (2000), for example, analyzed Irish poverty using the 1987 and 1994 Irish Household Budget Surveys for two intermediate values of the parameter, 0.5 and 0.7, and found that results were similar for the two.

Finally, by interpreting ρ as the extent to which society believes the poor should share in growth, we can view the selection of ρ as a normative decision requiring political discourse to obtain a solution. Regardless of the method for choosing ρ, the resulting tools allow a useful decomposition of poverty into an absolute poverty group (those below the absolute poverty line) and a hybrid or relative group (those above the absolute but below the hybrid poverty line). This is analogous to the above decomposition into the ultra-poor and the poor above the ultra-poverty line and likewise could be helpful in guiding differential policy responses for the two groups.

Atkinson and Bourguignon (2000) combine absolute and relative poverty lines in a different way. When mean income is low enough that $z_a > z_r$, they suggest that the absolute poverty line would be appropriate and hence the income elasticity of the poverty line is zero in this region. However, when incomes are high enough for $z_r > z_a$, the relative poverty line should apply, yielding a unitary income elasticity of the poverty line. The hybrid poverty line of a country is then the maximum of the absolute poverty line and the relative poverty line, or $z = \max\{z_a, z_r\}$. Atkinson and Bourguignon use data on poverty lines and mean incomes to calibrate the absolute and relative lines.

Ravallion and Chen (2011) argue that an income elasticity of one is implausible and posit a *weak relativity axiom* that requires poverty to fall if all incomes rise by the same proportion. They then provide the alternative hybrid poverty line formula $z = \max\{z_a, f + z_r\}$, where $f > 0$ is interpreted as the fixed cost of social inclusion. They set the three parameters of their proposed formula with the aid of data. Although the line of Atkinson and Bourguignon (2000) does not satisfy the weak relativity axiom for the standard scale invariant poverty measures, the lines of Foster (1998) and Ravallion and Chen (2011) do.

Categorical and Ordinal Variables

The previous analysis applies to any cardinal welfare indicator, where cardinality requires that values convey more information than just more or less. Nonmonetary examples of cardinal variables might include calories, years of schooling, or hectares of land. Many other variables are more appropriately interpreted as ordinal, because their values are only indicators of order. Others might be categorical and have no values or underlying ordering at all. Examples of ordinal variables include self-reported health and subjective well-being. Categorical variables include sanitation facilities or the floor materials in a house. What can be done if we want to evaluate the size, spread, or base of such a welfare indicator?

Allison and Foster (2004) describe ways of comparing distributions of self-reported health in terms of spread and, in the process, provide new approaches to evaluating size and base for this ordinal variable. The main tools are dominance rankings. Changes in size and poverty are evaluated using first-order stochastic dominance. Changes in spread are twin first-order dominance movements away from the median category. To calculate a mean, an inequality measure, or an FGT poverty index for $\alpha > 0$, one must cardinalize the ordinal variable, and hence the comparisons obtained are not generally meaningful (because a different cardinalization could reverse the ranking).

The headcount ratio, however, is identical for all cardinalizations and thus is an appropriate tool for measuring poverty when the variable is ordinal or even categorical. Of course, the headcount ratio provides no information at all about depth. Bennett and Hatzimasoura (2011) provide one approach to evaluating depth with an ordinal variable, based on a reinterpretation of the poverty gap as "average headcount ratios" across different poverty lines.

Chronic Poverty

Returning to the case of income, we saw how poor people can differ from one another in policy-relevant ways. For example, poor people with deeper income shortfalls are distinct from those just below the poverty line. Time is a second dimension for differentiating among the poor: *persistent* poverty is different from *temporary* poverty. Persistent poverty is usually termed *chronic* poverty, and there are two main ways of identifying and measuring it:

- The components approach of Jalan and Ravallion (2000) identifies as chronically poor someone whose average income across several periods is below the poverty line. This method rules out people whose incomes temporarily dip below the line in a given period, but who, on average, earn more than poverty line income. Chronic poverty can then be measured by applying a standard poverty measure to the average incomes distribution.

The use of average income implies that each period's income is a perfect substitute for any other period's income. Alternative methods that allow for imperfect income substitution across periods have been proposed: see Calvo and Dercon (2009) or Foster and Santos (2006).

- In the spells method, exemplified by Foster (2009), the chronically poor are those whose incomes are frequently below the poverty line, say, in two of four periods. People with fewer poverty spells are not chronically poor—their spells are censored out when chronic poverty is measured. Aggregation proceeds as in the standard FGT case, but now data on spells, normalized gaps, and squared normalized gaps are collected in matrices.

The dimension-adjusted FGT indices are simply the means of the respective censored matrices. For example, the dimension-adjusted headcount ratio is the number of spells experienced by chronically poor people divided by the maximum number of spells that could be experienced by everyone. This approach assumes there is no income substitution across periods, and, indeed, incomes are never aggregated as they are in the components approach. It also presumes that poverty spells have the same value, no matter the period or person.

Either approach to measuring chronic poverty allows the separate identification of chronic and transient poor and a corresponding decomposition of poverty into chronic and transient components. This can be particularly useful for tracking chronic poverty across subgroups for better targeting of the policy mix.

Note that chronic poverty measurement increases data requirements substantially. Panel data linked across periods at the individual or household level are needed to undertake this form of measurement; it is not enough to have multiple data cross-sections. Given the relative scarcity of panel data, substantial efforts are being devoted to find novels ways of constructing virtual panels from cross-sectional data. See, for example, Dang and others (2011).

Multidimensional Poverty

There is interest in developing and applying poverty measures that are multidimensional in that shortfalls from multiple welfare indicators are used to identify the poor and measure poverty. Several reasons exist for this interest:

- Sen's capability approach has received greater acceptance as a way of conceptualizing well-being and poverty. According to Sen (1999), poverty is seen as capability deprivation. Because many capabilities exist, an accurate assessment of someone's poverty requires a simultaneous assessment of multiple dimensions.
- The number of datasets that would support a multidimensional assessment has increased.
- Strong demand comes from countries, international organizations, and nongovernmental organizations for instruments that measure poverty multidimensionally. For example, since 2009 the official poverty measure in Mexico has been multidimensional, reflecting shortfalls in income and several other "social" dimensions as required by the relevant law (CONEVAL 2011). More recently, Colombia elected to supplement its official income poverty measure with a multidimensional poverty measure that is also used to coordinate social policy among its ministries and the presidency (Angulo, Diaz, and Pardo 2011).

The *World Development Report 2000/2001: Attacking Poverty* (World Bank 2000) expressed the generally accepted idea that poverty is inherently multidimensional. But as emphasized by Ferreira (2011), less agreement exists on how to measure poverty when it has many constituent welfare indicators. One way is to examine the nature of the indicators and how they relate to one another. Some variables—such as earned and unearned income—are easy to combine into a single aggregate. Others—such as health and employment outcomes—are not. It is helpful to distinguish between these cases.

When the variables can be meaningfully aggregated into a composite welfare indicator for each person, the distribution of the composite indicator could be evaluated using traditional poverty measurement methods. An aggregate cutoff could be chosen to identify who is poor, and their poverty could be measured using a poverty measure. In this way, the multidimensional case could be converted to the single dimensional environment, where well-known methods apply.

However, just because combining variables into one indicator is feasible does not necessarily mean it is the best way to proceed. Aggregate analysis conceals deprivations in individual variables that are compensated by higher levels in other dimensions. If missing deprivations are policy relevant, a more disaggregated approach may be needed. In India, for example, aggregate consumption is expanding and poverty headcount ratios are falling, yet a high prevalence of malnutrition persists among children. Because of this situation, shifting focus from shortfalls in aggregate consumption to shortfalls in food consumption, or to shortfalls in consumption of food by children, may be natural, if the data allow. When an aggregate welfare indicator conceals policy-relevant information, a lower level of aggregation may be preferable, even when full aggregation is feasible.

Now consider the case where all the key variables cannot be meaningfully aggregated into a single composite welfare indicator or where, for policy reasons, complete aggregation is not desirable (such as where deprivations in a certain variable are important to track). In this case, alternative approaches must be explored. One option is to limit consideration to a subset of the welfare indicators that can be aggregated and to drop the rest. This approach has the benefit of expediency but ignores key poverty components. Let us suppose instead that all variables must be used and that two or more welfare indicators remain after aggregation. How can poverty be measured?

Many recent papers have considered this question, including Tsui (2002); Bourguignon and Chakravarty (2003); Alkire and Foster (2007, 2011); Massoumi and Lugo (2008); and Bossert, Chakravarty, and D'Ambrosio (2009). As with chronic poverty measurement, the aggregation step used by each is based directly on traditional, single-dimensional poverty measures, appropriately expanded to account for many dimensions. For the identification step, all begin with a cutoff in each dimension—which might be called a *deprivation cutoff*. If the variable is below its respective cutoff, the person is considered to be deprived in that dimension. Most of these papers then adopt the *union approach* to identification, whereby anyone who is deprived in even a single dimension is identified as poor. Some also discuss the *intersection approach*, which is at the other extreme where someone must be deprived in every dimension to be identified as being poor.

As noted by Alkire and Foster (2011), the union approach often identifies a very large group of poor, whereas the intersection approach often identifies a vanishingly narrow slice, and this becomes particularly evident when the number of dimensions expands. They propose an intermediate approach to identifying the poor that depends on a simple measure of the breadth or multiplicity of deprivation the person experiences. In this approach, every deprivation has a value. The overall breadth of deprivation experienced by a person is measured by summing the values of deprivations experienced. A *poverty cutoff* is selected, and if the breadth of deprivation is above or equal to the poverty cutoff, then the person is identified as being poor. The union approach is obtained at one extreme where the poverty cutoff is very low, while the intersection approach arises at the other where the cutoff is very high. An intermediate poverty cutoff identifies as poor those who are sufficiently multiply deprived. This is the *dual cutoff* approach to identification suggested by Alkire and Foster (2011).

For aggregation, Alkire and Foster (2011) extend the FGT class of indices to the multidimensional context. They do this by constructing three matrices analogous to the vectors used in the FGT definitions, except that now each person has a vector containing information to be aggregated into the overall measure. The matrices are censored in that the data of anyone who is not poor are replaced by a vector of zeroes. The *censored deprivation matrix* g^0 contains deprivation values (when a person is deprived in a dimension and poor) or zeroes (when the person is not deprived in the dimension or not poor). The *adjusted headcount ratio* $M_0 = \mu(g^0)$ is its mean. The measure can be equivalently expressed as $M_0 = HA$, where H is the population percentage identified as poor and A is the average breadth of deprivation they experience. Analogous definitions yield the *adjusted poverty gap* M_1 and the *adjusted FGT* M_2, as part of a family M_α of measures where $\alpha \geq 0$. The methodology of Alkire and Foster combines a dual cutoff identification approach and an adjusted FGT index.

The adjusted headcount ratio has several properties that make it particularly attractive in practical applications. It can be used when the underlying data are ordinal or even categorical. Its interpretation as $H \times A$ is similar to the interpretation of P_G, the traditional poverty gap, because $P_G = P_H \times P_{IG}$, where P_H is the traditional headcount ratio and P_{IG} is the average normalized income gap of the poor. M_0 augments the information in H using A, which is a measure of breadth rather than depth. It is decomposable by population subgroup. It can dig down into the aggregate numbers to understand the key deprivations that are behind the measured poverty level. Related examples can be found in Alkire and Foster (2011) and the recent Human Development Reports of the United Nations Development Programme, which implemented the approach across 109 countries as the Multidimensional Poverty Index (MPI) (see also Alkire, Foster, and Santos 2011).

Measuring poverty in a multidimensional environment is challenging, and the dual cutoff, adjusted headcount ratio methodology has been subject to intense scrutiny. See, for example, Ravallion (2011) and the rejoinders by Alkire and Foster (2011) and Alkire, Foster, and Santos (2011). Ravallion (2011) offers an alternative approach that evaluates each dimension separately using a traditional single-dimensional method to generate a *dashboard* of dimension-specific deprivation measures. This approach provides useful information about who is deprived in a given dimension and the extent of their deprivation, and by using headcount ratios, it can also deal with ordinal or categorical variables.

However, the approach provides no answer to the central question of identification: Who is poor? In addition, the dimension-specific indices reflect only the marginal distributions of the separate dimensions and hence ignore their joint distribution. The methodology of Alkire and Foster relies importantly on the joint distribution to determine the extent to which an individual is multiply deprived. Their proposal is a first attempt at a practical methodology for measuring poverty multidimensionally. Given the demand for measurement methods that capture the multidimensional nature of poverty, we can expect greater use of these and related methods in the future.

Multidimensional Standards

How should a society measure progress? Per capita income or expenditure is well suited for indicating the resources available to an average member of the society. However, there are at least two substantive critiques of this measure as the sole indicator of progress. First, as noted previously in the discussion of income standards, per capita income or expenditure thoroughly ignores the distribution of resources among the population. Other possibilities, such as the Atkinson or Sen income standards, are sensitive to the distribution and might well be preferable as an indicator of societal progress.

Second, monetary resources are not the only resources important to a person's well-being. Without a more complete picture of the capabilities available to people, or at least of the levels of achievement in the various domains, we may be seeing only a partial view of progress. To be sure, income and other welfare indicators are often positively correlated, for both individual and country-level data, which may suggest that the nonincome indicators are not needed. But as emphasized by Sen (1999), notable exceptions to these regularities exist. A proper measure of progress should convey empirical realities in all eventualities, including exceptional cases. Correlation does not justify dropping important dimensions in assessing progress.

The Human Development Index (HDI) of the United Nations Development Programme was designed as an alternative to income per capita that includes health and education achievements in a country (thus addressing the second critique). The underlying structure of the traditional HDI is straightforward, even if the details of its construction are not. A country's achievements in income, health, and education are summarized in three indicators that are normalized to lie between zero and one. The traditional HDI is a simple mean of these components. The precise construction of the indicators—including the choice of "goalposts" for normalizing a variable and its specific transformation—can affect the HDI's picture of development across countries. As an example, the income indicator used in the HDI is based on a *logarithm* of income per capita; if the untransformed variable were used instead, the ranking at the upper end would more closely follow the income ranking of these countries.

This lack of robustness is indicative of the challenge of constructing component indicators that can be meaningfully combined into a composite indicator. One alternative to combining dimensions into an overall indicator is to provide a *dashboard* of dimensional indicators. If indicators were not being combined, normalizing goalposts and special transformations would not be needed; the variables could be presented in their original, more comprehensible forms. In particular, one could dispense with the log transformation, because average income itself would rank countries the same way—within this dimension.

However, many good reasons exist for using a composite indicator rather than a vector of components. A single numerical indicator is more salient and easier to track. A comprehensive measure emphasizes the point that we are more interested in overall progress than progress in any given dimension. Moreover, given that the aggregation formula is decomposable, it invites further analysis to identify which components are driving the overall results. The success of the HDI would have been unlikely if only a dashboard of dimensional indicators had been provided.

The mean is just one way of combining dimensions to get a measure of progress. Other forms are possible. Foster, McGillivray, and Seth (2010, 2013) use the weighted additive form of the traditional HDI but allow the weights to vary from the HDI's case of equal weights. They examine the robustness of HDI comparisons to variations in weights and derive conditions under which the original ranking is preserved.

A second aggregation formula can be found in the "new" HDI that appeared in the *Human Development Report 2010* (UNDP 2010). Instead of aggregating by using an arithmetic mean, the new HDI has adopted a geometric mean. Under this approach, component indicators are viewed as imperfect substitutes rather than the perfect substitutes implicit in an additive form. The rates of trade-off across dimensions now depend on the component levels, with indicators having lower relative levels being valued more highly. This approach rewards balanced development in which no one dimension lags too far behind or moves too far ahead of the rest.

In the *Human Development Report 2010*, the relation between the old and the new methodology is presented in a figure in the statistical annex (UNDP 2010, 217 figure T1.1). Although the old and new HDI rankings have a positive relationship, the ranks are not perfectly positively associated. The new HDI values tend to be lower than the old HDI values, mainly because the income component had been normalized with respect to a much larger value, in addition to applying a geometric mean instead of the traditional arithmetic mean.

By focusing purely on average achievements in a country, the HDI is also subject to the first critique of per capita income—that it ignores inequality across people. In a multidimensional setting, there are more ways for a concern for inequality to be incorporated into a measure. One aspect is inequality within each dimension. Hicks (1997), for example, uses the Sen (or Gini-discounted) mean to evaluate the distribution of each component, then averages across dimensions. Greater inequality with dimensions lowers the Sen mean and hence the overall measure.

Noting that the resulting measure is not subgroup consistent, Foster, López-Calva, and Székely (2005) propose an alternative class of distribution-sensitive measures. A general mean with fixed parameter $\alpha < 1$ is applied to each component, thereby discounting for within-dimension inequality using an Atkinson inequality measure. To ensure that the overall measure is subgroup consistent, they aggregate across dimensions using the same general mean (having the same fixed parameter $\alpha < 1$). The resulting formula can be viewed as a general mean of the *matrix* of individual welfare indicators and is an example of what might be called a *multidimensional standard*—which generalizes the notion of an income standard from a vector (of one welfare indicator across many people) to a matrix (of several welfare indicators across many people).

The approach has another advantage besides subgroup consistency: measures in this class are *path independent*, in that one obtains the same overall value whether one aggregates within each dimension and then across dimensions (as defined above) or one aggregates across dimensions for each person (analogous to a utility function) and then across people (as with a traditional individualistic social welfare function). The latter order of aggregation is more traditional in welfare economics, because it builds up from the individual. However, the alternate definition is easier to derive empirically, because the data need not be linked at the individual level. This convenient property was used in the construction of the Inequality-Adjusted Human Development Index (IA-HDI), which has been reported in the Human Development Reports since 2010 (see Alkire and Foster 2010 for a more extensive discussion). It is a member of the Foster, López-Calva, and Székely (2005) class using the geometric mean (or $\alpha = 0$).

The second aspect of multidimensional inequality concerns association across dimensions and is perhaps best explained using terminology from statistics. The distribution of welfare indicators across people can be summarized in the *joint distribution*, which indicates the prevalence of combinations of welfare indicators across the population. Each joint distribution has associated with it a marginal distribution for each welfare indicator, which indicates the prevalence of the various levels of a welfare indicator in the population. Two different joint distributions may have the same marginal distribution; the association or correlation between indicators can be very different even when the distribution within each indicator is the same.

For example, suppose two societies have the same marginal distributions of achievements, and the well-being is measured by two dimensions: income and education. In the first society the indicators are highly positively correlated, meaning that one with higher income has higher education. This may be due to a failure of governance in providing free public education. As a result, people with low income are unable to obtain higher levels of education. Now suppose in a second country, the marginal distributions of two societies are the same, but the correlation is much lower. This may have happened because the government arranged public provision of education.

To detect the difference between these two situations, we need to use a measure that is sensitive to association between dimensions.

Seth (2009) extended the method of Foster and others to a class of multidimensional standards that are sensitive to both forms of inequality: the welfare indicators of each person are first aggregated using a general mean of order $\beta < 1$; then these personal aggregates are aggregated using a general mean of order $\alpha < 1$ to obtain the overall measure. Note that when α is equal to β, the measure belongs to the Foster and others class and is neutral to the second form of inequality. When α is not equal to β, the measure is sensitive to association among dimensions. For the detailed methodology, see Seth (2012). This second form of inequality has also been discussed in the poverty measurement literature (see Tsui 2002; Bourguignon and Chakravarty 2003; Alkire and Foster 2007, 2011).

Given a multidimensional standard s incorporating one or both notions of inequality, it is then straightforward to define a multidimensional inequality measure as the percentage shortfall of s from the overall mean achievement, namely, $I = (\mu - s)/\mu$. It should be noted, though, that many assumptions are needed to construct s, which can make multidimensional inequality I hard to measure in practice. Key among these are assumptions pertaining to the cardinalization and comparability of the component indicators; changing the way a variable is measured and altering its value vis-à-vis other variables can change the rankings provided by s and the inequality measure. Particularly vexing is the case where one or more of the variables are ordinal, so that the cardinal form of each variable must, by definition, be arbitrary. One way forward is to restrict consideration to multidimensional versions of stochastic dominance (see Atkinson and Bourguignon 1982). However, the case that addresses this issue—first-order dominance—is precisely the case where the first form of inequality must be ignored. Further work is needed to construct robust multidimensional standards and practical indicators of multidimensional inequality.

Inequality of Opportunity

The previous section examined the general case where several welfare indicators contribute to a person's well-being. We now return to the simpler case of a single welfare indicator, but where other variables provide information on relevant characteristics or "identities" of the individuals. Recent work has moved from evaluations of inequality across all people to measures of inequality across groups of people, with the goal of isolating forms of inequality that are particularly objectionable or policy relevant.

Roemer (1998) divides identity variables into *circumstances*, which are unrelated to actions taken by the person and hence the person is not accountable for such circumstances, and *efforts*, which are under the person's control. He argues that inequality across groups of people defined by circumstances is particularly objectionable. For example, income inequality across racial groups or across groups defined by the education levels of one's parents should be of special concern because it reflects an underlying inequality of opportunity. Ferreira and Gignoux (2008) implement this approach by applying Theil's second inequality measure, or the mean log deviation, to a smoothed distribution defined by replacing each income in a group with the group mean. In other words, inequality of opportunity is measured as a between-group inequality term. This general approach can be applied for different circumstance variables, and hence ways of defining groups, to obtain different inequality of opportunity measures conditional on that choice.

Stewart (2002) contends that group inequalities, which she calls *horizontal* inequalities, can be more important than overall or *vertical* inequalities. But rather than invoking a normative notion of equal opportunity, she uses an empirical argument: horizontal inequalities, such as those across ethnic groups, tend to be more closely linked to conflict than are vertical inequalities. Stewart emphasizes that many possible dimensions of achievements could be evaluated. The horizontal inequalities in a given dimension for a configuration of groups can be measured and monitored using the associated between-group inequality term.

The World Bank's Human Opportunity Index (HOI) is another group inequality measure that uses an opportunity interpretation of group inequalities. Here the focus is on the provision of social services, so the underlying distribution is taken to be dichotomous, with a zero being posted for all people without access to the service and a one for those having access. The overall mean of this variable then corresponds to the *coverage rate* for the social service. The aim is to go beyond the mean coverage to account for differential coverage rates across population subgroups, where the groups are defined using circumstantial variables. An inequality measure is applied to the smoothed distribution (which replaces a person's actual value with the group's coverage rate) to obtain a measure of inequality of opportunity.

The HOI is the overall coverage rate discounted by the inequality of opportunity or, equivalently, a distribution-sensitive income standard applied directly to the smoothed distribution.

The inequality measure used in the original HOI was the relative mean deviation, a rather crude inequality measure that ignores transfers on either side of the mean (see de Barros and others 2009). However, it is easy to consider other inequality measures that generate between-group inequality measures that are sensitive to differential coverage across subgroups on the same side of the mean. For example, if we use the Atkinson inequality measure based on the geometric and arithmetic means, the resulting HOI will evaluate the smoothed distribution using the geometric mean. Note that every different social service can lead to a different picture of a population's opportunity to access social services. An overall view may require aggregating access to services at the individual level or aggregating HOIs into an overall index. In addition, the measure is dependent on the particular circumstances selected to define population subgroups. These implementation challenges are worthwhile because the measures can help reveal inequalities that are especially salient and unjust.

Polarization

The term *polarization* describes a situation where a population spreads apart into well-defined extremes of high and low and loses observations in the middle. It is related to inequality in that a regressive transfer from low incomes to high incomes (across the middle) increases both polarization and inequality. However, the process of observations coming closer together at the extremes and thereby raising polarization entails progressive transfers that *lower* inequality. The two concepts go in different directions for this form of transformation.

The concept of polarization is not the same as the concept of inequality and requires its own measurement approach. Several polarization measures have been proposed over the past two decades, but the two most frequently cited are those of Foster and Wolfson (1992, 2010) and Esteban and Ray (1994). The Foster-Wolfson polarization measure first divides the entire population into two groups: one with achievements larger than the median achievement and the other with achievements below the median. The polarization measure is the difference between the between-group inequality and the within-group inequality (as measured by the Gini coefficient) times the ratio of mean to median (where the ratio of mean to median is a measure of skewness of the distribution).

Foster and Wolfson (1992, 2010) also propose dominance orderings based on polarization curves that can determine whether unambiguous increases in polarization have taken place. First-order polarization occurs when there are first-order stochastic dominant movements away from the median. Second-order polarization occurs when there are second-order dominant movements away from the median. The Foster-Wolfson polarization measure is related to the area below the second-order polarization curve. This approach has been extended by Zhang and Kanbur (2001) and Chakravarty and D'Ambrosio (2010).

In contrast to the Foster-Wolfson approach, in which two groups of observations are endogenously defined using the median as the dividing line, Esteban and Ray (1994) assume that several groups of observations are exogenously given, each around its own pole. Their polarization measure rises when the groups pull apart from one another, or when observations within a group become more tightly clustered together. The measure is challenging to implement in practice because no clear way is given for dividing an overall distribution into relevant clusters. These and other practical problems of implementation are addressed in Duclos, Esteban, and Ray (2004).

References

Alkire, S., and J. E. Foster. 2007. "Counting and Multidimensional Poverty Measurement." Working Paper 7, Oxford Poverty and Human Development Initiative, University of Oxford.

———. 2010. "Designing the Inequality-Adjusted Human Development Index (HDI)." Working Paper 37, Oxford Poverty and Human Development Initiative, University of Oxford.

———. 2011. "Counting and Multidimensional Poverty Measurement." *Journal of Public Economics* 95 (7–8): 476–87.

Alkire, S., J. E. Foster, and M. E. Santos. 2011. "Where Did Identification Go?" *Journal of Economic Inequality* 9 (3): 501–5.

Allison, R. A., and J. E. Foster. 2004. "Measuring Health Inequality Using Qualitative Data." *Journal of Health Economics* 23 (3): 505–24.

Angulo, R. C., B. Y. Diaz, and R. Pardo. 2011. "Multidimensional Poverty Index (MPI-Colombia) 1997–2010." Department of Planning (Departamento Nacional de Planeación), Bogota.

Atkinson, A. B., and F. Bourguignon. 1982. "The Comparison of Multi-Dimensioned Distributions of Economic Status." *Review of Economic Studies* 49 (2): 183–201.

———. 2000. "Poverty and Inclusion from a World Perspective." In *Governance, Equity, and Global Markets*, edited by J. E. Stiglitz and P.-A. Muet, 151–66. Oxford: Oxford University Press.

Bennett, C. J., and C. Hatzimasoura. 2011. "Poverty Measurement with Ordinal Data." IIEP-WP-201114, Institute for International Economic Policy, Elliott School of International Affairs, The George Washington University, Washington, DC.

Bossert, W., S. R. Chakravarty, and C. D'Ambrosio. 2009. "Multidimensional Poverty and Material Deprivation." Working Paper 129, Society for the Study of Economic Inequality (ECINEQ), Palma de Mallorca, Spain.

Bourguignon, F., and S. R. Chakravarty. 2003. "The Measurement of Multidimensional Poverty." *Journal of Economic Inequality* 1 (1): 25–49.

Calvo, C., and S. Dercon. 2009. "Chronic Poverty and All That: The Measurement of Poverty over Time." In *Poverty Dynamics: Interdisciplinary Perspectives*, edited by A. Addison, D. Hulme, and R. Kanbur, 29–58. Oxford: Oxford University Press.

Chakravarty, S. R., and C. D'Ambrosio. 2010. "Polarization Orderings of Income Distributions." *Review of Income and Wealth* 56 (1): 47–64.

CONEVAL (Consejo Nacional de Evaluación de la Política de Desarrollo Social). 2011. "Coneval Presents 2010 Poverty Levels for Each Municipality." Press Release No. 015, Mexico, D.F., December 2.

Dang, H.-A., P. Lanjouw, J. Luoto, and D. McKenzie. 2011. "Using Repeated Cross-Sections to Explore Movements in and out of Poverty." Policy Research Working Paper 5550, World Bank, Washington, DC.

de Barros, R. P., F. H. G. Ferreira, J. R. Molinas, M. Vega, and J. S. Chanduvi. 2009. *Measuring Inequality of Opportunities in Latin America and the Caribbean*. Washington, DC: World Bank.

Duclos, J.-Y., J. M. Esteban, and D. Ray. 2004. "Polarization: Concepts, Measurement, Estimation." *Econometrica* 72 (6): 1737–72.

Esteban, J. M., and D. Ray. 1994. "On the Measurement of Polarization." *Econometrica* 62 (4): 819–51.

Ferreira, F. 2011. "Poverty Is Multidimensional. but What Are We Going to Do about It?" *Journal of Economic Inequality* 9 (93): 493–95.

Ferreira, F., and J. Gignoux. 2008. "The Measurement of Inequality of Opportunity: Theory and an Application to Latin America." Policy Research Working Paper 4659, World Bank, Washington, DC.

Foster, J. E. 1998. "Absolute versus Relative Poverty." *American Economic Review* 88 (2): 335–41.

———. 2009. "A Class of Chronic Poverty Measures." In *Poverty Dynamics: Interdisciplinary Perspectives*, edited by A. Addison, D. Hulme, and R. Kanbur, 59–76. Oxford: Oxford University Press.

Foster, J. E., L. López-Calva, and M. Székely. 2005. "Measuring the Distribution of Human Development: Methodology and an Application to Mexico." *Journal of Human Development and Capabilities* 6 (1): 5–25.

Foster, J. E., M. McGillivray, and S. Seth. 2010. "Rank Robustness of Composite Indices: Dominance and Ambiguity." Paper presented at the 31st General Conference of the International Association for Research in Income and Wealth, St. Gallen, Switzerland, August 22–28.

———. 2013. "Composite Indices: Rank Robustness, Statistical Association, and Redundancy." *Econometric Reviews* 32 (1): 35–56.

Foster, J. E., and M. E. Santos. 2006. "Measuring Chronic Poverty." Paper presented at the 11th Annual Meeting of the Latin American and Caribbean Economic Association (LACEA), Instituto Tecnológico Autónomo de México, Mexico D. F., November 2–4.

Foster, J. E., and M. Székely. 2006. "Poverty Lines over Space and Time." Unpublished manuscript, Vanderbilt University, Nashville, TN.

Foster, J. E., and M. C. Wolfson. 1992. "Polarization and the Decline of the Middle Class: Canada and the U.S." Unpublished manuscript, Vanderbilt University, Nashville, TN.

———. 2010. "Polarization and the Decline of the Middle Class: Canada and the U.S." *Journal of Economic Inequality* 8 (2): 247–73.

Hicks, D. A. 1997. "The Inequality-Adjusted Human Development Index: A Constructive Proposal." *World Development* 25 (8): 1283–98.

Jalan, J., and M. Ravallion. 2000. "Is Transient Poverty Different? Evidence for Rural China." *Journal of Development Studies* 36 (6): 82–89.

Massoumi, E., and M. A. Lugo. 2008. "The Information Basis of Multivariate Poverty Assessments." In *Quantitative Approaches to Multidimensional*

Poverty Measurement, edited by N. Kakwani and J. Silber, 1–29. London: Palgrave MacMillan.

Madden, D. 2000. "Relative or Absolute Poverty Lines: A New Approach." *Review of Income and Wealth* 46 (2): 181–99.

Ravallion, M. 2011. "On Multidimensional Indices of Poverty." *Journal of Economic Inequality* 9 (2): 235–48.

Ravallion, M., and S. Chen. 2011. "Weakly Relative Poverty." *Review of Economics and Statistics* 93 (4): 1251–61.

Roemer, J. 1998. *Equality of Opportunity*. Cambridge, MA: Harvard University Press.

Sen, A. 1999. *Development as Freedom*. New York: Knopf.

Seth, S. 2009. "Inequality, Interactions, and Human Development." *Journal of Human Development and Capabilities* 10 (3): 375–96.

———. 2012. "A Class of Distribution and Association Sensitive Multidimensional Welfare Indices." *Journal of Economic Inequality*, doi: 10.1007/s10888-011-9210-3.

Stewart, F. 2002. "Horizontal Inequalities: A Neglected Dimension of Development." Working Paper 81, Queen Elizabeth House, University of Oxford.

Tsui, K.-Y. 2002. "Multidimensional Poverty Indices." *Social Choice and Welfare* 19 (1): 69–93.

UNDP (United Nations Development Programme). 2010. *Human Development Report 2010: The Real Wealth of Nations—Pathways to Human Development*. New York: Palgrave-Macmillan.

World Bank. 2000. *World Development Report 2000/2001: Attacking Poverty*. Washington, DC: World Bank.

Zhang, X., and R. Kanbur. 2001. "What Difference Do Polarisation Measures Make? An Application to China." *Journal of Development Studies* 37 (3): 85–98.

Chapter 5

Getting Started with ADePT

This chapter provides basic information about installing and using ADePT. The instructions are sufficient to perform a simple analysis. More information is available:

- Detailed instructions for using ADePT are provided in the *ADePT User's Guide*, which you can download from http://www.worldbank .org/adept ▸ **Documentation**.
- Video tutorials are available at http://www.worldbank.org/adept ▸ **Video Tutorials**.
- ADePT provides online help through the **Help** ▸ **Contents** command.
- For help with using an ADePT module, see appropriate chapters in this book or in another book in the *Streamlined Analysis with ADePT Software* series.
- Module-specific instructions, and example datasets, projects, and reports, are available at http://www.worldbank.org/adept ▸ **Modules**.
- Examples of datasets and projects are installed with ADePT. They are located in the*example* subfolder in the ADePT program folder. Use the examples with the instructions in this chapter to familiarize yourself with ADePT operations.

Conventions Used in This Chapter

- Windows, buttons, tabs, dialogs, and other features you see on screen are shown in **bold**. For example, the **Save As** dialog has a **Save** button and a **Cancel** button.
- Keystrokes are shown in SMALL CAPS. For example, you may be instructed to press the ENTER key.
- Menu commands use a shorthand notation. For example, **Project ▸ Exit** means "open the **Project** menu and click the **Exit** command."

Installing ADePT

System Requirements

- PC running Microsoft Windows XP (SP1 or later), Windows Vista, Windows Server 2003 and later, or Windows 7; ADePT runs in 32- and 64-bit environments.
- NET 2.0 or later (included with recent Windows installations) and all updates and patches
- 80MB disk space to install, plus space for temporary dataset copies
- At least 512MB RAM
- At least 1024 × 768 screen resolution
- At least one printer driver must be installed (even if no computer is connected).
- Microsoft® Excel® for Windows® (XP or later), Microsoft® Excel Viewer, or a compatible spreadsheet program for viewing reports generated by ADePT is required.
- A Web browser and Internet access are needed to download ADePT. Internet access is needed to install program updates and to load Web-based datasets into ADePT. Otherwise, ADePT runs without needing Internet access.

Installation

1. Download the ADePT installer by clicking the **ADePT Downloads** button at http://www.worldbank.org/adept.
2. Launch the installer, and follow the on-screen instructions.

ADePT automatically launches after installation.

Launching ADePT

1. Click the ADePT icon in the Windows® **Start** menu.
2. In the **Select ADePT Module** window, double-click the name of the module you want to use (see arrow in screenshot below). To open a health module, double-click **Health**, then click **Health Financing** or **Health Outcomes**.

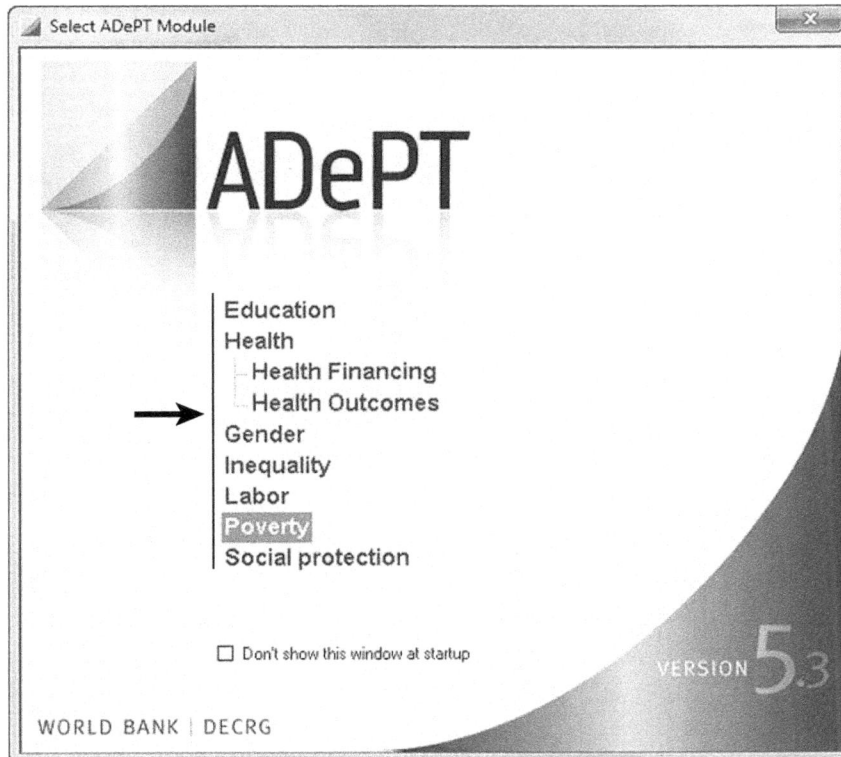

3. You now see the ADePT main window. (The example below shows ADePT configured with the Poverty module. The lower left-hand and upper right-hand panels will be different when another module is loaded.)

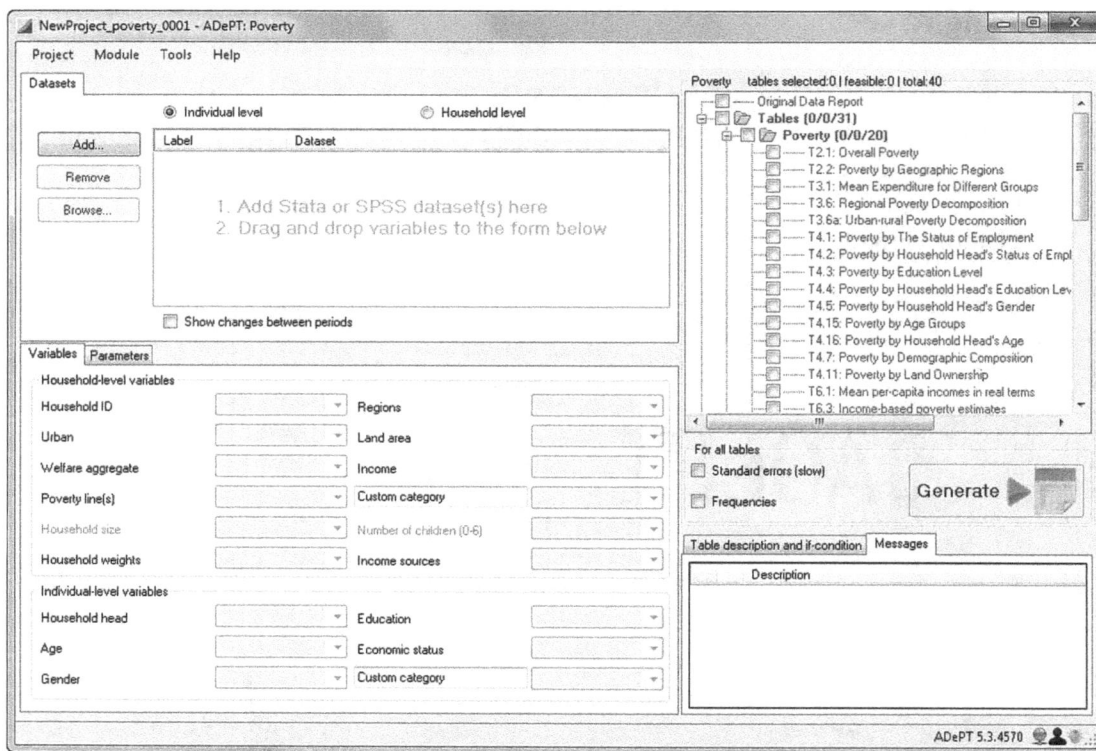

- *To switch to another module after launching ADePT:*
  a. **Module** ▸ **Select Module...**
  b. In the **Select ADePT Module** window, double-click the name of the module you want to use.

Overview of the Analysis Procedure

There are four general steps in performing an analysis:

1. Specify one or more datasets that you want to analyze.
2. Map dataset variables to ADePT analysis inputs.
3. Select tables and graphs.
4. Generate the report.

Perform each step in the ADePT main window:

1. Click **Add...** button to load dataset(s).
   Enter dataset year in **Label** column.

3. Select tables and/or graphs
   to be included in report.

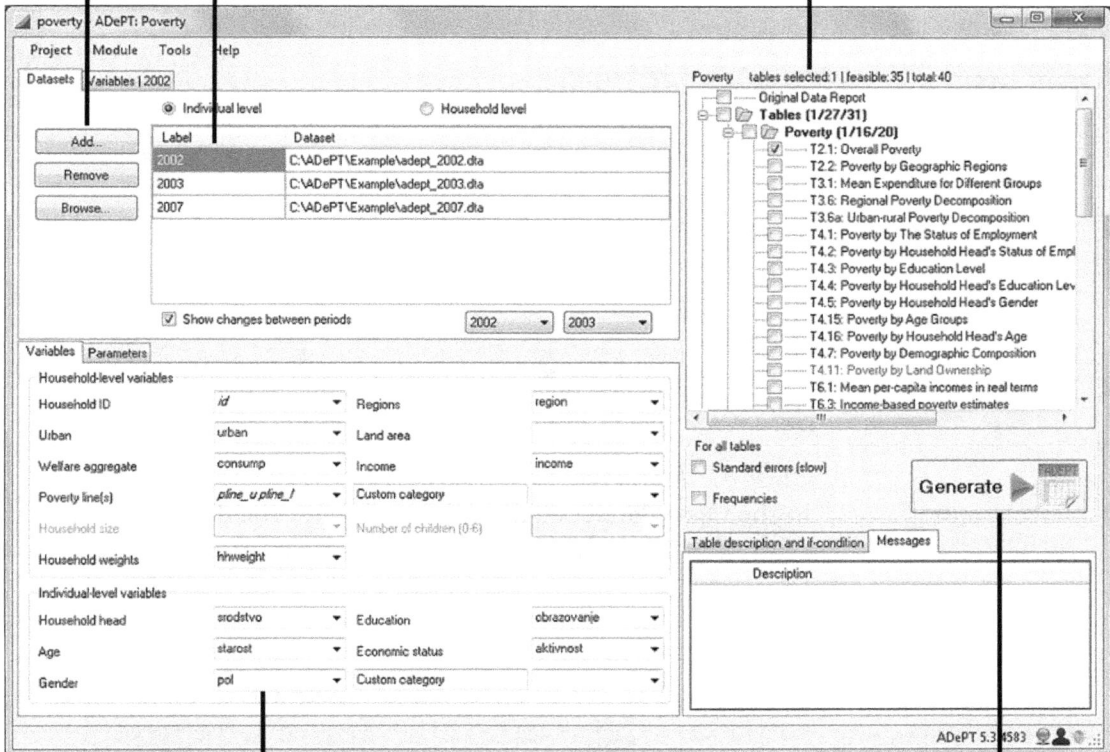

2. Map dataset variables to input variables
by selecting dataset variables in drop-down lists.

4. Click **Generate** button.

The next sections in this chapter provide detailed instructions for the four steps.

Specify Datasets

Your first task in performing an analysis is to specify one or more datasets. ADePT can process data in Stata® (.*dta*), SPSS® (.*sav*), and tab delimited text (.*txt*) formats.

Operations in this section take place in the upper left-hand corner of the ADePT main window.

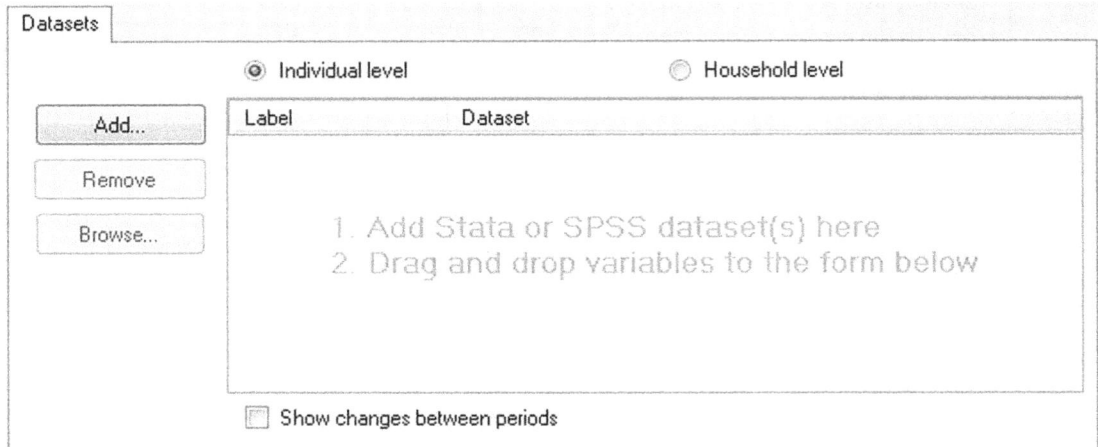

Datasets		
⦿ Individual level		○ Household level

	Label	Dataset
Add...		
Remove	1. Add Stata or SPSS dataset(s) here	
Browse...	2. Drag and drop variables to the form below	

☐ Show changes between periods

1. Click the **Add...** button.
2. In the **Open** dataset dialog, locate and click the dataset you want to analyze, then click the **Open** button. The dataset is now listed in the **Datasets** tab.

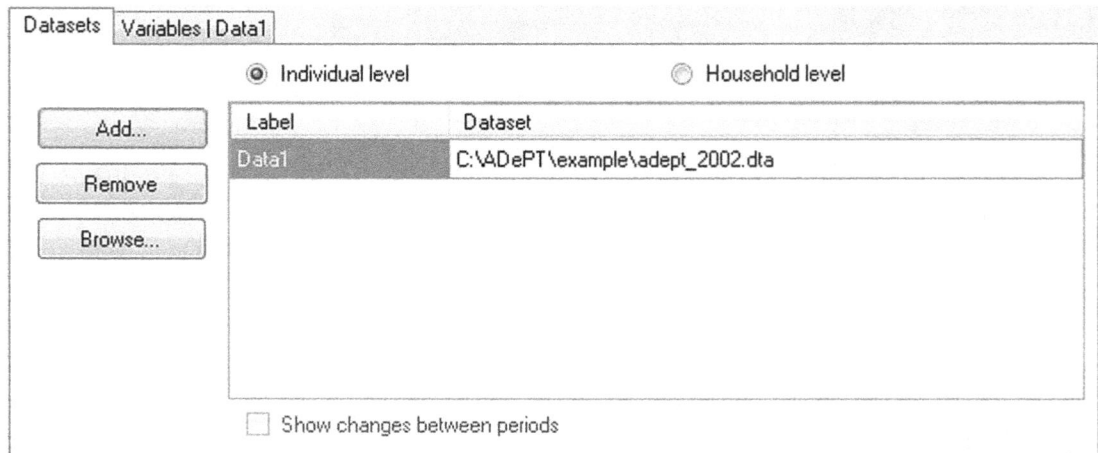

Datasets	Variables	Data1	
⦿ Individual level		○ Household level

	Label	Dataset
Add...	Data1	C:\ADePT\example\adept_2002.dta
Remove		
Browse...		

☐ Show changes between periods

Tip: While learning to use ADePT, you may want to experiment with sample data. You can find sample datasets in the *ADePT\ Example* folder.

3. Specify a label for the dataset:
   a. In the **Label** column, select the default label.
   b. Type a label for the dataset. Recommended: Label the dataset using the year the survey was conducted (for example, 2002). When labels are years, ADePT can calculate differences between surveys.
   c. Press ENTER.
4. Optional: Repeat steps 1–3 to specify each additional dataset.

   Note: If more than one dataset is specified, the datasets must contain only individual observations or household observations, not both.

   • *To remove a dataset:* Click the dataset, then click the **Remove** button. Three datasets have been specified in this example.

   Note: ADePT does not alter original datasets in any way. It always works with copies of datasets.

5. At the top of the **Datasets** tab
   • Select **Individual level** if the datasets contain one observation for each household member.
   • Select **Household level** if the datasets contain one observation for each household.
6. By default, the **Show changes between periods** option is activated.
   • If you want ADePT to calculate changes between two periods, select the periods to the right of the option. The left-hand

period must be earlier than the right-hand period, as shown here:

- If you do not want ADePT to calculate changes between periods, deactivate the **Show changes between periods** option.

Map Variables

ADePT needs to know which variables in the dataset(s) correspond to the inputs to its calculations. You must manually map dataset variables to input variables.

Operations described in this section take place on the left-hand side of the ADePT main window. These examples show the Poverty module loaded into ADePT, but the process is similar for the other modules.

There are two methods for mapping variables:

Method 1: In the lower input **Variables** tab, open the variable's list, then click the corresponding dataset variable, as shown for the **Urban** variable.

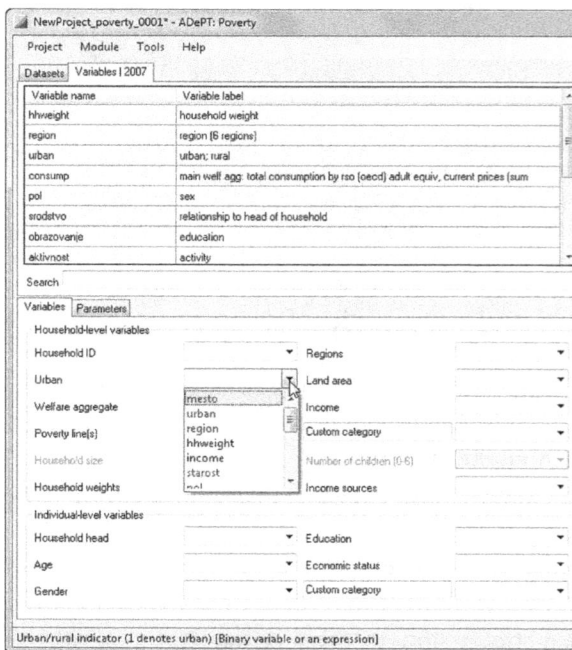

Method 2: In the upper dataset **Variables** tab, drag the variable name and drop it in the corresponding field in the lower input **Variables** tab.

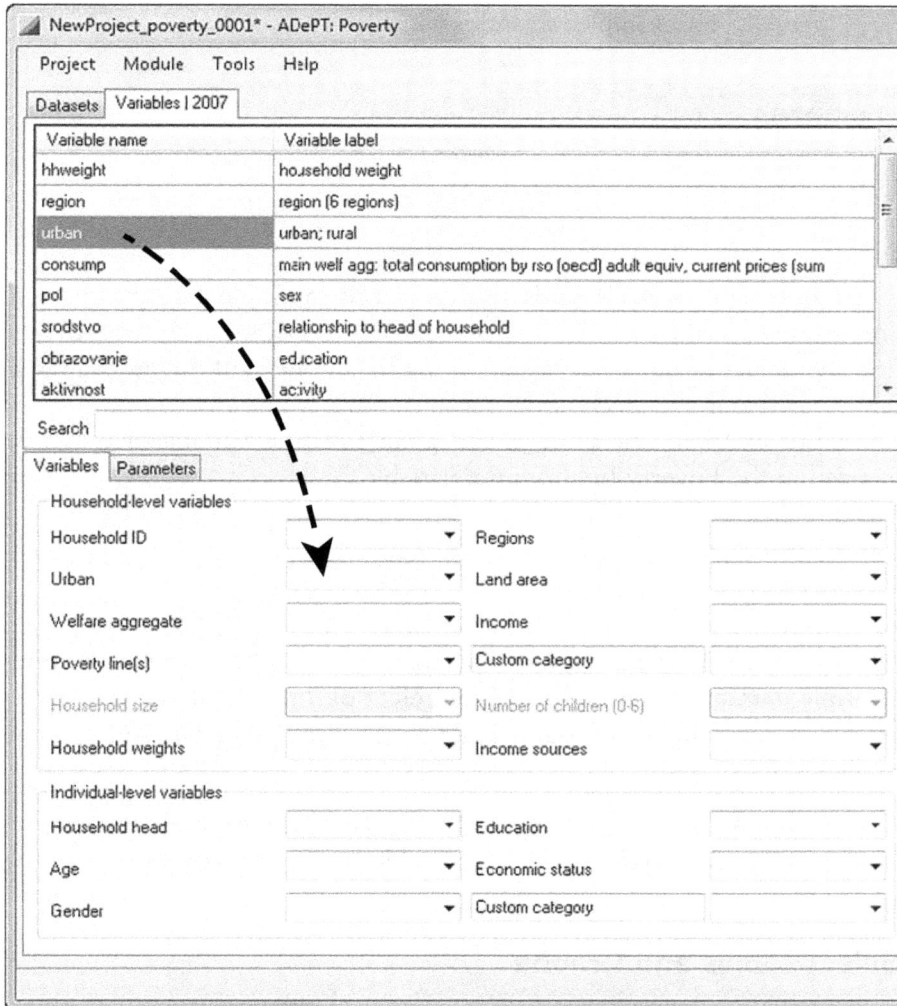

Note: You can also type dataset variable names in the input variable fields. The above methods are preferred, however, because typing may introduce spelling errors. A spelling error is indicated by the red exclamation point next to the input variable field.

- *To remove a mapping:* Select the variable name in the input variable field, and then press DELETE.

  Some modules have multiple input variable tabs. The Education module, for example, organizes variables in three tabs.

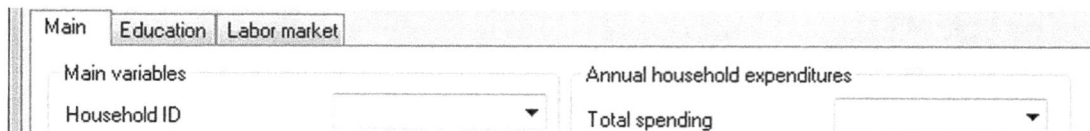

| Main | Education | Labor market |

Main variables

Household ID ▼

Annual household expenditures

Total spending ▼

In some input variable fields, you can specify multiple dataset variables. For example, in the ADePT Poverty module, you can specify two poverty lines (variables or numeric constants) instead of one, and the program will replicate all tables for each of the specified poverty lines.

In this example, the **pline_u** and **pline_l** dataset variables have been mapped to the **Poverty line(s)** input variable.

Poverty line(s)   *pline_u pline_l* ▼

The italic variable name indicates that this input variable field accepts multiple dataset variables. When you select or drag a new input variable to one of these fields, it is appended to the previous value rather than replacing it.

Tip: Open the example project (**Project ▸ Open Example Project**) to see the result of mapping dataset variables to input variables.

Select Tables and Graphs

After mapping variables, you are ready to select the tables and graphs you want ADePT to generate.

Operations described in this section take place in the right-hand side of the ADePT main window.

Poverty   tables selected:0 | feasible:35 | total:40

- ☐ Original Data Report
- ☐ 📁 **Tables (0/27/31)**
  - ☐ 📁 **Poverty (0/16/20)**
    - ☐ T2.1: Overall Poverty
    - ☐ T2.2: Poverty by Geographic Regions
    - ☐ T3.1: Mean Expenditure for Different Groups
    - ☐ T3.6: Regional Poverty Decomposition
    - ☐ T3.6a: Urban-rural Poverty Decomposition
    - ☐ T4.1: Poverty by The Status of Employment
    - ☐ T4.2: Poverty by Household Head's Status of Empl
    - ☐ T4.3: Poverty by Education Level
    - ☐ T4.4: Poverty by Household Head's Education Lev
    - ☐ T4.5: Poverty by Household Head's Gender
    - ☐ T4.15: Poverty by Age Groups
    - ☐ T4.16: Poverty by Household Head's Age
    - ☐ T4.7: Poverty by Demographic Composition
    - ☐ T4.11: Poverty by Land Ownership
    - ☐ T6.1: Mean per-capita incomes in real terms
    - ☐ T6.3: Income-based poverty estimates

For all tables

☐ Standard errors (slow)

☐ Frequencies

Generate ▶

| Table description and if-condition | Messages |

Description

ADePT 5.3.4583

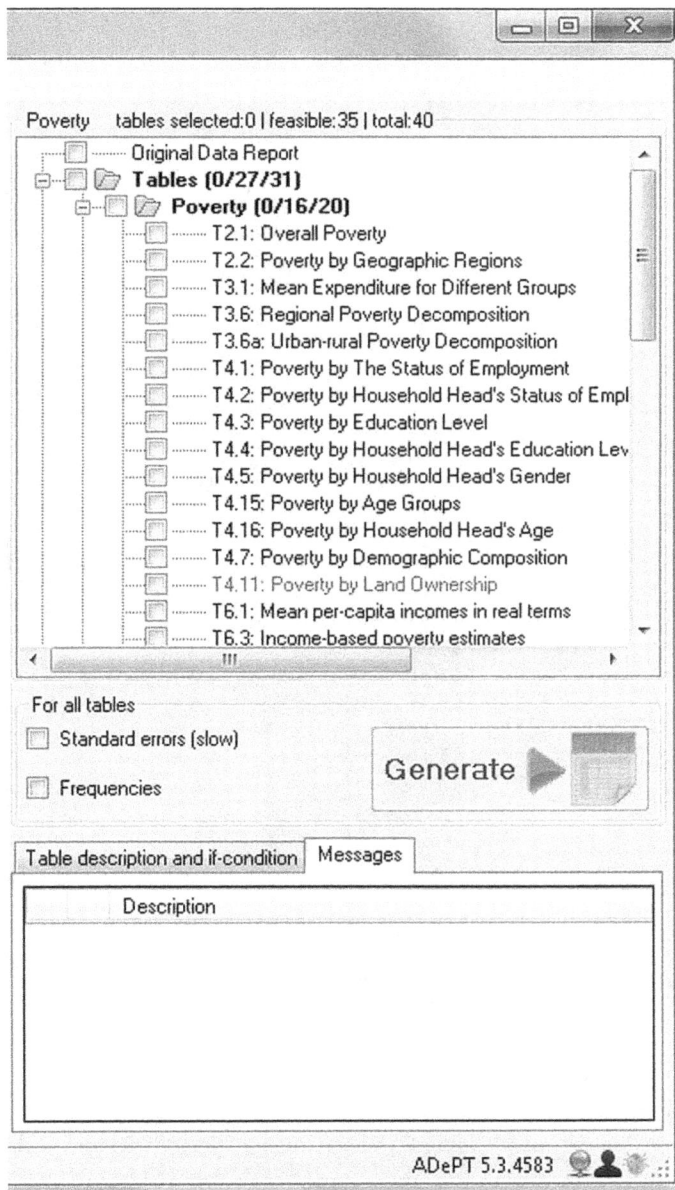

In the upper right-hand (outputs) panel, select the tables and graphs you want to generate.

Note: If a name is gray, it cannot be selected. These tables and graphs cannot be generated because required variables have not been specified.

- *To see a description of a table or graph:* Click the name. Its description is displayed in the **Table description and if-condition** tab in the lower right-hand corner of the ADePT window.

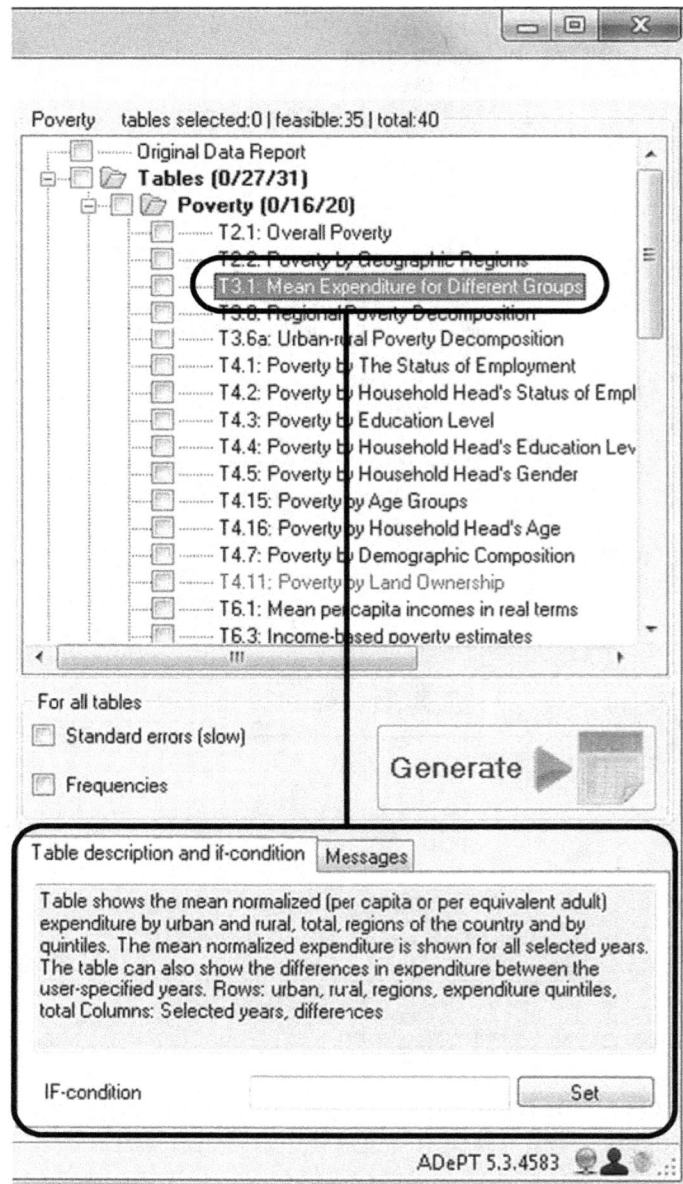

Generate the Report

You are now ready to generate your report:

1. Click the **Generate** button.

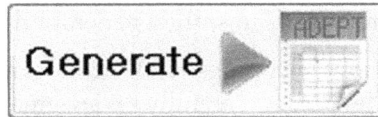

   Generate ▶

   • *To stop calculating:* Click the **Stop** button.

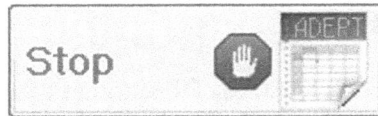

   Stop ✋

2. Examine items in the **Messages** tab. ADePT lists potential problems in this tab.

		Description	
ⓘ	11	Note: in variable pol value 1 was assumed to mean "Male"	▲
⚠	12	Suspected outliers with code(s): 1 3 - in variable aktivnost	
⚠	13	some respondents might be too young for education level - Primary school	
ⓘ	14	Number of years between the two periods is equal to 1	▼

ADePT can identify three kinds of problems:

    ⓘ **Notification** provides information that may be of interest to you. Notifications do not affect the content of reports generated by ADePT.

    ⚠ **Warning** indicates a suspicious situation in the data. Warnings are issued when ADePT cannot determine whether the data pose an impossible situation. Examples include violation of parameters, presence of potential outliers in the data, inconsistent data, and inconsistent category definitions. ADePT reports are not affected by warnings.

⊗ **Error** prevents the use of a variable in the analysis. For example, a variable may not exist in a dataset (in this case, ADePT continues its calculations as if the variable was not specified). If ADePT can match the problem to a particular variable field, then that field is highlighted in the input **Variables** tab.

3. As needed, correct problems, then generate the report again.

   Note: Notifications, warnings, and errors can negatively affect the results ADePT produces. Carefully review messages and correct critical problems before drawing conclusions from tables and graphs.

Examine the Output

When the analysis is complete, ADePT automatically opens the results as a spreadsheet in Excel® or Excel Viewer. The results are organized in multiple worksheets:

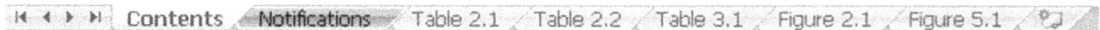

◄ ◄ ► ► Contents Notifications Table 2.1 Table 2.2 Table 3.1 Figure 2.1 Figure 5.1

- The **Contents** worksheet lists all the other worksheets, including titles for tables and graphs.
- The **Notifications** worksheet lists errors, warnings, and notifications that ADePT identified during its analysis. This worksheet may be more useful than the **Messages** tab in the ADePT main window because the problems are organized by dataset.
- **Table** worksheets display tables generated by ADePT.
  Tip: ADePT formats table data with a reasonable number of decimal places. Click in a cell to see the data with full resolution in the formula bar.
- **Figure** worksheets display graphs generated by ADePT.

Working with Variables

Viewing Basic Information about a Dataset's Variables

1. In the **Datasets** tab, click the dataset you want to examine.
2. Click the **Variables** tab.

Variable name	Variable label	
hhweight	household weight	
region	region (6 regions)	
urban	urban; rural	
consump	main welf agg: total consumption by rso (oecd) adult equiv, current prices (sum	
pol	sex	
srodstvo	relationship to head of household	
obrazovanje	education	
aktivnost	activity	

Datasets | Variables | 2007

Search

- *To search for a variable:* In the **Search** field, type a few characters of the variable name or variable label.
- *To view statistics for a variable:* Double-click the variable name or variable label. This opens the **MultiDataset Statistics** window for that variable.

Σ consump - MultiDataset Statistics

	2002	2003	2007
Number of uniques	6386	2548	5556
Number of missings	0	0	0
Number of non-missings	19725	8027	17375
Minimum	630.1021	1718.891	1937.104
Maximum	137441.6	84542.62	221147.1
Unweighted mean	10544.35	11206.01	20896.35
Unweighted standard deviation	6632.247	6409.684	12763.98

Filter: OFF

Viewing a Dataset's Data and Variable Details

1. In the **Datasets** tab, click the dataset you want to examine.
2. Click the **Browse...** button. This opens the **ADePT Data Browser**.

The **Data Browser** lists observations in rows and organizes variables in columns.

- *To see underlying data:* Click the **Hide Value Labels** button.
- *To see value labels:* Click the **Show Value Labels** button.
- *To view a variable's statistics:*
  a. Click in the variable's column.
  b. Click the **Show Statistics...** button Σ.

- *To view detailed information about the dataset's variables:* Click the **Variable View** tab in the bottom left-hand corner of the **Data Browser**.

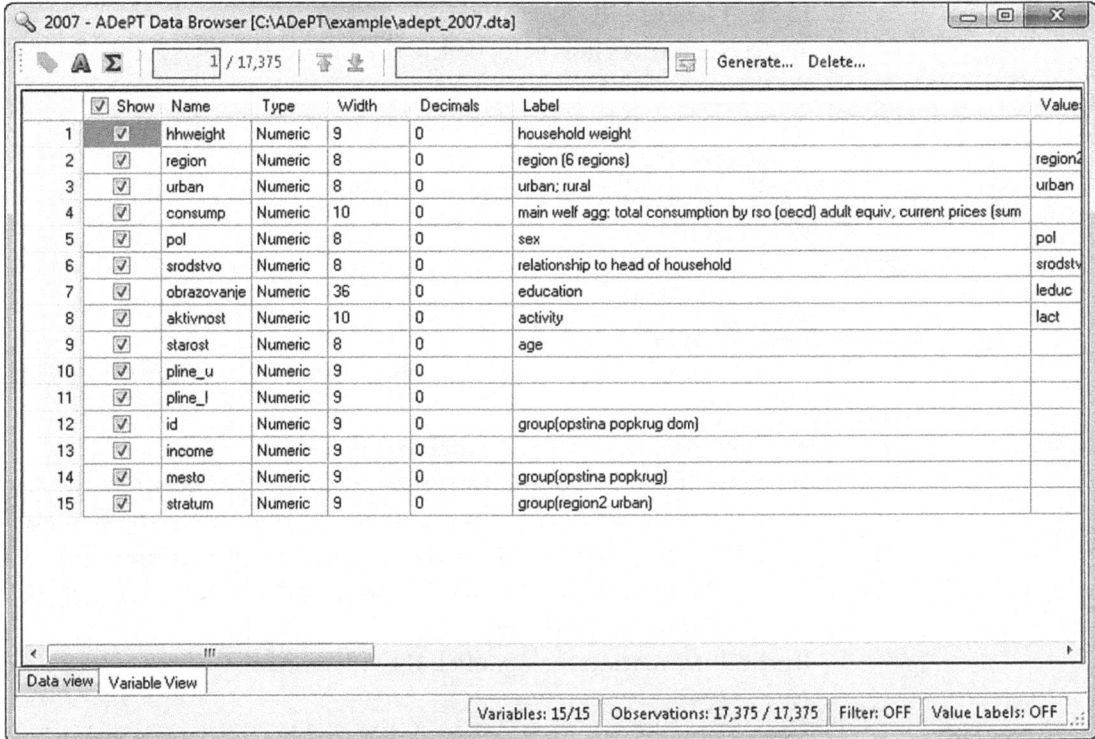

- *To hide or show variable columns in the **Data View** tab:* In the **Variable View** tab, click the checkbox next to the variable name.

  Tip: The *ADePT User's Guide* describes other functions available in the **Data Browser.**

Generating Variables

You can create new variables that are based on variables present in a dataset. This might be useful for simulating the effects of changes in parameters on various economic outcomes. For example, in the Poverty module you can model the effect of income transfers on some population groups on the basis of poverty and inequality.

1. In the **Datasets** tab in the main window, click the dataset that you want to modify.
2. Click the **Variables | [dataset label]** tab.
3. Right-click in the table, then click **Add or replace variable...** in the pop-up menu.

4. In the **Generate/Replace Variable** dialog:

    a. In the **Expression** field, define the new variable using the following syntax:

              <new_variable_name> = <expression> [if <filter_expression>], where

- <new_variable_name> is a unique name not already in the dataset(s).
- <expression> calculates new data for the variable (for more information about expressions, see "Variable Expressions" section below).
- <filter_expression> filters observations that affect the calculation (optional).

    b. Optional: Activate the **Apply to all datasets** option.
        Note: If you loaded multiple datasets but do not generate the new variable for all datasets, you will not be able to use the new variable in calculations. However, you may want to generate a new variable differently for each dataset in the project.

    c. Click the **Generate** button.

5. In the **Information** dialog, click the **OK** button.

The new variable will be listed in the **Variables | [dataset name]** tab and in the **Data Browser.** If the variable was generated for all loaded datasets, it will appear in the drop-down lists in the input **Variables** tab.

When you save a project, variable expressions are saved with the project, and the variables are regenerated when you open that project. Generating new variables does not change original datasets.

Replacing Variables

You can replace an existing numeric variable by following the instructions in "Generating numeric dataset variables." But in the **Generate/Replace Variable** dialog (step 4a), specify an existing variable name instead of a new variable name.

As with generated variables, these expressions are saved with a project, and the variables are regenerated when you open the project. Replacing variables does not change original datasets.

Variable Expressions

The following operators can be used in expressions:

Operator				Description
+	–	*	/	basic mathematical operators
abs	sign			
=	==			equality check operators
^	pow	sqrt		exponent (e.g., $x\char94 2$ is x squared), power (e.g., pow(4,2) is 42 = 16), and square root
round	truncate			shortening operators
min	max			range operators
ceiling	floor			

Variable expressions can include constants, and strings can be used for variables that are of type string.

Expression examples are as follows:

Expression	Description
$x = 1$	sets all variable x observations to 1
$x = y + z$	sets variable x observations to y observation plus z observation
$x = y = 1$	sets variable x observations to 1 (true) if y is 1; otherwise, sets variable x observations to 0 (false)
$x = 23$ if $z == .$	sets variable x observations to 23 if z is missing (.); otherwise, sets to.
$x = \text{Log}(y)$ if $z = 1$	sets variable x observations to log of y observations if z is 1; otherwise, sets to.
s = "test"	sets all variable x observations to the string "test"

Note: The periods (.) in the table above represent system-missing values. This symbol is defined in SPSS® and is used to indicate missing data in datasets.

Another example: To simulate the impact on poverty of a 10 percent increase in incomes of households with more than 4 members, replace the existing income variable using this expression:

income = income*1.1 if hhsize > 4.

Deleting Variables

You can remove variables from the working copy of a dataset that ADePT uses for its calculations. This operation does not change the original dataset. Native variables, as well as generated and replaced variables, can be deleted.

1. In the dataset **Variables** tab, right-click in the row containing the variable you want to delete, then click **Drop Variable [variable name]** in the pop-up menu.
2. In the **Confirmation** dialog, click the **Yes** button.

Setting Parameters

Some modules have a **Parameters** tab next to the input **Variables** tab. In the **Parameters** tab, you can set ranges, weightings, and other module-specific factors that ADePT will apply during its processing. A **Parameters** tab may also have input variable fields for mapping dataset variables, as shown in the drop-down list below.

The mechanics for setting parameters are straightforward: activate options, set values, and select items in drop-down lists. The analytical reasons for setting parameters can be found elsewhere in this book or in the appropriate book in the *Streamlined Analysis with ADePT Software* series.

Working with Projects

After specifying datasets and mapping variables, you can save the configuration for future use. A saved project stores links to datasets, variable names, and other information related to analysis inputs. Projects do not retain table and graph selections, corresponding if-conditions, and frequencies and standard errors choices because they are related to analysis outputs.

- *To save a project:*
  a. **Project ▸ Save Project** or **Project ▸ Save As...**
  b. In the **Save As** dialog, select a location and name for the project, then click the **Save** button.

- *To open a saved project:*
  a. **Project ▸ Open Project...**
  b. In the **Open** dialog, locate and select the project, then click the **Open** button.

ADePT supports Web-based projects and datasets.
- *To open a Web-based project:*
  a. **Project ▸ Open Web Project...**
  b. In the **Open web project** dialog, enter the project's URL, then click the **OK** button.

- *To add a Web-based dataset:*
  a. In the **Datasets** tab, SHIFT-click the **Add...** button.
  b. In the **Add Web Dataset** dialog, enter the dataset's URL, then click the **OK** button.

Adding Standard Errors or Frequencies to Outputs

- *To calculate standard errors:* Before clicking the **Generate** button, activate the **Standard errors** option.

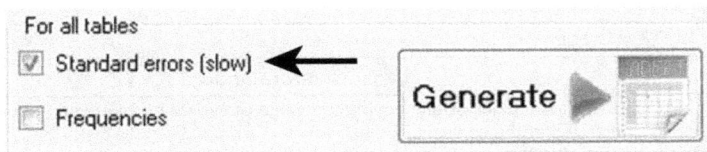

Calculating tables with standard errors takes considerably more time than calculating tables without them—possibly an order of magnitude longer. A good approach is to obtain the result you want without standard errors, then generate final results with standard errors.

- *To calculate frequencies:* Before clicking the **Generate** button, activate the **Frequencies** option.

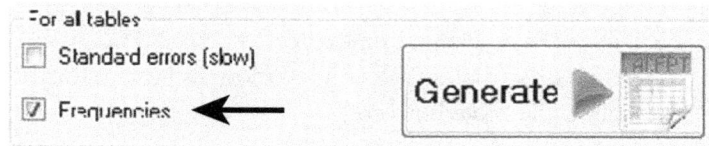

Tables with frequencies show the unweighted number of observations that were used in the calculation of a particular cell in a table. No significant additional time is needed to calculate frequencies.

Results of standard error and frequency calculations associated with a table are provided in separate worksheets, labeled **SE** and **FREQ,** within the output report.

Applying If-Conditions to Outputs

The purpose of if-conditions is to include observations from a particular subgroup of a population in the analysis. The inclusion condition is formulated as a Boolean expression—a function of the variables existing in the dataset. Each particular observation is included in the analysis if it satisfies the inclusion condition (the Boolean expression evaluates to value **true**). In many cases, the conditions we use are quite simple. Consider the following examples:

If-condition	Interpretation
urban=1	Only those observations having the value of variable urban equal to one will be included in the analysis.
region=5	Only observations from the region with code 5 are included in the analysis.
age_yrs>=16	Only those individuals who are 16 years old or older are included in the analysis.
sland!=0	Exclude from analysis those individuals who are not landowners (given that the variable sland denotes the area of the land owned).

1. In the list of tables and graphs, click the table or graph name.
2. Enter the if-condition at the bottom of the **Table description and if-condition** tab (see list of operators below).

If-condition operators include the following:

Operator	Description
=	equal
==	equal
>=	greater than or equal
<=	less than or equal
!=	not equal
&	logical AND
|	logical OR
inlist(<variable>,n_1,n_2,n_3,...)	include only observations for which <variable> has values n_1,n_2,n_3,...
inrange(<variable>,n_1,n_2)	include observations for which <variable> is between n_1 and n_2.
!missing(<variable>)	exclude observations with missing values in <variable>.

3. Click the **Set** button. A table or graph having an if-condition is highlighted.

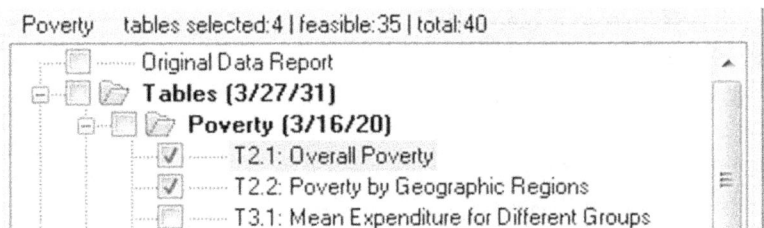

Generating Custom Tables

You can add a custom table to ADePT's output.

1. **Tools** ▸ **Show custom table** tab.
2. In the lower left-hand panel's **Custom table** tab, activate the **Define custom table option**.

3. Design the table by selecting items in the drop-down lists and by activating the options as desired.

   The **Custom table** tab in the lower right-hand corner of the ADePT main window displays a simple preview of your table design. This preview enables you to interactively modify the table to suit your needs.
4. In the upper right-hand (outputs) panel:
   a. Scroll to the bottom of the list.
   b. Select **Custom table**.

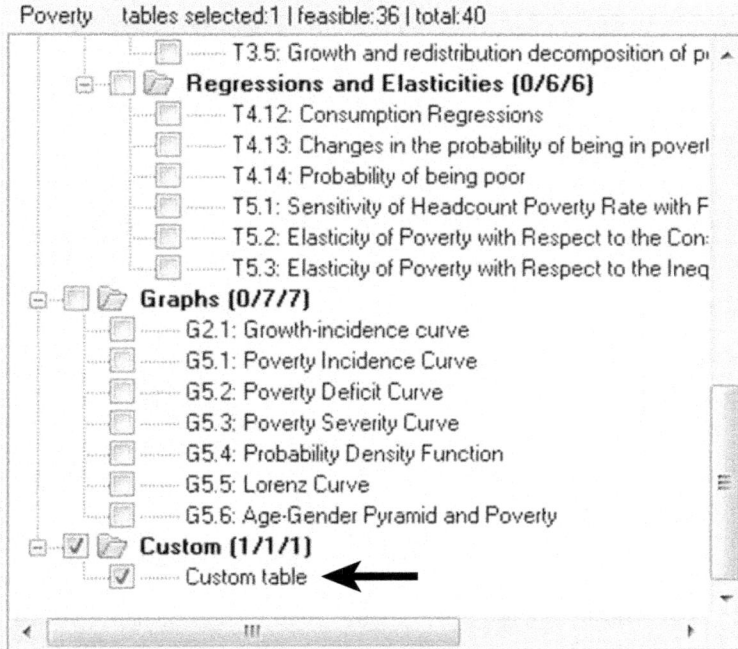

The custom table will be included in the report generated by ADePT.

Appendix

This appendix provides additional tables and figures that may be useful in understanding the concepts and results discussed in chapters 1–3. We use the same Integrated Household Survey dataset of Georgia for 2003 and 2006 that we used in chapter 3. Results in this appendix are reported at the national level, with rural and urban breakdown, and at the subnational level for 2003 only. Figures for a particular region cover both 2003 and 2006.

Income Standards and Inequality

In chapter 3, we examined income standards such as quantile incomes, partial means, and the arithmetic mean. Remember that quantile incomes and partial means, unlike arithmetic means, are not computed using the entire per capita expenditure distribution. So the arithmetic mean is the only standard among these three that depends on the entire distribution. However, it is not sensitive to any change in spread or inequality within the distribution. Given that any inequality index can be constructed using a higher income standard and a lower income standard, income standards can be used to construct the different inequality indices presented in chapter 3.

Table A.1 shows additional income standards that are sensitive to inequality across the entire distribution. Table rows report rural and urban areas and subnational regions. Row *13* reports the income standard for Georgia as a whole. The variable is per capita expenditure, assessed in lari.

A Unified Approach to Measuring Poverty and Inequality

Table A.1: General Means and the Sen Mean

lari

	Region	General mean					Sen mean
		$\alpha = 1$	$\alpha = 2$	$\alpha = 0$	$\alpha = -1$	$\alpha = 0.5$	
	Region	A	B	C	D	E	F
1	Urban	128.9	155.5	106.1	84.7	117.2	85.7
2	Rural	123.5	151.8	99.1	75.4	111.0	79.9
	Subnational						
3	Kakheti	107.9	131.6	87.2	65.7	97.4	70.7
4	Tbilisi	144.5	171.8	121.5	101.4	132.5	98.0
5	Shida Kartli	122.9	153.6	96.3	67.8	109.3	77.9
6	Kvemo Kartli	93.5	113.7	77.3	61.8	85.2	63.0
7	Samtskhe-Javakheti	116.5	142.3	96.2	76.8	106.0	78.2
8	Ajara	107.8	129.9	87.9	68.5	97.7	71.2
9	Guria	134.3	166.9	109.9	86.4	121.6	88.7
10	Samegrelo	117.2	142.3	95.7	75.8	106.1	77.2
11	Imereti	150.3	178.9	124.3	99.6	137.1	100.7
12	Mtskheta-Mtianeti	113.0	134.0	92.0	71.5	102.6	75.2
13	Total	126.1	153.6	102.4	79.7	113.9	82.7

Source: Based on ADePT Poverty and Inequality modules using Integrated Household Survey of Georgia 2003 and 2006.

Columns A through E show the general means for five different values of the inequality aversion parameter α: $\alpha = 1$ for the arithmetic mean, $\alpha = 2$ for the Euclidean mean, $\alpha = 0$ for the geometric mean, $\alpha = -1$ for the harmonic mean, and $\alpha = 0.5$. From our discussions of general means in chapter 2, we know that a distribution's general mean decreases as α increases. Column F lists the Sen mean.

Column A reports the mean per capita consumption expenditure when $\alpha = 1$. The other income standards, with the mean, can be used to construct a particular inequality measure. For example, the mean can be combined with the Euclidean mean to construct the generalized entropy measure for $\alpha = 2$. The mean and the geometric mean can be used to construct the Atkinson inequality measure A(0) and the generalized entropy measure GE(0). The mean and the harmonic mean are used together to compute the Atkinson measure of inequality A(-1). The mean and the general mean for $\alpha = 0.5$ are combined to compute A(0.5). Finally, the mean and the Sen mean can be used to compute the Gini coefficient.

For example, the mean per capita expenditure in Kakheti is GEL 107.9 [3,A], whereas the Sen mean is GEL 70.7 [3,F]. Thus, the Gini coefficient is easily computed as $100 \times (107.9 - 70.7)/107.9 = 34.4$, which can be verified from table 3.8. Similarly, the mean for Tbilisi is GEL 144.5 [4,A] and the geometric mean is GEL 121.5 *[4,C]*, so the Atkinson measure A(0) is computed as $100 \times (144.5 - 121.5)/144.5 = 15.9$, which can be verified from table 3.27.

Censored Income Standards and Poverty Measures

A distribution's censored income standard is computed by applying income standards to a per capita expenditure distribution that is censored at the poverty line. In a censored distribution, the achievements of those below the poverty line are retained, and the achievements of those above the poverty line are replaced by the poverty line itself.

The censored income standards shown in table A.2 are closely related to the poverty measures reported in chapter 3. Table rows report rural and urban areas and subnational regions. Row *13* reports the income standard for Georgia as a whole. The variable is per capita expenditure, assessed in lari.

Column A shows the doubly censored mean of a distribution, where censoring takes place at the distribution's upper and lower ends. In a doubly

Table A.2: Censored Income Standards
lari

| | Region | Doubly censored mean | General mean | | | Sen mean |
| | | | $\alpha = 1$ | $\alpha = 0$ | $\alpha = -1$ | |
		A	B	C	D	E
	Poverty line = 75.4					
1	Urban	54.2	68.9	66.9	62.9	63.6
2	Rural	51.6	67.4	64.5	58.6	60.9
	Subnational region					
3	Kakheti	46.1	65.3	61.8	54.4	57.7
4	Tbilisi	59.7	71.3	70.2	68.4	67.7
5	Shida Kartli	48.8	66.6	63.0	54.2	59.6
6	Kvemo Kartli	41.9	63.8	60.0	53.7	55.3
7	Samtskhe-Javakheti	52.7	67.9	65.3	60.4	61.8
8	Ajara	47.4	65.8	62.4	56.4	58.3
9	Guria	56.4	69.1	67.1	62.9	63.9
10	Samegrelo	50.2	67.1	64.5	59.7	60.6
11	Imereti	59.8	70.8	69.3	66.5	66.7
12	Mtskheta-Mtianeti	49.6	65.5	62.1	56.8	57.9
13	Total	52.8	68.1	65.6	60.6	62.2

Source: Based on ADePT Poverty and Inequality modules using Integrated Household Survey of Georgia 2003 and 2006.

censored distribution, people whose per capita expenditure is not less than the poverty line are assumed to have poverty-line income, and people whose per capita expenditure is less than the poverty line are assumed to have zero per capita expenditure. The doubly censored mean is the mean of the doubly censored distribution. The rest of the columns report income standards for distributions that are censored once at the poverty line. Columns B, C, and D show the arithmetic mean, the geometric mean, and the harmonic mean, respectively. Column E reports the censored distribution's Sen mean.

Those five censored income standards are related to five different poverty measures, as explained in chapter 3. If the poverty line is denoted by z and a censored income standard is denoted by a, then a poverty measure can be computed by combining each of those five income standards and the poverty line.

The poverty line in this exercise is z = GEL 75.4. If the censored income standard a is the doubly censored mean, then the headcount ratio is $(z - a)/z$. Similarly, if the censored income standard a is the censored arithmetic mean and the censored Sen mean, then $(z - a)/z$ would be the poverty gap measure and the Sen-Shorrocks-Thon (SST) index, respectively. If the censored income standard a is the censored geometric mean, then the corresponding poverty measure is the Watts index, computed as $\ln z - \ln a$. Finally, if the censored income standard a is the censored harmonic mean, then the corresponding poverty measure is the Clark-Hemming-Ulph-Chakravarty (CHUC) index, computed as $(z - a)/z$. Thus, a mere comparison of the censored income standards for the same poverty line can provide a good understanding for poverty comparisons.

Here is how different poverty measures can be obtained using each of these censored income standards.

- In table 3.2, Georgia's headcount ratio in 2003 for poverty line GEL 75.4 is 29.9. This can be obtained from table A.2 using the national doubly censored mean of GEL 52.8 [13,A]: 100 × (75.4 − 52.8)/ 75.4 = 29.9.
- In table 3.2, the national poverty gap measure is 9.7. This can be obtained from table A.2 using the poverty line and the national censored arithmetic mean of GEL 68.1 [13,B]: 100 × (75.4 − 68.1)/ 75.4 = 9.7.
- In table 3.26, the national Watts index is 13.9. This can be obtained from table A.2 using the poverty line and the national censored geometric mean GEL 65.6 [13,C]: 100 × (ln75.4 − ln65.6) = 13.9.

- In table 3.26, the national CHUC index is 19.6. This can be obtained from table A.2 using the poverty line and the national censored harmonic mean of GEL 60.6 [13,D]: $100 \times (75.4 - 60.6)/75.4 = 19.6$.
- In table 3.26, the national SST index is 17.5. This can be obtained from table A.2 using the poverty line and the national censored Sen mean of GEL 62.2 [13,E]: $100 \times (75.4 - 62.2)/75.4 = 17.5$.

Elasticity of Watts Index, SST Index, and CHUC Index to Per Capita Consumption Expenditure

Table A.3 presents a tool for checking the sensitivity of three poverty measures to consumption expenditure: the Watts index, the SST index, and the CHUC index. In the table, we ask what the percentage change in poverty would be if everyone's consumption expenditure increased by 1 percent. Results are compared across 2003 and 2006.

The percentage change in poverty caused by a 1 percent change in the mean or average per capita consumption expenditure is called the *elasticity of poverty with respect to per capita consumption*. The particular way in which we consider an increase in the average per capita consumption expenditure is by increasing everyone's consumption expenditure by the same percentage. This type of change is distribution neutral, because the relative inequality does not change.

Table A.3: Elasticity of Watts Index, SST Index, and CHUC Index to Per Capita Consumption Expenditure

		Watts index			SST index			CHUC index		
		2003	2006	Change	2003	2006	Change	2003	2006	Change
		A	B	C	D	E	F	G	H	I
	Poverty line = GEL 75.4									
1	Urban	−2.00	−2.11	−0.11	−1.81	−1.88	−0.07	−1.78	−1.91	−0.12
2	Rural	−1.76	−1.69	0.07	−1.57	−1.50	0.07	−1.48	−1.44	0.04
3	Total	−1.86	−1.87	−0.01	−1.68	−1.67	0.00	−1.60	−1.63	−0.02
	Poverty line = GEL 45.2									
4	Urban	−2.31	−2.49	−0.18	−2.31	−2.42	−0.12	−2.17	−2.41	−0.24
5	Rural	−1.89	−1.83	0.06	−1.81	−1.73	0.08	−1.78	−1.78	0.00
6	Total	−2.04	−2.06	−0.01	−2.00	−1.98	0.01	−1.93	−1.99	−0.06

Source: Based on ADePT Poverty and Inequality modules using Integrated Household Survey of Georgia 2003 and 2006.
Note: Change is shown between years 2003 and 2006. CHUC = Clark-Hemming-Ulph-Chakravarty; SST = Sen-Shorrocks-Thon.

Consumption expenditure is measured in lari per month, and the poverty lines are set at GEL 75.4 and GEL 45.2 per month. For the former poverty line, if a Georgian household is not capable of providing a monthly consumption expenditure level of GEL 75.4 to each of its members, then the household (and each member) is identified as poor. Columns A through I denote three different sets of poverty measures—Watts index, SST index, and CHUC index—each measure containing three columns. The first two columns within each set report the elasticities for 2003 and 2006, respectively, and the third column reports the difference between the two years.

Consider the results when the poverty line is GEL 75.4 per month. Note that the elasticities are negative, meaning poverty falls because of an increase in consumption expenditure, but the higher magnitudes imply higher elasticity even though signs are negative. The Watts index elasticity with respect to the mean consumption expenditure for the urban area in 2003 is –2.00 [1,A]. In other words, if the consumption expenditure increases by 1 percent for everyone, then the mean per capita consumption expenditure increases by 1 percent and the urban headcount ratio falls by 2 percent.

If the mean consumption expenditure is increased by 1 percent in 2006, then the Watts index falls to 2.11 percent [1,B]. A higher value implies higher sensitivity. The urban elasticity of the Watts index is less sensitive to consumption expenditure in 2003 than in 2006 by 0.11 percentage point [1,C]. Similarly, the SST index elasticity relative to per capita consumption expenditure for the urban area in 2003 is –1.81 [1,D], which increases by 0.07 point to –1.88 in 2006 [1,E]. The CHUC index elasticity in 2003 is –1.78 [1,G], which decreases by –0.12 point to –1.91 in 2006 [1,H].

Lessons for Policy Makers

Because poverty lines are set normatively, they are difficult to justify exclusively. A slight change in per capita consumption expenditure may or may not change the poverty measures by significant amounts. If the distribution is highly polarized or, in other words, there are two groups in the society—one group of rich people and the other group of extremely poor people—then a slight change in everyone's income by the same proportion may not have any impact on headcount ratio. In contrast, if there is a concentration of marginal poor around the poverty line, then a slight change in everyone's income by the same proportion would have a huge impact on poverty rates. Hence, this type of analysis may tell us how policy changes impact the poverty rate.

Sensitivity of Watts Index, SST Index, and CHUC Index to Poverty Line

The exercise in table A.4 is analogous to the exercise for checking the elasticity of poverty measures to per capita consumption expenditure, but it is more rigorous. It is always possible to find a certain percentage of decrease in the poverty line that matches the increase in the consumption expenditure for everyone by 1 percent. In this exercise, we check the sensitivity of poverty measures by changing the poverty line in more than one direction.

The table shows how the actual headcount ratio changes as the poverty line changes from its initial level, whether GEL 75.4 per month or GEL 45.2 per month. Rows denote the change in poverty line in both upward and downward directions. Columns report the change in three poverty measures: Watts index, SST index, and CHUC index. The variable is per capita consumption expenditure measured in lari. This table shows results for 2003 only, but this analysis can be conducted for any year.

Columns A and B report the national Watts index for different poverty lines, and column C shows the change in the index from the actual poverty line. The rows corresponding to +5 percent denote the results for a

Table A.4: Sensitivity of Watts Index, SST Index, and CHUC Index to the Choice of Poverty Line, 2003

		Watts index	Change from actual (%)	SST index	Change from actual (%)	CHUC index	Change from actual (%)
		A	B	C	D	E	F
	Poverty line = GEL 75.4						
1	Actual	13.9	0.0	17.5	0.0	19.6	0.0
2	+5%	15.4	11.0	19.2	9.6	21.3	9.0
3	+10%	17.0	22.4	20.9	19.2	23.1	18.0
4	+20%	20.3	46.1	24.3	38.5	26.6	35.8
5	−5%	12.4	−10.5	15.9	−9.3	17.8	−8.9
6	−10%	11.1	−20.4	14.3	−18.4	16.1	−17.6
7	−20%	8.5	−38.8	11.2	−35.9	12.8	−34.6
	Poverty line = GEL 45.2						
8	Actual	4.3	0.0	5.9	0.0	6.9	0.0
9	+5%	4.8	12.2	6.6	11.8	7.7	11.3
10	+10%	5.4	25.3	7.3	24.2	8.5	23.2
11	+20%	6.6	54.0	8.9	51.3	10.2	48.6
12	−5%	3.8	−11.6	5.2	−11.3	6.1	−10.8
13	−10%	3.3	−22.3	4.6	−21.9	5.4	−21.1
14	−20%	2.5	−41.5	3.5	−40.8	4.2	−39.7

Source: Based on ADePT Poverty and Inequality modules using Integrated Household Survey of Georgia 2003.
Note: CHUC = Clark-Hemming-Ulph-Chakravarty; SST = Sen-Shorrocks-Thon.

5 percent increase in the poverty line. Thus, when the poverty line is GEL 75.4, a 5 percent increase moves the poverty line to GEL 79.2. The Watts index increases by 1.5 points from 13.9 [1,A] to 15.4 [2,A], or by 11 percent from its actual level of 13.9.

Similarly, if the poverty line changes by –10 percent from GEL 75.4, then the poverty Watts index falls by 2.8 from 13.9 [1,A] to 11.1 [6,A], or by 20.4 percent from the actual level of 13.9. This index is more sensitive to change in the poverty line when the actual poverty line is lower at GEL 45.2. In fact, the SST index and the CHUC index are also more sensitive to change in poverty line when the actual poverty line is GEL 45.2 rather than GEL 75.4.

Lessons for Policy Makers

The table helps us understand how robust a particular poverty estimate is with respect to the poverty line. Selection of any poverty line is debatable, because it is set with normative judgment. On the one hand, if a poverty measure changes drastically from a change in the poverty line, then a cautious policy conclusion should be drawn from the analysis based on a particular poverty line. On the other hand, if a poverty measure does not vary much because of a change in the poverty line, then a more robust conclusion can be drawn.

Decomposition of the Gini Coefficient

Table A.5 analyzes the composition of inequality across different population subgroups using the Gini coefficient. Unlike the decomposable inequality measures containing a within-group term and a between-group term, the Gini coefficient decomposition usually has three terms: a within-group inequality term, a between-group inequality term, and an overlap term. The within-group inequality term is a weighted average of all subgroup inequalities. Note that the overlap term vanishes if the income rankings of the subgroups do not overlap. However, the residual term is nonzero when there are overlapping incomes.

Recall that the Gini coefficient lies between 0 and 1 (chapter 2 contains a detailed description of the Gini coefficient). When every household in a region has the same per capita expenditure, then the Gini coefficient is 0.

Table A.5: Breakdown of Gini Coefficient by Geography

		2003	2006
		A	B
1	Total	34.4	35.4
	Urban and rural		
2	Within-group inequality	17.2	17.7
3	Between-group inequality	1.1	0.5
4	Overlap term	16.2	17.2
	Geographic regions		
5	Within-group inequality	4.9	5.2
6	Between-group inequality	8.7	7.0
7	Overlap	20.8	23.2

Source: Based on ADePT Poverty and Inequality modules using Integrated Household Survey of Georgia 2003 and 2006.

Row *1* reports the overall Gini coefficients. Subsequent rows report Gini coefficient decompositions for two different population subgroups: rural and urban regions and geographic regions. The first row of each set reports the within-group inequality and the second and the third rows report the between-group inequality and the overlap term, respectively. The overall Gini coefficient in 2003 is 34.4 *[1,A]*, which increases to 35.4 in 2006 *[1,B]*. Thus, in terms of the Gini coefficient, inequality increased in 2006.

The first set decomposes the population into rural and urban areas. The total within-group Gini coefficient is 17.2 in 2003 and increases to 17.7 in 2006 *[row 2]*. However, the between-group inequality decreased from 1.1 in 2003 to 0.5 in 2006 *[row 3]*. The overlap term registers an increase from 16.2 to 17.2 *[row 4]*.

The decomposition of population by geographic regions has a similar story. The total within-group inequality increases from 4.9 in 2003 to 5.2 in 2006 *[row 5]*, but the between-group inequality decreases from 8.7 in 2003 to 7.0 in 2006 *[row 6]*, and the overlap term increases from 20.8 in 2003 to 23.2 in 2006 *[row 7]*. Note that the overlap term is larger for the decomposition across geographic regions *[row 7]* than across rural and urban areas *[row 4]*. A possible reason could be the number of groups: as the number of groups increases, the possibility of overlap increases.

Lessons for Policy Makers

This type of analysis is important for policy purposes and may affect policy recommendations. Both the overall inequality and the intergroup inequality may be detrimental to a nation's welfare. Suppose there are two groups in a region and the overall income inequality is moderate. After the groups are decomposed into within-group and between-group terms, if the within-group inequality is low and the between-group inequality is very high, then the society is polarized. This might increase the possibility of social conflict, as discussed in chapter 4. Thus, merely looking into the overall inequality figures may not reveal this potential problem to the policy maker. The type of analysis conducted in this table may turn out to be crucial.

Decomposition of Generalized Entropy Measures

The Gini coefficient is not decomposable in the usual way because it has an overlap term. Thus, it is important to look at the usual decomposition (within-group and between-group inequalities) using additively decomposable measures. With this objective, table A.6 analyzes the decomposition of inequality across urban and rural areas and across geographic regions. The analysis is based on three different types of generalized entropy (GE) measures: the first Theil measure denoted by GE(1), the second Theil

Table A.6: Decomposition of Generalized Entropy Measures by Geography

		2003			2006			Change		
		GE(0)	GE(1)	GE(2)	GE(0)	GE(1)	GE(2)	GE(0)	GE(1)	GE(2)
		A	B	C	D	E	F	G	H	I
1	Total	20.8	20.0	24.2	21.8	21.5	27.8	1.1	1.6	3.6
	Urban and rural									
2	Between-group inequality	0.0	0.0	0.0	0.0	0.0	0.0	0.0	0.0	0.0
3	Between as a share of total (%)	0.1	0.1	0.1	0.0	0.0	0.0	−0.1	−0.1	−0.1
4	Within-group inequality	20.8	19.9	24.2	21.8	21.5	27.8	1.1	1.6	3.7
	Geographic regions									
5	Between-group inequality	1.3	1.2	1.2	0.8	0.8	0.8	−0.4	−0.4	−0.4
6	Between as a share of total (%)	6.1	6.2	5.0	3.8	3.7	2.8	−2.3	−2.5	−2.2
7	Within-group inequality	19.5	18.7	23.0	21.0	20.7	27.1	1.5	2.0	4.1

Source: Based on ADePT Poverty and Inequality modules using Integrated Household Survey of Georgia 2003 and 2006.
Note: GE = generalized entropy.

measure denoted by GE(0), and the generalized entropy measure for $\alpha = 2$ denoted by GE(2).

Each measure can be decomposed into a within-group inequality term and a between-group inequality term, where the within-group inequality term is a weighted average of all subgroup inequalities. However, the weights (except for the two Theil measures) do not necessarily add up to 1. Chapter 2 provides a more detailed discussion of generalized entropy measures.

Row 1 reports the three inequality indices for 2003 and 2006 and the changes across these two years. In 2003, we see that GE(0) is 20.8 [4,A], which increases by 1.1 (rounded) to 21.8 in 2006 [4,D]. Like GE(0), GE(1) and GE(2) also increase between 2003 and 2006.

Now consider rows 2 through 4, which report inequalities across and between two years for urban and rural areas. The between-group inequality areas [row 2] appear to be negligible compared to the overall inequality [row 1] for all three measures for both years. Given that the share of between-group inequality is negligible, the within-group inequality [row 4] is almost equal to the overall inequality.

For the next set of results, the entire population is divided into 10 geographic regions. Unlike the previous results, the between-group inequality [row 5] is not negligible, but it is still much lower than the within-group inequality [row 7]. For example, the between-group inequality in 2003 for GE(0) is 1.3 [5,A], which is 6.1 percent of the overall inequality [6,A]. The between-group inequality for GE(0) fell in 2006 to 0.8 [5,D], which is 3.8 percent of overall inequality [6,D]. GE(1) and GE(2) show a similar pattern. However, the total within-group inequality increased between 2003 and 2006. The total within-group inequality for GE(0) increased from 19.5 in 2003 [7,A] to 21.0 in 2006 [7,D].

Lessons for Policy Makers

Policy recommendations might be driven by this analysis, because a nation's welfare could be negatively affected by overall and intergroup inequalities. Consider a case in which income inequality is moderate between two groups in a region. Decomposition reveals low within-group inequality and very high between-group inequality, indicating a polarized society and the potential for social conflict. Policy makers may overlook this critical situation if they focus only on overall inequality data.

Dynamic Decomposition of Inequality Using the Second Theil Measure

Among all relative inequality measures, the generalized entropy measures are additively decomposable so that overall inequality is the sum of overall within-group inequality and between-group inequality. Overall within-group inequality is the weighted average of within-group inequalities of population subgroups. Weights attached to within-subgroup inequalities do not necessarily sum to 1. It turns out there are only two generalized entropy measures for which the weights sum to 1: the first Theil measure and the second Theil measure.

For the first Theil measure, weight attached to each subgroup is the share of overall income held by that subgroup. For the second Theil measure, weight attached to each subgroup is that subgroup's population share. For dynamic decomposition of inequality, it is more interesting to understand the change in within-group and between-group inequality and also the change in subgroup population share.

Following Mookherjee and Shorrocks (1982), we use the second Theil measure and decompose the change in overall inequality into four components: (a) change in within-group inequality, (b) change in between-group inequality, (c) shift in subgroup population shares, and (d) relative variation in subgroup mean incomes. Let us examine the process mathematically before interpreting the empirical results. Recall from chapter 2 that the second Theil measure is

$$I_{T2}(x) = \ln\frac{W_A(x)}{W_G(x)} = \frac{1}{N}\sum_{n=1}^{N}\ln\frac{\bar{x}}{x_i}, \tag{A.1}$$

where $\bar{x}$ is the mean of the income vector x and N is the total population size.

Suppose the overall population is divided into $K > 1$ population subgroups. These population subgroups may be different geographic regions, ethnic groups, or rural and urban regions. For rural and urban decomposition, $K = 2$. We denote the income vector of subgroup k by x^k, the population size of subgroup k by N^k, and the mean income of subgroup k by $\bar{x}^k$. Let us denote the population share of subgroup k by $v^k = N^k/N$ and the income share of subgroup k by $\mu^k = \bar{x}^k/\bar{x}$. The second Theil measure can then be decomposed as

$$I_{T2}(x) = \sum_{k=1}^{K} v^k I_{T2}(x^k) + \sum_{k=1}^{k} v^k \ln\frac{1}{\mu^k}. \tag{A.2}$$

The first component is the population-share weighted average of within-group inequalities, and the second term is the between-group inequality.

Now, suppose we are interested in the dynamic decomposition of the second Theil measure between periods t_0 and t_1. The decomposition of changes in inequality between these two periods is

$$\Delta I_{T2}(x) = I_{T2}(x;t_1) - I_{T2}(x;t_0)$$

$$= \sum_{k=1}^{K} v^k(t_0)\Delta I_{T2}(x^k) + \sum_{k=1}^{K} I_{T2}(x^k;t_1)\Delta v^k + \sum_{k=1}^{K} \ln\frac{1}{\mu^k(t_1)}\Delta v^k + \sum_{k=1}^{K} v^k(t_0)\Delta\ln\frac{1}{\mu^k},$$

$$(A.3)$$

where Δ represents the change in the variables from time t_0 to t_1. The four components can be interpreted as (a) the intertemporal change in within-group inequality, (b) the change in the population shares of the groups in the within-group component, (c) the change in population shares of the groups in the between-group component, and (d) the change in the relative incomes of the subgroups.

Table A.7 provides a dynamic decomposition of the overall Georgian income inequality using the second Theil measure. Results in the table correspond to changes across years 2003 and 2006. The variable for our analysis is consumption expenditure in lari per month. Row 1 reports the change in overall inequality. Rows 2 through 5 decompose this change into four factors, as explained in the previous paragraph. Row 2 reports the change in overall within-group inequality. Rows 3 and 4 report the effect of changes in population shares on the within-group inequality and the between-group inequality, respectively. Row 5 reports the change in relative subgroup incomes.

Table A.7: Dynamic Decomposition of Inequality Using the Second Theil Measure

		GE(0)
		A
1	Change in aggregate inequality	−0.011
2	Within-group inequality	−0.015
3	Population shares of within-group inequality	0.000
4	Population shares of between-group inequality	0.000
5	Mean group incomes	0.004

Source: Based on ADePT Poverty and Inequality modules using Integrated Household Survey of Georgia 2003 and 2006.
Note: GE = generalized entropy.

The decrease in the overall inequality between 2003 and 2006 is −0.011 [1,A]. Row 2 indicates that this decline is mostly attributed to the decrease in the within-group inequality because it is evident from row 5 that the relative income share does not change in the same direction. The effect of change in population share on the within-group inequality [row 3] and the between-group inequality [row 4] is negligible.

Decomposition of Generalized Entropy Measure by Income Source

In table A.8, we first break down the single variable into several components, then we decompose the overall inequality across that variable into the inequality of its components. For example, the total disposable income of a household has several components such as male earnings, female earnings, benefits, and income taxes. Analyzing inequality across disposable income may not reveal inequality across these various components. This type of inequality decomposition into factor components was studied in detail by Shorrocks (1982), but only for a single period. Jenkins (1995) conducted a dynamic intertemporal decomposition analysis across the population. Following Jenkins, we use the generalized entropy measure of order

Table A.8: Decomposition of Generalized Entropy Measure by Income Source

	Mean (GEL)	Relative mean (%)	Correlation with total	GE(2)	Absolute factor contribution	Proportionate factor contribution (%)
	A	B	C	D	E	F
				2003		
1 Food consumption	76.9	61.0	80.8	27.2	12.7	52.3
2 Expenditures on nonfood goods	15.2	12.0	62.5	57.2	3.0	12.4
3 Utilities	8.4	6.7	35.5	140.0	1.4	5.9
4 Expenditures on services	17.4	13.8	55.4	140.5	4.8	19.6
5 Other expenditures	8.2	6.5	48.5	179.6	2.4	9.8
6 Per capita consumption expenditure	126.1	100.0		24.2	24.2	100.0
				2006		
7 Food consumption	72.8	57.8	72.3	26.2	11.3	40.5
8 Expenditures on nonfood goods	13.2	10.5	56.3	74.8	2.9	10.5
9 Utilities	10.4	8.3	40.2	161.3	2.3	8.2
10 Expenditures on services	20.2	16.1	62.9	221.9	8.4	30.2
11 Other expenditures	9.3	7.4	50.0	186.7	2.9	10.6
12 **Per capita consumption expenditure**	**126.0**	**100.0**		**27.8**	**27.8**	**100.0**

Source: Based on ADePT Poverty and Inequality modules using Integrated Household Survey of Georgia 2003 and 2006.
Note: GE = generalized entropy.

284

two for our analysis in this table, mainly because some components may be zero and the measure is additively decomposable, as discussed in chapter 2.

Before discussing the results, let us provide a brief theoretical background. Interested readers can refer to Shorrocks (1982) for a further theoretical discussion. The following theoretical brief was heavily drawn from Shorrocks (1982) and Jenkins (1995). Suppose the variable for our analysis is income and is denoted by vector x. Income has K components, and the distribution of the kth component across the population is denoted by x^k. The mean of incomes is denoted by $\bar{x}$, and the mean of the kth component is denoted by $\bar{x}^k$. Inequality across incomes is denoted by $I_{GE}(x; 2)$, and inequality across the kth component is denoted by $I_{GE}(x^k; 2)$. The overall inequality can be expressed as

$$I_{GE}(x; 2) = \sum_{k=1}^{K} S_k \; with \; S_k = \rho_k \chi_k \sqrt{I_{GE}(x^k; 2)I_{GE}(x; 2)}, \qquad (A.4)$$

where ρ_k is the correlation between x and x^k, and χ_k is the share of that component in the overall income. Thus, S_k is the absolute contribution of component k to the overall income. It turns out that the relative contribution of component k is

$$s_k = S_k / I_{GE}(x; 2) = \rho_k \chi_k \sqrt{I_{GE}(x^k; 2)/I_{GE}(x; 2)} \; and \; \sum_{k=1}^{K} S_k = 1. \quad (A.5)$$

Jenkins shows that the absolute change in $I_{GE}(x; 2)$ between time periods t and $t + 1$ can be decomposed as

$$\Delta I_{GE}(x; 2) = I_{GE}^{t+1}(x; 2) - I_{GE}^{t}(x; 2) = \sum_{k=1}^{k} \Delta S_k$$

$$= \sum_{k=1}^{k} \Delta \rho_k \chi_k \sqrt{I_{GE}(x^k; 2)/I_{GE}(x; 2)}. \qquad (A.6)$$

Similarly, the proportionate change in inequality can be expressed as

$$\delta I_{GE}(x;2) = \frac{I_{GE}^{t+1}(x;2) - I_{GE}^{t}(x;2)}{I_{GE}^{t}(x;2)} = \sum_{k=1}^{K} \frac{\Delta S_k}{S_k / s_k} = \sum_{k=1}^{K} s_k \frac{\Delta S_k}{S_k} = \sum_{k=1}^{K} s_k \delta S_k. \quad (A.7)$$

Table A.8 presents the results using the Georgian dataset for 2003 and 2006. Rows denote different categories of consumption expenditure on food items, nonfood items, utilities, services, and other expenditures for two years. Column A reports the mean consumption expenditure and the mean expenditure in each category. Georgia's mean per capita expenditure in 2003 is GEL 126.1 [6,A], which changes marginally to GEL 126.0 in 2006 [12,A]. The mean per capita expenditure on food in 2003 is GEL 76.9 [1,A], which decreases to GEL 72.8 in 2006 [7,A]. Mean expenditure on nonfood also decreases over three years. However, mean expenditures for the other three categories increase.

Column B reports the mean expenditure of each category as a percentage of overall per capita expenditure. The food category accounts for 61.0 percent of per capita expenditure in 2003 [1,B], which falls to 57.8 percent in 2006 [7,B]. Per capita expenditure on foods is highly correlated with the overall per capita expenditure—the correlation in 2003 is 80.8 [1,C] (the upper bound and the lower bound of correlation is 0), which falls to 72.3 in 2006 [7,C], while the correlation between per capita expenditure on utilities and the overall expenditure increases. Inequality of GE(2) for Georgia increases from 24.2 [6,D] to 27.8 [12,D]. Inequality in per capita food consumption expenditure does not change much, but inequalities in utilities and expenditures on services drastically increase.

Finally, we look at the contribution of each component to overall inequality. As expected, the food category contributes the most to overall inequality. This category's contribution is more than half of the overall inequality. Its proportionate contribution, however, falls to 40.5 percent in 2006. The proportionate contribution of expenditure on services increases from 19.6 percent in 2003 [4,F] to 30.2 percent in 2006 [10,F].

Lessons for Policy Makers

Table A.8 is helpful for understanding the source of inequality. This table can identify components responsible for changes in inequality across two time periods and the contributory factor to the overall inequality in a single period of time.

Quantile Function

Figure A.1 graphs the quantile function of per capita expenditure for urban Georgia. The vertical axis reports per capita expenditure, and the horizontal

Figure A.1: The Quantile Functions of Urban Per Capita Expenditure, Georgia

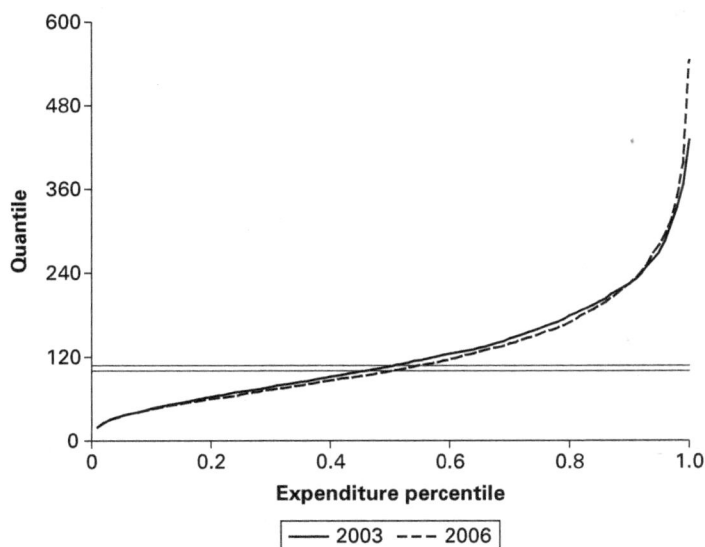

Source: Based on ADePT Poverty and Inequality modules using Integrated Household Survey of Georgia 2003 and 2006.

axis reports percentiles. A quantile function reports the level below which per capita expenditure falls for a given population percentage, when the population is ranked by per capita expenditure. The solid line represents the quantile function for 2003, and the dotted line corresponds to the urban distribution of consumption expenditure for 2006. The horizontal lines are poverty lines for 2003 and 2006.

If a distribution's quantile function lies completely above that of another distribution, then the situation is called first-order stochastic dominance. When a distribution first-order stochastically dominates another distribution, then every income standard reported ranks the former distribution better than the latter distribution. If two quantile functions cross each other, then a dominance relationship may not hold and ranking distributions would depend on the particular per capita expenditure standards used.

The curve with the solid line represents Georgia's urban quantile function in 2003, and the quantile function with the dotted line corresponds to Georgia in 2006. If a quantile function lies completely above another quantile function, then every lower partial mean of the former distribution is larger than the corresponding lower partial mean of the latter distribution. However, in the case of urban Georgia, the two quantile functions cross each other, which prevents an unambiguous ranking. As evident from the figure, the 90th percentile in 2006 is larger than the 90th percentile in 2003, whereas the 40th percentile in 2006 is smaller than that in 2003. Given that a quantile function is an inverse of the cumulative distribution function, the example implies that first-order stochastic dominance does not hold between these two time periods.

Generalized Lorenz Curve

Figure A.2 graphs the generalized Lorenz curve of Georgia's urban per capita expenditure for 2003 and 2006. The vertical axis reports the cumulative mean per capita expenditure and the horizontal axis reports the percentile of per capita expenditure. A generalized Lorenz curve graphs the share of mean per capita consumption expenditure spent by each percentile of the

Figure A.2: Generalized Lorenz Curve of Urban Per Capita Expenditure, Georgia

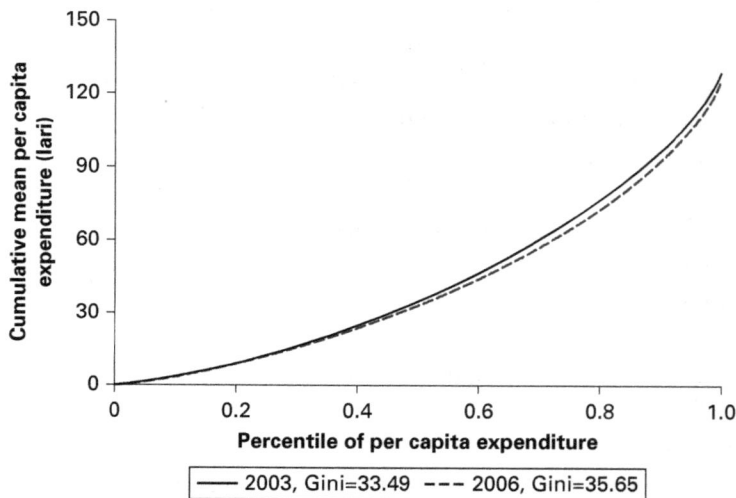

Source: Based on ADePT Poverty and Inequality modules using Integrated Household Survey of Georgia 2003 and 2006.

population. The curve graphs the area under the quantile function up to each percentile of population, or the height of the Lorenz curve times the mean per capita expenditure. Thus, the height of the generalized Lorenz curve is equal to the mean consumption expenditure when the percentile is one. In other words, the share of the total consumption expenditure spent by the entire population is 100 percent.

The curve with the solid line represents the generalized Lorenz curve for urban Georgia in 2003. The generalized Lorenz curve with the dotted line corresponds to urban Georgia in 2006. If a generalized Lorenz curve lies completely above another generalized Lorenz curve, then every lower partial mean of the former distribution is larger than the corresponding lower partial mean of the latter distribution, and the former distribution has a larger Sen mean than the latter distribution. Also, when one generalized Lorenz curve lies above another, the distribution corresponding to the former generalized Lorenz curve is said to second-order stochastically dominate the distribution corresponding to the latter. In this particular example, the distribution of per capita expenditure in 2003 second-order stochastically dominates the distribution of per capita expenditure in 2006.

General Mean Curve

Figure A.3 graphs the general mean curve of urban Georgia's per capita expenditure for two years. The vertical axis reports per capita expenditure, and the horizontal axis reports parameter α, also known as a society's degree of aversion toward inequality. A general mean curve plots the value of general means of a distribution corresponding to parameter α. The general mean of a distribution tends toward the maximum and the minimum per capita expenditures in the distribution when α tends to ∞ and $-\infty$, respectively.

Given that the largest per capita expenditure in any distribution is usually several times larger than the minimum per capita expenditure, allowing α to be very large would prevent any meaningful graphic analysis. So we restrict $\alpha = 1$ to be between -5 and 5, which we consider large enough. The height of the curve at $\alpha = 1$ denotes the arithmetic mean. Similarly, the heights at $\alpha = 0$, $\alpha = -1$, and $\alpha = 2$ denote the geometric mean, the harmonic mean, and the Euclidean mean, respectively.

Figure A.3: Generalized Mean Curve of Urban Per Capita Expenditure, Georgia

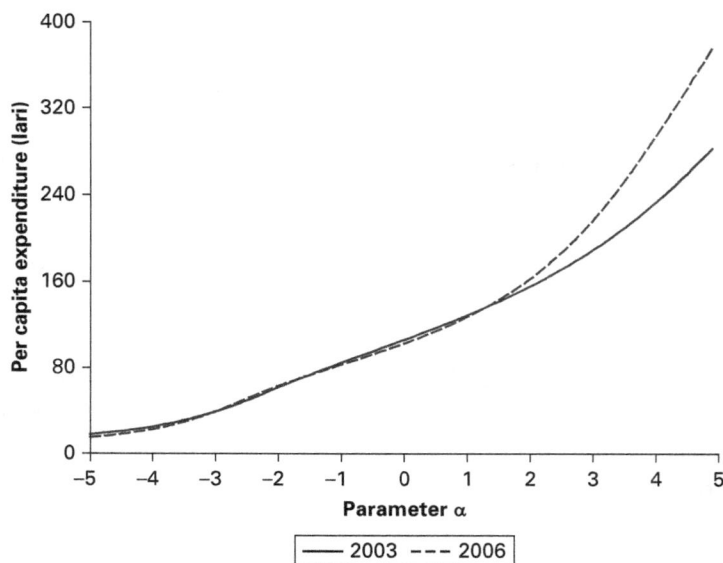

Source: Based on ADePT Poverty and Inequality modules using Integrated Household Survey of Georgia 2003 and 2006.

The solid line represents urban Georgia's general mean curve for 2003. The general mean curve with the dotted line corresponds to urban Georgia for 2006. If a general mean curve of a distribution lies completely above the general mean curve of another distribution, then every general mean of the former distribution is larger than the corresponding general mean of the latter. Then, for example, the former distribution would have a higher arithmetic mean, higher geometric mean, higher harmonic mean, and higher Euclidean mean than the latter distribution. Note that the standardized general mean curve can be obtained from the general mean curve by dividing the curve throughout by the arithmetic mean.

Generalized Lorenz Growth Curve

Figure A.4 graphs the generalized Lorenz growth curve for Georgia's per capita expenditure. The vertical axis reports the annual growth rate of

Figure A.4: Generalized Lorenz Growth Curve for Urban Per Capita Expenditure, Georgia

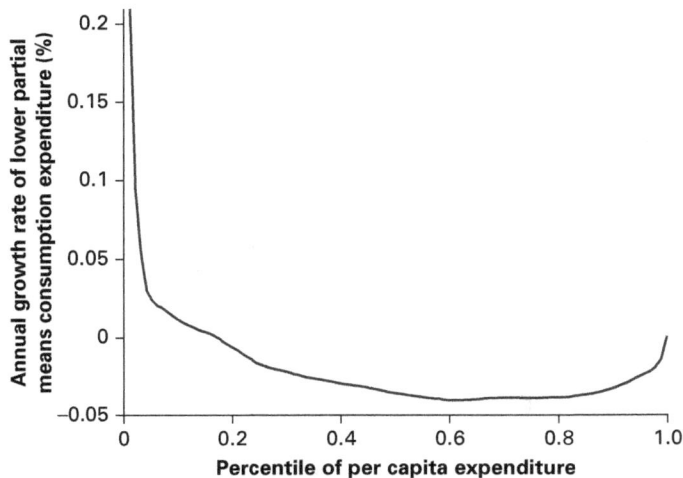

Source: Based on ADePT Poverty and Inequality modules using Integrated Household Survey of Georgia 2003 and 2006.

the lower partial mean consumption expenditures and the horizontal axis reports the cumulative population share. A generalized Lorenz growth curve graphs the growth of lower partial mean per capita consumption expenditure for each population percentile. Thus, a generalized Lorenz growth curve indicates how every lower partial mean is changing over time.

General Mean Growth Curve

Figure A.5 graphs the general mean growth curve for Georgia's per capita expenditure. The vertical axis reports the annual growth rate of the general mean consumption expenditures and the horizontal axis reports parameter α, also known as a society's degree of aversion toward inequality. A general mean growth curve graphs the growth of different general means and thus indicates how the general means are changing over time. The growth rate in mean per capita expenditure is the same as the growth rate of general mean at $\alpha = 1$.

Figure A.5: General Mean Growth Curve of Urban Per Capita Expenditure, Georgia

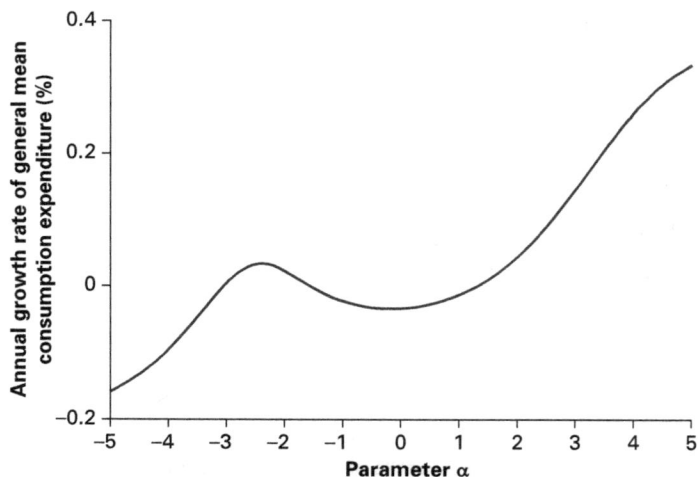

Source: Based on ADePT Poverty and Inequality modules using Integrated Household Survey of Georgia 2003 and 2006.

References

Jenkins, S. P. 1995. "Accounting for Inequality Trends: Decomposition Analyses for the UK, 1971–86." *Economica* 62 (245): 29–63.

Mookherjee, D., and A. F. Shorrocks. 1982. "A Decomposition Analysis of the Trend in UK Income Inequality." *The Economic Journal* 92 (368): 886–902.

Shorrocks, A. F. 1982. "Inequality Decomposition by Factor Components." *Econometrica* 50 (1): 193–211.

Index

Boxes, figures, notes, and tables are indicated by *b*, *f*, *n*, and *t*, respectively.

ECO-AUDIT
Environmental Benefits Statement

The World Bank is committed to preserving endangered forests and natural resources. The Office of the Publisher has chosen to print *A Unified Approach to Measuring Poverty and Inequality: Theory and Practice* on recycled paper with 50 percent postconsumer fiber in accordance with the recommended standards for paper usage set by the Green Press Initiative, a nonprofit program supporting publishers in using fiber that is not sourced from endangered forests. For more information, visit www.greenpressinitiative.org.

Saved:
- 13 trees
- 6 million BTUs of total energy
- 1,111 pounds of net greenhouse gases
- 6,030 gallons of waste water
- 404 pounds of solid waste

green
press
INITIATIVE

www.ingramcontent.com/pod-product-compliance
Lightning Source LLC
Chambersburg PA
CBHW080605270326
41928CB00016B/2932